The
Sixth Continent

By the same author

The

SIXTH CONTINENT

Russia and the making of
Mikhail Gorbachov

Mark Frankland

1817

HARPER & ROW, PUBLISHERS New York
Cambridge, Philadelphia, San Francisco, Washington
London, Mexico City, São Paulo, Singapore, Sydney

FIRST U.S. EDITION

Library of Congress Cataloging-in-Publication Data
Frankland, Mark, 1934–
  The sixth continent.
  Includes index.
  1. Soviet Union—Politics and government—1982–
2. Gorbachov, Mikhail Sergeevich, 1931– . I. Title.
DK288.F45 1987   947.085′4   87-45046
ISBN 0-06-015806-9

87 88 89 90 91 RRD 10 9 8 7 6 5 4 3 2 1

Contents

Foreword

At the beginning of 1982 the Soviet Union entered a period of great uncertainty. Leonid Brezhnev, for all his pretensions to immortality, was seriously ill and unable to govern in any purposeful way. No one knew who would succeed him. Nor could anyone predict with certainty what his successor's policies might be. The Kremlin's pronouncements, it went without saying in those days, did not allow that the country needed change. Many Russians, however, among them officials, in private thought otherwise (as did most of the world's specialists on Soviet affairs, but that is by the way). In *The Sixth Continent* I have tried to tell the story of the emergence of a new Soviet leadership which shared some of the private thoughts that could not be expressed openly while Brezhnev lived. It is a story of political struggle and intellectual confusion, of conflicts of both interest and outlook, and of moralities and manners. To borrow a well-known phrase from the history of Tsarist Russia, it was a 'time of troubles'.

These events took place in what was to all intents and purposes the world's sixth continent – hence the book's title. For years foreigners have puzzled over where the Russian empire and its Soviet successor belong in the family of nations and cultures. A geographer must place Russia both in Europe and Asia. André Malraux located it more meaningfully when he suggested it was in neither the one nor the other, but simply in Russia. A country that already had a singular history and way of life was wrenched further from Europe by the Revolution of 1917. This was the opposite of what some of its leaders expected, but Stalin made both a virtue and a necessity of it. The system he developed depended on isolating his subjects from the outside world and depicting that world as, for the most part, hellish. Under Stalin the old Russian empire (whose citizens had from time to time at least debated their political and cultural identity) was turned unambiguously into a 'Sixth Continent' and told to rejoice in the fact.

For those beyond this continent's borders the events that began in 1982 were watched mainly for their impact on Moscow's relations with this wicked foreign world. Many educated Russians, discouraged by their rulers' helpless conservatism and the increasingly obvious sickness of much of Soviet society, hoped most for internal change. In fact the foreign and Soviet hopes were connected: to change abroad Russia had first to change at home.

The prospect of a new leader could not fail to provoke anticipation. Soviet (and old Russian) experience suggested that the country had to have a new Tsar if it was to follow a new course. Brezhnev was only the fourth ruler of the Soviet Union since Lenin. Lenin had been the architect of the great palace of communism. Stalin was the builder who altered some of the architect's drawings as he went along. The result was vast and, after the victory over Hitler's Germany, solid. By the time of Stalin's death in 1953, however, it was plain that this building was unsuited for modern life, quite apart from its extensive chambers of horrors of which almost everyone was by then afraid. Khrushchov, an unexpected hero, closed down the worst of the latter. He also set about impulsively demolishing walls and putting in new windows in the hope of making the forbidding palace better suited to contemporary needs.

In 1964 Khrushchov's colleagues lost patience with his endless remodelling. They were frightened that one day he might go too far, knocking down a vital structural wall to bury them all. Brezhnev's policy was more cautious. He did not reopen the horror chambers. Where possible he repainted the rooms in prettier colours. He even bought some new furniture. But plans for more substantial, and possibly dangerous, changes were soon forgotten. Brezhnev preferred the easy way out: he called on the propaganda of make-believe to persuade Soviet citizens that, whatever the outside world might say, they in fact lived in the most modern dwelling possible.

After the false starts of Andropov and Chernenko, Mikhail Gorbachov emerged in 1985 as the leader who seemed to have the chance to continue Khrushchov's work. He was young enough; intelligent enough; and apparently possessed the necessary determination. Certainly those Russians who believed that Khrushchov on the whole had the right impulses wished Gorbachov well. Khrushchov, though, because he made mistakes and failed, was not usually mentioned in connection with the new leader. If a historical parallel was needed, even senior Communist part members did not think it odd to recall Peter the Great, who three hundred years earlier had insisted on rebuilding Russia's house although the majority of its inhabitants then, as is probably true today, did not fully understand the need for it.

So it was in 1982, for the first time in almost two decades that public political events in the Soviet Union acquired significance. The carefully rehearsed masque of Kremlin life was replaced by something recognizable as political battle. Both the chronology of events, and the characters who took part in them, acquired significance, throwing light on the changes that had taken place in the country's life in spite of – and sometimes because of – the immobilism of policy under Brezhnev.

My story concludes towards the end of 1986 when the first stage in the replacement of Brezhnevism was done. Mikhail Gorbachov and his like-minded colleagues had by then completed their first broad analysis of where the country had gone wrong. The years between 1982 and 1986 had provided overwhelming evidence of the poor condition of the country the new leadership had inherited. The state of mind of the Soviet Union at the start of the 1980s was to a remarkable extent demoralized.

These revelations, which were to be succinctly but damningly summed up in a survey of Leonid Brezhnev's career published in *Pravda* on the eightieth anniversary of his birth on 19 December 1986, explain the passion behind Gorbachov's bid for power. It is still unclear how far Gorbachov wants, or will be able, to carry his policy of change. We shall have to wait for several years to know what his Russia will look like: whether the Soviet economy can really find a place for initiative and enterprise; whether the Soviet state can tolerate a more open society in which not only an Academician Sakharov, allowed to return to Moscow from exile in Gorky at the end of 1986, but less eminent citizens too can openly criticize government policy; whether the Communist party can keep its grip on power while letting Soviet people have more control over their lives. A Soviet Union that could encompass such change would be a much more formidable country than Brezhnev's Soviet Union ever was. But whatever happens the years from 1982 to 1986 remain to remind us why the Soviet Union has to change if it wishes to remain a great modern state; and why the Soviet establishment, perhaps against the will of its majority, eventually produced a leader committed to change. Here lies the source of the passion that moved Gorbachov to bid for power. Here, too, lie many of the traps which his policies, which have still to take final shape, must avoid. Here, too, are some of the truths the rest of the world must grasp if it is to deal sensibly with the Soviet Union at the end of the twentieth century.

I have tried to tell the story of these years from the vantage point of someone who saw most of them from inside the Soviet Union and who was fascinated by how Russians reacted to them and talked about them, sometimes spinning theories wilder than any thriller writer might think plausible. Those reactions are themselves an important part of the story, which is why I have made a point of including them. They suggest the emotions, prejudices and hopes of a country that to its surprise found itself at a turning point in its history.

– Foreword –

My warmest thanks are due to Donald Trelford, the editor of the *Observer*, who encouraged and made possible my return to Moscow as the paper's correspondent in 1982. I am also deeply grateful to David Astor, the *Observer*'s editor who recruited me, when I was very young and quite ignorant, to go on my first posting to Moscow from 1962 to 1964. I am indebted, too, to many other members of the *Observer* staff for their help, advice and friendship over the years. Two people in particular gave me generous and unmatched guidance in coming to grips with Soviet affairs – the late Edward Crankshaw, and Robert Stephens, until recently the *Observer*'s foreign editor.

The
Sixth Continent

1

Peace and Quiet

When Leonid Brezhnev was buried at midday on November 15, 1982 the two men lowering the coffin into the grave by the Kremlin wall let it slip from its white cloth supports. It hit the frozen earth with a crack that sounded loud not only to privileged guests at the funeral but also to millions watching on television.

The incident was, inevitably, taken as an omen. A country in which power is so far beyond the reach of ordinary people is bound to be superstitious about the great and powerful, seeking clues to their fortunes wherever it can. Ninety years earlier St. Petersburg had shaken its head over the wife of Tsar Nicholas II who made her first appearance in the capital as Empress-to-be in the funeral procession of her father-in-law Alexander III: 'she has come to us behind a coffin.' The presentiment of ill fortune for Russia's last Tsar and Tsarina proved correct. And so would the presentiment that history might have something unpleasant to say about Leonid Brezhnev; indeed no less than the reputation of his reign was at stake. The royal allusion was not out of place for the Soviet Union had had, until Brezhnev's death, only four rulers since the October Revolution of 1917.

Few people watching the funeral could have predicted how thorough the assault on Brezhnev's reputation was to be. The ceremony that day – the unfortunate dropping of the coffin apart – suggested the strength and solidity of the country over which Brezhnev had presided for eighteen years. The disciplined ritual of the Soviet state took over from the moment the dead leader's body had been placed to lie in the House of Unions. Built at the end of the eighteenth century as the Nobility's Club this handsome light green and white palace had also received the corpses of Lenin and Stalin. For Brezhnev's lying-in-state the Hall's chandeliers and mirrors were covered with black crêpe. Soldiers from Guards' units stood sentry in the entrance and on the stairs, while in the Hall of Columns, where the open coffin lay, the great, the powerful and some carefully chosen representatives of the people took turns to stand as the dead leader's honour guard. An orchestra played, over and over again, Chopin's *Marche Funèbre*. A choir that relieved it merely hummed, communism having not yet found appropriate words of consolation for those gone to the next world. There were enough flowers to fill all Moscow's markets and enough medals, Brezhnev's medals, laid out on velvet cushions by the coffin, to make the most decorated soldier catch his breath. Brezhnev had liked medals. He acquired several Orders of Lenin and was a Hero of the Soviet Union four times over, but the most eye-catching of the decorations in front of the dead man was a five-pointed ruby star set in diamonds. The precious stones surrounded a platinum picture of the Kremlin clock tower inscribed with the word *Pobeda*, Victory. Stalin had devised this decoration when the Red Army began to beat back Hitler's soldiers. He awarded it only to the greatest of his commanders. Brezhnev had given it to himself.

The lying-in-state, the corpse's short journey on a gun carriage from the House of Unions to Red Square and the carrying of the still open coffin to the grave were all dominated by the military to a degree that would surely have puzzled, if not alarmed, the makers of the Russian Revolution. But there was no evidence that the nation Brezhnev had ruled over found it odd. Brezhnev himself had fought in 'the great patriotic war' as World War II is called officially in the Soviet Union. He had been a commissar, the party's representative among the soldiers. He rose to the rank of major general and took part in the great victory parade during which the battle standards of the defeated German army, after being made to lick the dust of Red Square, were thrown down before Stalin, standing on the Lenin mausoleum. Later Brezhnev promoted himself army general, and in 1976 (the year before he became President) marshal of the Soviet Union. But it was the country's as much as Brezhnev's military prowess that was being honoured that November day in Moscow. The victory over Hitler was the one achievement in over sixty years of Soviet power that no one disputed. It gave the Soviet régime a popular legitimacy it had until then lacked. It made it a rightful government for Russia and confirmed that the new Soviet army run by Communists was true heir to the old Russian army that had on occasions been turned against Communists.

Chief Marshal of Aviation Pavel Kutakhov, present at Brezhnev's funeral as commander of the Soviet Air Forces, once met a Western military attaché who told him he was about to visit Volgograd, as Stalingrad, scene of the battle that turned the war's fortunes, is now called. The Marshal, a wartime fighter pilot ace, waved a finger in the face of the foreign soldier. 'Go to Volgograd often,' he commanded, 'then you will understand what happens to people who aggress against the Soviet Union. Dmitri Donskoi showed

2

them, Alexander Nevsky showed them. And we showed them at Stalingrad.'

This assimilation of the heroes of old Russia (the two princes had defeated medieval invaders from East and West) no longer surprised anyone in Brezhnev's Soviet Union. Brezhnev himself had followed pre-revolutionary Russian statesmen in paying respectful and expensive attention to the armed forces. He had learned about them and their needs at first hand during the years he spent as party secretary supervising defence matters. As Soviet leader he presided, in the 1970s, over the emergence of Soviet military power as the nuclear equal of the United States. Brezhnev had only practised what a great Tsarist prime minister, Sergei Witte, had preached. What was it, Witte asked, that transformed Russia at the turn of the nineteenth century into 'the most influential, most dominant, grandest European power? Only the power of the bayonet'. The world might not be impressed by Russian culture and wealth but 'it bowed to our might'.

The world again bowed to the might of the Russia of Leonid Brezhnev. There was surely no chance that another Hitler (or Napoleon, since we are ignoring the revolutionary divide of 1917) would risk invading it or, today's equivalent, firing missiles at it. Brezhnev was the first Soviet leader to know the pleasure of military equality with the most powerful states of the Western world. For that reason alone it was appropriate that his funeral was such a military affair.

The soldiers in Moscow that day looked like members of a powerful, proud army. At the heart of the funeral ceremony in and around Red Square they were a very special sort of soldier, troops of the KGB, the Committee for State Security. Those at the Lenin mausoleum and the grave were in full dress uniform of knee boots, tightly-waisted light grey overcoat, gold belt and lanyard. Their hats were of grey Persian lamb. White gloves, which they did not put on until just before the funeral began, were carried by a non-commissioned officer in a little brown case. A Tsarist officer would have had no difficulty in recognizing them as Russian soldiers. The different, drabber uniforms of the revolutionary Red Army had been perhaps the only unlamented casualty of World War II.

Further from the centre soldiers of the interior ministry stood guard in fine long khaki greatcoats like those issued to their great grandfathers in the First World War. And on the outskirts of the ceremony construction troops shuffled down side streets on more lowly but no less necessary duties. These men, the scene-shifters and stage hands of great occasions of the Soviet state, wore stained padded jackets and had the faces and stubby build of Slav and Asian peasants.

Here, surely, was a classical army built on hierarchy, rank and discipline, an army to match the city in which Brezhnev and all the dead leaders of the Soviet state lie buried. Moscow, for those with eyes to see, was a military museum. The three roads that Brezhnev used most often on his journeys in

3

and out of the city all took him past monuments that stirred the Russian memory. Driving into the capital from the VIP airport of Vnukovo Brezhnev passed the memorial to Yuri Gagarin, the air force pilot from the heart of Russia who became the first man to fly in space. Gagarin stands on top of the tall column like a silver Superman about to take off into the air, a case of national pride swamping the straightforward, attractive man who performed the heroic feat. After hunting parties in the forests around Zavidovo to the north-west of the city Brezhnev came home down the Leningrad highway. To the right of this road, twenty-three kilometres outside Moscow, stands one of the simplest monuments of the last war – a row of giant anti-tank obstacles. The Russian army stopped the Germans here in the dreadful winter of 1941. The road Brezhnev drove along most often linked the city with his dacha in the western suburbs. It took him through the finest of all the entrances to Moscow, the beginning of Kutuzovsky Prospect which is marked by a classical arch in the style of London's Marble Arch and the Arc de Triomphe in Paris. The arch supports six bronze horses, a chariot and the winged figure of 'Glory'. No one could mistake it for anything but a monument to victory. The arch had been erected after the war of 1812 to commemorate the nation's defeat of Napoleon who, unlike Hitler, managed to enter the city, though little good did it do him. The arch originally stood outside the Belorussian station at what was then the entrance to the city. The Tsars drove through it when they visited Moscow from the capital, St. Petersburg. At the beginning of the 1930s the arch like many other old buildings and monuments fell victim to revolution's love of a clean canvas. Deplored as an unnecessary relic of the past and an obstacle to traffic it was pulled down but not completely destroyed. The sculptures were preserved in the gardens of a decaying Moscow monastery. After the war, when Soviet patriotism was no longer supposed to start only in 1917, the sculptures were recovered and the arch was re-built. Work was completed in 1968, four years after Brezhnev took over as head of the Communist party.

Brezhnev, coming into Moscow from his dacha did not, like the Tsars, drive under the arch. His convoy merely swept beside it and then past another monument to the 'patriotic war' against Napoleon, a huge nineteenth-century painting of the Battle of Borodino. Like the arch this had also fallen into neglect after the Revolution but was restored and put into a fine new building for Borodino's 150th anniversary in 1962. Brezhnev lived on Kutuzovsky Prospect (named after the great Russian commander of the war against Napoleon) a little further towards the centre of the city in a heavy block of flats built in Stalin's day. And it was while he was still alive that the decision was made to build the capital's biggest monument to World War II on the small hill almost opposite the Triumphal Arch where Napoleon had paused to survey the city before entering it. This memorial, planned on a gigantic scale, was to be the final reconciliation of Soviet and pre-Revolutionary Russian military glory.

4

Brezhnev's Moscow retained another link with the old city. A glance at a map of modern Moscow shows something like a spider's web with a very obvious centre. This is the Kremlin, and from most directions of the compass the main streets drive straight towards it. There can be few other cities in the world where the feeling is so strong of being carried towards the centre whether one wants it or not. The Kremlin is built on a hill at a curve in the Moskva river and in the days before the tall buildings of the modern city a traveller moving down one of the main streets was pulled into the heart of Russian history by glimpses of the tall swan's neck of Ivan the Terrible's bell tower and the domes and spires of the Kremlin cathedrals. When Lenin moved the Soviet government out of Peter the Great's capital on the Baltic and back to Moscow the Kremlin's pull became even greater than before. Its silent churches might lose their magic but another force, just as ambitious, occupied the old buildings. Power and wisdom, first in the shape of Lenin, then Stalin, took up residence there.

Stalin widened some of the streets that plunged towards the Kremlin. He lined them with heavy, humourless buildings turning them into canyons along which people seemed to flow even more inevitably into the centre. He renamed the chief of these re-made Moscow streets after Maxim Gorky, the Revolution's favourite writer (Gorky did not like it, complaining that such changing of names was a 'distortion of history'). Stalin tried to alter the city in other ways too but in spite of his pulling down and renaming he did not destroy – why should he have wanted to? – the feeling of a city that revolved around and was drawn towards its centre. Even the strange skyscrapers he put up after the war, although far taller than the Kremlin, did not rob it of its magnet quality. Stalin, like the leaders that were to follow him, moved round Moscow by car and quickly at that. He designed for himself and his successors a city that was to be seen from a fast-moving car window, not by the ordinary citizen on foot who is easily oppressed by the wide straight streets. The skyscrapers were Gothic castles from one of the realistic backdrops that Stalin liked to see at the Bolshoi theatre, flattering symbols of grandeur on the leaders' journeys to and from the Kremlin.

Every time Brezhnev passed through the city he saw a reflection of the system at whose centre he sat as the party's general secretary. Every journey he made through it flattered him. It is not surprising that by the time he died more had gone to his head than the medals, of which he acquired a bigger collection than even Stalin. Brezhnev had also become a writer, publishing in 1978 what was claimed to be his autobiography. The first part glorified his war experiences. The second told of his work as a party leader rebuilding the Ukraine after the war. *Virgin Land*, the last instalment, was the story of how Kazakhstan was turned into a new and badly needed source of grain for a country shockingly short of decent food (there was no hint that Nikita Khrushchov, then the party leader, had been chiefly responsible for that). The books won Brezhnev the Lenin prize for literature, though the usual rules for the award had to be bent a little, and praise from all public figures. The first volume, it was said, was

> not very large, but in the depths of its ideological content, in the breadth of the author's generalizations and opinions it has become a great event in public life. It has evoked a warm echo in the hearts of Soviet people, the delighted response of frontline soldiers . . .

The enthusiastic speaker was Mikhail Gorbachov, then the party leader of the Stavropol region but only a few months away from promotion to Moscow as a secretary of the Central Committee. Gorbachov's praise was no more outrageous than anyone else's. The leaders of the Republic of Azerbaidzhan, where the oriental art of flattery is not forgotten, commissioned a portrait of a thoughtful Brezhnev composing the great work at his desk. A film was made out of one part of the autobiography. A Kazakh composer (among her earlier works an 'Ode to the Party' and a symphony entitled 'Energy') turned *Virgin Land* into an oratorio. A stage version of the autobiography played even at the venerable Maly theatre in Moscow – until Brezhnev's death, when it fell promptly out of the repertoire. In unofficial Moscow the reaction was, to put it mildly, less charitable. There was scorn not just for Brezhnev's exaggeration of his life's achievements. It was his claim to literary genius that people who took their writing seriously found particularly ridiculous. What are the names of the four Soviet Tsars?, a joke went, Vladimir (Lenin) the Wise; Joseph (Stalin) the Terrible; Nikita (Khrushchov) the Miracle Worker; and now Leonid the Writer of Fables.

It was a characteristic of the last years of Brezhnev's rule that his entourage and the great machine of power were unable to stop the flattery even when it had become so obviously ridiculous. A fourth volume of memoirs appeared as well as more political works that no one supposed Brezhnev really wrote himself. A volume of photographs was published including many of his family. One in colour, across two pages, showed Brezhnev out hunting. Smiling, arms outstretched, he is wearing an American cowboy belt with a revolver stuck in it. The face, swollen with age and illness, still contains a hint of a vain and handsome younger man.

Brezhnev had immense power and that power undoubtedly went to his head, but it was surely the Soviet Union's good luck that he sometimes used it in frivolous ways. No one who rose up through the Soviet hierarchy under Stalin can be accused of softness, and at the time of Stalin's death Leonid Brezhnev was already a secretary of the Central Committee and a candidate member of its ruling Presidium. But he turned out to be the most undemanding, the sunniest ruler the Soviet Union had known. He began his speech to the Soviet Communist party congress in 1976 with a declaration no Soviet leader before him would have made: 'The world is changing before our very eyes and changing for the better.' This was partly a reference to the outside world. The Americans had just been humiliated in Viet Nam. Soviet equality with the United States had been for the first time publicly and officially confirmed by treaties limiting each side's nuclear weapons. But it also reflected delight at the late emergence of the Soviet Union into the long-awaited sunlight of a consumer society.

In 1965, the year after Brezhnev and his colleagues had engineered the overthrow of Khrushchov, only a quarter of Soviet families had television sets and far fewer – just one in ten – refrigerators. By 1978 four out of five families had both. The élite of the working class, those who worked in the heavy and defence industries, were even better off. In the great iron and steel works in the Urals city of Chelyabinsk almost all families would have both refrigerators and washing machines by 1985, and a quarter of them cars. The great majority would also have such decorative luxuries as oriental carpets and china dinner services. In Moscow and other big cities the new prosperity had set off a fashion for dogs, the bigger the better. Bulldogs, St. Bernards and Alsatians mixed with old Russian breeds, setting their owners apart as people of chic.

More than two million new flats had been going up each year for over twenty years. This programme, begun by Khrushchov, had changed the face of Moscow and most other Soviet cities and towns. The new construction had increased the impression that Moscow was a capital gathered round a sacred, powerful core. Outside that core was the old city, then Stalin's pompous additions and beyond them the *Khrushchoby* (a pun on *trush-choby*, slums), the simple prefabricated housing blocks thrown up as rapidly as possible in the 1960s. The last addition was the Brezhnev era's vision of what a communist city should look like. Seen from a distance these towers and blocks did indeed have something visionary about them, especially for someone who remembered the Moscow of bug-infested wooden houses and the communal apartments with their monumental, exhausting quarrels among families over shared kitchens and bathrooms. Closer up, the new estates presented another picture but the most important leaders seldom explored the world beyond their car windows and if they did the greatest care was taken, in the time-honoured Russian way, to show them the untypical best. Five and a half years after Brezhnev died a new leader, Mikhail Gorbachov, having made plain his distaste for such carefully prepared charades, visited the industrial area of Kuibyshev in central Russia. Nevertheless before he arrived the local leaders brought thousands of workers and students armed with shovels onto the city's streets for a 'panic clean-up'. They 'ironed the ashpalt' of the streets and painted over cracks in walls. Steps that had been broken for two years to offices the great man was to visit were rapidly cemented. The cement had no time to dry and had to be covered by planks.

Brezhnev must have known such things went on – every Soviet official who had ever tried to please a superior knew it – but it was his style to turn a benevolent blind eye. A Russian who worked with him said he developed the manner of a 'good-natured country squire'. He was optimistic ('The world . . . is changing for the better'). He thought he had earned a rest and some pleasure. And he was happy if his colleagues and the rest of the country too could enjoy something of the same. The leadership had lived a life apart from ordinary people since Stalin's day. Privileges grew as one rose in power. This was scarcely a secret and there were traditional justifications for it going beyond both the Revolution and Russia's borders. But Brezhnev seemed to take particular pleasure in the lighter side of power. He indulged a passion for motor cars which he drove fast but not too well. Stalin had been driven in a Soviet-made ZIL from the car factory named after him. It was armoured against bullets and bombs and said to weigh seven tons. It was a sign of happier times that Brezhnev liked smart, expensive foreign cars. He had both Rolls Royces and Mercedes Benzes. Either he or a friend crashed a dark blue Silver Shadow; after Brezhnev's death the wreck ended up in a car club in Latvia. During his first visit to West Germany he was presented with a Mercedes and promptly had an accident in it. Richard Nixon gave him a Lincoln Continental. On later visits abroad Brezhnev developed the habit of returning the cars he was given and ordering them resprayed a different colour.

Perhaps this was an inappropriate hobby for the leader of the self-styled world's first socialist state. Not so many years before Brezhnev's predecessor had pronounced a communist anathema on the private motor car. Khrushchov decreed that instead the Soviet Union was to have public transport and a system of car hire more efficient than anything devised by Hertz and Avis. But it was typical of Brezhnev that he did not keep his motoring pleasures to himself. He presided over the birth of a mass car industry and by the time he died most people who wanted a car badly enough stood a decent chance of getting one. The cars were old-fashioned and a nightmare to service but they brought the miracle of mobility to many Soviet families.

One may doubt that he ever thought of it for himself but Brezhnev's own relaxation in the pleasures of power arguably fitted the needs of the country. For almost fifty years after 1917 the Soviet Union had passed from one storm to another. Revolution, civil war, forced industrialization, the destruction of peasant Russia, Stalin's paranoid dictatorship, the war, the reconstruction after the war and Stalin's last bloody campaigns against enemies real and imagined – no other country has been through anything like it in this century. The Soviet Union was turned into what has been called a 'quicksand society' in which nothing was permanent and the ground fell away from beneath the feet of succeeding generations. The country did not properly quieten down even when Stalin died in 1953. Khrushchov had to make the system work without the old dictator. He moved the machinery of government around like someone re-arranging unprepossessing furniture in a house inherited from a grim old relative. Before he had it to his liking his colleagues got fed up and bundled him aside, to the relief of the larger part of the bureaucracy whose life he had made so uncomfortable.

Khrushchov, it was said, induced heart attacks in officials who displeased him, so elemental were the tongue lashings he dealt out. That was not Brezhnev's style. He even encouraged a certain familiarity among those who worked with him. He liked to be called Lyonya, the affectionate diminutive of Leonid. His good nature showed in the little public ceremonies he held to award medals to his colleagues. He addressed them affectionately and appeared genuinely moved by their successes. His telephone conversations to officials outside Moscow began with a friendly enquiry: 'Tell me, how are you down there?' Even with junior officials his preferred style was an avuncular word of advice with an arm around the shoulder, not the dreadful dressing down the Soviet bureaucrat had come to expect from his superiors.

The Brezhnev age, remarked the dissident historian Roy Medvedev, was 'the quietest period in Soviet history'. And no one appreciated that quietness more than the country's vast bureaucracy: the party officials, the government civil servants, and the men and women who ran the country's factories and farms. Most of them were the products of the chain of revolutions that had begun in 1917. Under Brezhnev for the first time in their lives they saw a chance to enjoy their power and privileges without fear of some new upheaval, be it a Khrushchov scheme to force bureaucrats out of Moscow or one of Stalin's more dire plans.

But like even the most good-natured squire Brezhnev had the power of the last word. He never pretended to be anything so mild as a constitutional monarch or the prime minister of a Western democracy. There had been a time in the mid-1970s when he was referred to in public as *Vozhd*, the Leader, an epithet with frightening associations for it had been used to describe Stalin. He had more successfully reclaimed Stalin's title of general secretary of the party. Khrushchov had preferred the less tainted one of first secretary. Careers depended on Brezhnev's favour. He did not like to break people but he could still make them. The problem, as he grew iller and older, was extracting the favours from him. Sometimes they were bestowed unasked. Increasingly sentimental in old age he was known, when moved by a song or a film, most likely with a war theme, to have an assistant ring up the author to convey his gratitude. And in spite of his good nature the knowledge of what he had the power to do still induced apprehension. A member of the Presidium of the Supreme Soviet (the collective constitutional head of state) recalled passing Brezhnev on the stairs of the Kremlin and being horrified when the old man waved a finger at him in what seemed a threatening way. He was so worried that he at once asked for a formal audience. 'What have I done wrong?' he asked. 'Nothing at all,' Brezhnev answered, 'but I haven't seen you for a long time and that's bad.'

These were the habits of an oriental court, not entirely a novelty for the Russia either of Stalin or the Tsars. And yet, towards the end of Brezhnev's life, some of the courtiers were making public if obscure gestures of unease. Almost exactly a year before Brezhnev died *Pravda* published a long article by one of the shrewdest members of the court, Aleksandr Chakovsky, editor of the intellectuals' weekly *Literaturnaya Gazeta*. A short man with an un-Russian fondness for long cigars, Chakovsky had played literary politics so successfully that he was one of the very rare writers to sit in the Central Committee. His article was curious, an acknowledgement that life was not improving as fast as some people expected it to but putting the blame safely beyond the doorstep of the Kremlin.

'We have become used,' Chakovsky wrote, 'to tomorrow being necessarily better than today. It's become an axiom of our thinking.' He outlined some of the country's achievements, pausing to stress the obvious improvement of recent years in the standard of living. Nevertheless none other than comrade Brezhnev had pointed out that there were difficulties too. 'And haven't we experienced these difficulties? Can we always buy in the shops what we want, be it so-called mass consumer goods or food products? No, by no means always.'

Brezhnev and other party leaders had begun to mention problems with food supplies which were of course no secret to Soviet shoppers. But it was odd for a Chakovsky to devote a long article to the subject of people's disappointed expectations. What is more he provided a very defensive explanation. In the first place, he said, it was because of the United States. 'Just think, comrades, how many millions, no, billions of roubles we could invest in improving the material standard of Soviet people's life if it wasn't for the arms race imposed on us by . . . the USA.'

This was very unusual. People were not usually asked to think about the real cost to the Soviet Union of catching up with American military might. The government never published the figures of what that real cost was. Chakovsky's other explanations for the 'difficulties' were no less intriguing. Nature had recently played cruel tricks on the country, first parching newly planted crops and then drenching the harvests. The whole world was being shaken by the energy crisis 'which to some degree or other can't help affecting us'. But some people were to blame as well, people who knew all about 'their rights guaranteed by the Constitution' but 'don't want to perform their duties to society, . . . people who know they won't be thrown out of their houses but are essentially parasites sitting round the necks of millions of Soviet people who have created and are creating wonders in the sphere of production and culture'.

Wasn't there something wild about this casting round for excuses which on examination were not very convincing? Difficult weather was nothing new in Russia. Just how did a foreign energy crisis affect the Soviet Union with its enviable reserves of oil and gas and coal? And who were these parasites and how exactly were they sitting round the necks of the virtuous hard-working millions?

Chakovsky called his article, puzzlingly, 'The Bells of History'. A few months after it appeared Moscow was to be alerted by bells of another kind, bells that to anyone with a political nose unmistakably signalled alarm.

2

Strange Stories

In August of 1982, a month when the Soviet Union is as much on holiday as any European country, a few lines in *Pravda* announced that Sergei Medunov, the party leader of Krasnodar, had been transferred to other work. It became known later that this was a posting to the Russian Republic's ministry of the fruit and vegetable industry. A Soviet citizen did not have to be very knowledgeable about Moscow politics to understand that this was a shaming demotion. The Krasnodar territory covered the area of a small country, 83,000 square kilometres of fine farm land and, in its southern part, the mountains and sea coast of the north Caucasus. Its population of almost five million produced grain and some of the country's finest tea. In the towns along the Black Sea coast they were developing a new and profitable business typical of Brezhnev's Russia – mass tourism.

The men who ran the over one hundred and fifty regions and territories into which the Soviet Union was divided had immense power and responsibility. A play that opened in Moscow the same year had as its hero a party boss of a territory even bigger than Krasnodar. It was called, without boastfulness, *Four times the size of France*. Although usually little known outside the Soviet Union the regional party leaders could be as experienced in government as many rank-and-file ministers in West Europe. Within the Soviet Union they were the modern equivalents of feudal lords, running their lands on behalf of the great prince in Moscow but also, as a group, with considerable power to frustrate him.

Medunov looked the baron's part. He was sturdily built and well-fleshed. With his big head, his jowls and his silver hair he came as close as anyone to meeting the common Russian taste for leaders who look solid. He was sixty-five, had governed Krasnodar for nine years and been a full member of the

12

Central Committee – the parliament of the Soviet Communist party – for six. He was known to be close to Brezhnev. At the party congress the year before Medunov had been singled out for distinction. His short speech there had contained ten admiring references to the Soviet leader: ' . . . the Soviet people's inexhaustible love for you, dear Leonid Ilyich . . . the clarity of genius with which you have revealed the rich practical experience of our party . . .' and so on. Medunov's praise was not unusual by the standards of the day. One of the leading members of what was to be Gorbachov's Politburo, Geidar Aliyev, was on the same occasion even more flattering of the old leader. But as chance had it the speaker who followed Medunov got by with half as many references to Brezhnev and also – again unlike Medunov – managed to air some problems of substance. Boris Yeltsin, promoted later by Gorbachov to be Moscow party leader and a candidate member of the Politburo, would have liked to say even more. At the next party congress, in 1986, he admitted that 'lack of daring and political immaturity' had made him bite his tongue in Brezhnev's presence.

It was a rare confession for a Soviet politician, and one that it is hard to imagine a Medunov ever making. Only nine years younger than Brezhnev, he also belonged to the generation that had made its careers under Stalin and fought in the war against Hitler. This generation's education had been patchy, usually through no fault of its own. Its climb to power was occasionally brutal in what were tragically brutal times. But the Medunovs, like Brezhnev himself, now had the chance to enjoy power, the first generation of Soviet rulers to have such a chance. Under Brezhnev they came to count on growing old in their jobs. They even considered it their right. The 319 full members of the Central Committee elected at Brezhnev's last party congress in 1981 were on average just a little younger than Medunov. The last Central Committee elected under Khrushchov twenty years earlier had had an average age of only fifty-one.

A generous Almighty would surely have understood some of the temptations these men gave way to. They were no longer young. They had expended a good deal of their mental and physical resources, for their life had been rough. Power in their early years often had a bitter taste. Was it surprising if they now wanted to relax? Unfortunately not all their temptations were innocent. Medunov and his like had to worry about pleasing Moscow but with their own people they could do much as they liked. The longer they stayed in their jobs the greater the number of subordinates whom they had picked. These men's dependence on them was almost absolute. If a Medunov went off the tracks few of those who worked under him would want or dare to protest – as long as they knew the great man kept Moscow's favour. And Medunov had shown his skill in retaining that. In 1979 an extraordinary scandal had driven a Moscow minister to resign and sent his deputy to the firing squad. The scandal was caviar, or rather an ingenious scheme for packing it in herring tins, passing it cheap to accomplices, and then sharing out the considerable profits from re-selling it at its proper price. One of the accomplices was a senior Krasnodar official, the chairman of the town council of Sochi where Medunov had once served ten years as party boss. Other Krasnodar officials close to Medunov were also rumoured to have been involved. A different series of investigations starting in 1979 revealed other sorts of official theft and bribery to be common in Krasnodar. In the countryside widespread use was also being made of illegal construction teams. But Medunov managed to contain these unpleasant problems and, as his prominent place at the 1981 party congress showed, he continued to flourish.

Sochi was the most famous of Krasnodar's seaside resorts, an obviously profitable target for sellers of boot-legged caviar. Stalin had turned the little pre-revolutionary riviera town into one of his characteristic fantasies behind whose screen he got on with the messy business of building up Soviet might. The country's very first resorts had been the seaside palaces that Lenin confiscated from the Romanovs and their aristocracy, and the traces remain to this day of the inherited belief that a worker deserves no less than vast buildings, chandeliers and marble when he goes on holiday. The Stalin-era architects of Sochi entirely subscribed to this style. In the poor, rough world of the Soviet 1930s their neo-classical palaces surrounded by richly planted gardens were perhaps a necessary mirage, bewitching many though reached by very few. The Sochi of the early 1980s was a very different place. Some meritorious workers still spent their allotted days in the 1930s Italianate splendour of Metallurg, the steelworkers' sanitorium, but hundreds of thousands of others managed either through their farm or factory but increasingly through their own initiative to get to its overcrowded hotels and narrow beaches. Brezhnev's economic experts had managed to give the Soviet people a great deal more money than attractive goods and services to spend it on. When a citizen went on holiday he did not mind paying a bribe or something extra to get somewhere to stay, to penetrate into a discothèque, or even to find a table in a café undistinguished in every possible way except that it was one of too few. In the West there would have been automatic adjustment, prices rushing up until demand was brought under control. Brezhnev's Soviet Union did not allow such 'anarchy of the market', as one of his colleagues on the Politburo called it. The adjustment was made nevertheless by a black market. In the Black Sea resort towns of Krasnodar there were fortunes to be made – illegally. And made they were.

It took several years for the story of what went wrong in Krasnodar to emerge and even now, under Gorbachov's policy of 'openness', there has been no attempt to publish a complete version. Pieces of the puzzle have appeared in one newspaper only to be ignored by all the rest. But it is obvious that the government of the territory went rotten. The seriousness of the situation may be guessed from the quality of the party officials drafted in to clean up Medunov's mess. The first, in the summer of 1982, was Vitali

Vorotnikov, later to become prime minister of the Russian Republic and a member of the Politburo. His successor, Georgi Razumovsky, after two years in Krasnodar became head of the organizational party work department of the Central Committee, arguably the most important section in the party's headquarters for it supervises all senior appointments.

Even while Medunov ruled in Krasnodar reports appeared suggesting all was not well in his kingdom. One visitor described going shopping in the territory's capital and finding on the black market 'everything I could not buy in the shops'. The black market with its network of merchants and clients and their joint protectors turned out to be astonishingly like the territory's real economy. The first revelation, after Medunov's departure for Moscow, was about Gelendzhik, a resort just up the coast from the more famous Sochi. The centre of the scandal was a woman called Bella Borodkina, director of Gelendzhik's cafés and restaurants. Iron Bella, as she was known in the town, ran a racket that was far from original. Her employees were encouraged and sometimes ordered to cheat customers by overcharging them or giving short weight (all portions in Soviet restaurants are meant by law to be weighed). The employees passed on part of this money to Iron Bella. She expected chefs in the biggest restaurants to pay her £2,500 a month at the height of the season. She used a good part of this money – almost half a million pounds – to bribe the men who supplied her restaurants. This ensured she had the pick of their store rooms. At her arrest she was found to have property worth nearly one million pounds. In April 1986 she went before a firing squad, the first woman to be executed in the Soviet Union for many years.

Why such a severe punishment? It was partly because of the huge amounts involved. When the director of Moscow's biggest foodshop was arrested later in 1982 it was learned that he had taken bribes worth only £250,000. But one may guess it also had to do with the thoroughness of Bella Borodkina's corruption of Gelendzhik's leading officials. She bribed the senior officers of the town's militia, the uniformed police. She even had in her pay the men of the department for combating the embezzlement of socialist property and speculation, the Soviet fraud squad usually known by its Russian initials as the OBKhSS. She secured the protection of the chairman of the committee of people's control, supposed to be the local public morals watchdog. But her most powerful patron was the head of the Gelendzhik party himself. Rumour had it that he fled abroad when the scandal broke. After that it was no surprise when other pillars of the community including the procurator (the chief legal officer) and the head of the militia were also implicated in the affair and sacked in disgrace.

Iron Bella's fall was a warning to all of Krasnodar where the clean-up after Medunov's departure was to take at least three years. Moscow had to appoint a new chief of militia for the whole of the territory. Carefully chosen members of the Communist party and of its youth organization, the

Komsomol, had to be drafted into the militia ranks, as many as a thousand of them in 1984 alone. In the two years after Medunov's replacement nearly half of the secretaries on Krasnodar's town and district party committees were removed and the same number of local government officials. Some were moved because they were inefficient or unsuitable for the job but many were sacked. There was also a thorough purge of the men and women who ran the territory's farms and factories.

It has never been explained exactly where Medunov himself fitted into the sleazy, secret world of Soviet Krasnodar; whether he was manipulated by it, or just turned a blind eye to it, or whether he played a more active part. At the very least he was guilty of a poor choice of subordinates; of ignoring numerous complaints from the public about what was going on; and of trying to protect some of the guilty. It is possible, though, that he was much more actively involved in wrongdoing than that. After a few miserable months in the fruit and vegetable ministry and Brezhnev was dead the Central Committee expelled Medunov from its own ranks and from the party. It is not known if criminal charges were brought against him. There has been no word of a trial.

But Sergei Medunov was never the real issue in the summer of 1982. He was a modest trophy in a hunt for much bigger game. At the time of Medunov's fall Moscow was already enjoying gossip about much more exciting people than a provincial party baron, whatever his importance in the hierarchy of power. The rumours had begun at the beginning of the year and by the spring extremely detailed accounts of the scandal were being published in the West although no documentary evidence existed for any of it. 'Death, Diamonds and Brezhnev's daughter,' said one foreign headline, as succinct a summary of the affair as could be wished for. Brezhnev's only daughter Galina was said to be having an affair with a minor administrator at the Bolshoi theatre called Boris Buryata. Buryata in turn was said to be involved in an illegal trade in diamonds with the director of the Soviet national circus Anatoli Kolevatov. Galina Brezhnev was already well known to Moscow gossips. She was fifty-three and 'so plump' according to one uncharitable Muscovite 'that if you pricked her butter would run out'. Her first two marriages had been to circus performers but she had now acquired a more appropriate husband – Yuri Churbanov, first deputy minister of internal affairs and the country's second most senior uniformed policeman. Buryata, also known as Boris the Gypsy because he had once sung in Moscow's Gypsy theatre, was nevertheless often seen with Galina and his way of life suggested he had another source of income beside his modest salary from the Bolshoi. He had a weakness for smart cars and drove a Mercedes. A handsome, big man, he also liked jewellery. Some Muscovites swear that when the police came to arrest him he was wearing a gold and diamond cross. Others insist that under his nutria bath robe he had a gold and diamond chain which he refused to take off saying it was a present from Brezhnev's daughter. The police rang Galina up and she confirmed it . . .

The most interesting thing about this and the other stories that were circulated at that time was not their truth. There was, and still is, no way to prove or disprove them. They were interesting just because they were being spread around. The Soviet leadership led a sheltered life. Their families seldom appeared in public. There was never any gossip about them in the press. The women in particular led lives almost as secluded as the ladies of the old Moscow court before Peter the Great forced Western ways on Russia. Brezhnev's wife Viktoria was an almost mysterious figure. Practically no one would have recognized her if she walked down a Moscow street, which of course she was most unlikely to do. Even the stormy Galina was not well-known beyond the privileged circle of capital gossips. And yet here was Moscow talking about the most intimate details of her life and even passing them on to foreign correspondents and diplomats with impunity. It was the clearest possible sign that *lèse majesté* was no longer dangerous. There were other signs too, not least the jokes.

Making jokes in the Soviet Union, as in any authoritarian society (an old-fashioned school, for example), need not signal daring, let alone rebellion. Jokes in that sort of world are more likely a gesture of resignation and even self-reproach. Russians have long known this. The nineteenth-century liberal Alexander Herzen called this sort of laughter 'self-flagellation'. It was, he said, 'our atonement, the only protest, the only revenge, that was possible to us'. But by 1982 the jokes about Brezhnev had become extraordinarily cruel, making much fun of his physical disability. Foreigners in Moscow had for several years argued about how competent the old man was to conduct the affairs of state. By the time of the twenty-sixth party congress in 1981 diplomats professed to be encouraged by reports that his attention span had lengthened from thirty minutes to a whole two hours. In many ways the foreign world conspired with the Kremlin to keep the truth about Brezhnev from the Soviet people. No foreign statesman who had an audience with him would admit the old man could do little more than read from a piece of paper, leaving real conversation to foreign minister Gromyko. To do so would have diminished the importance of the occasion and also the importance of the visitor. And the Russians became very skilful in propping Brezhnev up, either literally with sturdy men who followed him around or in other ways, for example abroad, when the resourceful Gromyko was ready almost to sing and dance to distract attention from his uncomprehending leader.

The Soviet people, however, did not need to be tactful. The little they saw of Brezhnev on television was enough to convince them he was getting gaga. They noticed he could no longer pin medals on people. His fingers could not manage the catch. Instead he gave the medals in a case and even then his hand was seen to shake. His speech was on occasions so slurred it could hardly be understood. People imitated it and laughed. He was given nicknames like Five Star Rotgut, a play on his fondness for medals and the

Russian slang for the cheap fortified wine that heavy drinkers favoured. Someone thought up a neat variation on the old slogan 'Lenin is dead but his deeds live on'. 'Brezhnev is dead,' the new one ran, 'but his body lives on.' (The pun in Russian was neat. The word for deeds, *delo*, was almost the same as the word for body, *telo*.) A popular generic joke of those years had to do with a tiny nationality called the Chukchis, an Eskimo-like people who live in the far north-east of Siberia. The Chukchis, for the purpose of these jokes, were taken to be stupid fellows but through their stupidity a truth was often revealed. A Chukchi goes to the Central Committee headquarters in Moscow's Old Square and knocks at the door. He tells the official who receives him that he wants to join the Politburo. The official gets very angry. 'What's the matter with you? Are you ill?' The Chukchi looks surprised. 'Oh, I didn't know. Do you have to be?'

A well-connected Moscow family, watching the usual end of year TV special for 1981, turned away in disgust when Brezhnev appeared on the screen to mumble his New Year greetings. A man who attended Central Committee meetings in Brezhnev's last years later admitted that he had sat there wondering how this puffing invalid could possibly control the huge machinery of the Communist party and Soviet state. And there were occasions when the disrespect was not kept private. A foreigner attending a public lecture on the Soviet space programme not long before Brezhnev's death was amazed to hear the cosmonaut German Titov say, in answer to a question, that 'the old man doesn't know how to do anything'. No one doubted that he meant Brezhnev.

Part of the problem was that the iller Brezhnev became the more he had to be glorified. By the end of the 1970s his private office had become almost a Kremlin version of the White House and had taken most of the burden off him. His assistants submitted only the most important matters for his decision and then always in simplified form. In spite of this, knowledgeable Russians never expected Brezhnev or any other of his senior contemporaries to retire. A man who knew the Kremlin at first hand predicted that 'the old men will stay on till they die because otherwise they would be thrown overboard. They just wouldn't have any more public respect.' The party had no way of dealing with this lack of any system for honourable retirement except to declare, in the face of the increasingly obvious, that the country was lucky to have in Brezhnev its wisest, most competent ruler since Lenin. This was dangerous not only because it was obviously untrue and contributed to the cynicism that was so marked a feature of the late Brezhnev years. It was dangerous, too, because it created an atmosphere in which Brezhnev and those round him felt free to practise the politics of whim. In 1980 Brezhnev made his forty-three-year-old son-in-law Yuri Churbanov first deputy minister of internal affairs though there were older and more senior men poised for the job. The next year he brought Churbanov into the Central Committee as a candidate member. In 1979 Brezhnev's only son

Yuri was appointed first deputy minister of foreign trade, also over the heads of older and more experienced men. And in 1981 Yuri Brezhnev, too, became a candidate member of the Central Committee.

The children of the Kremlin were not a new problem. Lenin was lucky to have had a childless marriage. Stalin indulged, sometimes spitefully, his sons and one daughter but never so far as to damage his own dignity. By Brezhnev's day it was thought quite proper to do the best one could for one's children. Their privileged education assured them entry into the intelligentsia to which the parents had never belonged. But it was not acceptable to thrust them into a political career. It was one thing for the leader of a country like Romania to put his family into positions of power but it still went against the Moscow grain. When it had been attempted it ended in tears. Khrushchov had transformed his journalist son-in-law Aleksei Adzhubei into a member of the Central Committee and deputed authority to him. This was later condemned as one of Khrushchov's so-called 'hare-brained schemes'. Adzhubei was removed from the Central Committee within a few months of the quiet coup against his father-in-law, and never allowed back into any job of importance. Brezhnev seemed to have forgotten this cautionary tale. Otherwise he might have foreseen that the first party congress after his death would drop both his son and son-in-law from the Central Committee, and that Yuri Brezhnev would also lose his government post.

And perhaps Brezhnev was becoming careless in other ways, too. He lived in luxury like most (if not all) of his colleagues but it was the state's luxury, the functional luxury that was arguably necessary for the ruler of any great country. His resort villa at Pitsunda on the Krasnodar coast (where Sergei Medunov had had an opportunity to do his obliging best for the old man) and his little palace at Oreanda in the Crimea were not Brezhnev's to hand on to his children and grandchildren. Was he to be blamed if he did want to hand something on? It was only after his death that there was talk of a gold dagger in a diamond-studded sheath that was found among his possessions. It was supposed to have been given to him during a visit to Azerbaidzhan, his last journey out of Moscow before he died. There was another rumour about a gold samovar weighing forty-two kilograms – the story was most precise about the weight – that was also said to have been discovered in one of his private safes.

Does such gossip have a place in history? Remove it from an account of the last years of the Brezhnev era and that account will thereby be distorted. It tells us something important of the time that such stories were often told and almost as often believed. It speaks volumes of the atmosphere of mystery and intrigue during the last part of Brezhnev's rule that they were so fearlessly spread and discussed. But, most important, they were a signal that someone had identified a serious illness in the Soviet body politic. It could have been someone who exploited it against Brezhnev and his friends just because it was the best weapon to hand. There were precedents for that kind of politics in the Kremlin. But it was the fate, and perhaps good luck, of the Soviet Union that the man who really made the politics of the last year of Brezhnev's life – the man who engineered the disgracing of Medunov and the whispering about Brezhnev's family – deeply cared about this illness. Yuri Andropov, the Politburo member who manoeuvred so skilfully to succeed Leonid Brezhnev, was a puritan.

3

Time of Troubles

It cannot be proved that Yuri Andropov managed to seize power in the Kremlin because he was a puritan, a throwback to the austere generation of Bolshevik revolutionaries who, while ready to make others suffer for their own good, were also ready to suffer themselves. But the Andropov puritanism and a more widely shared sense of dismay over the state of the country's affairs were to provide much of the emotional and moral power for the changes that began after Brezhnev's death. It is impossible to estimate how widespread this unease was. The politicians did not refer to it at all in their speeches while Brezhnev was alive, except to talk about specific economic and social difficulties. It was common, though, to hear members of the intelligentsia talk privately of their worries. These were not just the worries of everyday life, of the growth of bad social habits like drunkenness and drug taking (people knew the latter was becoming a problem but it was never admitted officially). They went beyond concern about the way bribery had become part of daily life or the growth of some crimes, particularly those associated with drunkenness.

Much more painful was the sense that the country, rather than developing, was decaying, falling apart like one of the blocks on the new housing estates because it had been badly built and was now being badly maintained by people who were losing their skills and no longer cared. The pain was all the greater because the leaders pretended everything was going splendidly, and were praised as though they were miracle-workers. A gifted actor turned *chansonnier*, most of whose songs circulated on scratchy, unofficial tapes, became for many Russians the hero of these last Brezhnev years. In 1986 a famous poet offered a lurid summary of what people felt they had been up against in the recent past – 'the monstrous strength of evil, of

21

lawlessness, of corruption, extortion, falseness and duplicity.' Vladimir Vysotsky's admirers considered him the antidote to this age of falseness. 'To listen to him,' a friend said, 'was like breathing oxygen.' He described how Vysotsky had once gone down a street in the new industrial town that was later re-named after Brezhnev and heard the sound of his own voice from almost every open window. People knew he was visiting and had put on their tapes of him in his honour. 'Imagine what power there was there.' Vysotsky sang about what people really thought and felt during those years.

> The grief that penetrated through his happiness brought together in the most astonishing way the most different kinds of people. And what could bring us, such very different people, together except conscience? [Vysotsky] was himself conscience laid bare. He was suffering itself.

Vysotsky was the anguished voice of those people who had believed change was possible in the first years after Stalin's death but were now no longer sure. He was angry, but loyal in spite of it. After his death during the Moscow Olympics, one could see army officers laying flowers at his grave as well as the teenagers who might stand for hours looking at their hero's photograph while playing his songs on a tape recorder. That was why one could even hear a senior party member say that to understand the Soviet Union one had to understand Vysotsky.

The black mood did sometimes find its way past the censorship, and nowhere more memorably than in a story called *Pozhar, The Fire*, by the Siberian writer Valentin Rasputin. He had won a considerable reputation in the Soviet Union and abroad as a chronicler of Russian country life. But above all he was a moralist and *The Fire* was nothing if not a moral tale for present Soviet times. It is set in Sosnovka, a logging settlement in Siberia – 'uncomfortable and untidy, not a town and not a village but a bivouac'. Its puzzled hero, Ivan Petrovich, is just about to retire as head of one of the lumberjack sections. His is the voice that comments on the story.

The fire breaks out at night in Sosnovka's warehouse but there is no fire engine because it has been cannibalized for spare parts. This and the unorganized attempt to fight the fire inspire Ivan Petrovich to a gloomy monologue. Why had everyone become so free and easy, so careless? It hadn't been like that in the war and the difficult years after it but the old customs and laws that had saved the villages then had been forgotten. Perhaps it was because Sosnovka wasn't really like the old villages. Six of them had been flooded by a hydro-electric station and resettled here as a logging settlement. There was something demoralizing in just cutting down timber. The new inhabitants of Sosnovka grew nothing for themselves. And the drunks who had always existed in 'old Russia' had now become a 'shameless' force, not afraid of anything or anyone. The last four years had seen almost as many deaths from drunkenness as the six villages that made up Sosnovka had known during all the war. The new people who came to work as loggers were a strange race. They had no family, no friends. They could not help themselves or others. They had in their eyes the look of men who were not living but serving out a life sentence. The old villagers had become corrupted too. They used the settlement's lorries for their private purposes. They had started to steal. They expected to be offered vodka before they would work.

How had it happened?

The world doesn't turn over at once, at one blow, but it's like with us: something wasn't done – now it is done, it wasn't allowed – now it is, it was considered shameful, a mortal sin – now it's considered smart, a triumph. And for how long shall we go on surrendering that to which we have held fast for centuries? Where, from what reserves, will the wished for help come?

He does not know the answer. The disorganized firefighters get drunk, looting vodka and bottles of Hungarian and Bulgarian wine which they mix with eau de cologne, a new village fashion. An old watchman tries to stop the looting and is killed. There had been one law in the watchman's life: don't steal. Stealing was for him the root of all evil. He sobbed when it happened but in Sosnovka he had had to get used to it.

Ivan Petrovich had tried to follow his own conscience but he ended up at war with both others and himself. The new workers who came to the settlement were getting worse and harder to manage. They sometimes terrorized him, putting sand in the tank of his lorry and tearing up his garden fence because he was the only one who complained about them. The rest 'put up with it, believing every change is for the better'. But surely what counted was a man's work. Good work was what lived on after you. Of course in the past people had never been entirely true to the good but they had known there was a clear line between the good and the bad; the number of them passing over to the good side had grown. 'But what happened then was impossible to understand. Who frightened them, the people who had already crossed the line and tasted good, why did they turn back?' They had started to 'wander back and forth between the good and the bad . . . Good and bad had got mixed up. Good in its pure form had turned into weakness, bad into strength.'

Why couldn't people see this? Perhaps because they had mistaken change and modernization for true progress. 'We have arrived at what for centuries we had been leaving behind. No, not arrived, but rather driven up in a motor car and declaring it the greatest victory of man precisely because we went away on foot and have come back in a car.'

The story has no happy end. The fire is put out. Nothing seems likely to change in Sosnovka. Ivan Petrovich's unease remains. The only place he feels he can look for guidance, for a final judgement, is the land. He walks deep into the forest but 'the land is silent, not greeting him, not saying goodbye'.

It is difficult to think of a more intense expression of disquiet about the condition of Soviet society and its direction. The logging settlement that eats up the surrounding forests and then moves on is an image of Brezhnev's Russia with its increasingly wasteful consumption of natural resources. The Soviet Union, like Sosnovka, had come to judge success in terms of meeting economic plans, but apart from those plans being possibly misguided what about other values? 'It would be better,' Rasputin's Ivan Petrovich thinks, 'if we had another plan – not just for cubic metres, but for souls! To work out how many souls are lost, gone to the devil, and how many remain!'

Shortly before Brezhnev died a very different kind of writer tackled the same themes of social demoralization and decay. Fyodor Burlatsky was a political scientist, author of the first Soviet study of Machiavelli, and an intellectual with unusually good connections to the world of power around the party Central Committee. He was to become a skilful public advocate of change and 'liberalization' in the post-Brezhnev era. Rasputin looked at his country from the point of view of someone whose values come from the traditional world of man living with nature – the world of the old Russian village. Burlatsky came from a different background, one highly educated both in the traditional Russian and modern Soviet sense. But the feeling of alarm was no less apparent in what he wrote.

> We are talking . . . about the broadest dissemination in society of immorality, inhumanity, untruth and disorder. In other words, of the destruction of the socio-psychological foundations on which the entire building of society stands . . . morality and family relations, daily living and mass psychology, legality and the forms of distribution of material goods.

This remarkable analysis got published because, ostensibly, it was not about the Soviet Union at all but a study, called *Interregnum*, of China after the death of Mao Tsedung. But the usually alert readers of the literary journal *Novy Mir* that published it could not fail to spot the Soviet likeness. It was a tradition to use China studies to make points about the Soviet Union. And with everyone waiting for Brezhnev to die it could be said that a Soviet interregnum had already begun. Burlatsky used the phrase 'Time of Troubles' to describe the Chinese events. Every Russian knew this was the name of the period of seventeenth-century instability before the establishment of the Romanov dynasty. Anyone with foresight had to expect something similar when Brezhnev, the ruler for a long eighteen years, at last departed.

The concern expressed, albeit guardedly, in these writings and which permeated the gravelly songs of Vysotsky went far beyond doubts about the conduct of the Brezhnev family and misbehaviour, however gross, in Krasnodar. It was a feeling that the moral purpose had gone out of public life and that private manners were threatened too. The cruelty of Stalinism had coexisted with, and would have been impossible without, a belief in the establishment that this was perhaps the only way to build a modern, strong Soviet state. The war had seen tragedy turn to a glorious recovery of national purpose. The post-Stalin years under Khrushchov may have ended in disarray but they had begun in hope, not just of a better material life but also of a better, more humane society. It had been 'a period of great illusions', according to a Russian who grew up during it, 'people felt that they were personally taking part in the creation of an upright, decent Motherland'. Brezhnev's rule killed many of those hopes, though by neglect rather than cruelty. It also unwittingly poisoned some of the fruits it did manage to harvest. The consumer boom over which Brezhnev so proudly presided created new demands among consumers which it then was unable to satisfy. There was nothing new about shops not having much to offer. The novelty was that shops did now sometimes have unheard-of delights like well-made shoes or Polish cosmetics or modern Yugoslav furniture. But who managed to buy them? And who were these people on the streets wearing obviously Western clothes? And how did the neighbours suddenly manage to buy a new Zhiguli car when you had been waiting five years for a chance?

The press was full of moralizing comment on the corrupting effects of shortages. And it is true that living with them was a strain. Decent people were forced to behave badly to keep up with the rest. This is the confession, surely not untypical, of a well brought-up Russian woman who was slow to learn the secrets of Soviet shopping:

It wasn't till I was thirty that I realised there was another way than standing in queues. As a schoolgirl after the war I used to queue for all the productions at the Arts theatre. One winter I was the only one in my group with proper winter boots so I kept places for my friends till the box office opened . . . And then I met our new neighbour Valya. We were in her flat and I said something about badly needing new winter boots and not knowing where on earth to find them. Of course it was useless just going round the shops looking for them. Valya said 'You want boots?' and started dialling a number on the telephone. She said to the person who answered 'Nina, have you got any good boots, a friend needs some? . . . All right, she'll be round tomorrow afternoon.' She turned to me, 'That's settled. Go round to this store, up to the fourth department, and ask for Nina Andreyevna. Say I sent you and remember to pay five roubles *on top*.' Of course this was some time ago. You'd have to pay much more on top these days. I went there the next afternoon, terribly nervous and hardly daring to ask for Nina Andreyevna. This woman appeared and took me into the back where customers aren't supposed to go. They kept all the goods there in great cages, like animals. She took me into a cage full of boots. 'Here,' the woman said. 'We've got Finnish boots, Austrian boots, even Soviet boots. Try them on.' I couldn't believe it and I was so scared I took the first pair that fitted. I was still in a panic because I had no idea how to give her the five roubles on top. She sent me to pay the bill at the cash desk and when I came back said straight out, 'Valya told you about the five roubles on top?' Yes, I said, so relieved I almost threw the five rouble note I was clutching in her face. But I've never stood in queues since.

Experiences like this, multiplied tens of thousands of times, explained why shop workers closely followed by the staff of restaurants, cafés and such service industries as existed invariably came top of the unpopularity polls. People not only felt at their mercy. Some also felt cheapened by having to deal with them on their own terms. The press and the political leaders encouraged this indignation. They were less keen to provoke an alternative debate on how the economic system itself, not the wretches who had to make it work, might be the true corrupter. That point was made, however, in an unusual novel, *Department Store*, by a writer who admitted modelling himself on Arthur Haley. The book's hero, Firtich, is director of a big city department store. He lives in a world, familiar to every Soviet citizen, of dishonest cashiers, speculators buying up goods in short supply to resell at a profit, crooked restaurant managers, and food shops that keep their best goods for special customers while bribing government inspectors to look the other way. Firtich's problem is that he believes in trade as an honourable way of life while most people round him do not. 'They don't know how to work. They're not professionals.' His biggest battle is to get decent goods to sell. The aim of his suppliers is the opposite. A factory bribes the head of Firtich's shoe department with diamonds to persuade her to accept a delivery of abominably made and quite unsellable shoes. Firtich has a brilliant idea. He should have his own quality controllers in the factories just as the Soviet military does in weapons-making plants – 'Do they let rubbish get through?'

The book got some hostile reviews. Its hero, one critic said, was no better than a crook, trying to persuade the readers that it was impossible to be both honest and to survive in Soviet trade. This happened to be true, as the Soviet press would later reveal. Much of retail trade was based on short-changing customers to create the slush-fund necessary to buy the good will of the trade bureaucracy. It was an inevitable consequence of shortages and the reluctance to let economic laws operate.

The publicity given to the wickednesses of the world of trade did not succeed in concentrating public unease on this easy target alone. In the more open years after Brezhnev's death sociologists produced fascinating lists of the most unpopular professions that went far beyond the wretched Firtiches. Among them were doctors, the renter-owners of private houses and flats in resort towns, workers in economic organizations, local government authorities, and the law enforcement agencies.

This list brings one closer to the causes of Soviet corruption. There was nothing surprising about the doctors and the renters of seaside houses being on the list. They both provided services often in short supply either for a bribe or an exorbitant price and were particularly resented ('I've discovered,' sighed a Muscovite whose husband had been dangerously ill, 'that there's nothing so expensive as a system of free medical help'). But the others on the list represented the government. Many of them would also be members of the party.

Few actions taken by Yuri Andropov produced such an effect as his sacking, a month after becoming general secretary, of the country's police chief Nikolai Shcholokov. Shcholokov, who had the rank of army general, had been appointed minister of internal affairs by Brezhnev in 1966. The two men were in fact old friends. The families lived in the same grand apartment building on Kutuzovsky Prospect. Nothing was said at the time of Shcholokov's removal to suggest he had done anything wrong. It was only at the twenty-seventh party congress, when he had been dead two years, that he was publicly accused of 'unworthy conduct, the most serious infractions of party discipline and socialist legality, of degeneration'. Not that unofficial Moscow had ever had any doubt about that. The militia, as was later to be admitted by the press, was widely thought capable of most kinds of villainy. No one was surprised by the rumour that Shcholokov had allocated to himself and his friends some new Mercedes Benz cars meant for the police force. An old story was revived about Mrs. Shcholokov being seen wearing in public fine jewellery remarkably like some known to have been stolen from the widow of the successful and rich writer Aleksei Tolstoi. Retribution also fell on Shcholokov's son Igor who had been making a career in the youth organization, the Komsomol. Within months of his father's dismissal Igor was voted out of his seat as a candidate member of the Komsomol's ruling bureau.

The purge continued far beyond the ex-police chief's own family. In the months and years that followed his dismissal the senior ranks of the internal affairs ministry were also thoroughly cleaned out, though it was never revealed how many of the men who left had been guilty of more than incompetence and neglect of duty. Most of the deputy ministers went, as did the heads of the OBKhSS, of criminal investigation, and of the traffic police (whose men's notorious susceptibility to bribes had long been a joke – and a comfort – to truckdrivers and motorists). A similar purge took place throughout the country. Tens of thousands of hopefully honest men and women were brought into the militia, among them no less than 55,000 communists drafted from local party organizations. And to help keep them honest the militia was for the first time given its own political officers comparable to the commissars the Soviet army has long had to live with. Their job would be to ginger up the militiamen's conscience, to 'increase the responsibility of personnel for the discharge of their duties'. A senior official from the Central Committee's administrative organs department that supervises the law enforcement agencies was appointed to head the militia's new political directorate: a clear sign that the change was meant seriously. (The purge was perhaps inevitably carried to excess and some innocent policemen were later reinstated in their jobs.)

There was nothing original about much that went wrong with the Soviet police force. It is natural for criminals to try to corrupt the one group of men who have unchallenged power over them. Krasnodar, not surprisingly, provided many examples of this. A captain in the territory's OBKhSS, investigating bribery on a collective farm, discovered that the foremen of construction gangs were paying their men less than they should and pocketing the balance. The captain summoned one of them for cross- examination. He stressed the seriousness of the case, said his superiors were concerned about it – in other words he played his victim along like the villain in a thousand novels about corrupt cops. The victim was a self-confident fellow who drove around in a Volga painted in the then fashionable light grey colour known as 'white night'. He at once understood the policeman's game and was happy to keep him quiet with payments that in the end came to more than £20,000.

Something like the policeman-criminal relationship was repeated outside the Soviet underworld. Power flowed down from the centre, from Moscow. A politician's or bureaucrat's career depended on him pleasing those above him, not those below, though they were the people whom he was meant to serve. An ambitious criminal like 'Iron Bella' Borodkina in Gelendzhik knew that if she was to be secure it was not enough to buy off the police. She had to buy off the party, in the shape of the town first secretary if possible, for it was the party that had ultimate power over the police as it did over every other part of Soviet life. All local party bodies had their administrative organs sections to supervise the militia. And even before the creation in 1983 of a political directorate in the ministry of internal affairs every police force had its party *aktiv* which was meant to be the party's eyes and ears as well as a source of moral and political leadership. As for a local party leader, the boss of Gelendzhik for example, once he had been tempted into protecting the criminal or the merely mildly corrupt, he had to make sure that he remained in favour with the one man who could make or break him – in this case, until August 1982, Sergei Medunov. Then he, too, was secure.

It was a system that bred excesses worthy of the Russian nineteenth-century satirists who of course were observing a similarly centralized system of power. Almost nothing, it sometimes seemed, was too ridiculous if it won the favour of a superior. Could it be possible that an important party leader like the head of a region would undertake to double production of meat *in one year*? Yes, it could. In 1959, when Nikita Khrushchov was trying to haul Soviet farms out of the mess they had been left in by Stalin, the first secretary of Ryazan promised exactly that. Ryazan eventually met an even higher target. Its first secretary was made a Hero of Socialist Labour and awarded the Order of Lenin. The feat was written into the school textbooks. The next year the truth came out. Almost all Ryazan's livestock had been slaughtered to meet the ridiculous target. The Ryazan party leader had sent his men into other regions to buy up their cattle, often illegally. A meat tax was levied on all local institutions forcing factories to send workers to buy meat in shops which was then sold back to the authorities as newly slaughtered. When the Central Committee finally sent out a commission to investigate the party secretary, the new Hero of Socialist Labour took a gun and shot himself in his office. This was not an odd, exotic episode. Similar if less spectacular stories were to emerge in the mid-1980s from Uzbekistan where local party leaders fulfilled routine farm plans by buying produce from their own shops.

The power of the party did not entirely explain why the perpetrators of these and other crimes thought they would get away with it. The party had its control mechanisms, starting with the Central Committee departments in Moscow. All party committees were elected. The statutes laid down the right of rank-and-file members to criticize, and of primary party organizations to supervise the implementation of party policy. But some of these safeguards existed only on paper. Party committees were in fact usually chosen from above, not elected from below. And there were almost infallible – although certainly not legal – ways of fending off criticism from ordinary party members or a rebellious low level party organization. Soviet television began in the summer of 1985 a new drama series about the adventures of an investigative reporter. The first instalment showed him trying to get to the bottom of a housing scandal in a small town. The local bosses tried to silence him by blackmail. First they photographed him drinking (Gorbachov's new anti-alcohol laws were by then in effect). Next they photographed him with a girl. Transfer it to America and it would have been unsurprising, but in the Soviet Union? The truth is that this sort of thing became routine under Brezhnev, and continued after his death. Even when Gorbachov had been in power almost a year some policemen in Baku, the capital of Azerbaidzhan, almost succeeded in having one of their colleagues sent to prison after he had accused them, correctly, of taking bribes.

The author of the 1985 TV series, Arkadi Vaksberg, was a journalist who had won fame by his legal investigations. They were printed at immense length in the intellectuals' weekly paper *Literaturnaya Gazeta* where even the stars of the literary establishment read them with admiration. Vaksberg knew at first hand the lengths to which local leaderships were ready to go to protect their discreditable secrets: in his case they had included threats of violence and hints of even worse. After the twenty-seventh party congress he published a remarkable analysis – remarkable not least because it was published – of the machinery of pressure and manipulation used to silence criticism. The Supreme Court, no less, had just listed the illegal ways in which powerful officials punished the over-critically minded. They could have them sacked. They could drive them to the bottom of the housing queue. They could stop them getting a garden allotment. In these and many other ways they could make someone's life a misery. And their chosen tool, Vaksberg revealed (though it can have been no revelation to the averagely aware Soviet citizen), was invariably the telephone. His law professor at university, he recalled, had always warned his students not to confuse the real law with 'telephone law'. 'How much water has gone under the bridge since then,' Vaksberg wrote, 'but "telephone law", alas, hasn't disappeared – it's only grown stronger. To such an extent that people are no longer ashamed of it. In one town after another respected jurists have expressed surprise at my surprise. "How could you?" I would say getting angry and thereby showing unpardonable naivety, "how could you do such a thing?" For an answer I got an easy nod of the head at the shameless telephone: what, do you mean to say you don't understand?'

According to Vaksberg there were still plenty of legal officials – and by implication officials of every other kind, too – 'for whom a telephone call from an "influential person", particularly someone "local", someone who is "one of us", is everywhere and in everything taken as more important than the law. Not only more important but also more necessary . . .'

A trial at the beginning of 1986 explained how easy it was for an ambitious and unscrupulous man to enrich himself under such a system. Vasili Vyshku had been appointed deputy prime minister of Moldavia at the young age of forty-one. The following year he became a full member of the Moldavian central committee. He appeared to be a man of the future. He went jogging every morning, scoring points by his modest sports outfit of a Soviet-made tracksuit and old running shoes (flashy Soviet joggers preferred Adidas or other foreign sports clothes). Vyshku made money, probably hundreds of thousands of pounds, by selling protection and favours to his friends. Why did people give him so much money, sometimes in packets of up to £10,000? 'I don't know exactly,' Vyshku told the court. 'Probably, for friendship . . . for my good will.' He was a skilled user of the telephone. A single call was enough to get his mistress a two-roomed flat she had no legal claim to. He sold jobs, even taking £9,500 from a man who wanted to be made manager of a warehouse.

The newspaper report of the Vyshku trial went on to make more general points. The deputy prime minister had used his power and his friends for illegal purposes. 'But it sometimes happens differently. A leader, having surrounded himself with "his" people doesn't go beyond the law. All he does is make a peaceful life for himself by creating an atmosphere that won't tolerate criticism. He smothers any initiative with routine.' Moldavia had been a stepping stone in Brezhnev's career. He made there many of the friends whom later he brought to supreme power with him. Sometimes known as the 'Moldavian gypsies' these included the ill-fated police chief Shcholokov and Konstantin Chernenko, the right-hand man of Brezhnev's last years. The Vyshku affair was not a complete surprise. The cloud of scandal had been hanging over Moldavia for some time. In 1980 Brezhnev appointed Ivan Bodyul, the Moldavian party leader who had once worked under him in the capital, Kishinyov, to be a deputy Soviet prime minister. Five years later Bodyul was 'retired'. At the end of 1985 the prime minister of Moldavia was also retired though he was only a year older than Vyshku. This was after a Moscow newspaper had revealed that many of the republic's economic managers had, on instructions from an unspecified 'above', been filing false performance figures.

Moldavia was an example of power misused for personal gain; of power misused to maintain oneself in power, if necessary by faking reports about one's achievements and sitting on anyone who tried to blow the whistle. It is fair to assume that Brezhnev's sentimental interest in a republic he had known as a younger man made this misuse of power easier. Kishinyov in return flattered the old man by displaying an inordinate number of his portraits in public places and turning the office he had used when he was Moldavian party leader into a museum.

Without Brezhnev's benign neglect the safety mechanisms that did exist within the Soviet system might have worked. It was not just a matter of the party's self-policing machinery. There was also the committee of state security, the KGB, which had the authority to investigate particularly serious cases of corruption. The evidence is that danger signals did reach Moscow – not just from Moldavia but even more urgently from the republics of Soviet Central Asia – but that they were ignored or consciously not acted upon. This was revealed at the twenty-seventh party congress in early 1986. The party's personnel offices (the organizational party work departments) had failed to do what they were supposed to do. Supervision was weak. They had been slow to make the correct moral judgements on the facts before them. That had to be the explanation, a speaker concluded, because it was impossible to suppose that no one in the Central Committee in Moscow had known what was going on.

This brings one closer to the sense of urgency in Yuri Andropov's bid for power. Corruption was not new in the Soviet Union. No less than three members of the Gorbachov Politburo, the party leadership elected at the twenty-seventh party congress, had made their name by cleaning the comrade rascals out. Vitali Vorotnikov had cleaned up after Medunov in Krasnodar. Eduard Shevardnadze, Gorbachov's foreign minister, was promoted from minister of internal affairs in Georgia to head the republic's party with the mission of purging an establishment that was as much Mafia as Marxist. A similar scandal had brought Geidar Aliyev, Azerbaidzhan's KGB chief, to leadership of the Azerbaidzhani party in 1969. Aliyev, it was said, had only managed to cut back the corruption in his republic by relying on his friends in the KGB, most of whom were very likely Slavs and not native Azerbaidzhanis. He had used helicopters to overfly the capital of Baku to spot the big villas built with illicit money. He even dressed up as a truckdriver to run an illegal load of tomatoes to Moscow to discover for himself how the system of pay-offs to the traffic police worked. One story has it that his truck was followed by a police car that picked up each of the unfortunate policemen who had extracted a bribe from Aliyev.

The worst scandals had been outside Russia proper. The Azerbaidzhanis with their Middle Eastern ways, the commerce-minded Georgians, and the even harder-to-understand Central Asians were bound to present special problems. But Medunov and Krasnodar were Russian. So was the neighbouring north Caucasus region of Rostov where disquieting rumours turned eventually into a show trial of a whole band of trade officials, including senior members of the Russian Republic's trade ministry in Moscow, fifty people in all (the leader, like Iron Bella, was sentenced to death). Here, too, there had been connivance by important party officials. The head of a department in the Rostov city party committee stopped one of the newly appointed trade officials in the corridor of the party headquarters. 'He asked me,' the official recalled in court, 'how work was, did I have any difficulties. He said – if there were any questions I could quite freely turn to him. Money was mentioned and I took out 200 roubles [almost £200] and gave them to him. He took the money and remarked that in general it was necessary to see something of each other. I replied – I'm always ready for that! I understood that seeing something of [him] meant picnics in the countryside.'

Buttering up a superior with picnics, even alcoholic ones as they very likely were, may not seem very dreadful. But, as the Vyshku affair in Moldavia showed, official connivance of mundane sorts of corruption easily turned into other kinds of abuse of power. The decision to publicize the Rostov trade scandal was widely taken to signal Moscow's disquiet about the way the whole Rostov region was being run. It came out (after Brezhnev's death) that the party leadership there had been guilty of major errors. They had allowed carelessness in the construction of Atommash, a huge new factory designed to mass produce the new generation of Soviet nuclear power reactors. Shocking disorganization was also revealed at Rostselmash, the country's biggest maker of combine harvesters. Typically an attempt was made – and it was successful at first – to silence the experienced agricultural journalist who wrote the report. Here the damage was obvious enough. Delays in the nuclear power programme, combine harvesters which left twenty per cent of the grain on the fields – these were palpably harming the economy. And yet, under Brezhnev, nothing – or nothing effective – had been done or said about them. Ivan Bondarenko, party first secretary of the Rostov region since 1968, was a senior member of the Central Committee and a Brezhnev man. As long as Bondarenko could rely on a warm greeting in Moscow it was probably not very risky being inefficient or corrupt in Rostov if you were one of his group. Significantly the man who replaced Bondarenko in 1984 (officially he retired for health reasons) was a sufficiently tough operator for Gorbachov later to promote him to be minister of internal affairs.

There were to be more revelations about party organizations that had gone rotten, notably the party in the Soviet capital itself. Most newspaper accounts still tried to explain the problem as a product of shortages. Bureaucrats lived off these shortages, it was argued. They extracted bribes in return for the always necessary official paperwork. They had the power to decide whether a delivery of first quality meat went to the canteen at Rostselmash or the hospitals for which it was originally intended. But it was also sometimes possible to find more profound, and much more worrying, explanations. One was provided by Fyodor Burlatsky in his study *Interregnum*. The Chinese, he wrote, had come to certain conclusions about the corrosive consequences of a cult of personality such as they had known under Mao. Mao's dictatorship had turned the party into a feudal organization. It had developed 'feudal traditions in the mechanism for the inheritance of power; feudal traditions in the distribution of jobs and the methods of selecting cadres; feudal traditions in the way of life of the political élite; feudal methods in intra-party struggle; and finally a feudal structure of political relations as a whole.'

Was not this description recognizable to a Russian reader even without the use of that code expression the 'cult of personality'? The Russians had invented this formula to signal, discreetly, the horrors and illegalities of Stalin's rule. If the 'cult' had had such an effect on China why should it have been less damaging in the land of its birth? When Burlatsky went on to describe in detail the various ways in which dictatorship perverted party members in China the similarities were equally striking. Party members turned into 'lords who thought only of their own advantage'. They conducted affairs as they wished without bothering to be well-informed. They were petty tyrants. They lied and deceived. They took revenge on their critics. They were narrow-minded and frustrated party policy if it suited them. They covered up their mistakes. They floated with the current. They wanted privileges. They practised nepotism.

Here was a more profound analysis of the state of affairs that worried Andropov and later Mikhail Gorbachov. But as an explanation of Soviet history it belonged to the Garden of Eden school: all was well until Stalin drove the Soviet Union out of the paradise that Lenin had so carefully planted. It did not face the question of to what extent the party even without Stalin was inevitably corrupting itself by its claim to absolute power. The Soviet Union, under the new constitution adopted in 1977, was no longer a dictatorship of the proletariat but a 'socialist state of all the people'. Nevertheless 'the leading and guiding force of Soviet society and the nucleus of its political system, of all state organizations, is the Communist Party of the Soviet Union. The CPSU exists for the people and serves the people.'

But who was to check up on the party? It was true that under Brezhnev abuse of power was more often frivolous and greedy than, as with Stalin, cruel. It was sometimes not so much power corrupting as power being delightful and absolute power absolutely delightful. What the country lacked was any constitutional recognition that party leaders were frail humans. There was not a hint that the institution of government itself might be 'the greatest of all reflections on human nature'. The worldly-wise makers of the American Revolution pointed out that 'if men were angels no government would be necessary'. The thought that followed was even more relevant to the Soviet dilemma: 'If angels were to govern men, neither external nor internal controls on government would be necessary.'

The party was indeed represented as being as close to an angelic body as the world had ever seen. Of course it had its machinery of control which on paper looked thorough. And no one could have accused the men of greatest power of being innocents. They certainly did not believe their subordinates to be angels. The politics they themselves practised within the Central Committee, though only hazily discernible by those outside, were as competitive as anywhere in the world. The struggle for Brezhnev's succession was to make that plain enough.

Nevertheless the foundation of the party's power was its claim to a monopoly of wisdom and public virtue. The party had absolute power because it was absolutely right. How did you prevent this astonishing claim born out of the scientific optimism of the nineteenth century and a Russian tradition of blessed autocracy from becoming a licence to laziness, negligence and even the grossest forms of injustice and misrule? The problem could not even be addressed openly. The principle of the party as the country's 'leading and guiding force' was beyond discussion. Yet awareness of this problem lay behind much of the political warfare that eventually brought Gorbachov to power. It gave it an urgency and significance that raised it above an ordinary struggle for power. It was too much, perhaps, to talk of the survival of the Soviet Union being at stake. But it was not an exaggeration that the survival of the Soviet Union as a great power into the twenty-first century was at stake. Gorbachov was to come close to revealing this anxiety in his closing speech to the party congress in March 1986. In his main report at the start of proceedings he had said 'our party is a healthy body'. But he nevertheless chose to leave the delegates with a very different thought of Lenin's. He reminded them of Lenin's words to the last party congress he attended:

All revolutionary parties that have perished up till now perished because they became too pleased with themselves and could not see in what their strength consisted, and were frightened to speak of their weaknesses. But we shall not perish, because we are not frightened to talk about our weaknesses and we shall learn to overcome those weaknesses.

Gorbachov was, like Lenin, an optimist. But by quoting these words he had signalled as clearly as Soviet political convention allowed how serious he judged the battle that lay ahead to be.

4

The Bolshevik

It is one of the misleading curiosities of the fight to succeed Brezhnev that the winner emerged from the KGB corner. Yuri Andropov had been appointed KGB chairman in 1967. He was Brezhnev's choice to replace a protégé of Dmitri Shelepin, a Politburo member who had himself once been head of the KGB but was perceived by Brezhnev as a rival to be disposed of, which he eventually was. As head of the internal and external security services Andropov made less public appearances than most other senior officials. But the work brought him promotion. A candidate member of the Politburo since 1967, Brezhnev advanced him to full membership – together with foreign minister Gromyko and the defence minister, Marshal Grechko – in 1976. The same year Andropov was promoted to army general, one below the most senior rank of marshal (the KGB uses military ranks). But by the beginning of the 1980s, when the succession to Brezhnev had become the most popular topic for Muscovite political speculation, it was being put around that Andropov should not be forgotten as a possible candidate. It was said that when he accepted the KGB posting he insisted it be seen as an episode in an essentially political career, and not as his transformation into a professional Chekist (the word, still much used, comes from the Cheka, the political police set up in 1917 and the father of the modern Soviet security services). Although the KGB had been cleaned up since the days of Stalin's lawlessness it still did not seem proper for its chairman to step straight into the supreme leadership.

Andropov was right. His career, until he took over the KGB, had been that of a successful party functionary. It began in Karelia where as a Komsomol leader he organized partisans during the war, using the code name Mohican. He was brought onto the staff of the Central Committee while Stalin was still alive, transferred to the foreign ministry, serving as ambassador in Hungary during the uprising of 1956, and then returned to the Central Committee, becoming head of the department that supervises relations with the Soviet bloc. In 1962 he was promoted to be a Central Committee secretary. With Brezhnev weakening this was the post to which Andropov needed to get back. Every Soviet leader from Stalin on had reached the top from the combined vantage point of Politburo membership and a place on the Central Committee secretariat. The secretaries, who in recent years have usually numbered around ten, supervise the party apparatus throughout the country. They prepare papers for the Politburo and execute its decisions. The senior secretaries are those three or four who are also Politburo members. It is easy to imagine the power this gives them: they are makers of policy as well as its executors, and conduits of information from both top down and bottom up.

At the beginning of 1982 there were no obvious vacancies on the secretariat. What was more, Konstantin Chernenko, who did occupy the advantageous twin positions of Politburo member and secretary, had every reason to keep Andropov from joining him in the secretariat. Chernenko was by then Brezhnev's shadow. The old man seldom appeared in public without him at his side. Foreigners who studied the form of possible Soviet leaders did not rate Chernenko highly. Nor did some people in Moscow. In late 1981 the one-time British diplomat and Soviet spy Donald Maclean wrote a paper on the state of the Soviet Union in which he forecast that if Chernenko were to succeed Brezhnev the country would continue to be run 'like an old gentlemen's club in which no change is allowed'. The Chernenkos and Brezhnevs, Maclean thought, were typical of the young men picked by Stalin. They had grown up without any real knowledge of the outside world. Their education never amounted to much more than cramming in order to get the necessary paper qualifications. 'Sort of Soviet Ernie Bevins' he called them. Maclean's opinion can be taken as typical of the Soviet intellectual world in which he lived. But this world had no influence whatsoever on the choice of party leader. Chernenko's appeal was to the men who did have such influence, men promoted up the party and government hierarchy by Brezhnev and now comfortably growing old in power. For them the prospect of life continuing as peacefully as in a fading London club could only have been attractive.

Andropov used the weapons to hand. If Brezhnev's family and friends were vulnerable, anything that came out about them would also damage Chernenko as Brezhnev's heir apparent. Andropov had in the KGB a machine one of whose functions was to put about stories, sometimes true, sometimes not, among the population. It cannot be proved that this is what happened. But the stories about the Brezhnev family were passed about so freely, particularly to foreigners, that at the very least the KGB must have been looking the other way. It is also striking that both then and in later

Kremlin struggles the damaging rumours almost always concerned those political figures who were targets of the Politburo member closest to the KGB camp. It is hard to recall a single damaging story about Andropov except the rumours about his health when he was already near death. And if it had been anyone else those rumours might have emerged much sooner.

Even Andropov cannot have foreseen how the anti-Brezhnev rumours and his bid to get into the secretariat would come together. According to one vivid account Andropov showed the dossier on Galina Brezhnev and her friends to Mikhail Suslov, one of the veterans of the Politburo and the secretary next to Brezhnev in seniority. Suslov – this version has it – in turn showed the papers to Semyon Tsvigun, Andropov's deputy at the KGB but first and foremost an old associate of Brezhnev. Tsvigun and Brezhnev were also related through their wives. Whatever the truth Tsvigun died soon after, in January 1982, (some said it was suicide) and Suslov, already an ill man, followed him to the grave at the end of the same month. Four months later Andropov was made a secretary of the Central Committee and left the KGB.

Andropov in theory took over Suslov's job of chief ideologist but it was a job that no one else could do, at least not in the same way. Suslov had reached the top of the party under Stalin and in the Brezhnev years supervised an intellectual enterprise unique to Moscow; covering the leadership's policies in intellectual clothes cut from one hundred per cent guaranteed Marxist-Leninist cloth. He was not a die-hard Stalinist. He had supported Nikita Khrushchov in his fight against his neo-Stalinist opponents. But he was a conservative who certainly thought it his right to lay into any foreign communists he suspected of deviating from Moscow's line. It would be a brave man who would now sit down to read Suslov's published works. If there is anything original in them it is one of the Kremlin's best kept secrets. It was also widely believed that Suslov did not actually bother to write much of what appeared under his name. That was the point of a popular story about his anger with a junior ideological official over an article that had caused political problems. Suslov was amazed to learn that the erring official had really penned the piece that bore his name. 'Did he write it himself?' he asked. 'Who does he think he is? Lenin?'

Some of those who worked under Suslov dismissed him, after his death, as a 'dried fish' who 'thought in categories of dogma'. But he was a sincere dried fish and the Brezhnev age demanded no more than that from its chief political philosopher. Tall and thin, Suslov looked like a don among his more solidly built Politburo colleagues. His value to them was his dogged skill in matching unoriginal ideas to an unoriginal age.

Andropov's likely emergence from the purdah of the KGB was signalled in April when he was chosen to make the speech delivered each year by a member of the Politburo on the anniversary of Lenin's birth. Under Brezhnev this and similar gatherings served to reaffirm established beliefs.

They were celebrations of the religion of the state. Repetition, not originality, was their purpose. Andropov, though, managed to include some unusually sharp remarks in his address, referring to people's 'justified indignation' over 'cases of theft, bribe-taking, bureaucratism . . .' At this time the rumours about the Brezhnev family were becoming more intense and there had been other queer signals of political intrigue. Moscow began talking about an article in a little-read Leningrad magazine which made fun of a supposedly great old writer who ought to be dead but just would not die. It was taken as a reference to 'Leonid the Writer of Fables'. Soon after Andropov joined the secretariat Soviet officials were explaining in private that he and Chernenko were jointly chairing its sessions, a job that had been Suslov's, and which was taken to confer the unofficial rank of second secretary or party deputy leader. And then in August, when Brezhnev was away from the capital on holiday, Medunov was summoned to Moscow and dismissed.

People were aware that Andropov was a formidable member of Brezhnev's Politburo. Some knowledgeable Russians considered him and the defence minister Dmitri Ustinov its two cleverest men, though Andropov's formal education had been no better than Brezhnev's. Born just before the outbreak of the First World War he was only eight years younger than Brezhnev and also came from a working class family not far removed from the peasantry. His railway worker father died in the famine in 1919. And yet he became an intellectual. Some odd things were written about him abroad: that he liked jazz and whisky and modern art. The details were on the whole wrong but the suspicion that this was an unusual man was right. His mother had been a music teacher. The Andropov family gave each other books as birthday presents. Andropov himself wrote poetry. Extracts were published after his death. A sympathetic poem to his wife on her birthday went:

> Let others laugh at the poet,
> But envy him twice over
> That I am writing sonnets
> To my own, not another's, wife.

He translated poetry too, including apparently Shelley, for he had a fair grasp of written English. Some Soviet poets said his work was good enough to be published but he never allowed that during his life. As for painting it seems that he had once commissioned painters out of favour with the official Soviet artists' union to decorate his villa in Sochi.

When Andropov succeeded Brezhnev there was to be an almost audible sigh of relief from part of the Soviet establishment. For some it was enough to have at last an apparently healthy leader. For others the relief was more profound. They welcomed Andropov's intellectual authority and personal honesty. The make-believe and sloppiness that were so often apparent in the Brezhnev era had been particularly painful to those Russians concerned with their country's standing abroad. In Andropov they felt they again had a leader to inspire respect amongst foreigners as well as at home. The Soviet system appeared able to regenerate itself.

The paradox of Andropov was that those years spent in the KGB which once threatened to bar him from the party leadership were the best guide to the nature of the man. They made his career a lesson for modern Communists for it brought them face to face with the underlying dilemma of Soviet communism – the supposed right, if occasion demands, to use force against people for their own good. During his fifteen years as chairman of the KGB Andropov had presided over the destruction of the dissident movement. His campaign was both canny and ruthless. By the time of Brezhnev's death organized dissent barely existed. Andropov never said anything to suggest he found this work distasteful. In his speeches as KGB chairman he spoke of dissidents as either doing the work of the Soviet Union's foreign enemies or as people so seriously misguided they could not be considered quite sane. There is no reason to suppose this judgement was entirely cynical. Khrushchov, a more straightforward man, had fallen on the same explanation for people who disagreed with Kremlin policies. It was the natural conclusion to draw from a major premise of Soviet politics – that the party represents in a concentrated form the wisdom and virtue of the proletariat, history's chosen class. Those who chose to oppose the party, it followed logically, were driven either by hatred of the working class or by an inability to understand what was best for them. The first courted punishment, the latter deserved treatment. The moral tension, for the old revolutionary Bolsheviks, had always lain in this apparent contradiction of doing good to people who might not see it as good at all. A life in the constant grip of this tension produced the well-steeled Bolshevik character; scarcely, in the eyes of history, a new psychological type but, because of the ambition, speed and dimensions of the Bolshevik experiment, displayed with unusual vividness in modern Soviet history.

The evidence is that this moral tension lay at the centre of Andropov's life. As far as can be discovered he led a modest, even austere, private life. His Moscow flat in the same block as Brezhnev's was quite small. He did not share the culpably human pleasures of Brezhnev and his cronies who hunted and played cards, smoked and drank as long as their health held out. Brezhnev liked being among people. Andropov was what Russians call *nyelyudim*, not easily sociable. Brezhnev loved publicity and being photographed. There seem to be very few photographs of Andropov except the most boring official kind. But Andropov was far from modest when it came to his right to rule as a communist. Andropov had a view of the modern, moral prince. His model, of course, was Lenin. He once said of him:

Spiritual warmth, cheerfulness, sincerity, kindness, charm – Ilyich had all these best of human qualities. He really loved people and therefore with all the strength of his soul hated everything that disfigured and twisted their life. He was merciless to enemies and traitors but revenge and cruelty were inherently foreign to him. Lenin's sense of principle never turned into blind fanaticism . . .

Merciless and loving: there was another Bolshevik prince Andropov greatly admired who combined those two qualities – Feliks Dzerzhinsky, the Polish gentleman who joined the Russian revolutionaries and created the Cheka, Lenin's political police. Andropov, according to a Soviet journalist in his confidence, never lost his admiration for Dzerzhinsky, 'the proletarian Jacobin' who as a seventeen-year-old swore an oath to 'fight against evil until his dying breath' and who 'remained true to that oath everywhere and always'. Another of Andropov's heroes was a young communist he had worked with during the war, a secretary of the Karelian Komsomol central committee who died leading a partisan detachment. What pleased Andropov was that when young partisans remembered their fallen leader 'they always added with pride: "He was a secretary of the central committee."'

It is hard to exaggerate the need of modern Soviet communism to find heroes, party members who lived through some of the terrible years of so often self-inflicted horror and yet emerged with honour, an honour that had to be reconciled with a communist's right, even obligation, to be ruthless in the good cause. A hero like Dzerzhinsky earned the right to power not least through self-denial. He ate the food of the rank-and-file Chekists; he sometimes fainted from exhaustion or hunger. He worked long hours seven days a week. He hated taking a holiday. It was his toughness to himself as much as his toughness to others that won him the nickname 'Iron Feliks'. The psychological type is again recognizable: the man who is ready to punish himself wins the right to coerce others. It was fitting that Andropov should have passed through the Dzerzhinsky school. He, too, it later turned out, destroyed his health by long hours spent in an old-fashioned, high-pillared office in the Lubyanka. It was generally accepted that he had tried to raise standards in the KGB. His message to the Soviet security services had been borrowed from Iron Feliks: 'Only the man with a cool head, a burning heart and pure hands can be a Chekist.' One of his deputies at the KGB said after his death that under Andropov the security service had 'acquired anew its original purity'. Gorbachov's KGB chief, Viktor Chebrikov, would speak of Andropov as the twin deity with Dzerzhinsky in the security service's pantheon.

All that we know of the man allows us to believe he did want a KGB with 'pure hands'. To the extent that he achieved this it was, in Brezhnev's Soviet Union, where organizations far less powerful than the KGB fearlessly misused their authority to make money, a considerable achievement. Andropov was the first KGB chief in many years to leave the job without any hint of mistakes or scandal. His suppression of dissent was of course considered by official Moscow to be an achievement.

The years at the KGB which had threatened to keep Andropov out of the mainstream of Kremlin politics also came to help his political ambitions in another way. It was to count for much that he had clean hands; that they were also strong was no disadvantage. But the KGB was also a unique vantage point from which to study the country. Andropov probably disposed of the best information available about the true state of the country. The KGB operated throughout the country. No other organization matched its powers of information-gathering. Some of this information Andropov was able to use in his early political forays, jumping on Medunov in order to set a frightening example, and weakening Brezhnev and Chernenko through the unhappy Galina. But the resources of the KGB also gave him the chance to reflect on what was really happening in the economy, and on popular attitudes and the morale of the establishment. Neither he nor anyone else could get an accurate picture of any of this from the Soviet press. The newspapers printed many critical articles but they were about specific and usually well-known problems. Weaknesses of strategy and principle could only be hinted at. It is doubtful that the mounting problems were discussed frankly at any meetings of the leadership chaired by Brezhnev or his allies. Andropov's first speeches as leader were to make it plain that he considered the situation he had inherited to be grave. This conviction based on special knowledge was to add powerfully to his campaign to win the leadership for himself.

In late September 1982 Brezhnev made the last of his great processions round the country. He went to Azerbaidzhan to award the republic an Order of Lenin for its economic achievements. It was an achievement of another kind for Geidar Aliyev, the Azerbaidzhani leader, to get Brezhnev there, and he gave his leader a particularly sumptuous and flattering welcome. Something odd happened at the ceremony at which Brezhnev conferred the award. He had spoken the first lines of his speech with the by now usual mumblings when his neat little assistant Andrei Aleksandrov appeared at his side, whispered and gave him a new text to read from. 'It's not my fault, comrades,' Brezhnev said to laughter, 'I'll have to start again.' Mistakes are rare at great Soviet public occasions and this one could not be hidden because the speech was being broadcast live. The incident has remained one of Moscow's minor mysteries. The suspiciously-minded have always pointed out that Aleksandrov, who began his career as a diplomat, was the only one of Brezhnev's assistants to be retained by Andropov. Intentionally or not, the episode confirmed the impression of Brezhnev as a man unfit to govern, who did not even know when he was reading from the wrong speech. But in Azerbaidzhan Brezhnev was otherwise treated as wisest of wise rulers. Aliyev, as was to be expected, poured compliments over him. Brezhnev's speech had been 'brilliant and heartfelt', a storehouse of 'wise advice and valuable suggestions'. Brezhnev was a sage who saw 'the clear contours of the communist tomorrow'. In sum he was 'the most influential and authoritative politician of our planet'.

At the end of October Brezhnev spoke to the senior commanders of the armed forces in the Kremlin. Chernenko sat on Brezhnev's right hand with Andropov beyond him, a clear signal of how the Soviet leader at least regarded the seniority of his Politburo. When Chernenko two days later went to the Georgian capital of Tbilisi to bestow another Order of Lenin he presented himself as Brezhnev's closest confidant, recounting a long conversation the two men had had before Chernenko's departure. Brezhnev had said that 'urgent affairs would not let me leave Moscow even for a short time. It would be a good thing if you' – here Chernenko used the familiar form of *ty* which is like *tu* in French – 'were just to fly down to Georgia.'

Brezhnev, as was expected, stood on the Lenin mausoleum to review the traditional military and civilian parade on November 7, the sixty-fifth anniversary of the Revolution. The weather was cold but clear. A special air unit near the capital had sprayed the clouds with granules of carbon dioxide forcing the snow to fall before it reached the capital. But the several hours in the winter air took their toll. Brezhnev looked in poor shape at the Kremlin reception after the parade. He died on November 10 but the public announcement was delayed until eight o'clock the next morning, just as the news of a tsar's death had often been delayed.

Some believe that the decisive Politburo meeting was the long and difficult one in May 1982 at which Andropov succeeded to Suslov's place on the secretariat. It is argued that this implicitly, if not openly, decided the succession. The Politburo and its proceedings were and remain an entertaining subject for speculation because it is impossible to disprove almost any version of what is said to have gone on there. Certainly Chernenko did not behave, in the months before Brezhnev's death, as though he had already conceded the succession to Andropov. The commonest guess, and there was some evidence for it, was that both Chernenko's and Andropov's names were put forward when the Politburo met after Brezhnev's death. Only eleven men were involved; taken together they were an illustration of the Brezhnev legacy. Most of them were in their late sixties or older. The Latvian Arvid Pelshe was eighty-three. The prime minister Nikolai Tikhonov, an old Brezhnev friend, was next oldest at seventy-seven. The youngest member, fifty-one, was Mikhail Gorbachov, Central Committee secretary responsible for agriculture. The next youngest, Grigori Romanov, party leader in Leningrad, was one year short of being a sexagenarian.

But not all the old men were replicas of Brezhnev. Brezhnev had not been, and probably could not have been even if he wanted to, a complete autocrat. He was the head of a great bureaucracy, the chairman of its board. Some Russians recognized in him the skills of an American politician – a reconciler of different interests, a builder of coalitions. This could be seen in the Politburo. Chernenko, Tikhonov and the Kazakh party leader Kunayev were Brezhnev's men, promoted because of their closeness to him. But Arvid Pelshe was there at least partly as a symbol. He had been a member of the Petrograd Soviet in 1917 and an early member of the Cheka. He had even known Lenin. Most of the other members represented an important constituency. Romanov had behind him the party in Leningrad, the country's second most important city; Vladimir Shcherbitsky had the Ukraine, the second most important republic. Gromyko's strength lay not so much in the foreign policy establishment he headed but in his own vast experience. He personified the foreign strategy of the Brezhnev era. Ustinov as defence minister spoke not only for the army but as a man whose life had been spent in the defence industry and who, at the start of the war against Hitler, had been appointed, at the age of only thirty-three, people's commissar (minister) for armaments.

How did the eleven men divide? The most believable version to be heard in Moscow was that Ustinov, Gromyko, Shcherbitsky and Romanov sided with Andropov. The last two, who had made typical party careers working their way up to the leadership of their fiefdoms, had nothing in common with a Chernenko carried to the top in Brezhnev's pocket. Little attention was paid at the time to Gorbachov, the junior member, but it is now obvious that he too was for Andropov. It is difficult to believe that Chernenko ever had a serious chance of beating Andropov. He had his constituency and it was powerful. These were the beneficiaries of the Brezhnev era in general and in particular that third of the Central Committee members whose careers had somewhere become entwined with Brezhnev's. Ever since Khrushchov had used the Central Committee to reverse a vote against him by his Stalinist colleagues in the Politburo, Soviet politics has been haunted by the possibility of its playing once more a similarly dramatic parliamentary role. But like many ghosts it has not been seen again and in November 1982 there were not even rumours of a sighting.

The contest might have been closer if Ustinov had not been so firmly on Andropov's side. Under Brezhnev the armed forces had reached the glorious peak of nuclear parity with the United States. But the Brezhnev cult had trespassed into sacred military territory. Brezhnev had exaggerated his own contribution to the war out of all recognition and the army was growing tired of the party's re-writing of its history. Worst of all, Brezhnev's self-award of the Order of Victory seemed to make him the equal of the very greatest wartime commanders. There was no ambiguity about who deserved the honour: senior commanders of one or several fronts whose actions had radically altered the course of the war. Brezhnev had only risen to be chief of the political department of a front, which was not the same thing at all. It was also said in Moscow that Ustinov saw eye to eye with Andropov about corruption. There was traditionally little love between the armed forces and the KGB but they had two things in common. They were represented throughout the country, their commanders in the field sitting on local party and government bodies. In places like Krasnodar and Rostov army officers could not have been entirely ignorant of what was going on. The anecdote-makers certainly believed Ustinov played a deciding role. A story soon went round Moscow about the Politburo meeting after Brezhnev's death. The members had sat in silence for two hours, looking uneasily at each other. Then Ustinov got up, went over to Andropov and put his arm round his shoulder. Everyone smiled. . . .

Within two weeks of Brezhnev's death the government announced that his memory was to be preserved for all time by renaming towns and districts, factories and ships after him. To the dismay of Muscovites who liked the pretty old name, the capital's Cheryomushki district in Moscow was turned into Brezhnev district. The new town that built the most modern Soviet truck, the Kamaz, became Brezhnev, as did the nuclear-powered ice-breaker *Arctic* and Star City, the settlement near Moscow where Soviet cosmonauts trained and lived. This considerable honour seemed to follow the spirit of the speech that Chernenko had made when proposing Andropov's name for the general secretaryship to the special plenum of the Central Committee on November 12. The first three-quarters had been emotional praise of Brezhnev. The party's duty was to 'treasure and develop . . . everything that was bequeathed us by Leonid Ilyich'. It had been a 'school for all of us who had the happiness of working hand in hand with Leonid Ilyich, to be by his side, to listen to him and to see at first hand the keenness of his mind, his quick wit and love of life'. The loss was so great – indeed Chernenko implied it was irreplaceable – that 'it is now twice, thrice more important to conduct matters in the party collectively'.

But the uncharitably-minded – and there were plenty, for Moscow relishes cruelty towards departed leaders – detected on the very day of Brezhnev's funeral a slight but significant diminution in his praise. Speaking in the presence of the open coffin in Red Square neither Andropov nor Ustinov called Brezhnev a 'great' leader. They referred to him only as 'outstanding'. The reception in the St. George's Hall of the Great Kremlin Palace after the funeral also sent a signal. No one knew what to expect of this gathering. Foreign ambassadors hosting important government delegations worried that it might interfere with their plans for lunch. But when the guests arrived it was clear to the foreign diplomats at least that the reception's chief purpose was to introduce the new leadership. Honour was done to Brezhnev by a quick bow to his portrait placed on a table, but the star of the occasion was the new general secretary.

Andropov stood with Tikhonov, Gromyko and V. V. Kuznetsov, Brezhnev's deputy as chairman of the presidium of the Supreme Soviet. It was hard, then, to know what to make of the new Russian leader. The long face was clever, a little owlish; the manner courteous and reserved. He was tall and well enough built but it was difficult to imagine him as the outdoors man that Brezhnev liked to pose as. The uncertainty about Andropov was matched by an uncertainty about how the city would react to Brezhnev's death and funeral. The last leader to die in power was Stalin. The crowds trying to see his body had panicked and men and women were crushed to death. This time the troops of the ministry of internal affairs took no chances. The officers kept their men on alert and the motors of their trucks running. But there was no panic, and for good reason. Few felt that the disappearance of Brezhnev mattered. What did matter was the rise to power of a man who aspired to revive Bolshevik traditions. But of that few people as yet had any inkling.

5

Waste

In the early 1970s, when the Brezhnev era seemed most full of promise, an elderly Frenchman travelled from Moscow to Khabarovsk on the Trans-Siberian railway. After only a few hours at the eastern end of the line he boarded the train again for the long journey back to Moscow. The Frenchman watched life through the windows of the train, commenting on what he saw to his wife and anyone else who would listen. The sights, as he saw them a second time, seemed even more fascinating and puzzling; and as the train passed yet another straggling town he took off his spectacles and addressed the carriage. 'There are only two words in the English language to describe this country. One is *messee* and the other is *sloppee*.'

Many Russians might have said the same. The writer Valentin Rasputin in his story *The Fire* expressed pain at the slovenly ways of the logging settlement of Sosnovka, seeing in its dreary life a falling off from old standards and virtues. His account of the local fire engine, useless when disaster struck because so many parts had been stolen from it, recalled another, older story about a fictional Russian village. There had been a summer fire and afterwards the local authorities took quick action. They procured a fire engine – a wooden barrel set in a wheeled cart – and issued the villagers boards painted with the pictures of such useful fire-fighting equipment as buckets and axes. The villagers hung up the boards, painted the fire truck, built a little shed over it and 'even poured water into the barrel'. It was hot and the water began to evaporate. The village children dipped into what was left to make mud-pies in the road. Cracks appeared in the sides of the barrel. A shaft went missing from the truck. A peasant who needed to take his produce into town discovered that one of the shafts in his own cart was broken. He looked at the fire truck 'and deciding you wouldn't get far with that barrel and only one shaft took the other'. A little later both the barrel and the shed protecting it vanished 'but with such gradualness that no one ever noticed'. Since nobody had taken more than one piece they were puzzled how the whole contrivance had managed to disappear.

'There you are. If you live among people like this,' someone said, 'you'll start stealing from yourself.'

'Yes,' they all said. 'You've got to keep your eyes skinned with these people – and even then you'll miss something.'

This was village life in 1914, recalled in the imagination of a Russian writer shortly after the Revolution. Long before the 1980s the Russians were analysing, laughing at and reproaching themselves for their capacity for sloppiness and dislike of prudent routine. The writer Ivan Bunin pondered in exile over the

eternal Russian need for a celebration! How strong are our feelings, how we long for life to give us ecstasy – not just enjoyment but precisely ecstasy – and how it draws us towards constant intoxication, to hard drinking, and how boring for us it makes everyday life and systematic work.

Russian carefreeness was partly a result of living in a country so vast it seemed to have no limits (and indeed did not until Tsarist expansion ended in 1917), and so extraordinarily rich in resources that they, too, seemed limitless. Brezhnev's Soviet Union had two-thirds of the world's likely reserves of coal. It produced more oil than any other country. It had a third of the global stock of timber and half of the deposits of iron ore. It possessed large supplies of most ferrous and non-ferrous metals. Gold and diamonds were as naturally Russian as caviar and vodka. Yet by the 1970s it was plain to some people that not even the Soviet Union could afford to go on using its immense resources in such a reckless way. The country produced huge amounts of goods with these riches but it was still short of almost everything. Soon after Andropov became party leader a Soviet economist took a walk down a Moscow street. He was admiring some new apartment blocks when he noticed a massive piece of construction equipment on which someone had written with red paint, 'When are you going to take this away? It's been lying here since 1979.' The economist did a calculation. The equipment was of reinforced concrete. It contained about a ton of cement and half a ton of steel into which some four tons of fuel and raw materials would have gone. There were transport costs too. The materials would have had to be brought several hundred kilometres to Moscow. How could such waste happen when there was an annual shortage of up to three million tons of cement? When steel supplies were always tight despite a favourite, and correct, boast of politicians that the Soviet Union produced more steel than any other country in the world? And where fuel was already as precious as in the West because of rocketing extraction costs in the new oil fields of Siberia?

After Brezhnev had gone similar questions were asked about every other form of Soviet economic activity. The country depended heavily on railways but year after year they were unable to cope with the traffic. Most of the timber, ores and fuel came from the eastern part of the country but production of freight wagons to carry them was going down. Rolling stock for the giant open-cast coal mines of Kansk-Achinsk in central Siberia had to be dragged in from distant corners of the country against all the rules of rational use. The cost of such inefficiency could be appalling. The Soviet Union has good reserves of apatite, a phosphorus-rich ore used for making mineral fertilizers badly needed by Soviet farmers. Since the war an immense investment had been made in developing the biggest apatite reserves which are in remote mountains inside the Arctic circle near the sea port of Murmansk. A whole new town, called Apatity, had to be built. It is a solid place, by Brezhnev era standards well equipped, and has a population of one hundred thousand. Labour costs there are twice the national average because incentives must be paid to draw people to a region where the average temperature is minus five degrees centigrade and the sun disappears for forty-one days in winter. Everything about Apatity is expensive, from the imported Japanese mining equipment to the food that has to be brought in from more temperate zones. But to meet the unsatisfied demand for fertilizers the mines are being expanded and a giant new enrichment plant built.

In 1984 it emerged that apatite production could be doubled almost overnight at little extra cost. The magic formula was to stop waste. Scientists had worked out that half of the phosphorus fertilizers made with Murmansk's apatite never reached the fields. It was lost during the processing of the ore and then in its transport, storage and packaging. But the chief culprit was transport. The apatite was simply trickling out of the ill-designed and badly-maintained freight wagons.

Horror stories of this sort were no secret to readers of the academic journals or even ordinary newspapers. They may not have known how much apatite was being wasted but they could have offered an educated guess for they knew of many similar stories. It was well known, for example, that between a quarter and a third of all farm produce was lost somewhere between the fields and the kitchen table. At the beginning of the 1970s the state committee for science and technology commissioned the Siberian branch of the Academy of Sciences to make a study of industrial equipment delivered to the northern parts of the country. The scholars concluded that much of it was unsuited to the north's severe climate and the consequent annual loss to the economy was almost £2 billion. The team made recommendations which led to some savings but when a similar study was commissioned ten years later, on the eve of Brezhnev's death, the situation was discovered to be much worse. The supply of unsuitable machinery to the north was by then costing the country almost ten times more.

Some Russians are still drawn to a romantic explanation of their country's disorder. There are macho overtones in the idea that 'everyday life and systematic work' are not appropriate for a real *muzhik*, as well as the more familiar scorn for a measured way of life that leaves no room for feats of the spirit. But there was also a Soviet version of this old cast of mind. Nothing since the Revolution had delighted Soviet publicists so much as a feat, a fine *podvig*. Feats, of course, were no longer spiritual in the old sense. They were revolutionary. They were heroic. The revolution itself had been a historic, collective feat. So, according to official mythology, were the collectivization of farming and the forced industrialization of the 1930s. The Second World War – the 'great patriotic war' – had been the greatest feat of all.

In the year of Brezhnev's death a new Soviet film cast a cold eye on this cult of the heroic exploit. It told a simple story. An express train runs into some goods wagons at a railway station. The driver tries to stop the train but fails. He is killed but no one else is badly hurt. The driver lived in the town where the accident happened and he is given a hero's funeral. But a railway investigator arrives on the scene and after poking around comes to a different conclusion. The accident was the result of chronic carelessness. The signalmen had not been doing their job. The driver knew he had a faulty speedometer and was going too fast. His co-driver, who had been treated as a mini-hero, had in fact panicked and jumped out just before the collision. No one in the town wants to hear the inspector's version. The local authorities bribe the driver's widow with the offer of a new flat and she asks the inspector to close the case. Someone kills the mongrel dog the inspector has made a pet of. Eventually even the town party secretary asks him to go. He walks out of the town watched by workers and old women with hate in their eyes. A journalist with pretensions to being 'modern' and 'liberal' writes an article in the town newspaper glorifying the dead man's *podvig*. The film ends as the town gathers by the side of the railway track to unveil a monument to its new hero.

The message of *A train stopped* was uncomfortable. Heroes, it suggested, were at best people who cleared up the mess made by others. More usually, though, they were themselves messy, careless people trapped by mistakes of their own making but which it suited no one to admit. Sloppiness was the stuff of which heroes were made. But the explanation could be taken further. From 1983 onwards Soviet economists and sociologists had more freedom to argue that the system itself bred carelessness and sometimes made it inevitable. The system created emergencies in which heroic feats were needed. The system needed to cover up its own deficiencies by making heroes out of its victims. Soviet farming, for example, was often described as a battleground where heroes fought to plant crops in time, to bring in the harvest and to extract record yields from apparently hostile cows. And there was good reason for this. Much had been done to rescue farming from the ruins left by Stalin but the system still condemned many farmers to what in the West would have been bankruptcy. Prices paid to farmers for the crops they had to deliver to the state often still did not cover their costs. Farmers were for the first time beginning to get decent supplies of equipment and fertilizers but they were not getting the chance to pay for them. By 1975 one in five collective farms and a staggering fifty per cent of all state farms were unprofitable. In 1982 the debts of collective farms came to £40 billion even though the government had written off state and collective farm debts totalling £20 billion over the preceding seventeen years. There were other reasons, most of them rooted in the past, for the poor state of the country's farms, but it is easy to understand the irresponsibility bred by a system that condemned so many farms to unprofitability and stood ideas of cost, prices and just reward on their head.

Brezhnev had fathered the slogan 'the economy must be economical'. It was to be met with everywhere, on street hoardings and in factories. The leaders repeated it in almost every speech. But how the economy was to be made economical was quite unclear. Brezhnev and his senior colleagues had grown up and come to power in the command economy created by Stalin. Its essence was that political considerations overrode economic ones. The party did as it thought best, not as old-fashioned economic laws allowed. How else could it have achieved industrialization and a revolution in the countryside at the same time? Nevertheless even in the complacent seventies it was obvious that economic trends were bad. The leadership had always prided itself on high growth rates which seemed proof that the country would inevitably overtake a slower growing capitalist world. But the five-year plans of the Brezhnev era recorded a steady decrease in the rate of growth. In the eighth five-year plan national income grew by over seven per cent each year. In the ninth it grew by five per cent a year. By 1982, already in the eleventh five-year plan, the annual growth rate of national income was only a fraction more than three per cent.

Three per cent was better than some capitalist countries could manage but what did the Soviet three per cent mean? Was it all usable wealth? Certainly not. Some was quite useless – faulty equipment, unsellable shoes. Some of it was simply lies, creative book-keeping. But even when it represented a real increase in usable goods it was not necessarily a cause for rejoicing. The Soviet economy had reached the point where it could damage itself by producing more. The command economy had brought labour and raw materials together: and while the Soviet Union was struggling to build a modern industry whatever was produced represented a needed increase in the nation's wealth. But this was no longer true. Raw materials, though still plentiful, were in the wrong place. The old deposits of coal, oil and ores had been conveniently at hand for the country's industry which was concentrated west of the Ural mountains. The new oil and coal fields were in the north and east, as expensive to get at as to develop. As a result oil production was below target (and in 1983 would actually decline). The greater cost also meant it was more economical to devise ways to reduce the consumption of oil rather than to produce more of it. The phenomenon was quite new to the Soviet Union and a new slogan was produced to tackle it. The economy could no longer continue along extensive lines. It had to develop intensively. A leading economist who became a Gorbachov adviser gave an example of what this meant. The production cost of a tractor represented as little as three per cent of the total cost of using the machine throughout its working life. The way to economy was to make a tractor that needed less fuel, less repairs and servicing. £50 more spent on making the tractor better would save five times that amount in running costs.

Imagine the reaction of the leadership when this sort of argument was presented to them. They were being asked to make a considerable intellectual effort. They were being asked to consider the economy not as a piece of putty they could shape at will but as a complicated organism with its own laws of operation – the same lesson that the monster had taught an over-confident Frankenstein. But worse followed. If the economy turned into something no one had expected, then much of Soviet life would have to change to put it right. The political system was based on the assumption that the country needed constant bossing from the top. Never mind that economists had calculated that there were one billion economic links of one kind or another between organizations and factories, and that the number of items produced by the whole economy came to at least twenty-four billion. The central government presumed to be able to command all this. If the system were to change what would become of the bureaucracy? There were over eighty ministries or their equivalents in Moscow and many more in the capitals of the republics. And what would happen to the party apparatus which sat, like Sinbad the Sailor, round the necks of the bureaucrats and businessmen to make sure they carried out the orders received from the centre?

To change all this would be to change the Soviet way of life. If the slogan 'the economy must be economical' meant anything it was surely that the country should take seriously economic criteria like cost, price and profit. Otherwise it would be impossible to extract better work from the labour force. Labour productivity was very low. In industry, according to Soviet calculations, it was half that of the United States. In agriculture it was up to five times less. Of course it was still possible on occasions to make people work hard by a combination of command and patriotic appeal. But without real economic criteria it was impossible to tell whether spurts of this kind actually benefited the economy. There was no point in heroically over-fulfilling production of wastefully inefficient machinery – for example, making miles of pipes out of steel rather than much cheaper plastic – though the old system could reward people for just such questionable feats.

Change was a frightening country to enter. The Stalin economy that Brezhnev inherited was a solid thing. It recalled a building so massively constructed that the cost of pulling it down is prohibitive. It had formed attitudes of mind that were just as hard to erase. Stalin performed economic conjuring tricks. He produced cheap food in a country where farms had been impoverished by government policy. He made housing inexpensive at a time of acute housing shortage. Unable to provide plenty he created its illusion by lowering prices. By the 1980s the government had to pay over twenty billion roubles (approaching £20 billion) a year to cover the difference between the cost of meat production and the price it was sold at in the state shops. All agricultural subsidies were costing, by 1984, fifty-four billion roubles a year. Rents on state housing were so low they did not even cover an apartment building's maintenance cost. Bread was so cheap it paid to feed it to pigs and poultry. Soviet public transport would have gone bankrupt at once if its only income had come from passengers' fares. This low cost of basic goods and services was as much part of the Soviet myth as heroic feats. Soviet propaganda boasted that the price of bread had not gone up for twenty years and that the five kopek (about 4p) ride on the Moscow metro was as permanent as the red stars on top of the Kremlin towers.

Brezhnev had been brought up to believe that an economy was there to produce more goods. It was as simple as that. This was implicit in the Communist party programme adopted, under Khrushchov's inspiration, in 1961. The programme forecast that by the 1980s 'an abundance of material and cultural goods will be reached for all the population, and the material conditions will be created for the transition, in the following period, to the communist principle of distribution according to need'. The goal was essentially uneconomic: communism was offering liberation from the cramping, inhuman laws not just of capitalism but of any economics. The means to the glorious goal of distribution according to need were also uneconomic. Money had little meaning in Brezhnev's Soviet Union. You could have money but no opportunity to buy what you wanted with it. What counted was access, which could either be by chance (coming across a shop that had just had a delivery of Hungarian apples) or by privilege (working for an important organization or factory that had better than average supplies). A cynic might say that the Soviet Union's trouble was that it had developed communist attitudes before even remotely achieving communist abundance. Outside their own homes people treated what in fact were scarce or expensive machines and products with the carelessness of millionaires. The system was reinforcing an old pattern of fecklessness that was itself partly produced by the unjust and often irrational economy of the tsarist empire. As a result the great would-be modernizing Revolution of 1917 was in danger of being inherited by Oblomovs ignorant of the realities of life, and not by the enterprising, penny-pinching Shtoltzes (Shtoltz was the friend but psychological opposite of Goncharov's hero) whom nineteenth-century Russian liberals had seen as the men of the future.

Is it surprising that Brezhnev failed to devise a programme of reform? His skill was as the manager of a going enterprise, as chairman of the board of the Soviet Union Inc. He reconciled the interests of the great bureaucracies. An attempt had been made in the mid-1960s to bring more rational economic pressures to bear but it petered out. The government had neither the energy nor inclination to try seriously again. It seemed to hope the problem would go away. That, at least, was the judgement of the anonymous creator of one of the best-known jokes about Brezhnev. It imagines Stalin, Khrushchov and Brezhnev travelling together in a train which suddenly stops. They descend to see what can be done to get it moving again. 'Shoot the driver,' Stalin says. Khrushchov disagrees. 'No. We must reorganize the train. The driver must be replaced by the guard and the guard by the driver.' Brezhnev looks pained. 'Comrades, I think you're being hasty. I have a better idea. Let's get back in the train, pull the blinds down, and pretend we are moving again.' Not the smallest price the country paid for this was the growing nonsense talked about questionable economic achievements and the poverty of the public debate about the real gravity of the situation. *Ot vranya vsya beda* – 'All our troubles come from lying' – remarked a character in a 'new era' television drama that caught the bitterness with which the falsity of the Brezhnev years would later come to be regarded. A leading economist, surveying after Brezhnev's death the economic writing of the recent past, could only exclaim: 'Exhaustion and boredom – that is all one can get from reading these efforts. There is nothing to contradict and no one to argue with because everything is so elementary, so wearisomely bland, so imperturbably calm.' The comment was all the more wounding for being borrowed from a nineteenth-century critic of tsarist orthodoxy.

Great natural riches that made it possible for the Soviet Union to tolerate waste at home so long had also allowed the leadership to avoid painful choices about its relations with the rest of the world. Soviet trade reflected the Politburo's preference for living as a Sixth Continent, a self-contained world with only the most controlled dealings with countries beyond its limits. The pattern of Soviet trade reflected this choice: it was bizarre compared with that of other industrial giants. The Soviet Union's chief exports were raw materials, notably oil and natural gas. It did export machinery and equipment but in 1984 they made up only twelve per cent of foreign sales and mostly went to the captive markets of other communist countries. Except in its arms sales the might of Soviet industry was scarcely felt in the outside world. Soviet gas and oil were anonymous once they entered the pipeline, whereas people knew at once when they were using a Japanese tape-recorder or riding in an American jet. The Russians were sensitive about this, but resigned. In Khrushchov's time they debated whether to buy foreign equipment from one of the great European motor companies or to make a small car of their own design. Justifying the decision to go Russian Khrushchov is supposed to have said, 'Never mind. One's own shit always smells of raspberries.'

Not having to compete abroad and protected at home, Soviet industry came to look like a creature from an earlier stage of the world's industrial revolution. Some Soviet industrialists hid from this truth by comparing the new machines they produced with obsolete models that foreign companies were no longer making. Some officials and economists were even ready to argue that competitiveness was a 'capitalist category that has no relation whatsoever to our socialist industry'. But there were others who understood very well the dangers of the situation. They knew that Soviet engineers had been discussing the advantages of diesel engines for twenty years but that still less than a quarter of all Soviet lorries and practically none of the buses were diesel-powered. If the industry had tried seriously to export it would have had to meet the foreign demand for diesel vehicles and thereby also done a power of good to the Soviet economy. With conservation the order of the day the old-fashioned petrol engines of most Soviet heavy vehicles were an extravagance the country could no longer afford, wasting eight million tons of petrol a year. The economy was also damaged by industry's inability to produce small lorries. Three-quarters of foreign lorries had a capacity of only up to two tons. Soviet lorries were on average much bigger and so spent most of their working time half-full. Again the Soviet economy would have been the first to benefit if its lorries had kept up with world standards.

The ordinary citizen could arrive at the same conclusion by using his eyes. Contacts with the West grew in the 1970s. More foreigners lived, worked and studied in the Soviet Union. More tourists went both ways. In the 1960s obtaining Western goods had been a minority pursuit of the very adventurous or the most privileged. By the time Brezhnev died Moscow and Leningrad were not far behind the West at least in the knowledge of pop fashions. Most large cities had a black market where Western jeans could be bought for £240 a pair, twice the average monthly salary at the official rate of exchange. The Moscow 'markets' like the one at the metro station near the race course were so well known that even provincials came to do their shopping there. Mothers would make the journey to find something fashionable for a daughter. Young men just out of military service made the pilgrimage to buy the jeans and running shoes without which they felt they could not impress their contemporaries. Soviet industry sometimes tried to catch up. It eventually produced jeans (despised) and imitation Adidas shoes (more acceptable). But it was a hopeless battle. People's attention was always caught by something new from abroad – miniaturized recorders, compact discs, videos, personal computers.

Naturally people asked why their own country could not produce such things. It might not matter if a teenager burst into tears because she could not buy the baggy jeans young Russians called 'bananas' and which all her schoolfriends wore. But when university students realized how far ahead the

West was in computing skills the damage to the Soviet government's image was more serious. The leadership had trapped itself. Self-imposed isolation had allowed it not to compete with the rest of the world. To end that isolation would reveal how far behind the Soviet Union was in the competition of nations which communists said was the substance of history. By the 1980s this far from new problem had taken on an even more worrying aspect. The backwardness of so much of Soviet industry threatened the achievement Brezhnev had most reason to pride himself on – military equality with the United States.

A year before Brezhnev's death Marshal Nikolai Ogarkov, chief of staff of the Soviet armed forces and spoken of as the most brilliant Soviet officer of the post-war generation, warned that developments in military technology were changing modern warfare. Weapons systems, he said, only had an effective life of about ten years. (He was to repeat this warning even more strongly after President Reagan's decision to develop anti-missile defences which – if they worked – would depend largely on America's supremacy in computers.) Ogarkov was raising the possibility that the Soviet Union might one day not be able to match American military advances. He implied that some leaders had not understood that the technological race had entered a new stage.

The Soviet Union had been wasting time. Yuri Andropov was to admit this in his public comments on the state of the country almost as soon as he took over the party leadership. Later it became the political fashion to date the economic decline from the end of the 1970s – this was the Gorbachov formula. But it was not clear why the start of the troubles was not dated even further back. Only one of the senior leaders has tried to do this. Mikhail Solomentsev, promoted to full membership of the Politburo by Andropov, told the twenty-seventh party congress that the failure of the old economic strategy was already obvious at the end of the 1960s. He said that specialists and party and government officials were arguing then that the time had come to modernize the economy and bring its technology up to date. Solomentsev was well-placed to know for at the time he was head of the Central Committee's department for heavy industry. Modernization had not happened, he said, because 'a lack of a sense of the new and the inertia of thought that held many people in thrall did not allow the correct conclusions to be drawn . . . As a result we lost time. Oh, how we miss it now!'

It was an unusual admission unusually phrased but few doubt now that wasted time and opportunities are among the main charges to be brought against Brezhnev and his associates. The loss of time was to have another consequence: the man whom the more far-sighted members of the establishment hoped would make up for the wasted years soon proved to be one of their victims himself. Yuri Andropov had waited too long for power. When the leaders of the world and their diplomats examined him in the Kremlin on the day of Brezhnev's funeral he was already an ill man with only a few months' active life left.

6

A Crack of the Whip

Yuri Andropov was elected general secretary on November 12, 1982. On November 29 the minister of railways, Ivan Pavlovsky, was transferred to 'other work' – a Brezhnev era way of saying he had been sacked – and replaced by his first deputy Nikolai Konarev. Almost a month to the day after Andropov's election *Pravda* made an unprecedented first-page announcement. Under the heading 'In the Politburo' it reported that the leadership had discussed letters sent by workers to the Central Committee and the Presidium of the Supreme Soviet. The item began sweetly enough. The workers, no one can have been surprised to learn, had expressed their support for the party's policies. The tone changed sharply a third of the way through:

> Questions are legitimately being asked about the need for strict observance of the party and government's demands for strengthening state, labour and production discipline, and for bringing actively to bear legal and social measures of persuasion on those who infringe it. Many letters contain facts showing that in a number of places the necessary struggle is not being carried out against people who tolerate waste, deception, fiddling the books, the uneconomic use of material resources, extravagance. Signals are also being received about the need to strengthen the fight against those who disturb public order and against the theft of socialist property.

The letters had raised other problems too: about the distribution of public housing and its upkeep; about food supplies and the quality of the health service. This, the announcement went on, was to be taken as evidence of 'the workers' political activeness' and as their 'instructions' to the party and government. Local authorities should pay heed to the 'justified criticisms and complaints of Soviet citizens'. In particular:

The attention of the procuracy of the USSR and the ministry of internal affairs of the USSR is drawn to the need for taking measures to strengthen the preservation of law and order in towns and villages taking into account that these questions are being raised with particular sharpness in the letters of workers who are seriously worried by them.

It was a most unusual document. Who would have imagined the leadership admitting that law and order had deteriorated so far that ordinary working people had become alarmed? The media in Brezhnev's day had never suggested that the country had a crime problem on this scale. And why was there this surge of proletarian anger against inefficient and dishonest officials? The party and government bureaucracy presided over by Brezhnev had, judging by the length of time they stayed in their jobs, been performing well enough. Andropov did not give the country long to puzzle over these contradictions. Within a week of the Politburo communiqué he removed Nikolai Shcholokov from the ministry of internal affairs that he had run for sixteen years. The real sting was in the choice of Shcholokov's successor. Andropov did not search for an up-and-coming policeman or a senior party official as might have been expected. He picked Vitali Fedorchuk, the man who had succeeded him as chairman of the KGB. It was the clearest possible signal to the Soviet militia that the easy old days were over. The KGB and the ministry of internal affairs were great bureaucratic rivals. The Chekists, it was generally supposed, looked down on the uniformed cops whom they could, when necessary, boss around. And if anyone knew the true state of affairs about corruption and inefficiency in the militia it was the KGB.

Fedorchuk was a stocky man with a reputation for toughness. He had been a Chekist almost all his adult life, specializing in military counter-intelligence, but from 1970 until he replaced Andropov as head of the KGB in the spring of 1982 he had run the security services in the Ukraine. The second largest of the Soviet republics, the Ukraine had chronic problems with nationalists, religious dissenters and a Jewish community that inevitably contained refuseniks who wanted to leave the Soviet Union but could not. In twelve years in the Ukraine Fedorchuk left his painful mark on all these groups. It had become an axiom that only the brave provoked the Ukrainian KGB. No appointment was more likely to scare policemen with something to hide, and Fedorchuk's arrival at the ministry building at No. 6 Ogaryov Street must have been a scene of panic and prayerful repentance worthy of the greatest Russian satirists.

Fedorchuk quickly made his mark on Moscow. Within days of his appointment police started to turn up in unexpected places. They went to shops, cafés and cinemas and demanded identity papers of anyone who seemed to be of working age. Those suspected of being absent from their job without leave were put in a bus and taken to a police station. The police held them there until their employers had been contacted and their absence from work explained. As a result some people were sacked. Everyone had their story to tell about the police sweeps. There were a lot of complaints. It had become a custom for office workers to take it in turns to go out to the shops, in working hours, for themselves and the rest of their colleagues. Given the well-known difficulties of Soviet shopping this was regarded as a normal activity for which no one should be reproached. Only the minority who did not have to be at work found the new situation delightful. The shops had never been so uncrowded, which seemed proof that Fedorchuk's men were attacking a real problem. Public excitement reached its peak in the middle of January when it became known that the police had pounced on one of the capital's most famous establishments – the Sandunovskaya *banya* or bathhouse. One of the small number of Moscow institutions that survived the break of the Revolution, the baths had been built at the beginning of the nineteenth century by an actress who was determined they would be Moscow's best. They offered rooms of unheard-of comfort for the nobility and even a special section where ladies could go with their dogs, the latter to be bathed by maids. The baths were rebuilt at the turn of the century even more splendidly in the most up-to-date European style. It was to this grand Beaux Arts building on Neglinnaya Street in the centre of the city that Fedorchuk's police came one January day. Whom they discovered in the by-now slightly shabby luxury of the Sandunovskaya was never revealed. But it was widely believed that several dozen men including some senior government officials were caught and unable to explain why they were not at their offices.

Nobody minded about that. But police harassment of ordinary people as they went about what they had come to consider their rightful business in the shops was not popular. Nor were people happy when they were told that they would not be allowed time off from work to go to the doctor or dentist, a well-established way of taking a free day. The most serious criticism was that the police sweeps had no legal justification, relations between employer and employee being no more a matter for criminal law in the Soviet Union than in Great Britain. The matter may have been thought serious enough to be discussed by the Politburo in late January. The police sweeps came to an end. Shop opening hours were made more flexible – a more sensible, though still not perfect solution. Two months later a factory manager was reported saying to his workforce, at the end of a lecture on discipline, 'Of course, it doesn't mean you can't do a little shopping.'

Fedorchuk had perhaps not understood that Muscovites, for all their sinfulness, could not be treated like Ukrainian dissidents. The national discipline campaign, though, continued. In January the procurator general revealed that law and order was in such a poor state in the city of Gorky (where Academician Andrei Sakharov lived in exile) that workers were afraid to walk home after nightshifts and citizens' patrols had been attacked by hooligans. Newspaper captions changed in an odd way. The worker standing in front of a machine tool looking at his watch would, in the old days, have been saying something like, 'We've finished the job with two hours to spare.' The new-style caption went: 'The lunch break ended half an hour ago but three lathes are still standing idle.' There were also a few more changes at the top. The minister of trade was retired in January. He was seventy-seven and had held the job since 1965. The deputy heads of two other ministries were sacked in the next two months and it was made plain, most unusually, that they had gone in disgrace. One had failed to stop embezzlement by his subordinates, the other used state materials to build a house for himself.

In Moscow, when the excitement over the police sweeps had died down, people seemed on the whole to approve the new atmosphere. It was largely a matter of having an active leader again. 'The biggest change,' a foreign ambassador remarked, 'is that now someone is in charge.' The Russian proverb about the peasant only crossing himself when he hears thunder was back in fashion. Even liberal-minded Russians spoke of the country's need for a *khozyain*, a master. 'The Soviet economy,' one intellectual remarked, 'is not like a machine where you push a button and it starts to move forward. It is like a horse and cart. If you stop whipping the horse the whole thing comes to a halt.' The message, that Andropov had picked up the whip which Brezhnev never properly grasped, was conveyed in many different ways. After attending a meeting with Andropov a newspaper editor called his staff together. Leonid Brezhnev, he told them, had been a kind man. He had been a very kind man. He had been an exceptionally kind man. The editor paused before concluding meaningfully, 'And too many people took advantage of his kindness.' Andropov's years in the KGB were not a disadvantage here. People of course made jokes about that past but they were not the dismissive, destructive anecdotes that had been aimed against Brezhnev. What did Andropov say when there was a knock at his door? 'Bring him in.' A Pole and Russian discuss their country's new dances. Martial law Poland has the Jaruzelska. The Pole puts his arms to his sides and hops around the room at attention. 'That's nothing,' the Russian replies. 'We have the Andropolka and it goes like this.' The Russian leans forward, puts his hands behind his back as though manacled, and does a convict's shuffle across the floor.

People listened because it was Andropov, former head of the KGB, who was talking about discipline. They also listened because they suspected that the performance of some parts of the economy could indeed by improved just by tightening discipline. As far as the railways were concerned they were right. Andropov not only put in a new railways minister. He appointed a Politburo member as troubleshooter for transport problems. His choice was the Azerbaidzhani party leader Geidar Aliyev who had been brought into full Politburo membership at the November Central Committee plenum after Brezhnev's death. Two days later Aliyev was made one of only two first deputy Soviet prime ministers. It was an unexpected and at first not very popular promotion, even though Aliyev could claim that he had turned the mess he had inherited in Azerbaidzhan into a success story. There was prejudice against the Muslim Azerbaidzhanis both among their Christian Armenian and Georgian neighbours in the Caucasus, and among Slavs.

Aliyev seemed to owe his rise to Brezhnev rather than to Andropov. He had endlessly cultivated and flattered the old man and his promotion was very likely agreed on after Brezhnev's visit to Baku in September. But Aliyev was to handle himself well in Moscow. He exchanged his Azerbaidzhani name – Geidar Ali rza ogly Aliyev – for a Russianized version, Geidar Aliyevich Aliyev. His spoken Russian was almost accentless (unlike that of the Georgian party leader Eduard Shevardnadze). Like all the other non-Slav leaders he had, of course, always paid ritual homage to the Russian people as an 'elder brother'. Aliyev was a handsome man, tall and well built, and a smart dresser who handled himself with a certain elegance. Unlike many senior party figures he read his speeches as though he meant them. It was said that people always left a meeting with Aliyev with a better opinion of the man. He amazed and flattered foreign diplomats by remembering their names: not a social skill usually associated with Politburo members of the time.

But Aliyev had another side. He had, after all, 'cleaned out' Azerbaidzhan. It was not just as a charmer that people there remembered him. Some time after his promotion to Moscow a Russian found himself in a taxi driving past Aliyev's residence in Baku and was surprised when the car slowed down. The Azerbaidzhani driver explained. 'The Shah,' he said apprehensively, 'is still the Shah.' One foreigner who talked with Aliyev remarked that he gave the impression of a man no one had cared to argue with for a good many years. This was the side of Aliyev to attract Andropov. Aliyev and the new railways minister Konarev imposed discipline. They sacked inadequate senior railway officials and gave the sackings full publicity in the railwaymen's newspaper *Gudok*. Under such encouragement the railways began running bigger and heavier trains than had previously been thought possible. Average train weights started to grow. More traffic was carried by fewer trains which meant that trains could also go faster. When the severe winter of 1984–5 hit the railways they were for the first time in many years able to make a quick recovery.

Railways, as the jokes about dictators remind us, respond to firm centralized authority. Andropov had made a point that no Soviet leader can afford to overlook. One of the advantages of the Soviet system was its ability to concentrate attention on particular crises and to ease them by imposing order from the centre. It had the bureaucratic machinery for this, and both governed as well as governors were used to such methods. And it had in men like Aliyev politicians with the training and talents to oversee the task. But discipline had its limits. It was one thing to make the railways as they existed work better. Other parts of the economy and society needed to be changed. So did many of the country's senior officials. And it was here that Andropov met resistance.

He was, however, able to impose from the beginning his own style of personal leadership. He had it put about that he did not like the flatulent publicity that had surrounded Brezhnev. He did not want to see his name quoted at the beginning and end of every major article in the press as had been the custom with Brezhnev. A story went round that in his first days in power Andropov rang up the editor of *Pravda* and asked if he had a copy of Lenin's works in the office. The editor of course said he had. In that case, Andropov is supposed to have replied, try quoting him instead of me. He did not want to see his photograph everywhere. He did not want his portrait on the ikon-like banners it had become the practice to issue to audiences at political meetings. He would not allow television to be present at every formal public appearance he made. When on February 1 *Pravda* reported Andropov's first sortie among the people – a tour of the Ordzhonikidze machine tool factory in Moscow – it printed not a single picture of what everyone at once knew was a major political event.

Andropov introduced a different sort of publicity. At his suggestion the Politburo began to issue a communiqué after its weekly meeting each Thursday. The communiqués gave little away except an indication of some of the topics discussed by the leadership but it was nevertheless a symbolic revolution. It had never before been officially admitted that the Politburo met once a week, let alone on what day. Other senior party figures did not at first welcome this. The leaderships of the republics and regions did not hurry to follow the Politburo's example. It became common to read of party members complaining they knew more of what was going on in the Politburo in Moscow than among their local leaders in Omsk and Pinsk. Andropov also let it be known that his own public pronouncements would be infrequent but weighty. He was to follow the advice Pushkin imagined Tsar Boris Godunov giving to his son: 'Speak little. The Tsar's voice must not be lost emptily on the air. Like a holy chime it must announce only great sorrow or great celebration.' This restraint in public word and deed was a relief after years in which the rituals of Soviet power had been devalued by repetition. It was not surprising that myths grew around the man. By early summer one could hear people whispering that Andropov had renounced all his Politburo privileges and was living a spartan life on his salary alone.

Such changes of style were in Andropov's power. Everything else was much more difficult, as the fate of police chief Shcholokov showed. The ex-minister of internal affairs who was eventually to be expelled in disgrace from the Central Committee was at first treated very differently. In January 1983 he was appointed to the main inspectorate of the ministry of defence where he joined such elderly war heroes as Marshals Kirill Moskalenko and Pavel Batitsky. This was the most honourable retirement possible – indeed perhaps the only form of honourable retirement available in the country – and brought almost no loss of privileges. Yet Shcholokov had never been a professional soldier and during the war only rose to being a middle-rank political commissar. There was no reason why he should join the most distinguished group of old soldiers in the country – except that he still had powerful friends. There was also the puzzle of the empty presidency, or chairmanship of the presidium of the Supreme Soviet. Brezhnev had had himself elected head of state in 1977. It marked his final triumph over rivals. In his and his supporters' eyes it was a coronation. It was assumed that when the Supreme Soviet gathered for its regular winter meeting at the end of November Andropov too would become head of state. But no new chairman was elected, and the country was to remain without one for over six months. His duties were performed by the first deputy chairman of the Supreme Soviet presidium V. V. Kuznetsov, who was eighty-one but spry. It was difficult to see that this temporary arrangement in any way impaired the workings of the Soviet state.

Brezhnev had used the presidency as a symbol of power but it was and remains doubtful whether a strong party leader needed it. Khrushchov had never been president; nor, for that matter, had Lenin or Stalin. The post was in theory prestigious. In practice it could be a political trap that even endangered a posthumous reputation. For Brezhnev's two predecessors in the job – Anastas Mikoyan and Nikolai Podgorny – it had been the equivalent of walking the Kremlin plank. These perils of the presidency were to be advertised in January 1983 when Podgorny died and was not given a state funeral, an honour also denied the much more formidable Mikoyan on his death in 1978, to the fury of his eminent family and friends.

Some people argued that Andropov had not wanted the job. It fitted what was already known about his distaste for ceremonies and parading himself in public. One explanation had it that Andropov and Chernenko agreed, before Brezhnev's death, to split the two posts with Chernenko becoming head of state. But, this version went, Andropov now felt sufficiently strong to withdraw the offer. Chernenko, to explain this setback, was putting it around that he no longer wanted to be head of state, preferring to remain as Central Committee secretary, and in all but name the number two figure in the party. But in that case why was someone else not chosen? Gromyko and Ustinov, it was assumed, could have had the job if they had wanted it. The mystery has not been cleared up and probably never will be. But undoubtedly part of the explanation was that the presidency only guaranteed increased prestige to the party leader while for any other Politburo member it threatened to be more like a slow-acting poison.

The affair of the empty presidency sharpened awareness of the likelihood of power battles in the Kremlin. People seized on references in the press in

December and January to the dangers of opposition and 'factionalism', both of which were of course forbidden by party rules. One newspaper even seemed to hint indirectly at damaging 'conflicts' between 'small groups' within the Central Committee. Andropov's problem was that, unlike the newly-elected leader in a Western democracy, he carried almost nobody else into power on his coat tails. He could get rid of Brezhnev's personal assistants, which he promptly did with the one exception of little Andrei Aleksandrov, the man who gave Brezhnev the wrong speech to read in Baku. To staff his own private office Andropov looked to the Central Committee apparatus and, in at least two instances, to the KGB (Viktor Sharapov and Pavel Laptyev). But that is where the changes stopped. He did not have the power to change government ministers off his own bat. The government was run by premier Tikhonov, an old friend of Brezhnev who remained faithful to ministers who like him had flourished under the old leader. At the November plenum Andropov criticized the minister of ferrous metallurgy almost as harshly as the railways minister who was replaced a week later. But the former was to be kept on until 1985 when he finally retired, ostensibly for reasons of health, after twenty years in the job. Only when Tikhonov retired in late 1985 would the real post-Brezhnev reshaping of the Soviet government begin. Andropov had no greater power over senior party officials. He had inherited the 'Brezhnev Central Committee' elected at the 1981 party congress. He would not be able to alter its membership until the next party congress, in 1985 at the earliest. The regional party leaders were also for the most part Brezhnev men. There would in theory be a chance to make changes at that level sooner, for the regions held party elections once every two or three years. But it was one thing to hold an election of this sort and another for it to amount to more than the formal re-selection of the old leadership.

The new leader's difficulties started in the Politburo. At the end of 1982 the Politburo had eleven members apart from Andropov. Chernenko, who had made such a pointed speech about the need for collective leadership when proposing Andropov as general secretary, could count Tikhonov and the party leader of Kazakhstan, Dinmukhamed Kunayev, as allies. This trio represented the three episodes in Brezhnev's career – Moldavia, the Ukraine, and the breaking in of Kazakhstan's virgin lands – during which he accumulated the friends through whom he was later to exercise his power. On whom could Andropov count? No one in the Politburo owed their career to him. Ustinov, Gromyko, the Ukrainian leader Vladimir Shcherbitsky and the Moscow party boss Viktor Grishin had at least the same weight of experience and seniority as Andropov (the most senior Politburo member, Arvid Pelshe, the eighty-three-year-old Latvian who had known Lenin, seems to have been too ill for power politics. He died in May 1983). Of the three youngest members, Aliyev and the Leningrad leader Grigori Romanov (both were aged fifty-nine) stood to benefit from change but not perhaps equally. What if Andropov favoured one over the other? In fact his favourite turned out to be the Politburo baby Mikhail Gorbachov, a choice that spelled destruction for Romanov.

They were an odd bunch and only made sense as a group as long as Brezhnev was alive. But they were united in one thing: they were in the Politburo and, one must presume, wanted to stay there. The temptation to push out a colleague was always held in check by self-interest, for the harder it was to make changes the safer everyone was. In the Kremlin, at least, there should have been no surprise that when Andropov died in February 1984 all the members of the Politburo that survived Brezhnev – with the exception of Pelshe – were still in their seats.

Andropov's attempt to establish himself ran into other obstacles. How did he know whom to trust and whom to advance? For thirty years his work had been first with the Soviet Union's communist allies, then with the secrets of the KGB. He had not had much opportunity to cultivate the men of power within the country, especially the barons who ran the republics and regions. But, as Brezhnev had shown, contacts throughout the country were the best means to building up a reliable following. A politician anywhere in the world could understand that but in the Soviet Union this age-old technique had peculiar importance. In a one-party state, where any sort of group or faction even within that party is banned, the only way to find out who is like-minded is through personal contact. In the land where everyone is meant to think the same it is dangerous to assume that anyone agrees with you. It can be said in defence of the astonishingly Mafia-like quality of some of the politics in Brezhnev's day that it was necessary to keep the business of government going. Friendships, favours, alliances and the more shady dealings to which these can and did lead were to a considerable extent a substitute for a politics in which people can be openly identified as friend or foe by their political colours.

It was Andropov's good luck that there was another man's network of political contacts waiting to be picked up. It had been put together by Andrei Kirilenko, an associate of Brezhnev who was considered his possible successor until Chernenko pushed him aside. Kirilenko's resignation from the Politburo – on the usual grounds of ill health – was announced at the same time as Andropov's election as party leader. The Kirilenko protégés had nothing to hope for from Chernenko. They needed Andropov as much as he needed them. The success of the marriage may be judged from the Gorbachov Politburo of 1986. Its two most important members (after Gorbachov himself) were the party number two Yegor Ligachov and the prime minister Nikolai Ryzhkov. Both came from the Kirilenko stable and both began their climb to the very top thanks to Andropov.

Coming to power in a one-party state had another disadvantage. The orthodoxy of the previous leadership (of which of course Andropov had been an important member) had never been tested in open public debate.

What were the policy alternatives open to a Soviet government? The most the media and academic press could do was make hints about what was wrong, but they were not empowered to search methodically for alternative policies. Party rules did allow for 'discussions on controversial or insufficiently clear questions'. They even laid down that this was 'necessary' if several regional or republican party organizations were of the same opinion; if there was an insufficiently strong majority within the party 'on the most important questions of party policy'; or if the Central Committee itself decided to consult with the general membership. But a discussion of this sort, the rules stressed, had to be conducted in such a manner as to avoid splitting the party or in any way damaging its unity.

There were cases of quite heated argument over projects that the leadership had not made up its own mind about. It was plain from speeches made at the 1981 party congress that there was no unanimity about the immense scheme for diverting river water from north Russia to the Ukraine and Central Asia. But the problems now facing the country were immediate and fundamental. The viability of the old economic, political and social systems was at stake. The careers of the party and state bureaucracy were at stake. These were not matters to be thrown out for even controlled debate within the party. One cannot tell whether Andropov had, before Brezhnev's death, discussed such matters or with whom. Did he hold policy conversations within the privacy of his office in the KGB? Had he already sounded out Gorbachov and found him like-minded? What had Andropov been reading? How seriously did he take the ideas and facts presented in the translations available to senior officials of articles from the foreign media about the Soviet Union? There was a sobering precedent for any Politburo member who might have been tempted while Brezhnev was alive to develop criticism of the leadership's adopted policies – Khrushchov's destruction of the anti-party group in 1957. Brezhnev was at least as strongly placed as Khrushchov then in the Central Committee, and far better supported than he had been in the Politburo.

There had also been, in the spring of 1982, a political scandal among the Moscow intelligentsia that must have cooled enthusiasm for anything like organized discussion of possible reforms to the system. In April (when Andropov was still at the KGB) six young intellectuals from well-connected families and some if not all party members, were arrested and threatened with prosecution under articles 70 and 72 of the Russian criminal code. These were the anti-dissident articles that punished 'anti-Soviet agitation and propaganda' and 'organizational activity directed towards commission of especially dangerous crimes against the state and also participation in anti-Soviet organizations'. Two of the arrested worked at the senior Soviet policy think-tank, the Institute for World Economy and International Relations (known to Russians by its initials as IMEMO). Others worked at major scientific research institutes. The young men were connected with little-known underground political journals with names like *Variants* and *Left Turn*. They argued that reforms might be made from above – i.e. by the party – if there was sufficient pressure from below. They accepted a Marxist outlook as natural for the Soviet Union and had no interest in restoring capitalism. Their chief ideas seem to have been that the Soviet Union was not a true socialist society; that only democracy could stop the ruling oligarchy becoming the virtual owners of state property; that the party bureaucracy was an exploiting class, though no longer a brutal one; and that economic efficiency could only be achieved if the bureaucracy's powers were cut back. They had much in common with the West's Euro-Communists and indeed studied European left-wing writing as best they could.

It is plain enough now that these young men were saying more forcefully what some older people were thinking but keeping to themselves and their closest friends. When the arrests became known some people feared that to bring the group to trial would have a crushing effect on the intellectual life of the party. Similar alarm was to be heard from the British diplomat-spy Donald Maclean. Donald Donaldovich, as he liked to be called in the Russian style, himself worked at IMEMO. He had not met the two men from there who had been arrested but he knew some of their friends. He was sure they were 'very serious types' who would not do anything 'outrageous'. More to the point 'they were asking all the questions that ought to be asked'. Economic efficiency, the over-great powers of the bureaucracy and the lack of meaningful democracy in an increasingly well-educated society were to be the central and inter-linked themes of policy debate in Gorbachov's Soviet Union. Perhaps not surprisingly the young men who seemed, while Brezhnev was alive, likely to get long prison sentences found their trials being postponed until, at some time in early 1983, they were released. They were given a warning not to see each other or talk about what had happened. They were also expelled from the party, lost their prestigious jobs but were found other work of a not too unsuitable kind.

The incident said much about the changing times. In April 1982 Andropov had wanted, or could not stop, the Moscow Euro-Communists' arrest. In 1983 he was able to prevail, possibly over opposition, to have them released. It also suggests that Andropov, when he succeeded to the leadership, did not have a clear idea of the changes that would be necessary. The half-dozen major policy speeches he was to have time to make suggest a man feeling his way out of a world he knew well into one he was not sure he fully understood. In that at least he was like most of his fellow countrymen. A generation had grown up under Brezhnev. The society that Andropov was preparing to criticize was the most stable, most agreeable world most Soviet citizens had known since the Revolution. A film that appeared in early 1983 was a useful reminder that while young intellectuals might flirt with Euro-Communism most people were busy getting the best out of life as it was. The heroine of *The blonde around the corner* is a ravishing girl who works in a

66

supermarket, a princess of the barely hidden underworld of the black and grey markets. Her friends, including her motor mechanic brother, are all people with access to goods and services in short supply. She falls in love with an intellectual – an astronomer – because he is so innocent of the facts of life. She cannot resist a man who thinks there is no sausage to be bought just because there is none in the shops and who only knows how to get an air ticket to the Crimean coast in the summer by standing in a queue. The film was made ostensibly as satire and the heroine is in the end quite unconvincingly transformed by the hero's innocence. But audiences rushed to see it, recognized the life they saw there, and laughed with the enchanting heroine rather than at her. They did not look or sound like people who felt they needed a crack of the whip.

7

The Master's Thoughts

Andropov led the Soviet Union for fourteen months, and during that time made little more than half a dozen major statements on policy. People had grown accustomed, in the Brezhnev years, to repetitive speeches flabby with the clichés of self-congratulation and the same ineffective criticism of apparently eternal problems. Style was the first novelty of Andropov's pronouncements. He spoke simply. He used very little party jargon. It seems to have been his way as a young man too: his first speeches as Komsomol leader were in plain, straightforward language. The style matched the directness of the content. The best evidence that Andropov had not been able, before his election as general secretary, to prepare an agenda for the country is to be found in what he said after Brezhnev's death. His first major speech, at the Central Committee plenum on November 22 contained, a most unusual admission for a Soviet leader:

> In general, comrades, we have many urgent problems in the economy. Of course I do not have any ready recipes for their solution. It is up to all of us in the party Central Committee to find these answers. To find them, generalising from our own and world experience and accumulating the knowledge of the best practical workers and scholars. All in all, slogans won't get us anywhere.

This did not sound like a man who had access to an already-prepared alternative set of policies. Quite apart from the political problems of trying to prepare any such document there was the difficulty of finding people able to answer the questions that troubled Andropov. The signs are that when he did turn to the country's academics and experts after becoming party leader they were of much less use than he expected. By mid-summer he was complaining about this in public. It was time for the social sciences, and above all economics, he said in June, to aim for a much higher standard and to take a 'decisive turn towards real practical tasks'. So far they had failed to do this. The party needed advice on how to improve the efficiency and quality of production, the country's central economic problem. The academic community had been unable to give it and was no better poised, Andropov implied, to help solve the other new problems thrown up by a changing society. It is not surprising he moved cautiously. He noted at the November plenum that a lot had been said about giving factories and farms more independence from the central planners. But he seemed to consider the matter still so beset by uncertainty that he warned it would be necessary to 'move cautiously' and to experiment first. An experiment to give factories greater freedom of initiative was not to begin until 1984.

Andropov gave the impression that at first he was not even fully aware of the range of social and economic problems he had inherited. This may explain the tentative way in which he developed his criticism of Brezhnev's record. There were political reasons for this, too. Andropov had not beaten Brezhnev in an election. As far as the public were concerned he had succeeded him as one pope follows another. Along with the office he had inherited the dogma and policies. To criticize the dead leader too roughly would make the party, and even more so the surviving members of the Politburo, look foolish. At the November plenum Andropov made seven flattering references to Brezhnev. He recalled 'Leonid Ilyich's winged words' about the economy having to be economical. He cited unpublished memoranda Brezhnev had written to the Politburo about the need to switch the economy away from extensive to intensive development. A month later, speaking to the Supreme Soviet, Andropov mentioned the dead leader only once. After that there were no more references to Brezhnev by name and growing hints that he was responsible for many of the difficulties now besetting the country. In February 1983 Andropov referred to 1981 and 1982 as lost years. In August, at almost his last appearance in public, he explained that the roots of the problem went even further back. Decisions taken at past party congresses (which meant a time frame of at least six years) had not been carried out and so the economy had simply continued along the old, wasteful lines. 'There are various reasons for that,' Andropov said, 'but it obviously showed that we did not look sufficiently energetically for ways to solve new problems, that we often took half-hearted measures and could not overcome sufficiently quickly the inertia that had built up. Now it is necessary to make up for lost time.'

By saying 'we' Andropov tactfully identified himself with the Brezhnev establishment which remained in place after its leader's death. It was sound politics given the establishment's strength. But the ideas Andropov began to develop in public implied the need to wage a war against everyone who was unable to overcome the 'inertia' of the past. The urgency with which Andropov regarded this problem was hinted at by an unusual series of articles in the newspaper *Sovietskaya Rossiya*. The first appeared on November 21, the day before Andropov made his first policy speech to the Central Committee. The headline read 'Measure a hundred times' (an expression Andropov was to borrow for a later speech) and the key to it lay in the rubric: 'Reading Lenin anew.' Sixty years ago to the day Lenin had spoken to the Moscow Soviet in the Bolshoi theatre, his last speech in public before his death in January 1924. Not the least surprising aspect of the article was its style, quite unlike the usual scholastic essays on Lenin's life and thoughts. This piece tried to draw the reader into the excitement and anguish of the already-ill leader's reflections, and was written as though Lenin himself was thinking aloud. 'It wasn't far to the Bolshoi,' the article began, 'but first it was necessary to have a preparatory conference with one's own thoughts, even though he had been thirsting for this meeting for so long. That was the word, thirsting! . . .' What followed were Lenin's ideas about how to save the Revolution.

> One must know how to speak simply and clearly . . . and abandon the heavy artillery of complicated expressions . . . Painful questions must not be avoided . . . but tackled head on . . . The truth, however bitter, must be looked straight in the face . . . It is important to explain how vast the gap is between the old and the new tasks . . . This does not mean any break in our line, in the continuity of policy . . . Among all our difficulties the *apparat* [the bureaucracy or machinery of state] has become a real misfortune. We are changing to entirely new tasks and rules but the *apparat* remains old. And often it controls us, not we it . . . The point is not decrees and institutions but practice and practical people . . . It is necessary to search out literally one by one people who can do business and step by step clean out our Augean stables, drive away the bosses who just mean well and close down the enterprises that have gone to sleep . . . The proletariat is not afraid to admit that some things have worked splendidly in the Revolution while other things have not. All revolutionary parties that have perished up till now have perished because they became too pleased with themselves and could not see in what their strength consisted, and were frightened to speak of their weaknesses . . .

It was these same phrases of Lenin that Mikhail Gorbachov was to use three years later at the end of the twenty-seventh party congress. Many of the other ideas in this and later articles by the same author, Valentin Chikin, were to appear in Andropov's speeches. Chikin was a Lenin scholar and deputy editor of *Sovietskaya Rossiya*. The paper was important – it came under the Central Committee. Its editor, Mikhail Nenashev, was an able man and considered to be in the new leader's confidence (Gorbachov was to promote Nenashev to be head of Soviet publishing. He would make Chikin

Sovietskaya Rossiya's editor and a candidate member of the Central Committee). In the 'Reading Lenin anew' series Chikin was playing an old game: associating the party leader with Lenin and thereby buttressing his authority. He was able to use Lenin's words to express ideas more sharply than Andropov could. Chikin could repeat Lenin's acid opinion of the bureaucracy – 'It is only slightly painted in Soviet colours on top but in everything else it remains typically old.' It would have been impolitic for Andropov to say this was true of the present *apparat* even though the evidence is that he, like Lenin, thought the great bureaucrats had become 'the pampered "grandees" of the Soviet Republic'. Chikin heightened the drama of the present day with his implied comparison between Lenin trying to take the country by the scruff of the neck into the unfamiliar world of his New Economic Policy (NEP) and an Andropov who understood the Soviet Union was again at the start of a new journey for which the old maps and methods were useless.

Andropov presented Moscow with an unusual and absorbing spectacle. For the first time since Khrushchov it was possible to watch a Soviet leader thinking aloud about the problems facing the country. After Andropov's death his son Igor was to talk of his father's fascination with Lenin and his habit of referring to Lenin's writings when he came home in the evening. Andropov was an orthodox Soviet Leninist. He was too intellectual to make the wild jumps of a politician of instinct like Khrushchov. The landmarks of his mind were conservative. Marxism-Leninism was sufficient to the country's needs and should not be tampered with:

> Voices may be heard sometimes saying that new phenomena in social life 'do not fit' into the concept of Marxism-Leninism, that it is living through a 'crisis' and that it should be 'brought to life' by being injected with ideas drawn from western sociology, philosophy or politology. The problem here, however, is not at all any alleged 'crisis' of Marxism. The problem is something else – the inability of some theorists declaring themselves as Marxists to encompass the true scope of the theoretical thinking of Marx, Engels and Lenin and to use the tremendous intellectual power of their teaching in the process of the concrete study of concrete questions . . . It is unworthy of communists to be attracted by trenchant phrases of all sorts of 'perfectors' of Marxism and to catch at fabrications of bourgeois science.

He was just as conservative on some of the long-ranging ideological problems of the Soviet state. What was to be the eventual relationship between the different nationalities in the Soviet Union? Some Soviet scholars believed that the original idea of a complete merging of the nations was unrealistic and even damaging. But Andropov held to the view that eventually the Soviet Union's component nations would, as Lenin predicted, merge into a new single one. He also occupied the conservative corner in the apparently abstruse debate about what would happen to collective farms. Andropov insisted that at some point they would be absorbed into the system of state ownership, even though it was well known that the collectives, where the farm was in theory the collective property of its member-workers, were usually the more efficient of the two.

The heart of Andropov's conservatism was his attitude to the party, and here at least he was at one with the Soviet establishment, the men in whose hands power lay. Andropov, alone of the Soviet leaders, knew the Soviet Union's European satellite-allies well. He had been closely involved in East European affairs from 1951 to 1967, serving as Soviet ambassador in Hungary during the 1956 revolution and finally as Central Committee secretary supervising the communist bloc. During those years he showed that mixture of ruthlessness and common sense that seem to have been the stuff of his communism. He had fought to keep the Hungarian party in power but once it was secured he was not dogmatic about how the Hungarians used that power, as long as the Party's control remained beyond dispute. When Andropov was chosen as Soviet party leader no one was more pleased than the Hungarian Communists who felt he understood the experiments they were making. Andropov's feelings for Hungary might not have been so friendly without the magical political skills of the Hungarian leader Janos Kadar. Kadar managed to strip some of the unpleasant attributes from the dictator-party but his control of the country was never in doubt. Andropov had nothing but scorn for other East Europeans who misunderstood what Kadar had done.

> In politics you have to pay for your mistakes. When the leading role of a Communist party weakens the danger arises of a slide towards a bourgeois-reformist path of development. The link between the party and the people is lost – and self-styled pretenders to the role of representatives of the workers' interests appear in the vacuum that arises.

Andropov spoke about the party as the moral instrument of history. It was the story of St. George and the dragon on a global scale. The hero-party had the mission of destroying the dragon of private property. 'The communists can express their theory in one concept: Abolition of private property' – Andropov quoted this sentence from Marx's *Communist Manifesto* in his most important statement on the principles and practice of the Soviet state. But the dragon was not easy to kill. Even when its body was slain its corrupting memory lived on in men's minds:

> The historical experience of real socialism shows that the turning of 'my own', privately owned, into 'ours', common, is no simple matter. The revolution in the relations of ownership by no means reduces to a single act as a result of which the basic means of production become the property of the whole people. It is far from the same thing to obtain the rights of a

master and becoming a true, wise and thrifty master . . . People . . . have for a long time . . . to shape themselves for it both economically, politically and, if you wish, psychologically, developing a collectivist mentality and behaviour.

Those who stand outside Soviet political orthodoxy may see in a different light this vision of the party as the necessary educator of a people still studying for communism. What else was to be expected after making a socialist revolution in a country that was not ready for it (a charge that Andropov himself would presumably have dismissed)? It does not mean his belief in the moral justification of the party's right to rule was not genuine. The indignation was real enough when he talked of communists who allowed themselves to be tempted by unorthodox ideas as 'unworthy'. Andropov spoke as a demanding teacher who knows that truth is only reached by discipline and self-denial. The oddity was that such a man had emerged from the easy-going Brezhnev world.

Andropov's Soviet admirers insisted that for all his orthodox beliefs he thought 'in categories of reality', not of dogma. They might have added that he kept a remarkably open mind about practical matters for a man whose formative years had been during the 1930s, the *belle époque* of Stalinism. It was indisputably a good mind. He had an ability to question and probe that the other leaders of his age seem not to have had. To a remarkable extent it was Andropov who laid the intellectual groundwork for many of the changes his protégé Gorbachov was to introduce. By doing so he showed the country that it had been taken in hand again, and that alone did much for Soviet self-confidence.

In the few public statements Andropov made he began to ask the right questions. Why was capital investment, particularly in agriculture, bringing such bad returns? Why were factories reluctant to introduce new technology even though so much of industry was out of date? Why did people's self-interest so often conflict with the interest of the state? Why was there much more money in circulation than goods to buy with it? Why was there a damaging shortage of labour when mechanization could lead to a rapid redeployment of the workforce to where it was most needed? (He produced the shocking figure that forty per cent of labour in manufacturing industry alone was still manual.) It was Andropov who rubbed home the uncomfortable truth that the Soviet Union's ability to influence the world depended first and foremost on its economic achievements: a perception entirely shared by his successors today.

Andropov's practical economic experience was small compared to most of the other Soviet leaders. Before becoming general secretary Brezhnev had worked on important economic programmes as a senior party official in the Ukraine, Moldavia and Kazakhstan. He had also done a spell as Central Committee secretary supervising the defence and heavy industries.

Andropov had behind him only four years as a party official in Karelia, a Soviet backwater, and that was as long ago as the late 1940s. It was not surprising that when he did take charge he became fascinated by the working of Gosplan, the state planning committee. How could such an organization not attract a man like Andropov? So much of the Soviet myth became flesh in Gosplan: the power of science, properly understood, to perfect society's development; the prerogative of Communists to control that power. Andropov seems to have believed that if he could discover how to rub Gosplan's magic lamp correctly the result would be a healthy, efficient economy. He is said to have visited the committee's office on several occasions to study its work. His hopes for it seem to have been reflected in one of Valentin Chikin's Lenin monologues:

> A step must be taken in the direction of increasing Gosplan's competence. Matters must be arranged so that its decisions are not overturned by anyone who feels like it . . . Its success will be determined by erudition plus independence plus conscientiousness . . . [It needs as] its head a significant personality, a major authority in technology or agronomy, a scientifically educated man with great practical experience . . . possessed not so much of administrative qualities as the capacity to win people over . . .

Andropov did not have time to find such a person himself but in 1986 Gorbachov was to appoint a new chief of Gosplan who answered this description. His choice, Nikolai Talyzin, was a professor of electrical engineering, had served as minister of communications and as Soviet representative to Comecon (the Soviet bloc common market). Unlike his predecessor, Talyzin was given the rank of first deputy prime minister and also made a candidate member of the Politburo.

By the end of 1983 Andropov had mapped in outline the wider changes the economy needed. He made these known to the Central Committee in December. He had decided that nothing less than a programme to improve the whole economic machinery of the state would do (at this time neither Andropov nor any other party leader talked of a 'reform' of the economy, let alone the 'radical reform' that was to become the slogan under Gorbachov). He spelled out the elements of such a programme: a new structure of management to produce a clear definition of the rights of ministries on the one hand and factories and farms on the other; a more effective system of central planning; more use of economic levers such as prices and credits; and a better way of measuring economic performance. Only an integrated approach to these problems, he concluded, could make 'fullest use of the advantages intrinsic in the socialist method of production'.

Soviet politics, like politics in any other country, appears to be chiefly about economics. But for Andropov, the Communist who believed that 'ours' should replace 'my own' in people's thinking, economics was only a means to an end. The party had a responsibility even greater than assuring prosperity. It had to prepare people morally for life in a society embarked on the journey towards communism. Andropov's rules for the present stage of Soviet society in one respect echoed those of two very different but equally moralistic leaders – Ronald Reagan and Margaret Thatcher. Under communism, when it came at some time in the still distant future, citizens would contribute whatever they could to society and take what they needed from it. But the Soviet Union was only at the stage of socialism. 'The greatest and indisputable gain of socialism,' Andropov said, 'is that it has created conditions that ensure every person the right to work.' But rewards under socialism should go to those who worked hardest.

Marx was strongly against the levelling down of wages and categorically rejected demagogic or naive talk, which was not infrequent in his time too, about socialism as 'general equality' in distribution and consumption. [As for] complete equality in the sense of the identical enjoyment of material goods [that would only be possible under communism]. But we have a long way to go before then. For that it will be necessary to have both a much higher level both of the economy and of people's consciousness. But today . . . each of our citizens only has a right to those material goods that correspond in quality and quantity to the socially useful work he performs. Only to that. And here it is important to have strict accounting and a strict observance of this principle.

This was more than a general statement to the effect that the government favoured wage differentials. It promised a change, important in its social implications, from the practice of the recent past when salaries had undergone a levelling process. In the early 1960s the average salary of an engineer had been one and a half to two times greater than the average wage of workers. By the mid-eighties engineers in manufacturing industry were being paid the same as workers. In the construction business they were getting even less than the average labourer. As a result many young engineers after graduating scarcely bothered to look for work that fitted their qualifications, preferring to take easier non-skilled work, particularly if it also offered a chance to make money unofficially on the side. Now the skilled and hard-working were to be paid more and the incompetent and the slackers were to get less. This, Andropov explained on several occasions, was the main purpose of the discipline campaign which some people had misunderstood. 'When we speak of discipline,' he said on the one visit he was able to make to a factory, 'we have in mind the whole chain of production. And of course all our efforts will go to pot if the battle for discipline that's been begun slides along the surface, is wasted on trifles: someone was five minutes late, another person took too many smoking breaks. Of course no one should be praised for that. It's necessary to impose order everywhere that working minutes are being lost. But we are talking about a serious attitude to every aspect of production discipline.'

Discipline meant seeing that people who contributed little felt this in the wages they received. Salaries had to be structured so that everyone would understand it would be 'unprofitable to work in the old way'. Andropov did not have the time to take this to its logical conclusion: that if a factory performed badly its whole workforce should suffer. This line was to be pursued under Gorbachov and surely Andropov would have approved. After all, Chikin had quoted Lenin suggesting the time might come to shut down 'factories that had gone to sleep'. Andropov's socialism was severe in another way. Soviet communists protected themselves against the attractive abundance of the West with two arguments. The first was that Western societies shared their wealth unequally. The second was that the West was prisoner of a 'consumerism' that destroyed true human values. Andropov was now proclaiming the need for a much greater measure of wage inequality in the Soviet Union. But he was also keen to warn people that communist abundance did not mean a society of gleaming supermarkets. Soviet 'consumerism' – the Russians called it *veshchizm*, 'thingism' – was already a favourite target of moralists in the Soviet media. Andropov tried to raise their moralizing to a more philosophical level. He was worried that some young people had become infected by 'the dangerous fungus of petty bourgeois attitudes'.

We must teach our successors an attitude to life in which material goods (and with time there must and will be more of them) should not dominate a man but serve to satisfy his highest needs. Only the spiritual riches of man are truly without limit. And though you cannot put them in a purse or hang them up on your wall for prestige that is the sort of accumulation we are for. It is the only one worthy of man, of Soviet man.

He explained more of what he meant to the Central Committee in June 1983.

We often use the expression 'raising the living standard'. But sometimes it is interpreted in an over-simple way and is taken to mean just an increase in people's incomes and the production of consumer goods. In reality the concept of standard of living is much broader and richer. It includes the continuous growth of people's consciousness and culture, including the culture of daily life, of conduct, and of what I would call the culture of sensible consumption. It includes social order of a model kind; a healthy and rational diet; and a high quality of services available to the population . . . It also means the worthwhile use – from a moral and aesthetic point of view – of one's spare time.

To imagine the impact such words had one has to remember how Andropov's predecessors spoke and behaved. Khrushchov, in the new party programme he had written in 1961, boasted about catching up America within two decades in the production and consumption of almost everything. He may have done himself an injustice by seeming to equate communism with infinite mountains of sausage but that was the embarrassing impression the programme made. As for Brezhnev, many people who did not actually know that he was far from practising the 'culture of sensible consumption' himself must have suspected that might be the case. When Andropov said such things it was easy to believe that he was ready to follow his own counsel.

Andropov raised another theme that was to be developed under Gorbachov. Speaking to the Central Committee at its June meeting he used for the first time the word *glasnost*, which means openness or publicity. 'Surely wouldn't it help us,' he asked, 'to bring the activities of party and state organs closer to the needs and interests of the people if there was more openness in their work, and also a regular accountability of leading workers to the population?'

Andropov had begun the practice of issuing communiqués about the Politburo's weekly meetings. He also re-introduced the Khrushchov practice of publishing a verbatim account of Central Committee meetings though he only managed this for the June plenum called to discuss ideology. It contained few surprises. Apparently the only impromptu moment was a question by Andropov himself to the minister of culture about the number of professional pop groups in the country (the answer was almost seven hundred). Gorbachov did not follow Andropov here: mystery has once more settled on most of what goes on at the Central Committee's meetings. But the idea of *glasnost* in general did survive and for good reason. Andropov was feeling his way towards one of the biggest problems facing the Soviet state at the end of the twentieth century. He had inherited a political system that gave immense power to the leader at the centre. It was a matter of belief that he and the party had the history-given right to exercise that power. But he was also aware that Soviet society was changing. People were better educated. Much more skill and initiative was needed from them in their work than even twenty-five years before, let alone than in Stalin's time. The day would come when old-fashioned manual labour, of which Andropov knew there was still far too much, would disappear. People were different, would become even more different, and had to be treated differently. The young already could not be talked down to. 'The young generation is in no way worse than ours. It is only different and new . . . And in general, comrades, we have to admit – though it's not easy for everyone [he was talking to old-time party members] – that each new generation is in some way stronger than the one that went before. It knows more. It sees further.'

It was almost revolutionary, in a country run by a gerontocracy, to suggest that young people might know best. But how should they and the new, better-educated workers be allowed to express themselves? What should be done, in other words, about Soviet democracy? The key to Andropov's thinking was suggested by another of his remarks on openness. It was necessary, he said, 'to speak with people seriously, frankly and not avoiding difficult subjects' for this was the only way to make them 'conscious participants in social life'. There should be more public discussion about important government decisions. 'I have in mind a broader discussion of the plans for such decisions in work collectives . . . as considerate an approach as possible to workers' suggestions.' More power should be given wherever possible to local authorities, especially to the soviets, the local government councils. The law on work collectives adopted by the Supreme Soviet in June 1983, the first such legislation in the country's history, was a step in the same direction. But if Andropov understood that the new generation had to be treated in a new way he could not contemplate any form of democracy that threatened the party's control. 'It goes without saying that an interpretation of self-government as leaning to anarcho-syndicalism, to splitting society into rival corporations independent of each other, to democracy without discipline, to the notions of rights disassociated from duties is deeply alien to us.' What was necessary was to 'combine successfully the free creativity of the masses with the advantages of a single system of scientific guidance, planning and management'.

Anyone who failed to understand the correct balance between these two apparently contradictory ideas could expect trouble. There was no 'flouting of human rights' in the Soviet Union as enemies in the West alleged, 'but regrettably there are people as yet who are trying to set their selfish interests against society and its other members. In this light it clearly becomes necessary to carry out work for the education, sometimes for the re-education of some persons, for combating encroachments upon socialist law and order and the norms of our collectivist life.'

This was not just a warning. Andropov made several important changes to laws that could be used against dissenters. On October 1, 1983 a new law was added to the Russian criminal code which made it possible to re-sentence prisoners, even while they were still serving an old sentence, if they 'maliciously disobeyed' camp authorities. The new sentence could be as high as five years for prisoners guilty of 'particularly serious' crimes against the state. Anti-Soviet agitation and propaganda, the charge brought against many dissidents, belongs to this 'particularly serious' category. The first sentence known to have been given under the new law came a year later, in October 1984, and the practice has now become common, as it was once before under Stalin. A decree of the Supreme Soviet published in January 1984 laid down heavier punishment for anyone charged with anti-Soviet agitation and who had received money from abroad, regardless of the source. Another change brought in a punishment of up to three years' imprisonment for 'passing on to a foreign country information that constitutes a professional secret'. Almost any information about almost any Soviet organization could be fitted into this definition.

Andropov, in his fifteen months in power, was forced to approach the contradiction at the heart of the Soviet system. As head of the KGB, wielder of the cleansing sword forged by 'Iron Feliks' Dzerzhinsky, his responsibility had been simpler: to protect the party's power. As party leader he had to consider both sides of the Soviet paradox because the country's survival as a great power depended on no less. The party had the right to rule but the Soviet Union would not be a modern, industrialized state worth ruling unless its citizens had more freedom to make decisions for themselves. This tension had been less obvious in the decades when the Soviet Union was still developing, changing from a largely rural society to an urban one. It had been covered up, too, by the non-stop display of intellectual conjuring that Soviet citizens knew as 'ideology'. But now ideology was itself in danger of becoming a brake on necessary changes and here Andropov, for reasons perhaps not least of age, showed a hesitancy that would mark the leadership until a younger generation took over in the Kremlin.

8

The Science of Belief

Ozhegov, the standard Soviet Russian dictionary, carries the following entry for *Ideologiya*, ideology:

A system of views, ideas, characterizing a social group, class, political party, society. *Marxist-Leninist ideology*, adj. **ideological**. *Struggle with ideological distortions*.

The Soviet Union's ideology is Marxism-Leninism, the ideology, according to its adherents, of the working class. As practised by Moscow, it is an all-embracing system of ideas and values. It takes all mankind and his works into account. It is as possessive as a jealous lover, venomous in its attacks on any system that appears to be competing with it. Marxism-Leninism has served many purposes. It rallied the Bolsheviks and their allies during the Revolution, providing both a path of action and the passion with which to pursue it. Later it gave a disorganized society which had apparently severed all links with the past a new set of intellectual and moral landmarks. It gave and still gives some, at least, in each new Soviet generation irresistibly clear answers to the questions the new generation in every country asks. The young 'must have generalizations, conclusions, incorrect if you like but still conclusions . . . Try and tell young people you cannot give them the whole truth and they will not listen to you.' The novelist Turgenev was explaining the attraction of the anarchist Bakunin for young Russians of the last century. Generalizations and conclusions was what Marxism-Leninism offered in abundance.

Most societies live either without a clear ideology, or with a variety of intellectual and moral systems that coexist in defiance of logic. The exceptional qualities of Soviet Marxism-Leninism – its sharpness of definition and its exclusiveness – are one of the most powerful reasons for the 'difference' of the Soviet Union, the feeling that it is a Sixth Continent where foreigners are easily lost. Those qualities, though, serve another purpose that is much more important to the system. The ideology must be tough and combative because it provides the justification for the Communist party's power. If the ideology shows weakness, what of the party's right to rule?

The party rules because it is the 'vanguard' of the working class, which is in turn history's chosen class. According to the revised 1986 programme of the Soviet Communist party the party is 'the inspirer and organizer of the historical creativity of the masses and the leading and guiding force of our society'. The party may be powerful now but it will be even more important in the future: 'the party's leading role,' the programme says, 'naturally grows.' Since the right of the party to speak for the working class can no more be scientifically proved than kings could prove their right to represent God on earth, unscientific faith and fervour must play an important part in Soviet ideology. Marx's insertion of moral beliefs into his great science of society was the first step towards a million dramas of faith lost and found in the land of the first proletarian revolution.

Greetings, esteemed editorial staff!

I want to address this question to you and through your paper to your readers: do I have the right to bear the name of *Komsomolets* [a member of the Komsomol] if I have stopped believing in communism?

I genuinely believed in it before and I tried to uphold the name of *Komsomolets*. But with the years, when I left school and acquired a trade and came really up against life my faith began to waver and then completely disappeared. Putting it in a nutshell, life itself, reality, crushed this faith in me. And one day I asked myself: Sergei! Why do you bear the name of *Komsomolets*? After all in your soul you have ceased to believe sincerely in communism. And if you don't believe sincerely in your soul it means you won't be able to produce any results in this field because without faith all you'll get is concern for yourself and you will try to take more from society than you give it.

And so I have decided to leave the Komsomol at my own request in order to try to make at least a bit of sense out of life and first of all out of myself, and then decide if I can be a *Komsomolets*. And now all the time I keep asking myself: why did your belief dry up? After all, the foundation for it was solid enough. I have been rejected by life and feel that I'm not living but just existing and life itself isn't allowing me to be resurrected in faith, that's what has to be reckoned with first and foremost.

That is my confession. I hope that people will respond to it and help me.

Minsk   Sergei V.

Who would doubt that this letter, published in the youth newspaper *Komsomolskaya Pravda* at the beginning of 1985, spoke of a genuine crisis of belief? In another sort of person Sergei's crisis would end not in a dark night of the soul but in a new illumination. An intelligent, sensitive girl of twenty-four, brought up in an educated but conventional Soviet family, manages for the first time to read the poetry of Mandelstam, Marina Tsvetayeva and Boris Pasternak. The experience 'knocked me off my feet, physically'. She lies in bed, feverish and delirious. The 'electric shock' administered by these voices whose existence she had not suspected eventually leads her to a passionate Christianity, to conflict with the authorities, prison and, in 1986, release to the West.

The poet Irina Ratushinskaya and Sergei V. from Minsk occupy the extremes. Sergei loses his faith; Irina acquires a new one. And because man is so fickle in his faith Soviet teachers try to stress the scientific nature of Marxism-Leninism while still making use of the moral charge contained in the old socialist ideal of freedom in equality. *Komsomolskaya Pravda* turned to a member of the staff of *Kommunist*, the Communist party's journal of theory, to explain to Sergei where he had gone wrong. The trouble, this learned man wrote, was precisely that Sergei had *believed* in communism. Communism was 'too serious a thing for it to be enough only to believe in it'. Believing in communism was not only unnecessary: it was 'also extremely harmful and dangerous'. Communism, said the expert, belonged to the sphere of knowledge and this was diametrically opposed to that of faith. One could believe in anything, including the existence of God or the malevolence of black cats. There was no way to prove one faith right and another wrong. But communism could be proved to be correct, though a Soviet citizen had to be prepared to work hard to grasp the compellingness of this proof. Poor Sergei from Minsk; if he read the reply to his letter he would have learned that to understand 'scientific communism' properly he had to have a knowledge of the problems that had absorbed 'Plato and Aristotle, Descartes and Spinoza, Locke and Leibnitz, Diderot and Helvétius, Smith and Ricardo, Saint-Simon and Fourier, Kant and Hegel, Belinsky, Herzen and Chernyshevsky. Don't think,' the expert on ideology kindly added, 'that I want to dazzle you with this stream of scholarly names. It is just a very short list of those names and ideas which every *class-conscious worker* must have an understanding of.'

It is not necessary to be a great sceptic to suppose that most Soviet citizens go through life with only a slight understanding of Aristotle and Leibnitz. And because the guardians of Soviet ideology know very well that human beings are driven as much by belief and prejudice as by knowledge they maintain a constant watch for breaches by rival faiths into the fortress of Marxism-Leninism. In recent years they have particularly struggled against the notion that morality founded in religious belief produces better behaved people. The argument has cropped up often in debates about drunkenness.

Good Christians tended not to drink, at least not to excess, and didn't that prove something? (In Soviet Central Asia the argument received an Islamic twist. After Gorbachov began his anti-alcohol campaign in 1985 mullahs rejoiced that the Communist party was returning to the abstemious ways of the Prophet.) The ideologists have had to be particularly vigilant about the powerful current of Christian morality in pre-revolutionary Russian literature and culture. It is so easy to get the 'wrong' ideas from writers like Dostoyevsky and Tolstoy. It is even possible for errors to be spread by books that have passed through the fine sieve of Soviet publishing. Shortly before Brezhnev's death a new book appeared in a series called 'Problems of moral philosophy'. Entitled *The Ethics of Love and the Metaphysics of Free Will* it set the alarm bells ringing in the same journal that had been called upon to advise Sergei about the lack of knowledge that he had mistaken for a loss of faith. The book's author, Yu. N. Davydov, was rash enough, in his opening pages, to declare that 'Dostoyevsky can give much, infinitely much, to our present day youth'. *Kommunist*'s horror crackled off the page as it summarized up Davydov's ideas about morality

- true morality is absolute;
- its basis is always the principle of love;
- it also signifies self-sacrifice and self-denial;
- the denial of moral absolutes is nihilism.

These were very naughty thoughts. Marxist-Leninists knew that morality was historically shaped and was a class phenomenon, yet here was a scholar who had written a number of 'solid Marxist works' suggesting that a society perished without absolute moral standards. It was, *Kommunist* concluded, a 'serious ideological mistake' to publish such a book.

Suspicion of religion's power to corrode ideology even affected the performance of music with religious associations. A leading light in the Soviet music world hoped in vain that the June 1983 Central Committee meeting called to discuss ideology might make it possible for religious works by great Russian composers to be heard in main concert halls like Moscow's Conservatoire. It was permitted to perform a Mozart mass or a Haydn oratorio but Rachmaninov's Vespers, though it had been issued on record, could only be performed in churches and few had a choir of sufficient skill. Judging by the enthusiasm with which religious music was greeted when it was performed it was a wise precaution. At a Moscow concert at Easter-time in 1981 Yevgeni Nesterenko, the star bass of the Bolshoi opera, roused an audience with a performance of the Merezhkovsky song 'Christ is Risen' (the stage of the Tchaikovsky hall where he was singing was decorated with the slogan 'Let the name and deeds of Lenin live for ever' and the concert was attended by the then head of the Central Committee's propaganda department who at the concert's end went to congratulate the great singer). At the time of the June plenum a tiny opera company working in what was once a basement cinema had just brought into its repertoire an ancient musical mystery play last performed by Russian soldiers during the First World War. This was tolerable only because so few people would ever get to see it.

At a more popular level party theorists understood the difficulty of convincing the young that class consciousness was the only basis for the morality of the present and the future. The Soviet Union no longer knew what class struggle was. Since the adoption of the Brezhnev constitution of 1977 the country had officially been a 'state of the whole people'. The dictatorship of the proletariat was over. The Soviet Union still had classes – a working class, a peasantry and an intelligentsia – but the differences between them were small and supposed to be getting smaller. And since there was no private ownership of the means of production these class differences could not lead to conflict. That, at least, was the theory but, as an adviser to Konstantin Chernenko was to admit, it created problems for the educators of Soviet youth: what shall they know of class struggle, who only the Soviet Union know? Vadim Pechenev noted with what seemed like regret that there were already several generations in the Soviet Union

who do not have any experience of their own of participation in class struggle with the exception of a few, mainly ideological kinds connected with the class struggle on the international arena. The consciousness of these people, unlike the consciousness of veterans of the Revolution and the first five year plans . . . is formed inside the country without any direct conflict with the class enemy.

Here was the sort of paradox loved by Soviet Marxist-Leninists. The absence of class conflict in the Soviet Union meant even greater efforts had to be made to inculcate class-consciousness into each new Soviet generation. Fortunately the class enemy was not far away. He was a couple of hours' drive from Leningrad in neutral, friendly Finland. He was massed to the west of Moscow's East European allies and across the Atlantic ocean. The border guards (who are part of the KGB) were on the look-out as much for hostile ideas as for spies and smugglers. They were charged with stopping the entry of 'tendentious literature, television films preaching moral licentiousness, the cult of force, occultism and permissiveness' and any other scrap of what the border troops' chief of staff called the outside world's 'ideological waste-paper' (the modern traveller, offended when his news-paper or magazine is confiscated at Moscow airport, should remember that Baedeker was advising visitors to pre-revolutionary Russia not to line their trunks with newspaper if they wanted to avoid delays at the Russian border).

It is one of the most important characteristics of the Sixth Continent that its borders are as much intellectual as geographical. Ideas no less than people need visas to cross them. They are – according to Soviet theory – the frontiers of class and their existence is a powerful justification of the need for rule by the Communist party, the wisest and most resolute element of the proletariat. Pechenev repeated what Lenin had said about every worker needing to understand the 'economic nature and social-political appearance of the landowner and the priest, the high official and the peasant, the student and the vagabond, [and] to know their strong and weak sides, to understand . . . all the sorts of sophisms with which each class and social layer *covers up* its egoistic instincts and its real "insides".'

The Soviet media made up for the lack of class struggle inside the country by regularly describing its ferocity abroad. The nine o'clock evening television news programme *Vremya* kept to a format that exactly reflected the concept of an entirely different world beyond the Soviet frontiers. The first part of the programme showed combine harvesters sailing across great wheatfields and steelmen gazing without a flinch into blazing furnaces. Then the capitalist world was portrayed in all its recidivist horror: striking workers, tramps under bridges, violent policemen charging peaceful demonstrators. This formula was to be criticized in the Gorbachov era as 'monotonous' but it remained to be seen whether any new one would be less Manichean.

At home the ideologists looked for positive, emotional symbols to attract the young. In a country where institutions and groups have often flourished most strongly around 'great men' the cult of Lenin was inevitable.

We shan't get lost on the road to our dreams!
Lenin will light the way.
Strive to learn as Lenin learned.
Learn to work as Lenin worked.
Know how to dream as he did.

The motto of Artek, the grandest of all Soviet young pioneer camps (children from the Chernobyl area were sent there after the nuclear accident of 1986), is one example of the many ways in which Lenin is imprinted on people's minds. It is difficult for a foreigner to assess the cult. Aspects of it that Soviet people take for granted make even the Soviet Union's communist friends uneasy. In the 1970s a Soviet children's book about Lenin as a boy was unwisely translated into Polish. It became a bestseller until the authorities realized Polish students were buying it as a joke and hurried to withdraw it from the shops. But every country needs a point of reverence and when, on January 21, the anniversary of Lenin's death, the papers print photographs of him (the headlines proclaiming 'To Lenin!') and the queue to get into his mausoleum loops like a necklace across Red Square the reverence is unmistakable. The Russian capacity to revere the dead as though they have not entirely vanished from earth plays a part here too, and other dead heroes, not all to the official taste (like the actor-singer Vladimir Vysotsky, poet of the rough reality beneath the smooth official surface), benefit from it as well as Lenin.

By the time of Brezhnev's death it was obvious that ideology was suffering from the same disease that was damaging the economy. It was producing quantity, not quality. The shops were full of books stuffed with irreproachably Marxist-Leninist sentiments that few cared to read. Seven hundred million copies of the Marxist-Leninist classics had been published since 1917. Party leaders could expect the latest edition of their collected speeches to be printed in editions of a hundred thousand but it was a mystery who bought them. The cities and villages were decorated with slogans that had not been changed for years. The one on the roof of the headquarters of Intourist, looking across to the Kremlin, proclaimed 'Communism will conquer'. The slogan on the post office in Gorky Street announced, like thousands of others, *Slava KPSS*, praise to the Communist party of the Soviet Union. No one seemed to notice them any more. On May Day, and on the anniversary of the Revolution, the party officials responsible for 'agitprop' – agitation and propaganda – would hang the streets of every town with red flags, with pictures of the trinity of Marx, Engels and Lenin and yet more slogans. They could report a job well done but it was hard to measure what effect, if any, their work had. It was noticeable that in the Baltic republics, where the way of life was approaching Scandinavian sophistication, there were far fewer banners and slogans to be seen. The local leaders doubted their usefulness.

Some party officials, at least, realized that more needed to be done to justify the party's power than to repeat, *ad nauseam*, Lenin's boast that it was the 'mind, honour and conscience of the age'. The big city intelligentsia had always been a problem. Their children, unlike the provincial Irina Ratushinskaya, were brought up from an early age in two intellectual worlds. It was necessary to know the geography of the official world, not least for passing exams in the obligatory political subjects. But the life of the mind was mainly lived in a much bigger and freer world of Russian and Western ideas and culture. It did not necessarily clash with the official world. Many intellectuals managed to contrive a coexistence between the two. But it meant that some of the intelligentsia, while never doubting the party's power, could not accept it as the authority that ideology proclaimed it to be.

A newer problem was how to dominate the minds of ordinary people, especially the young, at a time of growing contacts with the outside world. There was a school of thought in the party that regarded the possession of almost any Western product as evidence of a heretical mind. Some local party officials certainly thought they would gain credit by organizing lightning raids on young people in town centres to check whether they were wearing foreign teeshirts or crosses round their neck. Even carrying a plastic bag with the name of a foreign firm or product (as useful as it was fashionable, because Soviet shops were unable to provide such convenient things) was, in these circles, considered undesirable. The military, too, was beginning to have doubts about the class-consciousness of at least some of its national service recruits. The chief of the general staff, Marshal Nikolai Ogarkov, had warned before Brezhnev's death that young people were no longer always approaching questions of war and peace 'from class positions'. He complained that instead they sometimes accepted the oversimplified idea that 'any peace is good, any war bad'. Nothing could be more serious, in the eyes of the Soviet establishment, than for the party to lose its power to mobilize the country's young men.

There is no doubting Andropov's keenness to put some life into ideology. Before 1982 was out he had appointed a new head of the Central Committee's propaganda department and was planning to hold the June plenum on ideology. Some people in Moscow thought this odd, given the country's serious economic problems. But it was evidence of how seriously Andropov took his Leninism that he should want to get political theory right first. The editor of *Sovietskaya Rossiya*, Mikhail Nenashev, tried to set out some new guidelines for the party's propaganda experts before the Central Committee met. Ideological work, he said, was in a rut. It was a victim of 'clichés and conservative attachment to the old and familiar' and was losing touch with everyday Soviet life and the problems that worried ordinary people. When ideological workers did try to improve matters, all they could usually think of was to organize more lectures or put up more of the old slogans. Then they complained that they had done their best but that no one wanted to go to political lectures any more. The public lecture, organized in the main by an organization called Knowledge, was a familiar feature in the life of most Soviet towns. The lecturers, often well-qualified young specialists making extra money by their talks, would usually hold forth in some unattractive little hall before a small audience of which the retired and slightly dotty often made up the majority. It was not unknown for lectures to be cancelled for lack of an audience.

Nenashev insisted people would go to the right sort of lecture. His paper, for example, had published an account of a meeting between students and Boris Yeltsin, the man who was later to be promoted fast by Gorbachov but who at the time was still only party boss of the Sverdlovsk region in the Urals. Two thousand young people turned up and sat for five hours while Yeltsin answered their questions. That showed, according to Nenashev, that young people were not 'inert' or suffering from an 'information overload' as some propagandists suggested in self-defence. The secret was that Yeltsin had answered 'those questions which aroused the particular interest of Soviet people'. This was the opposite of what usually happened at ideological meetings, when all that took place was the convincing of the already-convinced. Party committees would 'urge high labour discipline on – leaders of production, they would unmask the harmfulness of religion – in front of nonbelievers, and expose drunkenness – to the sober'.

Re-thinking the ideology was also difficult because the existing orthodoxy always had its powerful supporters. There was that part of the establishment which flourished in the system as it was and for which any change was likely to be for the worse. There were the philosopher-priests, the scholars and vulgarizers of Marxism-Leninism who for mixed reasons of intellect and temperament were always ready to fight off any attempt to alter an ideology they considered immaculate. One suspects that some of these men were happiest when the intellectual theories they propounded were most out of touch with the realities of Soviet life. Claiming to be scientists of society they also seemed to need to test their own and others' faith. It was certainly hard to see how anyone without faith could argue that the country's twenty-two thousand state farms (*sovkhozy*) were superior to the twenty-six thousand collective farms (*kolkhozy*). Studies showed that on average they were much less efficient. Yet orthodoxy demanded that the collectives become state farms because Marxism-Leninism held the cooperative form of property to be 'inferior'. The merging of the two forms of property would be the final step towards a classless society, the great goal of the Revolution. The *kolkhoz* farmers were peasants while the employees of the state farms, by a trick of ideological book-keeping, were considered members of the working class. No more collective farms meant no more peasants – classlessness at last. Nor was this a distant goal. The country's chief source of economic wisdom, the Institute of Economics of the Academy of Sciences, had for the past decade been insisting that this great event would take place no later than 1990.

Soviet farming had been haunted all its years by theoretical communists who flinched from the realities of Russian country life. Khrushchov, no theorist himself but who had absorbed simple communist notions as a young man, genuinely believed he was taking the Soviet Union closer to the good society when he cut back the number of household plots that farmers were allowed to cultivate themselves. He had been taught that private property was bad, so surely it was right to start eliminating the most significant form of private property remaining in the country. The result, Soviet economists later estimated, was that food production fell by as much as a third.

From 1984 on those Soviet specialists who believed that current orthodoxy about the collective farms was damagingly unreal began to fight back. But it was only one of a number of battles that were developing in the pages of academic journals and in turgid newspaper articles, and which occasionally even the leaders referred to in their speeches. The central quarrel was about practical measures to improve the economy's perform-ance. The orthodox asserted that 'economic man' was a creature of capitalism and therefore had no future in the Soviet Union. It followed that economic concepts such as commodity relations, cost and price had no usefulness in themselves and would eventually disappear into the history books. To stress them now would slow down the advance towards communism. They could be dangerous, too, if they prevented the party exercising its political will over the economy. This school of thought supported central planning not least because it symbolized political domination of the economic process.

But behind this was another debate that was just as fundamental but whose implications were even more disturbing. Could there be a serious political and social crisis in the Soviet Union; a crisis in which the party lost authority in the eyes of the people? The possibility of 'contradictions' in the Soviet system had been argued over for several years. The officially accepted formula was that while there could indeed be contradictions between individuals and society, or even groups of individuals and society, the absence of classes based on property meant that such contradictions were no longer 'antagonistic'. But there was a more radical formula. This allowed that there could be conflicts between 'managers and managed' under socialism. Differences between them were 'non-antagonistic' as long as the interests of both generally coincided. But what would happen if the managers lost 'contact with the managed, if they begin to use their position to implement their own selfish group interests at the expense of public interests and the working people's interests'? This would be an 'antagonistic' situation. Those who put forward this possibility did not say so outright, but the pitting of managers against managed seemed uncomfortably like a socialist version of class war.

This debate was carried on in journals that few people read and in a language that made little sense to the uninitiated. Arguments about whether contradictions were antagonistic or non-antagonistic may at best have made Soviet citizens think back to distantly remembered school lessons on Marxism. But the purpose of the arguments was much more than academic. The conservatives were the chaplains of the establishment. They justified tradition, and played down the need for change. It was not clear at the time whether the conservatives' opponents had connections to men of power within the party. It is now obvious that they did. That they certainly spoke for a significant part of the intelligentsia who wanted to catch the attention of the powerful was plain even then. The remedies they were proposing could not yet even be referred to by their proper name of economic and social reform. But with the coming to power of Andropov the leadership seemed more disposed to think about such matters, and less inclined to be lulled by assurances that nothing was fundamentally wrong.

At the twenty-seventh party congress Gorbachov accused the party's ideologists of 'a certain remoteness from life's requirements'. Later in the year a Central Committee resolution castigated the ideological world for 'scholasticism, dogmatism and quotation-mongering'. It ordered more enquiry into cooperative forms of production, commodity-money relations, prices and other financial levers. This was an attempt to get air into a world grown stuffy. But it did not suggest any alteration to Marxism-Leninism's status as the science of belief that justified both the Soviet state and the Communist party. Intellectual guns were to remain trained on foreign ideas.

9

Promise Deferred

By March 1983 Andropov's supporters were admitting that the pace of change had slowed. The new leader had taken the easy first steps. The campaign for discipline caught people by surprise and signalled a strong will to govern. But there were now much more difficult problems to tackle. The first was to decide what economic reforms were necessary. The second was to put the right people in the right jobs. Both were essential. It was no good altering the way the economy was managed but leaving the same party and government officials in charge of it. Brezhnev had presided over two limited attempts at economic reform without changing the economic and political managers. The result was that the system digested the reforms and continued as though nothing had happened. Some experiments were smothered by the bureaucrats who were meant to supervise them. An attempt had been made for fifteen years to show that factories could increase production while at the same time cutting their labour force – the acute shortage of labour made this a matter of national urgency. But by early 1983 Moscow ministries were manipulating financial regulations in such a way as to make this experiment pointless even in the factory chosen for the first pilot scheme. This was a common pattern. Later in 1983 the Georgian party leader Eduard Shevardnadze, who had made a name for himself by his readiness to try out new ideas, complained that it was only intervention by the Politburo and Andropov personally that had saved two experiments in his republic from being stifled by bureaucrats who found them inconvenient.

Andropov was cautious in the development of his economic policy. But as the weeks went by he began to show increasing irritation over this stodginess in the bureaucracy. In his first speech as party leader in November 1982 he had told the Central Committee that it was necessary to 'deploy cadres correctly so that in the decisive sectors there are people who are politically mature and competent, who possess initiative, the ability to organize, and that sense of the new without which in our time it is impossible to direct modern production successfully'.

A little later he raised the matter of cutting back the bureaucracy. This had been proposed in the party programme of 1961. 'We are doing something in that direction but not enough.' Andropov was sure it was possible 'to cut considerably the staffs of many institutions and organizations without any harm to business'. But his strongest warning to the bureaucracy at large and to its many representatives who had grown old in important jobs came at an unusual gathering in the Central Committee headquarters in August. Almost a hundred long-time members of the party were summoned to attend this meeting. Dressed in their best dark suits and heavy with medals (there were only two or three women among them) they found a formidable trio from the Politburo to greet them. Andropov was there, and to his right sat Grigori Romanov, the party leader of Leningrad who had been brought to Moscow as a Central Committee secretary in June. The youngest Politburo member, Mikhail Gorbachov, sitting on Andropov's left, opened the proceedings. The leadership had invited them, he said, to discuss how best to make use of the knowledge and experience of the men and women who like them had served many years in the party. 'Of course,' Gorbachov added, 'this kind of conversation presupposes raising questions, critical judgements and the analysis of shortcomings.' He then gave the floor to a very old gentleman who had joined the Bolshevik party in 1915, the year after Andropov was born.

What was Andropov up to? As one old man after another rose to speak a pattern emerged. They were all in favour of the high moral standards and hard work the new leader had been preaching. But they were particularly obsessed with the problem of senior managers and bureaucrats. A party member since 1918 who had taken part in the first country-wide programme of electrification recalled that in his youth the young had not had to wait years before being given responsibility as was often the case today. Wasn't this a reason, he asked, for the 'social passiveness' of some young men and women? Another veteran said that while it was right to bring pressure to bear on undisciplined workers 'indiscipline and irresponsibility among some of our leaders causes our economy no less damage'. The trouble was that even when senior managers failed to meet the plan nothing happened to them. 'They get off scot-free. They sit in the same job for years making a mess of things. We should make more severe demands on such leaders, and those who cannot learn how to work should be sacked.' The old men returned again and again to this theme:

People watch their superior's behaviour very carefully and the smallest misdemeanour on his part earns their censure. It must be said that some people have understood the [policy of] consideration for cadres like this: sticking in one place for decades and thinking more about yourself than about your work. It has even become difficult to move some chiefs on to another job.

The last of the party veterans to speak had formidable credentials: forty-five years' service in the Red Army and two encounters with Lenin. The father of the Revolution, he said, had always insisted on strong discipline from the party and made the most severe demands on leading communists. 'We say that Lenin was kind,' the old soldier went on, 'and that is true. But when the party's and the people's interests were involved he never allowed anyone to play the liberal with those who acted contrary to those interests. We are very pleased that the party Central Committee is conducting business in a Leninist, Bolshevik way. And we beeseech you – do not play the liberal with those who do not think about their work and the general good but only about their personal well-being.'

The soldier who had met Lenin sat down. *Pravda* reported there was long applause when Andropov at once replied, 'We promise you that.' The drama of the next six months lay in Andropov's attempt and failure to keep that promise. Closing the meeting, he told them they had been right to say there was such a thing as a 'moral right to lead people . . . but of what moral right can one speak if a man uses his official position to build a dacha, or enriches himself at the expense of his enterprise? . . . With such people we must be implacably severe.'

The very device of summoning these ancient communists to the Central Committee hinted that Andropov was finding it difficult to be as severe as he wanted. If a Soviet leader needed the support of party pensioners to teach the ruling establishment that decent moral standards and hard work were expected of it he was obviously having trouble getting his message through. Why was this, when so much of what he was saying seemed common sense?

Valentin Chikin, who often seemed to be speaking Andropov's thoughts out loud, had written about Lenin's ideas for keeping a balance between generations in government. According to Chikin, Lenin thought this particularly necessary in the Central Committee to guarantee 'continuity' in its work. But it was also important in the people's commissariats (as the ministries were called in Lenin's day) where young people should be brought in to gain experience. Andropov certainly came up against old age's resistance to the argument that the young be given a chance in time. But he was stating the problem more urgently than that. He was talking about the 'moral right' to rule. There is no way of knowing if Andropov followed the academic debate about 'contradictions' in Soviet society, let alone whether he accepted the possibility advanced by the reform-minded theorists that the Soviet Union risked – if changes were not made – its own version of class war in which 'managers' would be pitted against 'the managed'. But his knowledge of the hidden side of Soviet life gained during his years at the KGB and the austerity of his own habits suggest he was sincere about the campaign to purge those who were not morally fit to rule. The establishment, while apparently in awe of Andropov (as long as he seemed likely to live), could not be expected to see matters as he did. The great bureaucrats and regional party barons had prospered in a system which they had been taught was the best in the world. They were unlikely to believe it was heading for a crisis. As for morality, those in power knew that that problem was more complicated than the boy scout language used by the old party members in August had suggested.

The elaborate system of privileges for those in power, the privilege of power itself in a one-party state, were delicate subjects. Everyone knew that if a government minister or a local party leader was replaced on some charge of unworthy or immoral conduct his successor would immediately assume the privileges of the man who had been dismissed. He would inherit the Chaika, or the even more prestigious ZIL car and chauffeur; the better access to scarce domestic and imported goods; the bigger country dacha. It was not always easy to distinguish between privileges that were earned and those that were unearned. And what happened to the man who was sacked, who might, for many years, have done good work but given into one temptation like using his influence to get scarce building materials for his private country cottage? Honourable, let alone dishonourable, retirement was regarded with horror by Soviet officials for it spelled loss of standing as well as privilege. Andrei Gromyko once joked to a foreign visitor about what he called 'the Bermuda Triangle' of Soviet politics, the way in which a man who was important one day could the next vanish into utter oblivion, never to be seen or heard of again. It is not surprising that career patterns and routine retirement were unmentionable subjects, and when a Soviet paper first summoned up the nerve to tackle them – more than two years after Andropov's meeting with the party veterans – it at once touched off an emotional debate. The general director of a big factory in Leningrad, exceptional in that he had retired of his own accord, tried to explain how difficult a decision this was for people like him. Imagine, he said, that you are summoned by some senior official and put on the carpet by him. You leave his office feeling like a child that has been ticked off, but then your chauffeur opens the car door for you, people touch their caps to you in the corridor, there is a crowd of people waiting to see you in your office – and then you forget about the "carpeting" and the gratifying feeling of a director's weight and significance returns . . . Add to that the salary, and the honour. It's not easy to give it all up, to break an established way of life. And it's not only you, your family has also got used to it.'

The country's men of power knew that whatever Andropov might say the Kremlin could not conduct its politics on principles of pure morality. Kremlin politics were unusual chiefly because of the hidden manner in which they were practised, and the reluctance to admit publicly that expedience and compromise played a part in them. The Soviet attitude to politics, in the Western sense of give-and-take between different groups and interests, recalled Victorian attitudes to bodily functions. They were necessary and perhaps even enjoyable but as little as possible should be said about them in public. Sophisticated Russians would admit that the only way to get a real education in politics in the Soviet Union was to see it from the inside, preferably in the Central Committee itself. But an expert could recognize the Soviet leaders for what they were. After his one and only meeting with Stalin Harry Truman remembered him being 'as near like Tom Pendergast as any man I know'. Tom Pendergast was the boss of the Democratic party machine in the president's home town of Kansas City. But it was typical that Stalin took great pains to conceal his mastery of old-fashioned political techniques from his subjects. It was said in party circles in Moscow that he was even prudish enough to send to the Lenin Library for a copy of Machiavelli's *The Prince* each time he wanted to refer to it rather than keep a copy of it on his own bookshelves.

Andropov's public moves had soon signalled that a crafty political mind was at work. His manoeuvring to win the general secretaryship, and his rough tactics against Brezhnev (the Galina gossip) which also damaged Konstantin Chernenko, were not the behaviour of a boy scout. By bringing Grigori Romanov from Leningrad in June to be a secretary of the Central Committee in Moscow he showed readiness to promote old-style members of the establishment when it suited his purpose. No one would have accused Romanov of sharing the Brezhnev weakness of being too good-natured. He was widely regarded as the epitome of the over-bearing party boss. A little man with a solid body and a bad-tempered pout on his face, he was the Politburo member about whom almost everyone seemed to be able to tell an unflattering story. Romanov had thrown his weight around in Leningrad. He was notorious for driving in large and fast convoys through the city streets regardless of the inconvenience it caused. He had obstructed the shooting of a film the officially praised director Sergei Bondarchuk made of John Reed's *Ten days that shook the world*. Apparently he disliked seeing film crews and crowds of extras cluttering up his city. He had brow-beaten the Leningrad intelligentsia and took every chance he could to lecture them on their faults. When handing an award to one of the city's best-known theatres he found it necessary to deliver a lecture on the pitfalls waiting for even well-intentioned Soviet artists. 'Like parish, like priest' was a Moscow intellectual's comment on how Romanov had cowed Leningrad's world of culture. He was considered as much a hardliner on foreign as on internal policies, and could be famously harsh-tongued in conversations with Western visitors.

Romanov was thought to have run Leningrad efficiently. He had got the most out of the immense industrial and scientific resources concentrated there, and had in particular hammered away at the need for technological progress. His recipe was not experiment or reform but strong management, discipline, and rewards for the hard-working. There were the foundations there for a meeting of the minds with Andropov. Those managerial skills qualified Romanov to do the Central Committee secretary's job of supervising the defence industries. He was also useful as a representative of the party leaders of the Russian heartland around and to the north of Moscow with whom Andropov himself had no old or close links. And, lastly, it was logical to suppose that Romanov had supported Andropov in the Politburo in the battle for Brezhnev's succession.

Nevertheless Romanov's promotion looked odd against the background of Andropov's demands for impeccable behaviour among the leadership. Romanov was known to be a hard drinker. The story of how he had forced the director of the Hermitage Museum to lend him a tsarist dinner service for the wedding of his daughter, and how some of the pieces got broken, was so often retold that it verged on folk history. Almost as well-known was the married Romanov's friendship with a popular singer. In early 1983 Muscovites were enjoying an account of how Romanov and his girl friend had gone to a concert by the unchallenged star of Soviet pop music, Alla Pugachova. Singing one of her most popular numbers about how kings can do anything except make you love them, Pugachova turned and directed the refrain at Romanov. It was said that he stormed out of the theatre and ordered Pugachova's remaining Leningrad concerts cancelled, which can scarcely have increased his popularity in the city. It was odd for such vivid anecdotes to be spread about Politburo members and it was hard not to wonder whether the KGB had a hand in them. The story of the breaking of the tsarist crockery was several years old. Romanov had been a possible candidate for the party leadership whom it was then in Andropov's interest to check. Knowledgeable people could be excused for supposing that Andropov, while demanding impeccable behaviour from others, was ready to make use of the less than angelic Romanov when it was to his advantage.

Experience told the Soviet establishment that party leaders could launch high-sounding campaigns to get rid of political enemies: this was yet another of Stalin's legacies. It was only to be expected that people would watch Andropov develop his theme of morality in high places and wonder what he was up to. In early summer, before Romanov's appointment as Central Committee secretary, there was talk of Andropov having suggested to the Politburo that a list be drawn up of all the valuable presents they had been given. Mention was made of the precious dagger that the Azerbaidzhanis had given Brezhnev in 1982. Later in the year Andropov was reported to have begun a campaign against the private dachas built around Moscow by the governing élite. Unlike the country houses allotted to senior officials while in government service these privately-built villas could be handed on to families. Some were extremely luxurious, and it might have been embarrassing to ask how the money and materials for their construction had been acquired. Andropov, it goes without saying, did not have a private dacha. According to one version the Moscow party leader, Viktor Grishin, proposed that these country houses be sold back to the Moscow city or regional soviet at a fraction of their building cost. Not a word was said about this in public but Russians who got to hear of it pointed out that Brezhnev had never touched anyone's private property even when they had been guilty of serious misbehaviour, like the minister of the fish industry replaced in 1979 after the caviar scandal. The business, they said, was unpopular and it was making Andropov enemies.

Stories of this sort were all the more disturbing – for those with any reason to fear the new leader – because in April Andropov had made another important appointment. He moved Ivan Kapitonov, head of the Central Committee's organizational party work department since 1965, to supervise light industry and put in his place a Siberian regional first secretary, Yegor Ligachov from Tomsk. This gave Ligachov supervision over the files of senior party members and the country-wide system of appointments of party and state officials which made it possible for the Politburo to control the country from the centre. It was a rule of Soviet politics that a party leader needed his own man to run this department. Two things were striking about Ligachov. He had been away from the centre of power since he was sent to Tomsk in 1965 from a job at Central Committee headquarters: his career having made no progress under Brezhnev, he owed everything to Andropov who at the end of 1983 was to promote him higher still, to the post of Central Committee secretary. And second, he gave every sign of being a self-assured, self-righteous bruiser.

Ligachov looked right for the role of party strong man. He had a short, strong body. His manner suggested severity, in spite of white hair and a pink face. In Tomsk he had acquired a reputation for disliking drunkenness as much as he liked discipline. He had recently decreed that all party and other meetings in his region should be held on Saturdays to avoid the loss of working time. His style had mixed populism with severity. He was well-educated, graduating at the beginning of the war from the well-known Ordzhonikidze aviation institute in Moscow where his fellow students included the Soviet ambassador to Washington, Anatoli Dobrynin, and Leonid Zamyatin, head of the Central Committee's international information department and the Politburo's spokesman to the outside world. Ligachov had distinguished himself from most local party leaders by the attention he paid to preserving fine buildings and monuments in Tomsk, which was one of Siberia's oldest cities. It was hard to imagine a better man to cast a puritan eye on Andropov's behalf over the party's personal files.

One of the oddities of Andropov's brief rule was that his campaign to restore order in the lackadaisical empire he inherited picked up speed as his own chances of physical survival declined. The photographs of Andropov at the August meeting with the old party members showed a man who in a few months had lost weight and become almost frail. Three days later Andropov received a group of American senators in the Kremlin. It was to be his last appearance in public. From that day he was to rule unseen till his death the following February.

Strong rumours about Andropov's health began as early as March. He missed some important public functions that month and the news soon went round that he had been in hospital. As if to support Andropov's own argument that more openness was needed in Soviet life one version was misleadingly sensational. A woman was said to have shot and wounded him in the shoulder. She had in turn been shot and killed by a bodyguard. The truth was that the kidney trouble that eventually led to his death had forced Andropov into hospital. His kidneys had failed in February when he was for the first time put on dialysis. His mind and will-power, though, were untouched – the French foreign minister, after a meeting with him that month, called it a 'computer mind'. For the visit of President Koivisto of Finland in June Soviet protocol was altered to allow Andropov to meet the foreign guest in the Kremlin and not, as Brezhnev liked to do on such occasions, at the airport. It was a sensible change: goodness knows how many hours Brezhnev had spent on such time-wasting ceremonies. But the Finns at once saw that Andropov would not have been physically capable of it. He delivered his speech at the banquet for Koivisto sitting down. Two men had to help him get up for the toasts. At his meeting with Chancellor Kohl of West Germany in July he was scarcely allowed to walk a step but he still spoke energetically and sharply, like a man who really wanted to win over and convince. Later that month Janos Kadar came to Moscow. It was an occasion when Andropov had to be seen on television and the cameras showed him holding on to the back of a chair all the time he stood to make a short speech before presenting the Hungarian with the Order of Lenin. Like Brezhnev in his infirm days he made no attempt to pin the medal on Kadar's lapel. Kadar later spoke about that visit:

> When I met him for the last time, he spoke to me quite frankly. He told me about his illness, without complaint, as if he were just stating a fact. And when I think that this man did a tremendous amount of work at a time when he was ill for a whole year, so ill that anyone else in his place would have cared only about his illness and ceased to care about anything else, I realise that what was needed was communist conviction and human greatness.

In September Andropov became seriously ill and the next month had one of his kidneys removed. He moved from the official dacha he had been using (it had been Khrushchov's before) into specially adapted quarters in the Kremlin hospital at Kuntsevo in suburban Moscow where he was to pass the last months of his life. And yet he still managed to make himself felt from there. By early summer an investigation had been started into the case of the ex-minister of internal affairs Shcholokov, in spite of his prestigious appointment at the beginning of the year to the inspectorate of the defence ministry. At its June plenum the Central Committee expelled from its membership both Shcholokov and Medunov, the ex-party leader of Krasnodar, for unspecified 'mistakes in their work'. Moscow was swept by the news – never officially confirmed – that Shcholokov's wife had committed suicide. In July Shcholokov's son Igor lost his place as a candidate member of the Komsomol Central Committee bureau. His reputation as a playboy had apparently caught up with him. It was some time after the middle of 1983 that Andropov and his men managed to break through resistance to a proper investigation of one of the major, and most politically sensitive, networks of corruption. A senior detective later recalled that when Yuri Sokolov, the manager of Yeliseyev's, the most famous foodshop in Moscow, was arrested in 1982 it was a sensation because the case was considered exceptional. It was only in October 1983, when the decision was made 'not to hide our heads in the sand' and to continue the investigation 'without any consideration for the jobs people held and their patrons', that the full extent of the Sokolov network (it involved most of the Moscow trade system) began to be uncovered. By the winter Lefortovo prison was reported to be full of senior officials under investigation by the KGB on major charges of corruption. Among them was the Russian Republic's minister of light industry, sacked for 'misconduct' in October.

Andropov could not get people out of the Politburo but he was able to get some of his own men in. In June he introduced as a candidate member Vitali Vorotnikov, the man he had plucked from the Soviet embassy in Cuba to clean out Krasnodar, and also made him prime minister of the Russian Republic, whose territory runs from Leningrad on the gulf of Finland through Siberia to the Pacific ocean. In December Vorotnikov and Mikhail Solomentsev, head of the party control commission, were promoted to full Politburo membership. It was an example of the strange ways in which Kremlin alliances were made. It had never been clear why Brezhnev banished Vorotnikov to Cuba. Vorotnikov, who was only five years older than Mikhail Gorbachov, was said to be bored by a diplomatic job that looked like the beginning of the end of his career. When he did get back to Moscow he showed himself to be a man of the new era. He had a straightforward style; on trips abroad he asked his own questions and made his own notes. He struck visitors as intelligent and showed a sense of humour. Before long his face was to take on the sag of a man who drives himself to work too long hours – a familiar enough type in the history of Russian government. It was harder to understand the reason for Solomentsev's rise. He had been Russian premier before Vorotnikov and was Andropov's age, though much fitter. In his case power had acted as a preservative. But Solomentsev also had a grudge against Brezhnev who had kept him in the same job for over ten years. It was from this dapper old man who superficially seemed to fit the do-nothing Brezhnev years that some of the most acid criticisms of the wasted opportunities of the seventies later came.

The December Central Committee meeting produced two other significant appointments. Ligachov became a secretary of the Central Committee, reinforcing his authority to cast his demanding eye over party officials. And the head of the KGB, Viktor Chebrikov, was brought into the Politburo as a candidate member. That made people sit up. Little was known about Chebrikov except that his photographs appropriately showed the sort of intelligent face that gives nothing away. He had been put at the head of the KGB when Vitali Fedorchuk was transferred to scare the militia into good behaviour. It is likely that Andropov had always had that move in mind. Fedorchuk seemed too much of an ordinary tough cop to make a suitable head of the KGB of which at the time of his appointment he was not even one of the most senior members. Chebrikov was a different animal. After starting a conventional career as a party official he had been made a deputy chairman of the KGB soon after Andropov's appointment as its chief. If anyone knew him well it was Andropov. In June 1983 Andropov awarded Chebrikov the Order of Lenin. In November he promoted him army general, the same rank Andropov had held when he was running the security services. The historically-minded noted that leadership of the KGB seemed now to be recognized as one of the dozen most important political jobs in the country, automatically bringing at least candidate membership in the Politburo. This had not been the case until Andropov had moved to the KGB in 1967. An apprehensive establishment had to draw a more immediate conclusion from Chebrikov's unforeseen rise – that Andropov had improved his chances of remoulding it to his liking. If anyone could provide damaging information on stubborn senior officials Andropov wanted out of the way it was Chebrikov and the KGB. Although it could not be guessed at the time Chebrikov was himself in favour of radical changes in both domestic and foreign policy, which made him an even more formidable ally for Andropov.

The Soviet leader also managed to begin the necessarily slow business of legislating change in society and the economy. In June Aliyev, as first deputy prime minister, introduced into the Supreme Soviet a new law on labour collectives, the first of its kind the country had ever had. This legislation (which is described in the next chapter) suggested that the leadership had at last begun to admit that all was not well between government and the working class. July brought the publication of the decree on the new economic experiment which was to be conducted in five ministries from the beginning of 1984. Two of the ministries were 'all-union', covering the whole country: heavy and transport machine-building, and electrical equipment. The other three were less important, each confined to a part of light industry in a single republic. The modest scope of the experiment disappointed those

Russians who believed nothing short of far-reaching reform could rescue the country from its profligate habits. There was little sense that the changes Andropov proposed meant the start of a new era. But he signalled his seriousness about them by putting at the head of the heavy and transport machine-building industry one of the most experienced administrators of the Soviet defence industry. Sergei Afansyev, who switched to his new job in the spring of 1983, had as head of the innocently-named ministry of general machine building supervised the design and manufacture of Soviet missiles since 1965. The experiment was a cautious and possibly quite inadequate step in what almost everyone agreed was the right direction – the development of a management system that induced thrift, discipline and quality in Soviet factories without throwing them to the wolves of a free market. Whatever its limitations the Andropov experiment changed the economy: from 1987 all Soviet industry began working under its rules.

Andropov only had time to introduce the last change in the form of draft proposals. They, too, concerned Soviet man as worker – this time, his education for work. The draft of a reform of general and vocational education was published in January 1984, and for several months it became the subject of a controlled debate in the media. The chief purpose of the changes was to make the schools the sort of places that would turn out new Soviet generations with the need to work hopefully bred into them. In this, as in the other new measures, it was not hard to detect Andropov's puritan instincts.

In other ways Andropov's absence from public life did make itself felt. It is possible that he decided in the end to take the Soviet presidency in June hoping it would add weight to an authority already beginning to be sapped by public awareness of his failing health. But, once elected chairman of the Supreme Soviet, he had only a few weeks left to be seen in the office. The growing suspicion that the Soviet leader was very ill inevitably told on Soviet foreign policy, whose main purpose, since Brezhnev's death, had been to stop the deployment of Pershing 2 and Cruise missiles by the Nato allies in response to the earlier Soviet deployment of new and more formidable medium-range missiles of its own. The drama of the Soviet shooting down of the South Korean jumbo jet at the end of August had to be acted out with no visible intervention by Andropov, which only increased foreign speculation (almost certainly unjustified) that the Soviet military was not just incompetent but also out of control. There is no reason to suppose that an active Andropov could have stopped the new Nato missiles being deployed on schedule but his invisibility from August onwards certainly made poor Soviet prospects worse. Statements by an unseen Andropov to the Soviet press were all very well, but there was bound to be suspicion that Andropov, like Brezhnev before him, was turning into a Wizard of Oz whose power depended on pretence. The queue of foreign leaders wanting to come to Moscow was growing and no one could inform them when they might be ·

100

received. The inability of Soviet spokesmen to tell the truth when asked about Andropov's health – quite possibly they did not know it – added to the confusion abroad.

A more active Andropov might have managed Soviet diplomatic tactics better. Soviet negotiating behaviour towards the end of the missiles drama was sufficiently odd for some people to suggest a split between the military and the diplomats. A Soviet writer who was known for his mastery of the oblique set people talking with a dramatized version of President Kennedy's part in the Cuban missile crisis. This stressed Kennedy's rejection of military advice that he solve the crisis by force. Some people took it as a hint that similar battles were being fought in Moscow. Soviet propaganda against the Nato missiles had reached the proportions of hysteria, suggesting that deployment might start the next world war. Reagan was compared to Hitler and 'the history of militarism' was said to be repeating itself. There was the hint of a campaign for 'vigilance' against foreign spies and a warning that careless talk cost lives. 'Chatterers must be called to order,' said an article in *Pravda* which also reported receiving a photograph sent by schoolchildren in Krasnodar captioned, 'We shall be the motherland's watchful sentries.' It was at this time that a well-known Soviet journalist who often talked about foreign affairs on television began getting anxious letters from viewers about the likelihood of war. One woman asked him if she should have another child. He was able to answer yes with more authority than the woman probably realized because he knew that the propaganda campaign had got out of hand. The Soviet government had wanted to scare West Europe into stopping the missiles but had ended up frightening its own people more. It was not a glorious performance.

By the beginning of winter people were making fun of Andropov's illness. The jokes were as cruel as the old ones about Brezhnev. Why could Brezhnev travel and this one – a tip of the head towards the Kremlin – can't? Because Brezhnev worked on batteries but this one has to be plugged in. It was a wretched come-down for a leader who a few months earlier had been respected, if not always welcomed, for his firm hold on the whip of government. And, as if to remind Brezhnev's followers that his old standard might one day fly again, *Pravda* broke with precedent to publish a long article about him on the first anniversary of his death. The usual practice was to celebrate anniversaries only of the birth of public figures. The same evening Soviet televison screened a documentary film, based on Brezhnev's autobiography, about his part in the post-war reconstruction of the Ukraine. It showed Brezhnev as the handsome and energetic party manager he once had been. This could only make the invisible Andropov seem more decrepit. The commemorative article poured out all the old epithets of praise that were no longer in fashion under Andropov. It recounted Brezhnev's career, from the boy nourished on 'all the best qualities of the working class' to the statesman-architect of détente between East and West.

Half-way through, the tone changed. The article went on to survey the past year since Andropov's election as leader. This had assured continuity but 'continuity in politics does not mean being satisfied with what has been achieved'. It was as though the piece had been written by two people. Andropov's absence from public ceremonies reinforced this feeling that the country had two different leaderships. Chernenko had led the Politburo onto the Lenin mausoleum for the usual November 7 parade to mark the anniversary of the Revolution. Although he had been ill in the early summer, and was overshadowed by Andropov at the June plenum on ideology, which was meant to be Chernenko's preserve, he was noticeably active from the autumn on. In January he published a second revised edition of his collected speeches which *Pravda* was to review at length the day before Andropov died. In oblique ways of this kind the Chernenko camp was able to signal its resilience.

Though the Andropov team did their best to keep the seriousness of their leader's condition a secret everyone who had reason to fear him could take hope. Certainly this hobbled Andropov's attempt to replace the men who stood between him and control of the local party machines – the one hundred and fifty-seven first secretaries of the regions and territories. More than eighty of them were full members of the Central Committee, easily the most powerful bloc there. At the end of August Gorbachov and Ligachov presided over a meeting in the Central Committee to set the guidelines for elections to be held the coming winter in party organizations from factories and farms up to the regions and territories. Under Brezhnev these elections, which were held every two to three years, had not much disturbed those already in power. But it was clear from the tone of the August meeting and the reporting that followed it in the press that Andropov hoped this time to get rid of people he considered obstacles. Gorbachov and Ligachov insisted that this election campaign was to be outspoken, with 'the fire of criticism' turned on 'concrete people who are breaking discipline or not working full out'. The elections should produce new and better party committees. Local party authorities were warned not to prepare a scenario for the meetings in advance as was the custom. Local leaders should not try to censor speeches from the floor that contained unfavourable comments on them and their work. This resulted in some places in a 'flood of criticism' which, it was admitted, frightened some apparatchiks but Moscow considered healthy. It was even possible to mock the old-style leaders, the sort of man who on election to head a party organization 'turned into bronze, began to keep his distances from colleagues . . . and to consider himself an exceptional figure. Even his walk wasn't the same. There was the sound of metal in his voice and he began to talk condescendingly to his subordinates. He took revenge for criticism, not only on those who made it but even on the critic's relations . . .'

But the election results were disappointing, as Gorbachov later admitted.

They produced less than twenty new regional first secretaries, more than was usual under Brezhnev but not nearly enough to change the balance of the Central Committee or to bring a powerful force of new brooms to the country at large. In several cases a deal seems to have been done with the departing leaders. They were given the chance to retire, keeping as many benefits as possible, rather than be booted out in disgrace. Nevertheless men Andropov would surely have liked removed fought back successfully. There was particularly sharp criticism during the campaign of the state of affairs in the south Russian region of Rostov where there had been scandals of both mismanagement and corruption. But the Rostov party leader survived for another two years until Gorbachov at last managed to prise him out.

It would not be the first time that the leadership was frustrated by the stubbornness of the traditions that Brezhnev, apparently without thinking, had left behind him. Did Andropov believe, by the beginning of 1984, that he would still have time to dismantle them? Some say he did, and the medical report published, as was the custom, after his death seems to bear this out, for it suggests the treatment he received since February was producing satisfactory results until a quick decline set in in late January. Not long before his death he talked with one of the leading official writers. He is supposed to have said that he expected to be back at work and that the doctors had told him to count on living five more years. One version had it that Andropov paused there; five more years – he needed twice as long to do all that had to be done. Five years would have given him time to prepare the next party congress; to re-make the Central Committee; to produce at least an outline of the changes needed in the country.

Everything was done to make it look as though he would recover. The speech that had to be read out for him to the Central Committee plenum in December began with a disingenuous apology about his absence for 'temporary causes'. At the end of January, when his condition was already deteriorating, it was announced that he had chosen a Moscow constituency to represent at the spring elections for a new Supreme Soviet. Very few people seem to have known the truth about how ill he was. Information was kept to his family, his closest colleagues and assistants. He dealt with the Politburo through Gorbachov who commuted back and forward between Moscow and Kuntsevo. It is unclear which, if any, other Politburo members Andropov saw in his last weeks. He took the precaution of using as his regular physician a doctor from the KGB. A more discreet medical man could hardly be imagined. His team of assistants continued to work normally at the Central Committee building so that the affairs of state were not held up, as they had been whenever Brezhnev was ill. Andropov responded to material sent to him, held telephone conversations, and, via Gorbachov, despatched memoranda to the other leaders. One of his last notes to the Politburo is said to have recommended a twenty per cent cut in the party and government bureaucracy.

There was a precedent for ruling almost invisibly, by will-power. Stalin had been a sick man in his last few years. He showed himself rarely, and then only when the appearance could be stage-managed to make him look impressive. But why should Andropov have felt compelled to cling to power, thereby shortening his own life, as Stalin had? Stalin had stamped his will on the Soviet Union. He had helped reduce it to near chaos and then moulded it to his will. It was his country, as much as any country can be said to belong to one man. Everyone knew he would rule it till his death. Even his hidden opponents were fearful about what would happen when he died. No one took Andropov for Stalin but they were both obsessed men: Stalin lest there be change; Andropov lest there be not. In the end he could only hope that others would continue his work, a hope he expressed in a poem published after his death that gave a rare insight into the man's austere Hegelian faith.

We are fleeting creatures in this world 'under the moon':
Life is only an instant; non-existence is for ever.
The earth's globe revolves in the Universe,
Men live and disappear.
But the real, born in darkness,
Cannot be destroyed on its path to the dawn.
Other generations on earth
Will carry life's baton further.

Soviet communists like to say they are optimists. Andropov gave the feeling of a man who knew the huge price that sometimes had to be paid for optimism. In another country, at another time, one can imagine him as a great prelate who understood that man had to be chastised for his weakness. Andropov had seen the enemy and he knew its strength. Valentin Chikin might again have been speaking for him in an article he wrote in January on the sixtieth anniversary of Lenin's death. The two leaders' anxieties seemed indistinguishable in Chikin's urgent prose. Irresponsible people were dragging the party into needless arguments while 'stepping on the brakes in their daily political work'. But the main problem was discipline, in the country as well as the party. There had to be 'the most severe centralization and discipline' even if people who had got used to living in sloppy dressing gowns and slippers did not like it. The problem was to overcome inertia: 'it is hardest of all to overcome the terrible force of habit of millions, the force of inertia.' Andropov's battle was not just with a ruling class that had grown lazy and irresponsible. He had to take on the whole country. The Soviet worker in whose name a terrible revolution had been made had become used to the comfortable slippers and dressing gown socialism of Brezhnev. What if the working millions did not want to change their habits any more than some of their leaders?

10

Getting the Workers
to Work

In June 1983 Geidar Aliyev, as first deputy prime minster, introduced the promised new law on labour collectives into the Supreme Soviet. Few Soviet documents of recent years have caught so well the ambiguity of a leadership whose conservative habits were battling with an understanding of the need for change. The law appeared to give Soviet citizens more control over their life at work than ever before. A general assembly of every factory work force was to be held at least twice a year. The brigades into which many factory workers were divided were to have the power of consent over the management's appointment of their leaders, and also to request a leader's removal if he performed unsatisfactorily. The general assemblies could discuss all aspects of a factory's life: its plan, the system of pay and bonuses, work safety, general living and social conditions (many factories provided housing and some social services, such as crèches and kindergartens, for their workers).

Balancing these rights was the insistence that the factory's management retained the right to manage. The workers' assembly could discuss almost everything to do with the factory but the workers' power to make decisions that were binding was limited to what funds should go on housing, kindergartens and other social and cultural facilities. On all other matters the law gave the assemblies the right to propose, discuss, and ratify but not actually to decide. Their opinion was only to be 'taken into account' when a new factory director was appointed. But the greatest limitation of all came in the law's very first article which affirmed the Communist party's leadership over all work collectives and the latter's duty to carry out the party's decisions. It would have been truly revolutionary if this clause had been left out. But the need to re-assert the party's powers (enshrined in the 1977 constitution) pointed to the dilemma the post-Brezhnev leadership was to face each time it tried to give people more control over some aspect of their lives. Like good schoolmasters they wanted their pupil-citizens to have as much power as possible to take decisions – provided only they were the right ones.

The schoolmasterly purpose of the new law rang very plain in the speech Aliyev made when he introduced it to the Supreme Soviet. He might have taken as his text the old Marxist dictum about socialism – 'from each according to his ability, to each according to his work.' Its first half, he said, was proving much the more difficult to achieve. People were not working as hard as they could. The new law's purpose was to make it possible for collectives to give all they were capable of. A combination of more responsibility, more effective material rewards and the pressure of collective opinion would develop citizens' inner compulsion to work. He explained that the law gave workers more power to exert influence over lazy colleagues, especially through the brigades into which more and more factories were dividing their workers with the encouragement of the government.

The government quickly followed up the law with more measures to strengthen labour discipline. Punishments were increased for absenteeism, indiscipline and drunkenness. These were to be met with loss of holidays, transfer to lower-paid jobs and, perhaps toughest of all, losing one's place in the queue for better housing. The aim was to make it harder for an undisciplined worker to quit and move to another job where he would be welcomed because of the general shortage of labour. The brigades were encouraged to put every pressure possible on colleagues who slacked. Experiments seemed to have shown that a brigade which was paid according to its results worked with far greater productivity because it was in each of the brigade members' interests that his fellows did a proper job. This stress on the coercive side of the new legislation rather than on its modest democratic potential meant there was no revolution on the Soviet shop floor. Three years later Aliyev himself was to admit that the new law had not produced the results expected from it. Workers' assemblies, he said, still seldom discussed their factory's plans. Some managements continued to manage in the old way, paying no attention to the opinion of their work force. Many workers did not know how to use the rights the law had given them and some did not even know what those rights were.

The problem of why the workers in the world's first workers' state often worked sloppily went far too deep to be solved by one or two new laws. The hardest problem for the leaders to acknowledge in public was, to many people, the most obvious one. Workers often did not want – and perhaps no longer knew how – to work conscientiously. They behaved as though they were – to use an old Marxist term – alienated, although theoretically this should not have been possible in a socialist country that had abolished private ownership of the means of production. But the evidence was there and if the leaders did not refer to it openly some did, like the writer Valentin Rasputin in his story *The Fire* or an equally well-known colleague, Yuri Bondarev, who had talked in public about it just before the passing of the 1983 law on labour collectives:

> I am convinced that with the years we have forgotten something, that something has been lost from the nation's storehouse, from the traditional roots of our land. Our attitude to work has sometimes become very superficial, as though it were something optional, and as if someone else on earth will do it for us. What a delusion that is, what a weakening of the spirit . . .

People puzzled over how this had happened in ways that recalled Rasputin's fictional Ivan Petrovich. An engineer remembered how he had started work in the 1950s under a factory foreman famous for being 'severe and just'. When this man appeared at the start of the morning shift the workers were already waiting, 'neat and ready like soldiers'. Their lathes shone, the floor had been swept. There were only two breaks for smoking in the course of the day's work. If anyone worked badly or went absent the foreman sacked him. Many years later the engineer went back to his factory and met the old foreman. He was sitting in his office, looking 'tired and confused', a bottle of vodka on the table in front of him. There was a job that needed doing urgently but one of his lathe operators had refused it. The foreman had bought him a half-litre of vodka to make him change his mind but it hadn't helped. The workman said he knew somewhere else where he could get a litre of vodka and off he had gone.

Anyone who bothered to read the papers knew this was no isolated incident. Drinking at factories was widespread and Mondays and Fridays were notoriously bad days for serious work. One scholar calculated that an alcohol-free Soviet Union would increase its labour productivity by ten per cent overnight. As for people no longer standing at their work bench 'like soldiers', that applied to white collar workers, too. Young scientists were just as likely to spend their time idly, except in their case they played chess or invented games to play on the computer while their women colleagues got on with the shopping. The phenomenon of theft from the work place was so common that a new word had been coined to describe it. It was possible to find factories whose products were illegally traded outside the plant fence.

Increasing discipline had been the traditional response since Stalin's time. Lazar Kaganovich, one of Stalin's toughest assistants, had declared that 'the earth should tremble when the director walks round the plant'. Some modern managers were still keen to produce the same effect. The play *Four times the size of France* that was running at the Vakhtangov Theatre in Moscow in 1983 contained a character of whom Kaganovich would have approved. An old and senior party official, his credo was that 'people must submit . . . It was always thus in Russia: I am the prince and you are my slaves. That is how it was and how it will be.' The style was still common enough in industry for a widely-admired dramatist who specialized in themes from the business world to construct a whole play round the character of an industrialist whose dictatorial drive destroys his family. A senior manager of a big construction firm, he forces the pace of work on a building site to meet the plan causing his student son, labouring on the site in his vacation, to have a crippling accident. The construction boss's faith is simple: 'It is my holy duty to fulfil the plan.' Audiences applauded loudly at his one moment of doubt: 'I can't be a human being and a boss at the same time.' The type was obviously familiar to them.

Education was the twin of discipline. It was necessary to give the workers firm instruction because they were very likely not yet worthy of membership in the working class. Lenin himself had said that it needed many years' moulding by 'collective industrial labour' before a worker acquired a reliable 'proletarian psychology'. An adviser to Konstanin Chernenko explained that it was quite wrong to suppose that young Soviet people leaving school, because they were better educated and with higher skills than their parents, already had the necessary proletarian frame of mind. On the contrary, many of them were politically immature and had an entirely irresponsible attitude to work. Each new generation of workers had to be educated to be real workers. The crisis with the Solidarity movement in Poland was given as proof of this, though the Soviet authorities did not fear a similar working class explosion at home. The Polish events had remarkably little echo in the Soviet Union. There is even some impressionistic evidence that many, perhaps even most, people were hostile to them. From Pushkin onwards Russians had more often reacted against the Poles than with them. Disputes did take place in Soviet factories but they were usually about conditions of work and other local matters. Sometimes though not often they were reported in the press. On one possibly unique occasion during the first months of Andropov's rule, a central newspaper printed a photograph of obviously angry workers who had stopped work after being asked to handle dangerous materials. There was no evidence that such incidents had, in recent years, got seriously out of hand.

Anxiety about the quality of the proletariat's education lay behind the draft law on school reform introduced while Andropov was still alive. The schools were to put greater emphasis on practical work in order to accustom pupils to a life in factories and farms. Some educationalists believed in manual work from the earliest possible age as the essential first step on the long path to proletarian enlightenment. They did not get their way completely in the reforms but their proposals were revealing. They wanted 'real work' to take up four hours each day of the school curriculum as opposed to the existing maximum of four hours a week. They argued that 'productive labour becomes the creator of a new, socialist type of personality only if it is not reduced to a game . . . but is a permanent daily duty'. They suggested that schools use their pupils' labour to become financially self-supporting and forecast this could add 'tens of billions of pounds' to economic production. And in Moscow they found a 'factory-school' called the Seagull that appeared to fit their ideal. It had been set up in 1963 (when Khrushchov had been similarly enthusiastic about teaching children to get their hands dirty at 'real' work while at school) and in twenty years had sold electrical goods worth twenty million pounds. It was attended, part-time, by children from different schools in the capital. The school formed them into proper production brigades, made them work shifts and meet a real plan.

The proletarian romanticism of these reformers showed in their belief that the best, most educative labour was physical. They praised the Seagull's director for insisting that work there remain largely unmechanized. They argued that even children destined for professional careers as musicians or surgeons should do 'a definite period of compulsory labour' at a traditional production job. Without this they were likely to become 'consumers' and 'parasites' in society, and an infectious danger to others with their 'petty bourgeois ideology and psychology'. But in spite of the energy with which they argued their case they sometimes struck the wistful note of men who, while they believe they are right, fear that time has overtaken them. After the war, one of them recalled, when he had been a lad, no self-respecting girl would go out with boys with soft hands. 'No callouses meant you weren't a man.' Was this what Soviet girls thought at the end of the twentieth century? Was it desirable that they should still think like that? The answer to both questions was almost certainly no, but it was not easy for everyone to admit it.

It is not surprising that attitudes to work and workers were confused, for both had been the subject of myth-making since the Revolution. A famous part of the myth could be seen outside the entrance to Moscow's exhibition of economic achievements – two great steel figures of a handsome, strong young woman and man, holding up a hammer and sickle to the sky. The Worker and *Kolhoznitsa* (a collective farm girl), made by the socialist realist sculptress Vera Mukhina in the terrible year of 1937, were first put on show in Paris, and perhaps some innocent foreigners did believe that this was what the workers of the new Soviet state were really like. That some young Russians believed in those years that they were like, or becoming like, the glorious steel couple is beyond doubt. The myth was necessary to hide the gap between reality and the communists' plans. Unfortunately the workers' revolution had occurred in a mainly peasant country. Only sixteen per cent of the population of the Russian Empire lived in towns in 1910. Even sixty years later that had risen to only a little more than half, the same degree of urbanization reached by America on the eve of the First World War, or by France before the outbreak of the Second. The management style recommended by Kaganovich was designed for a workforce that was chiefly peasant in origin and had not yet been broken into the discipline of industrial life or acquired many of its skills. Like most other industrial revolutions the Soviet Union's was harsh, but its harshness was peculiarly great for being crammed into such a few years and managed by such a powerful, single-minded government. The boss's power over his workers was symbolized by the way he addressed them as *ty* while they had to call him by the polite form *vy*. He could control them by their 'labour books' (the record of a man's working life that was introduced in 1939) and by criminal laws which could send a man to prison for absenteeism or leaving his job without permission.

Until recently it had been taboo to mention the grimness of those years; not the grimness of Stalin's political crimes but of the impoverished ordinary life that was one of the sacrifices made to the god of industrialization. Most wages were only just above the living minimum. The welfare state barely existed. It was true that a man went hungry if he did not work and this remained true even in the first years after the war. When a film director, in the early 1980s, did make a movie in which he tried to recreate, for the first time ever, what it really felt like to live at that time, he was accused of having 'slandered the beautiful and bright generation of our fathers'. The authorities refused to release the film, called *My friend Ivan Lapshin*, and did not pay the director's salary for two years. Not the least of his crimes was to show up the official films of those years – cinematic equivalents of the Worker and *Kolkhoznitsa* – for the glossy fairy-stories they were. When the film was finally released perceptive Russians watched it with the horror of people who were at last learning the truth about their family. It shattered them. 'After a film like that,' a Muscovite remarked on the first day of its screening, 'there is only one thing left to do – hang oneself.'

The unfairness of it was that by the 1980s, when the Soviet Union was at last an industrialized country, Vera Mukhina's ideal couple were as out of step with the realities of life as they had been with the old reality of the 1930s. There was of course a large industrial working class – almost forty million men and women – and only a fifth of the labour force still worked on the land. But splendid young women were the exception on the farms of Russia. They had gone to the towns, leaving the fields and the cattle to old men and women, and to the children. As for the classic industrial worker, he certainly existed in the steel mills and coal mines. But it was already plain that he belonged to a dwindling species and one that – in the cause of up-to-dateness – ought to dwindle even faster. There was still a large amount of manual work in industry – almost forty per cent – but it was not performed by men like the one who modelled for Mukhina. Dressed in dirty overalls (the pockets conveniently big for a bottle of vodka) and as often as not equipped with the industrial tools of the last century they looked like grudging recruits in a dispirited army.

What had gone wrong? Part of the answer was that much had gone right. There was full employment and – for the industrial worker – at wages that covered the necessities of life and allowed for some luxuries. The social services state was at last established. The Soviet working class had never been so well off. It appeared to have absolute security. But other evidence suggested it was very far from contented. Labour productivity was increasing at a slower and slower rate. From almost seven per cent a year in the mid-sixties it had sunk to two and a half per cent by 1981. And, for all the mythology about the proletariat, most people did not want their children to join it. It was to be expected that most parents with higher education were not keen to see their children become blue collar workers. But surveys showed that over half of all parents from all backgrounds wanted their children to go to ordinary secondary schools rather than the vocational-technical ones which taught a trade as preparation for a factory life and from which entry to university was far less likely. As for the pupils of the vocational-technical schools the evidence was that they too despised the classic working class professions and the old-fashioned technology they were linked to. Some of the older managers called them lily-fingers and said they did not want to work, but it had no effect. The situation was common enough in the rest of the industrialized world. A working class wants 'better' for its children as it becomes better off itself.

The Soviet Union was imprisoned in a traditional understanding of what workers were. According to this the cream of the working class were operators of lathes and milling machines, men who stood behind heavy bits of machinery in greasy overalls and sweated at the job – the very professions that the new generation of workers despised. This was the working class that the Communist party had been trained to lead. A group of economists and sociologists were trying to persuade the leadership that this was one of the main problems facing the country. The argument was put most forcefully by a leading sociologist, Tatyana Zaslavskaya, one of only some dozen academicians in the economics department of the Academy of Sciences. In a paper written for a seminar held jointly by the Academy and Gosplan (and inspired by Andropov's need for answers to the country's economic problems) she offered an alarming analysis of what was wrong in the factories. The country's economic system, she said, was still essentially the one created by Stalin in the 1930s. It had been designed for a badly-educated workforce which was regarded as something to be 'managed', as though it were a passive object like any other raw material. The hardship of the Stalin years had made it possible to sustain 'almost military measures of labour discipline'. The workers had no alternative but to knuckle under. The economy of the 1980s was much more complicated than in Stalin's time, and so was its labour force. Workers were better educated. In the early 1960s few workers had completed more than six or seven years of school and peasants even less. Twenty years later most young people starting work had at least a proper secondary education. What was more, they came from families that were decently off, knew they were absolutely safe in their jobs and could easily change them if they wanted to.

The shortage of labour powerfully increased the worker's hand against employers. There were by the most modest calculations 700,000 vacant jobs. The cause was partly the inefficient use of labour but there was also a genuine demographic reason. Over five million youngsters finished eight-year schooling in 1975. Five years later there were just four million such school-leavers. Only towards the end of the century could the country expect an increase in the size of the labour force. The pattern of population movement made the labour shortage even worse than it need have been. Some thirteen million people moved every year, mainly from east to west and north to south, exactly the opposite of what was required by economic policy. A vital area like the Pacific Far East had almost as many emigrants as immigrants in spite of the wage differentials that were meant to encourage workers to move to the north and east. It was typical of the way in which Soviet workers managed to exploit the system to suit their interest that when the north Siberian differential had been raised it failed to ease the labour shortage. The government did not understand that workers went there to earn a certain amount of money and left when they had it. The new differential allowed them to earn it quicker and so they stayed an even shorter time than before. Barriers to movement seldom worked. Seventy thousand migrants managed to establish themselves each year in Moscow in spite of all the legal restrictions, causing considerable social problems and also a growing amount of crime.

And yet the system still treated Soviet workers, Zaslavskaya wrote, as though they were *vintiki*, little screws who could be manipulated at will by the management. In truth today's young worker was a far more demanding person than his father, and with a far wider range of interests. Nevertheless he was often expected to work in conditions that were only tolerable to the more ignorant and submissive workforce of fifty years ago. Most corrupting of all was the common practice of 'storming', completing the month's target with a rush in the last week because some necessary raw material or parts had arrived late. It was becoming common to read in the press angry complaints by workers about the jerky production rhythm of their factories. The rule seemed to be that half the work was done in the first twenty days and half in a frantic rush, in which considerations of quality had to be forgotten, in the last ten. Conveyor lines could be halted for the lack of one component and the men put to washing the floor. Some managements looked the other way when workers with nothing to do went absent or drunk. Sacking a worker was no punishment since he could so easily find another job, but the factory also dared not do it for reasons of its own. The management needed everyone it could lay its hands on at the end of the month when it speeded production to make up for lost time.

This was the chief explanation for the hoarding of manpower, the resulting under-employment and the demoralization of a large part of the work force. The 'work books' Stalin had introduced to keep a disciplinary check on workers' records had become a joke. They were still meant to be marked if a worker was sacked for bad work or drunkenness. But it was easy to say a book had been lost and get a duplicate. Managers in chronic need of labour did not ask too many questions if a new worker appeared at their door. Zaslavskaya drew up a depressing list of the qualities the system was breeding: poor labour discipline, indifference to the job, bad workmanship, little understanding of work 'as a means of self-realization', greed, and a 'low level of morals'. The bad effect this had on the economy was compounded as technology became more complicated. A drunk worker could not do much damage with a wheelbarrow. He could cause damage worth thousands of pounds drunk at the wheel of a bulldozer. The higher the technology the greater the loss caused by sloppy workmanship. Man, the academician sighed, 'had often become the weakest link in the technological chain'.

Younger, better-educated workers were particularly sensitive to the conditions in which they worked and to conservative methods of management. Surveys showed that their discontent centred round the practice of 'storming', but they also complained of the low level of mechanization, of lack of a chance to improve their qualifications and to show initiative on the job. In some cities anger over bad conditions of work was the cause of as many as three out of four conflicts between workers and management. An improvement in working conditions at once produced smoother, more disciplined work. The younger worker's tastes also marked him out as a different species. It was no longer odd for him to wear the jeans and running shoes already adopted by the children of the big-city intelligentsia. His favourite music was rock, followed by disco – almost the same preferences as those of students at universities and institutes. He had little interest in the traditional Soviet light music played endlessly on radio and television and which his parents had been brought up on.

What worried Zaslavskaya and her like-minded colleagues was that much of the working class was being conditioned by the system to see work only as a way of making money while channelling their real energy into their private lives. She believed that the progress of Soviet society depended on offering the individual stimulating and rewarding work. For a Soviet worker to understand that he was part-master of the country's wealth it was 'necessary to make him a real, if only partial master, of that small area in which he works: to give him a certain freedom of choice in the way he fulfils his task and improves technology, to give him both responsibility for and an interest in the finished results'.

113

The paper Zaslavskaya wrote in the spring of 1983 caused a stir because while never published in the Soviet Union it was leaked to the foreign press. The incident confirmed what everyone knew – that Soviet debates on problems and policies were more lively in private than they were usually allowed to be in public. After Gorbachov had become party leader, the academician was to re-state much of her case in open publications. In 1986 she offered some interesting examples of people she thought the economic and social system was preventing from working full out:

Workers who are systematically made to stand idle because of a lack of raw materials, energy or spare parts; teachers who do not have the opportunity to teach as they consider necessary and correct; actors who for years have not been given a part suitable to their talents; industrial managers who have initiative but who are bound hand and foot by instructions that forbid business-like behaviour.

The debate about the Soviet worker was only part of a wider but often subterranean debate about the Soviet citizen and his place in a society whose regulations dated from fiercer times. The puzzle was how to modify them without disturbing a Communist party with the pretensions of a preacher and powers of a policeman and little inclination to give up either. This haunted any discussion on how to make workers more productive as it was to haunt all other debates on change. Zaslavskaya and those like her, including many of her colleagues at the Siberian branch of the Academy of Sciences, were enthusiastic for anything that increased a worker's sense of personal responsibility. In farming they supported the so-called collective contract system under which a group of farmworkers took complete responsibility for a piece of land and its cultivation throughout a whole season. With pay geared to results, this was believed to make for more diligent farmers. The Siberian branch was itself running another farm experiment designed to make people aware of the cost of their work and the materials they used. Farmworkers were given chequebooks, a novelty in themselves, since private checking accounts are not available at Soviet banks. A herdsman had to write cheques for the fodder he needed for his cattle. In return he would be paid by cheque for the milk he produced. The experiment was highly artificial for the farm itself had not met its plan for fifty years. It was in debt, but was paying higher wages, a dreadful example of the system's tolerance of economic indiscipline. Those who devised the experiment were well aware of the precariousness of trying to teach workers to be efficient against such a background.

In industry labour brigades became the object of a great deal of cautious social engineering. The brigade itself was not a new invention. What attracted attention in 1983 was a type of brigade that had first seen light on a Moscow construction site in the 1960s. Its work was organized in such a way that its useful production could be measured. Brigade members' wages were set by what they produced as a team instead of by the usual system of individual piece rates. In spite of encouragement from the government the idea of 'self-financing' brigades, as they were called, had caught on slowly. By 1983 only a quarter of all workers in industry belonged to them. A method called the Coefficient of Labour Input (CLI) was devised to measure each brigade member's contribution. Starting work late or taking too long over a smoking break brought the coefficient down. This was the brigade working as a stern teacher who punished bad behaviour and rewarded good, and just as Mikhail Gorbachov, for one, hoped it would. In their most refined form brigades were envisaged as a school for labour and for all of adult life. Enthusiasts tried to think of ways of taking into account in the CLI all a worker's qualities, including his performance as a citizen and family man.

There were other voices in the debate belonging to what might be called the industrial democrats. They pointed out that before the 1983 law on labour collectives there had been several ways to consult with a workforce and give it a feeling of participation in decision-making. Factories, for example, had 'permanent production conferences' with a country-wide membership on paper of over six million workers. In reality these conferences were often dominated by a small group of trade unionists who also turned up on every other factory committee. Attendance by ordinary workers was poor. It was important, therefore, to make sure that the brigades under the new law did not become yet another formality. One way was to give workers a voice in management decisions and not just in the distribution of funds for housing and other social needs, for that would be to encourage the 'parasitical' attitude that the workforce only had to bother about distribution while leaving the management to look after production. As for brigades, they should have the right to elect their leaders, or brigadiers. The 1983 law ignored both recommendations but the latter were evidence of the way in which old socialist principles which had inspired the early Bolsheviks could still reappear, like flowers that grow again on a field wasted by years of war. The experts who made these suggestions were looking forward to the time when the workers themselves would take production decisions, only 'turning for their execution to the special knowledge of the managers'.

The industrial democrats knew that their hopes depended on a more far-ranging reform of the whole economic system. There was little point in trying to put workers on the same footing as their bosses if factories remained bound by commands from the centre. But it was not so certain that they understood what life on the factory floor was really like, and in particular what it meant to work in a new-style brigade. It was left to a scholarly journal to produce in the autumn of 1985 a fine piece of investigative reporting that suggested brigades might not be so desirable after all, and were certainly not helping workers feel they were masters of the shop floor. *Eko* was the monthly magazine of the Siberian branch of the Academy of Sciences and arguably the most interesting periodical in the whole country. The size of a pocket book, it displayed some of the best Soviet brains in an unusually relaxed way and even, at times, with wit (it had published the first horoscope in the Soviet Union, albeit a humorous one that foretold the troubled careers of industrial managers).

Eko's investigation into brigades had been conducted over the better part of two years at five heavy industrial plants. The author discovered all sorts of brigades but not a single one fitted the ideals of either the educators or the industrial democrats. Many workers only joined brigades at the insistence of management. Industrial democrats considered this made nonsense of the very idea of the brigade. Managements had reason to like brigades. 'The workers have become more obedient,' they said. In some cases the miraculous had been achieved. There was practically no more absenteeism or drunkenness. But where was the morality in it all? 'One should not forget that production was created by man and for man, or lose from sight the ordinary, time-honoured human understanding of good, and evil and justice.' Did new techniques for making workers work harder have to bring tension into what, after all, were described as labour *collectives*? Was there any way in which it was possible to advance towards a richer, more modern society and still pay heed to socialist ideals?

There was another experiment that suggested a different approach. It produced excellent results for workers. Employers, too, were usually delighted by it. But it was unofficial and – in many people's eyes – even illegal. The story of how it came about and its existence at the edge of legality revealed how tangled was the knot of moral and economic problems in getting the workers of the world's first workers' state to work harder.

They had several names. They were called seasonal workers, and more colourfully 'cranes' or 'rooks' because they did indeed come and go like migrating birds. But most people knew them as *shabashniki*, shabashniks, one of those words that hint at the vigorous unofficial world that exists beneath the prim surface of Soviet life. The name itself had a shady ring to it. The dictionary said it meant someone who concludes 'private deals at high prices for construction, repair and other work'. The shabashnik movement – it was a major social phenomenon for all that it was unplanned – had been developing since the late 1960s. Groups of workers had appeared in rural regions offering to do building work or to manage part of a farm's crop. Among the first were Koreans from Central Asia who hired out their skills as vegetable growers to farms in southern Russia. By the beginning of the 1980s the shabashniks were an important force in the Soviet economy, though few cared to admit it officially. They did not exist in published statistics but at the very least they must have totalled over a quarter of a million men. Most of them came from the Caucasus, but there were others from Moldavia, the western Ukraine and Belorussia, and from the Baltic states. They still worked in the Russian south but they had also penetrated to Siberia, to the north, and to the so-called non-black earth lands of central Russia. No one seemed to know what their contribution to farming amounted to. But in the rural areas where the shabashnik builders were active they were doing a third, and sometimes two-thirds, of all construction work. They were famous for their productivity. A man in their building brigades could do in a six-month season as much as an ordinary construction worker in a year. A shabashnik team contracted to grow onions would expect to get fifty tons from a hectare of land in Central Asia, and in a good season almost double. Most farms thought they were doing well to grow twenty.

To official eyes everything about the shabashniks was embarrassing even when it was not downright undesirable. In the first place, who were they? Many of them, especially those coming from the Caucasus, were the rural unemployed or at best under-employed. It was possible to find districts in Armenia where as many as four thousand men were without a permanent job. Such industry as existed in these areas offered work mainly to women. The existence of the shabashniks was an unwanted reminder of flaws in the policy of full employment that was the cause of so much justified pride. Shabashniks from the western part of the country included well-qualified engineers and even scientists. This caused considerable public indignation but the reason for it was obvious. The failure, under Brezhnev, to maintain wage differentials between workers and qualified technical staff led to both discontent and hardship among the latter. An engineer could not even increase his wages by better productivity as a worker on the shop floor could. Some white collar workers turned shabashniks had also got fed up with the minimal and boring work they were given to do in their old jobs:

'If you knew what a terrible feeling I experience each evening when I open the door of my flat,' one of them complained. 'My wife and son greet me happily: papa's home from work. If only they knew what papa had been doing all day. I've gossiped, smoked, drunk coffee, moved papers from one file to another . . . Is that worthy of a man, of a head of a family?'

The system did not find it easy to accept that educated men who wanted to work hard only found satisfaction in an occupation that bordered on the criminal. The opponents of the shabashniks made much of the fact that the farming brigades had to hire occasional additional workers at harvest and other peak times. The teams then took on pensioners and housewives but, if they had to, they also hired the tramps and layabouts, sometimes but not always drunkards, who managed to survive in quite large numbers in spite of the many regulations and punishments designed to drive them into regular work.

Authority tolerated the shabashniks because it needed them. The official construction industry was notorious for its sloppiness and slowness. Many farms were short of labour, and what labour they had was seldom highly productive. The unofficial brigades also alleviated what, in parts of the Caucasus, would have been quite severe, though localized, unemployment. If shabashniks had official support anywhere it was in Armenia, the republic that suffered most from unemployment, and whose migrant workers were popularly known as 'the Armenian Construction Company'.

What was seldom said in most public discussions of the problem was that it did not matter if shabashniks worked hard, built good roads and grew record crops of onions. They just did not fit into the system. What kind of a labour collective was it that did not take part in socialist competition, those contests in which one group of workers vied with another for the good of the collective cause and the delight of the politicians? What kind of worker was it who did not need to be watched over by ministries, managements, trade unions and above all the Communist party? The party was doing its best to see it had members in the new labour brigades it was encouraging. It took it for granted they would only perform at their best under stimulus from a conscientious party cell. But the shabashniks could produce excellent results without any of this. The thought must have occurred to some people that they managed it precisely because they were free of the apparatus of teachers and controllers that accompanied the ordinary Soviet workman throughout his life.

These were murky waters and only the self-confident and the not easily shocked were tempted to enter them. Somewhere in those waters might be hidden answers to important questions: what made a man work? When was self-interest good and when was it bad? Could a wage be too big for a Soviet man's good? Did the country really want to work hard, or did it prefer an easier life, secure, not very demanding but not very rewarding either, in which those with bigger appetites and greater energy would always be seen as a threat and therefore had to be kept within reach of punishment?

11

A Temporary Tsar

Yuri Andropov died on the evening of February 9, 1984. Within twenty-four hours the Politburo had agreed on Konstantin Chernenko as his successor. The signal that agreement had been reached was the announcement that Chernenko was to head the funeral commission which, according to Kremlin protocol, would preside over the dead leader's funeral. The reaction to this rapid choice was both unexpected and original. The leaders of the establishment had seemed to fall in quietly behind a new general secretary who no one supposed was the equal of his predecessors. But ordinary party members and some of the public met the news with a mixture of scorn and horror and, just as remarkably, seemed not to mind if anyone knew. It was partly that Andropov's death had taken the country by surprise. The secrecy about the real state of his health, the misleading hints that he would soon reappear, had – as they were meant to – allowed Andropov to keep the aura of leadership even when no one saw him. But Chernenko himself was the cause of most of the dismay.

His first appearances as leader were disastrous. He seemed unsure of himself standing at the head of the Politburo on the Lenin mausoleum for Andropov's funeral. At one point foreign minister Gromyko could be heard telling him not to take off his hat. Chernenko moved his right arm stiffly, and read his short speech badly. On that strangest of political stages, the gap-toothed battlements of the Kremlin wall behind him and Lenin's name stamped in admonishingly large letters on the mausoleum beneath, the old man looked lost beside his sturdier colleagues, an ageing understudy who had never been up to the part. His first major speech, in early March, turned out even worse. He was breathless and often stumbled over the words. The voice was light whereas the Kremlin had come to expect one heavy with authority and wisdom. At one point he lost his place and was silent for almost thirty seconds while he looked for the next sheet of his text. It was not long before the world had correctly diagnosed his emphysema, which had been aggravated by a bout of pneumonia the preceding year.

People realized they had another old, ill leader and did not like it. It had much to do with the Russian attitude to leadership, and the belief that peasants needed to be frightened into action by the sound of thunder. A young Russian, no better than he ought to be, caught this mood. Andropov, he said, had not been 'a bad *muzhik*. This country needs a strong leader, and it would have taken him ten years to clean the place up. But now we've got this old man who can't even lift his arm to salute properly. From him we'll just get more eyewash.'

A man standing in a queue snapped at a salesman who mumbled at him: 'What are you mumbling for? You're not making a speech on the mausoleum, are you?' There were reports of mocking interjections at party meetings held after Chernenko's election of the 'so he's made it at last, has he?' variety. More sophisticated Muscovites who had scarcely been warm to Andropov now mourned his honesty. They forecast, and dreaded, a return to power of the Brezhnev crowd. The first sign of it was a much talked about celebration that the family of the ex-police chief Shcholokov threw as soon as they heard of Andropov's death. It was said that the relatives of the Moscow underworld figures who had been pursued under Andropov also threw parties. Other people with cause to be pleased included some of the most unpopular groups in the country: the militia, for example, whom Andropov had humiliated by setting the KGB on them, and the unloved party and state bureaucrats with whom everyone had to deal at some time and about whom almost all had damning stories to tell.

Someone recalled the gossip about the gold samovar rumoured to have been found in Brezhnev's private safe after his death. It seemed that Chernenko had one exactly the same only he kept his on display in his dacha, assuming no one would guess what it was made of. But the most damaging stories were about his failure to fight in the war. Chernenko was an official in the party headquarters of his home region of Krasnoyarsk when Germany invaded the Soviet Union and he stayed there most of the war without joining the army. It was a measure of the disenchantment his choice as party leader caused that this was taken as evidence of cowardice. 'The only people who didn't fight,' said an intellectual who had joined up when still a boy, 'were the sick, the old, and those who were scared for their life.' In fact the only members of the Chernenko Politburo who fought in the Red Army during the war were the Ukrainian leader Shcherbitsky, and the KGB's Chebrikov who was at Stalingrad and ended the war as a twenty-three-year-old battalion commander. The others, if they were old enough, held posts in the party or industry which at times were almost as gruelling as fighting at the front. But some people were so angry they chose to forget this.

In this atmosphere it was to be expected that the Chernenko jokes would soon follow. An epithet applied to Lenin – 'eternally living' – was rewritten for Chernenko as 'eternally living, eternally ill'. The frequency of funerals was a popular theme for anecdotes. The television is playing sombre music and a mournful announcer appears. 'Comrades,' he says, breaking into a smile, 'you're not going to believe this, but another general secretary has just died.' And there was the simplest of all the many Chukchi jokes. A Chukchi goes to Moscow because he wants to become party leader – and the Central Committee elects him.

Disappointment at the choice of Chernenko was all the more obvious because of the genuine grief caused by Andropov's death. It was expected that a great official's family would show their sorrow at his burial, and this was plain enough on the faces of Andropov's wife Tatyana and his son and daughter when they waited by his open coffin in the Hall of Columns and during the ceremony in Red Square. But grief was also unmistakable in some of the official reports on Andropov's death. Several tributes in the press suggested an emotion that went far beyond the usual formal phrases of praise and regret. Valentin Chikin was the author of the most striking of these. It was printed under a rare photograph of Andropov as a twenty-eight-year-old Komsomol leader during the war. Wearing a high-necked sweater, fist clenched in communist salute, it showed him presenting a banner to a group of frontier troops. Chikin called this picture 'a precious relict' and described how journalists at *Sovietskaya Rossiya* had passed it around among themselves, each poring over it and reluctant to hand it on. 'We called it,' Chikin wrote, 'the BOLSHEVIK. That is just how the Bolshevik was, the commissar, when he raised the fighters to the storm of Perekop or the Hungry steppe, to work on the iron-ore mountain of Magnitogorsk or the launching pad of the Baikal-Amur railway line.'

By these references to famous feats of military and economic might Chikin put Andropov in the true line of Soviet succession, a succession that badly needed new heroes, at least from among the politicians. Chikin, who was writing just before the funeral, stated Andropov's claim to inspire the country from beyond the grave as a hero should:

Only a few hours remain till the sorrowful farewell. We shall carry him from the Hall of Columns to the grey Kremlin and we shall bury him in the Revolution's necropolis behind Lenin's mausoleum. But the summoning image of the party's standard-bearer will remain with us for ever. We shall gather the very last grain of his thoughts, his parting words, his precepts, and place them not in the quiet of a museum but in our hearts; so that they might always inspire us with their tirelessness, nourish us with their initiative, and unite us by their invincible party will.

For such people Andropov had been much-needed proof that the system was still able to produce leaders who could spot and rise above its weaknesses. Why did this realization that such a necessary leader had been lost not translate into determination to find a more worthy replacement? Within the higher levels of the party there were people who hoped that Andropov might be succeeded by someone who could continue in his style. For such people this meant Mikhail Gorbachov. But outside senior party members few knew much about Gorbachov. He was best known for having supervised farming for several years and this was scarcely seen as a recommendation. Qualities he was to reveal later were then still hidden from most of the public, and perhaps from some of his colleagues too. As a result some even doubted that Gorbachov was made of strong enough stuff: a good number two, it was said, but never a number one. Others pointed to his provincial origins, his lack of experience not only of the outside world but of most of the Soviet Union too. Even Gorbachov enthusiasts did not reject entirely the charge of inexperience, and it seems to have told conclusively against him when the Politburo met after Andropov died. 'They thought,' a Gorbachov supporter explained with a reference to the Soviet ten-year school system, 'that he was, so to speak, still only in the eighth or ninth class. And we've the custom that a long period of training is expected from a man.'

There was no evidence of a great battle over this. Some thought it odd that the Central Committee that formally elected Chernenko did not meet until Monday, February 13, four days after Andropov's death. The innocent explanation offered was that the weekend had intervened and that it was a happy measure of the country's development that weekends were now considered sacred. It was odd, too, that Gorbachov's brief closing remarks to the Central Committee plenum were not printed in the next day's papers. Gorbachov had stressed that Chernenko had been unanimously elected and urged the Committee members to return home in a spirit of unity and determination. These few paragraphs were published shortly afterwards but the incident suggested a meanness and lack of self-confidence in the Chernenko camp towards the man who they knew – even if most of the country still did not – was the strongest heir-apparent. But that attitude did not seem to be the result of a rough election debate in the Politburo. It was hard to see any circumstances in which the leadership could have picked Gorbachov to succeed Andropov, and indeed the election was a lesson in the realities of politics at the Soviet top. Among his eleven colleagues Gorbachov may have had allies in his near contemporary Vorotnikov, the Russian premier, and in the much older but disgruntled Solomentsev. Chernenko, though, could count on the Soviet premier Tikhonov, like Chernenko also a Brezhnev friend and appointee; on Kunayev, the party leader of Kazakhstan, a man in the Brezhnev mould; on the Ukrainian Shcherbitsky who, it was thought, had been angered by the Andropov-Gorbachov attempt (quite successful in this case) to purge some of his regional party leaders at the recent local party elections; and on Viktor Grishin, the Moscow party boss for over fifteen years, a man who in public gave as little away as a bishop walking in procession but who, it turned out, had reason to fear Andropov and may already have understood he would have reason to fear Gorbachov even more.

The behaviour of the other two younger Politburo members was probably determined by traditional arguments of self-interest. For Romanov, Gorbachov was a rival. By supporting Chernenko he won time to strengthen his own claim to the succession. Aliyev, as an Azerbaidzhani, had little hope of becoming party leader. It was hard to see that he would choose to damage his prospects under Chernenko – who, although seventy-two, might live for another five years – by fighting hard for Gorbachov. But the two men who seemed to have set the tone as the leaders gathered on February 10 to choose Andropov's successors were Andrei Gromyko and Dmitri Ustinov. Nobody supposed that either man had a high opinion of Chernenko. American officials at the Brezhnev-Carter summit in Vienna in 1979 had been struck by the lack of respect with which they and other senior members of the Soviet delegation had treated him. Of the two, Ustinov's voice carried the more weight. Some people had spoken of him as a possible general secretary himself and there were stories, as unprovable as all stories about what went on inside the Politburo, that he had refused to be a candidate. It was widely believed that Ustinov's support for Andropov had been decisive. But it had been easy to pick Andropov over Chernenko. It was not nearly so easy to prefer Gorbachov who was from another generation and, compared to his elderly colleagues, unquestionably inexperienced. What is more, by picking Chernenko Ustinov and Gromyko ensured their own influence. It was difficult to imagine Chernenko blocking Ustinov on defence matters, and the marshals should have no reason to complain as long as Ustinov was in the Politburo as defence minister. Gromyko was widely supposed to be condescending in the extreme about Chernenko's grasp of foreign affairs (one story had it that he once exploded over Chernenko's inability to distinguish between Libya and the Lebanon, whose Russian names are very similar). And in the months to come Gromyko would be found sitting beside Chernenko at most of his meetings with foreign statesman, treating him with the ease of an equal and on occasions dominating the talks himself.

These explanations missed the part of the puzzle that was Chernenko himself. He misled because he fitted too well the picture of a country with, as a scornful diplomat put it, 'an inexhaustible supply of old men'. The question was – how had Chernenko managed to grow old in power? And this was more than a clue to his choice as leader. It was also a clue to the nature of the Soviet political machine, to its good and bad qualities, to its durabil ty and its resistance to change. To understand an Andropov or a Gorbachov it was necessary to understand a Chernenko too.

He was born in 1911 in a village in Krasnoyarsk territory, almost in the middle of Siberia, into a peasant family that was large and poor. His mother died when he was still a child and he got only the scrappiest education, though it was said later that the village schoolteacher had marked him out as promising. At the age of twelve he was sent to work for well-to-do peasants. The first collective farm in the whole of Krasnoyarsk was organized in Chernenko's district in 1928, a year before the start of Stalin's all-out collectivization campaign. Chernenko, by then a teenager working for the Komsomol and in his own recollection 'underfed and poorly clothed', took part in this battle which was to leave a wound in the Soviet countryside that has not healed to this day. Peasants resisted collectivization in Krasnoyarsk as they did in almost every other part of the country. There was strong dislike of the policy of identifying and exiling kulaks, the supposedly better-off peasants. In Chernenko's district angry peasants killed some of the party activists and new collective farm leaders. This was the time when the country produced a new hero, inexplicable to the outside world, hated now by many Russians, but believed in by many then. Pavlik Morozov was a fourteen-year-old village boy killed by relatives after he had denounced his own father and mother for helping kulaks to escape the wrath of collectivization. A statue was erected to the young boy in his home village and there are still children's clubs and parks named after him throughout the Soviet Union.

Stalin needed such disturbing saints if he was to impose his will on the country. But he also needed an army of ordinary followers, and it was here that Chernenko belonged. It is easy enough to understand why. Born an underdog, he had as a boy seen bloody scenes from the Civil War as it swept back and forwards across Siberia. For him the Bolsheviks meant change, excitement and opportunity; and they offered, too, a theory – more marvellous than that, a science – that was not too hard to grasp but which explained everything in the world and seemed to bestow intellectual power on those who accepted it. Apart from military service as a frontier guard along the border between Soviet Kazakhstan and China, Chernenko spent most of the next thirty years of his life trying to persuade others of the truths he believed he had experienced as a boy and a young man. His background, his bad education, his extremely limited knowledge of a bigger world made him typical of the men Stalin ruled through – only one in five communists in 1939 had a full secondary education or better. Two years at the Higher Party School in Moscow during the war and a later degree (either by night classes or correspondence) from a teachers' training college in Moldavia cannot, at that period, have been of much help in broadening the mind.

If Chernenko had not met Brezhnev in Moldavia in 1950 and made friends with him he might have remained a provincial apparatchik all his life. It was a hard existence, with constant pressure from superiors and in turn the need to press heavily on those below. Add to that the hysteria essential to Stalinism, the fear that demons lurked wherever you least expected them, and you got what one perceptive writer on that period has summed up as a 'cunning and dodgy character, unscrupulous and conformist, who had learned the hard way the disadvantages of taking any initiative without orders from above'. Brezhnev's choice of Chernenko, from the late 1950s on, as his *chef de cabinet*, seems proof of his mastery of these unattractive but vital bureaucratic skills. The dismay over his election as party leader and the fun made of his infirmity missed the point that he had proved himself a formidable operator in the hidden world of Soviet power. Rising with Brezhnev gave him the chance to develop his bureaucratic muscles and eventually to bring them to perfection in the most testing arena, the Central Committee itself. Ustinov and Gromyko may have condescended to him but as head of the Committee's general department since 1965 (the job made him Brezhnev's manager of party headquarters) Chernenko had had more of a chance than most to learn how the system bequeathed by Stalin really worked. There was no doubt that he did the job to Brezhnev's satisfaction. A year before he died Brezhnev had publicly praised Chernenko for his 'tactfulness . . . responsiveness . . . and unlimited selflessness', and spoke warmly, too, of his 'restlessness' in the good of the cause and his memory – 'I can remember no occasion on which you ever forgot anything.'

When Chernenko appeared at Andropov's funeral and was unable to raise his right arm in salute, people chose not to remember that he had usually struck people as a tough customer. He certainly looked it, with his stocky peasant build and high cheek-bones that protected narrow, watchful eyes. Flattering memoirs of his early career published after he had become party leader stressed how even then he had been considerate to subordinates, as the Brezhnev style was supposed to demand. 'Unlike some of the leaders at that time,' a contemporary said of the young Chernenko, 'he did not raise his voice at people.' A Soviet official who knew him many years later as Brezhnev's right hand described another man altogether – 'demanding, rude, authoritarian, arrogant and dictatorial'. Arkadi Shevchenko, the Soviet diplomat who broke with the Soviet government in 1978, added that Chernenko was 'generally taciturn, . . . [tended] to speak in sharp abrupt sentences, frequently interrupting others, inspiring timidity in his subordinates, whether they are affected by his strong physical presence or connected to it only by telephone'.

As for ideas, Chernenko seemed to have none that went beyond the orthodoxy of the post-Khrushchov years. He published more books than any other member of the Brezhnev Politburo (apart from Brezhnev himself) and the Soviet embassy in Washington was instructed to pay an American publisher to bring out an English edition of his work even before he became a Politburo member, an indication, surely, of both vanity and ambition. The collection of his speeches published in Moscow in 1984 was remarkable chiefly for containing little about the country's economic problems and a great deal about propaganda and the machinery of party and state government. But a few bottles with interesting if not always intended messages were to be found in this ocean of words. Chernenko returned again and again to the theme of treating 'cadres', the permanent party and state officials, with respect. On no account should they be restlessly 'shuffled around'. This was essentially a defence of the Brezhnev generation's right to stay at their jobs: considerateness was to be shown above all to those already at the top. He also defended elderly officials with a quotation from Yakov Sverdlov, the first Soviet head of state: 'Youth is far from being measured only in years. A man may be young at fifty and old at thirty.'

He tried to make himself out to be a Soviet-style democrat. This was partly a dig at Andropov the disciplinarian. In fact it showed up what a cautious, communist view of democracy Chernenko had. His hobby horse were the letters that members of the public sent to the Central Committee and other party organizations. While Brezhnev was alive Chernenko had fathered a new department in the Central Committee to handle them, and put a septuagenarian in charge of it. He spoke about this as a great achievement in bringing more democracy into Soviet life, but it was a bureaucrat's solution which did little to narrow the gap between government and governed. The bureaucrats produced the statistics of letters received and letters answered but the methods and mentality that drove people to write the letters in the first place stayed the same (the letters department was abolished by Gorbachov, making it the shortest-lived department in the history of the Central Committee). One sensed with Chernenko, as with Brezhnev before him, a genuine enough desire to make people's life better but only as long as power, privilege and the established ways of conducting business remained undisturbed. That the two might no longer be reconciled was the one thing he and the traditionalists in the establishment could not bring themselves to admit.

Chernenko matched the Soviet system. They had grown old together, though neither admitted that their age was a disqualification. They had started out by destroying the kulaks, the farmers Stalin had demonized. Now they were ready to read any letter the citizenry (safely cleansed of kulaks) might care to send them. All those years ago they had been hungry and poorly clothed. Now they were stout, had eaten and drunk more than they ought to have done (Chernenko, unlike Andropov, had joined Brezhnev in his merry-making), and wore suits tailored from the best dark cloth. Stalin had accustomed them to the privileges that power brought just as he had taught them to obey and exact obedience in turn. The problem was that they were now left with only themselves to obey, and they had no new commands to give. This explained the curious atmosphere of Moscow during much of Chernenko's leadership. The Kremlin was to behave like an old soldier who compulsively dresses up in the imposing uniforms of the past but cannot hear the guns of the new battle that is building up.

Signs that the fashions of the past might return were quick to come. Brezhnev, whose name had been pushed discreetly but firmly to the back of the nation's memory, reappeared in descriptions of Chernenko as his 'true companion-in-arms'. The Kremlin's hunting lodge at Zavidovo, ignored by

Andropov, came to life in expectation that the good old days had returned. Two days before Chernenko gave his first and disastrous major public speech his wife Anna hosted the traditional Women's Day party for the wives of foreign ambassadors. Held in one of the big houses on the Lenin Hills overlooking the Moskva river that Stalin built for his closest colleagues, this was the one day in the year the Politburo ladies came into public view together. There was always a meal, some light entertainment, and then – to the alarm of those foreign guests who were unprepared for it – the ladies danced together. Few Moscow rituals caught so well the clumsy, tentative way in which the old Soviet establishment tried to hold out a friendly hand to the ill-understood, and ill-understanding, outside world. The news that day was that Mrs Chernenko had invited Brezhnev's widow and his daughter Galina to the party. The Soviet ladies had treated Mrs Brezhnev with the respect due a dowager empress. It was a dramatic and significant defiance of the old Kremlin practice of ignoring those who had lost their link with the world of power.

There were other, older ghosts afoot. It only became known a few weeks later but in March, on his ninety-fourth birthday, Vyacheslav Molotov was re-admitted into the Soviet Communist party from which he had been expelled in 1961. The news was greeted with alarm by those in the city who were already waiting nervously for signs that Chernenko and his supporters meant to take the country back into the past. No one was sure what Molotov's rehabilitation meant. Optimists suggested that the old Stalinist was on his deathbed and that giving him back his party card was Communism's equivalent of extreme unction which it would have been inhuman to deny him. But Molotov was not dying. Nor was he in the slightest repentant, not for his opposition to Khrushchov, not even for what he had done under Stalin. Until recently he had been spry enough to go to the Lenin Library, next door to his Moscow apartment. He had written his memoirs there, sending each chapter as it was finished to the Central Committee – under the circumstances a gesture of loyal reproach. He spent his summers at the Stalin-era dacha colony of Zhukovka where he went for walks but spent most of the day reading and making notes in the Marxist classics. He horrified Russians whom he met with his diatribes against the present day leadership which he said was 'revisionist'. He argued that the trials of the 1930s had been justified, and insisted that men like the great soldier Tukhachevsky, whom Stalin had shot, had been plotting against the Soviet state and should never have been rehabilitated. Molotov and Lazar Kaganovich were the only associates of Stalin (apart from the secret police chiefs) to be named by the official history of the Communist party as guilty participants in the purges. Some wondered whether Gromyko, now at his most influential, had wanted to repay a debt to the man who had been his patron at the start of his diplomatic career. Whatever the explanation it was understandable that Molotov's partial return to grace should cause alarm.

The authorities tacitly conceded this, for the news of his readmission to the party was never published inside the Soviet Union.

Chernenko sent a signal of his own the day after the Brezhnev women had appeared at the party on Lenin Hills. He summoned the staff of the Central Committee and delivered a long speech. It was full of the usual exhortations and admonitions – 'for a communist work in the party apparatus is a great honour but at the same time a great responsibility.' But that he delivered a speech to this audience was a comfort to the party's senior bureaucrats, many of whom had sat in the same job since Brezhnev's coming to power. They had seen Andropov remove some of their colleagues and, as Gorbachov's first year in power was to show, had excellent reason to fear for their own future too. Further encouragement for the establishment came at the meeting of the new Supreme Soviet in April. Hopes had grown while Andropov was alive that this would be an appropriate occasion to retire prime minister Tikhonov, a Brezhnev follower who was approaching eighty years old and who no one imagined would want to, or be capable of, bringing energy to reshaping the economy. But Tikhonov was re-elected, and so, almost without a single change, were his ministers. A more dispiriting message to the reformers would have been hard to imagine.

Few were surprised when Chernenko was elected chairman of the presidium of the Supreme Soviet at the same session. It was hard to imagine him resisting the honour as Andropov very likely did. Nor was there any evidence that his colleagues opposed his appointment. They were trapped by the system. Well aware that Chernenko was neither an impressive nor popular leader abroad or in the country at large they could not undermine his authority by stopping him becoming head of state. Tradition and popular attitudes all demanded that the party's authority be symbolized in one man, rather than in the collective leadership about which so many pious words were spoken. Khrushchov had not needed the presidency: he was strong enough without it. Brezhnev, who as general secretary in his first years had to cope with colleagues of equal authority, used the presidency to give himself an advantage over them. Chernenko needed it even more; not to dominate the Politburo but in order not to bring it into too much disrespect.

It fell to Gorbachov to propose Chernenko's candidacy to chair the Supreme Soviet presidium and in one of the first public demonstrations of his political skills he produced what sounded like powerful reasons for it. He said the Central Committee considered it necessary, in view of past experience, for the two jobs to be held together (he glided over the difficult truth that the past experience had been very short). This reflected the party's leading role in Soviet society, as enshrined in the new constitution, and it also had 'huge significance' for the conduct of Soviet foreign policy.

In little over a year Gorbachov was to destroy both these arguments by proposing that Andrei Gromyko, rather than himself as party leader, should succeed to the presidency. Chernenko was happily ignorant of that and he at once showed signs of meaning to enjoy the presidency as much as Brezhnev had. Kremlin ceremonies came back into vogue. Chernenko proved himself to be a keen giver of medals. Within a week he was presenting awards to two Politburo colleagues, Ustinov and Solomentsev, which they had been given according to protocol on their birthdays the preceding year. He also gave Viktor Chebrikov, the KGB chief, a 'Marshal's Star' made of gold, platinum and thirty-one small diamonds. This was an award, not a rank, though there was inevitably some inaccurate and panicky talk about the country's security services having a marshal at their head for the first time since the days of Stalin's appalling policeman Beria. Whether this was thanks, or a bid for Chebrikov's support, there was no way of telling.

These Kremlin ceremonies reached the peak of Chernenko image-building in September when Ustinov presented him with the Order of Lenin – his fourth – on the occasion of his seventy-fourth birthday. It was unusual to give such a decoration on a routine birthday, though Brezhnev had had the rules of medal-giving bent for him. Ustinov's praise of Chernenko was unusual too. He spoke of his 'truly heroic path of labour', and mentioned Chernenko's stint as a young frontier guard as one of the steps along it. But he also referred to Chernenko as the 'leader of the party and state, chairman of the Defence Council and Supreme Commander-in-Chief', a formula that was all the more impressive for being so rarely used. The occasion seemed designed to show the Soviet leader in the best possible light. It was attended by most of the Moscow-based Politburo members and also by heads of Central Committee departments associated with Chernenko, by his chief doctor, and by all his assistants. The effect was like one of those acrobatic acts in which the smallest member emerges unsteadily at the top of a pyramid made by the bigger ones, but the occasion was certainly meant as a signal of strength – to the West (which was making mischief with talk of invalids in the Kremlin), to the country at large, and not least to the Soviet armed forces.

Within weeks of Chernenko's election as party leader the Kremlin had shown signs of being worried about his unimpressive military credentials. It is impossible to say how widespread the damning talk about his failure to fight in the war had been, but Chernenko himself knew it could hurt him. In an autobiographical introduction to an English edition of his speeches published before he became leader he explained that when war broke out he had at once volunteered to fight at the front 'but all my requests were turned down'. There was no evidence that this was not true but it was not an easy theme for his propagandists to develop since his wartime occupation had not been out of the ordinary. Nothing, that year, so showed up the bankruptcy of the old techniques of leadership as the attempt instead to build the two years the young Chernenko spent as a frontier guard into a feat of heroism. In April readers of the army newspaper *Krasnaya Zvezda* found on the second page a letter from a mother whose son was serving at the same frontier post in eastern Kazakhstan that Chernenko had joined, as a volunteer, in 1930. Under the pretext of pleasing a fond mother the paper revealed that when Chernenko served there the post had been in constant action against 'the enemies of Soviet power'. Chernenko had shown 'bravery and courage', had been a good shot with rifle and submachine gun, and 'always hit the targets throwing hand grenades'. He showed himself a good horseman, too, but most significantly had been elected unanimously as secretary of the post's party cell. In his spare time he read a great deal and studied. The article was accompanied by a photograph of the young Chernenko with other delegates to the district's party conference. This one remaining piece of evidence of his military prowess shows him in the back row, an old point-topped Budyonnovka cap on top of jug ears, narrow-eyed, unsmiling.

It was hard to imagine thinner material for the propagandists to work on but they did their best. In the winter some Moscow film-goers were surprised to be shown, before the film they had paid to see, a documentary called *Outpost of Youth*. With a script written by Kazakhstan's best-known writer this was none other than the story of Chernenko's frontier post. Its scoop was an interview with a man who had served with the party leader and could give an account of an engagement in which they had both fought. Some half a dozen of them had set out to track down a foreign gang that had crossed the border. One of their troopers was killed and another wounded but they 'wiped out' the gang and rescued the cattle that had been rustled.

Goodness knows how much further the tale would have been embroidered had Chernenko lived. If people had laughed at the cult of Brezhnev how should they keep a straight face while an even less convincing one was being built around Chernenko? It was evidence of how out of touch with the country's mood Chernenko's supporters were. It was also evidence of a nervousness about the army. There had been one most unusual guest at the ceremony in September at which defence minister Ustinov had handed Chernenko his out-of-turn Order of Lenin – Marshal Sergei Akhromeyev, appointed chief of the general staff earlier the same month to replace the brilliant Marshal Ogarkov. Where the latter had gone no one knew for sure. The official announcement, which took everyone by surprise, merely said that he had been moved to 'other work'. Everyone supposed there had been a row. And if there was one thing that made the Soviet establishment nervous it was signs of discord between the Kremlin and the army, the one Soviet institution that could legitimately claim links with a glorious past going far back beyond 1917, the nation's saviour in 1941 and its protector today against an enemy – or so the party said – that was tireless in his plots against the country.

12

Men of Might and Morals

The disappearance of Marshal Nikolai Ogarkov in September 1984 was the stuff of which scandals are made. The most accomplished of the post-war soldiers could scarcely have been found wanting as chief of the general staff. The only possible explanation was that he had quarrelled with the political leadership. Communists are nervous about soldiers. The French and English revolutions taught them to be wary of generals riding white horses. Soviet Communists knew that generals had their political uses. On several occasions since the war the politicians had needed at least their tacit support: against Beria and the secret police after Stalin's death; on Khrushchov's side against the Stalinist anti-party group; with Brezhnev and his colleagues when they in turn decided to get rid of Khrushchov. But this only made them more wary of soldiers who might turn into someone else's useful ally.

Ogarkov was no ordinary Soviet marshal. He was brilliant and strong-minded: 'one hell of a smart soldier' in the opinion of a Western officer who knew him. He was the first engineer to rise to the top of the Soviet army, having survived a disaster when towards the end of the Second World War he lost his unit clearing a minefield on the Karelian front. He did not look an obviously military figure. Of only average height, his authority was in his sallow face with its Roman nose and full cheeks. His pretensions were considerable. At the beginning of 1983 *Pravda* published a long article in praise of Marshal Tukhachevsky who perished, with several members of his family, in Stalin's 1937 purge of the army. Tukhachevsky, a young Tsarist officer who went over to the Red Army, had been the most influential soldier in the pre-war Soviet army. An original military thinker, he had urged the army to adopt new technology and tactics, correctly foreseeing the importance of rapid armour and airborne operations in any future European war. He had also argued that a strong general staff should act as the single planning centre for the armed forces. The article, written by one of Ogarkov's first deputies, made the dead Marshal sound remarkably like the present chief of the general staff. To the discomfort of some of his colleagues, Ogarkov had managed to increase the general staff's importance by reorganizing the whole Soviet military structure. Arguing that a new war would be fought over a far wider area and at far greater speed than the last world war, Ogarkov divided the armed forces for war-fighting into big new theatres of military operations, and pushed the service branches towards operating as single all-arms units. This did not make him popular with service chiefs who felt their prestige was being damaged. The strategic rocket forces were said to have been particularly put out. So was Marshal Petrov, commander of the ground forces, who reportedly threatened to resign rather than let the classic infantry formations be disbanded.

Tukhachevsky had been a man of great charm. Ogarkov was better known for arrogance and acerbity. The reorganization of the armed forces was Politburo policy. But the Marshal had also been arguing as openly as was possible in the Soviet system for great attention to be paid to new military technologies. He was happy with the US-Soviet balance in nuclear weapons and ridiculed the value of acquiring new ones. But he seemed haunted by the chance that the Soviet Union might wake up one day to find itself defenceless before some entirely new Western weapon. He and his supporters again and again tried to explain that military technology knew no pause. The vigour of his argument – he said those who ignored it were making a 'serious mistake' – and its implication that a bigger defence budget was needed made this a matter of high politics. It did not seem a coincidence when, at the time of Ogarkov's disappearance, both *Pravda* and the army newspaper *Krasnaya Zvezda* printed editorials declaring that government programmes to improve living standards could under no circumstances be cut.

Some suspected there was more to Ogarkov's disappearance than that. Defence minister Ustinov had put him in the job but it was rumoured that the two men had often quarrelled. According to this version the last straw had been Ogarkov's behaviour during the summer's Warsaw Pact manoeuvres, over which Ustinov himself had presided. In discussions afterwards Ogarkov had infuriated the defence minister by questioning the professionalism with which the manoeuvres had been conducted. True or not, enough was known about Ogarkov to suggest that he was more uppity than the Politburo liked its soldiers to be. Had Ustinov been a younger man that might not have mattered. But he was in his mid-seventies and not well. When he went, the soldiers could be expected to want one of their own number appointed defence minister and Ogarkov, until his disappearance, was the obvious candidate. As with many Kremlin dramas the details were vague and most likely will remain so. One of the mysteries was the role of that permanent odd man out Grigori Romanov, party secretary supervising the defence industry. He was abroad when Ogarkov was removed – which, some suspected, had robbed the Marshal of support in the Politburo. But the overall plot was plain enough. Moscow was coming to the end of an era. Since 1945 the country had had leaders who could legitimately claim a share in the glory of Germany's defeat. Khrushchov and Brezhnev had been senior military commissars. They had seen battle and, perhaps as important, knew many of the victorious generals well. Khrushchov had known his defence minister, Marshal Malinovsky, for years (though Malinovsky went along with the quiet coup against him). Brezhnev and Marshal Grechko, Ustinov's predecessor, were old friends. Brezhnev had done him the great honour on his death of having the extension of Kutuzovsky Prospect leading out of Moscow named after him.

Ustinov was the last of the politicians with those close army ties made during the war. His experience was extraordinary, unmatched by few contemporaries, quite unmatchable by younger men. Of peasant stock, with a big Russian face that was featureless except for the turned-up nose, he was caught up as a child in the revolutionary whirlwind, and at the age of only fifteen was fighting anti-Bolshevik Muslims in Central Asia. Stalin's whirlwind (purges of real and imaginary enemies, promotions for the survivors) swept him in 1938, aged thirty, into the directorship of one of the biggest arms factories in Leningrad. Soviet scientists told a story of how Stalin made Ustinov people's commissar of armaments after the outbreak of war. Officers from the NKVD, as the secret police was then called, arrived at Ustinov's flat in Leningrad and told him he was to go to Moscow with them. Ustinov assumed he was being arrested. He had privately criticized the quality of some new Soviet weapons, in those days more than enough reason to be jailed. He packed a case and kissed his wife but when the train arrived in Moscow the NKVD men drove him to the Kremlin where Stalin and some senior defence officials were waiting. Stalin questioned Ustinov, insisted he tell his true opinions about arms production and sent him back to Leningrad. Several weeks later another group of NKVD officers turned up at his home and again took him off to Moscow. Ustinov was more than ever convinced he would be taken to the Lubyanka but this time, too, the secret police drove him to the Kremlin. He was taken before a Stalin this time surrounded by the Politburo. Stalin explained who Ustinov was and said he was proposing him to be commissar of armaments. 'I am for,' Stalin concluded. 'Who is against?'

Ustinov's introduction into the terrors and responsibilities of serving Stalin was not out of the ordinary. It is said he discovered on his first day at the commissariat how close he had been to disaster. The head of the department that kept secret documents showed him a paper written by a senior official denouncing him as an enemy of the people. So many men and women had been in jail or close to it that it was no longer a stigma. Several of the soldiers and experts Ustinov worked with had been in camps or prison when war began. Some, like the aeroplane designer Yakovlev, and Korolyov, the genius behind Soviet missiles, were put to work for a time in prison laboratories. Stalin did not hold a prison sentence against a man he needed, remarking (according to one popular anecdote) that he too had once 'been inside', albeit under the Tsar. Ustinov, as people's commissar, on at least one occasion extracted a man from prison to appoint him director of a factory making anti-tank guns. A story Ustinov himself used to tell conveyed the Gothic atmosphere of working for Stalin. Ustinov loved motorbikes and in 1943 had a serious accident riding one in Moscow. After three months in hospital he was called, still on a stick, to see Stalin and the other members of the State Defence Committee. 'Comrade Ustinov,' Stalin said, 'do you know there is a war going on?' Ustinov froze, only to be more frightened by Stalin's next words. 'As people's commissar you represent a specific sort of government property. And do you know that in wartime those who damage government property are punished?' Ustinov, now expecting the very worst, heard Stalin conclude, 'Well, and we shall punish you.' He turned to the others and asked what they suggested. There was silence, broken in the end by Andrei Zhdanov, the Leningrad party leader who knew Ustinov well. 'Comrade Stalin, let's give Ustinov a new motor cycle.' Everyone laughed and there the matter ended except that, when he said goodbye, Stalin told Ustinov that if he sat on a motorbike again before the war was over 'we shall talk to you in a different way'.

A man who served his country under Stalin during the war, and who after it, as Romanov stressed in his funeral oration, had been one of the brains behind the military programmes that gave the Soviet army parity with the Americans, was not someone the Marshals could patronize. But Ustinov was old and ill and may have known he was soon to die. It was not comfortable to imagine Ogarkov as Chernenko's defence minister. Elderly party leaders presented a peculiar problem in an age of nuclear missiles. How quickly could Brezhnev, Andropov or Chernenko have responded in a crisis? Some well-informed Russians believed that in a major emergency the army would have bothered only to evacuate the ailing Brezhnev, not try to consult with him. The shooting down of the Korean jumbo jet in 1983 (after which Ogarkov appeared for the first time before the foreign press to make a defence of the Soviet action) had concentrated people's minds on this problem. It made it all the more important for relations to be impeccable between the party leader, who was the constitutional commander-in-chief, and the senior military officer.

When Ustinov died in December 1984 an unspectacular soldier, Marshal Sergei Sokolov, was chosen as new minister of defence, but given only candidate membership in the Politburo. Ogarkov did not vanish into disgrace as at first seemed likely. He was put at the head of the western theatre of military operations, the most important of the new command organizations he had devised when running the general staff. He still published articles. Most significantly, he kept his seat on the party Central Committee.

The Politburo probably saw Ogarkov as a nuisance rather than a threat. But did not the army as a whole present a more subtle kind of threat? It was not likely to escape from the party's control. The machinery to supervise the armed forces was elaborate and apparently in good working order. The party is directly represented in the army by the main political directorate, staffed by soldiers but to all intents a department of the Central Committee. The directorate's political officers serve as deputy commanders in every unit down to company level. Just as important, four out of five Soviet officers are party members, and most of those who are not are likely to be in the Komsomol. Like party members everywhere they are organized into cells and are expected to conduct regular political discussions and activities. No other professional group in the Soviet Union has such a high percentage of party members. Finally the KGB provides a safety net through its third directorate which has departments in every military district, army and division. Each regiment also has several KGB officers reporting on signs of serious disagreement or dissent.

But there was one thing about the soldiers that neither party nor KGB could control – their image as the most successful part of the Soviet system, and the one most unambiguously identified with a Russian past that no longer seemed as deplorable as the Bolsheviks had once believed. That point was made, unintentionally, by a film that appeared at the end of 1984 about the greatest of the wartime commanders, Marshal Georgi Zhukov. Stalin was present too, but he was only allowed to haunt the documentary like the Cheshire Cat. The film showed his wartime office in the Kremlin, with the long table where the battle maps were laid out and his desk with an empty pipe and a box of the Hercegovina Flor cigarettes that he crumpled up for tobacco. Like Zhukov's own memoirs, the film made it plain to anyone with a little knowledge that if one man's will had been decisive in the war it was Stalin's. But this was no longer in keeping with the official line that the party had been both 'inspirer and organiser of victory'. Anyone wanting a single great hero to identify with the war was left with Zhukov, who happened to fit the heroic mould as well as any of the great Russian soldiers of the past. And when the next year a big art exhibition was organized in Moscow to honour the end of the war Zhukov inevitably emerged as its hero too. Two vast works, one an oil painting, another a relief chiselled in marble, showed him on the white horse he had ridden to inspect the 1945 victory parade on Red Square.

The irony was that the leadership had not trusted Zhukov. Stalin moved him almost straight from the victory parade into an obscure command. Khrushchov, after finding him a useful ally and creating a precedent by

135

making him defence minister and bringing him into the political leadership, had also had to get rid of him. Zhukov had committed the worst crime a Soviet soldier could commit: he tried to cut both the number and influence of the political officers in the army. If he had got his way not one would have risen above the rank of colonel (today's senior commissar is an army general, one rank below marshal). The giant oil painting at the victory exhibition explained why Zhukov had nevertheless gone from strength to strength in death. It placed the Marshal on his huge, rearing horse in front of St. Basil's Cathedral and the statue of Minin and Pozharsky, heroes of the seventeenth-century defence of Moscow against the Poles. A large red banner decorated with ikon-like heads of Lenin and Stalin cut across the top of the picture. The Ogarkov generation of officers had not inherited just a victorious army. They had inherited an army which in the course of that victory had re-established its links with pre-revolutionary Russia, the first Soviet institution to be allowed to do so. The painting summed it up. Zhukov was Lenin and Stalin's soldier; but he was also the most recent in a long line of soldiers who had fought the enemies of Russia.

One of the oddest pieces of evidence of the marriage between old Russian and modern Soviet feats of arms is in the museum of the Patriarch of the Russian Orthodox church at Zagorsk, north of Moscow. A big lacquer box, decorated with scenes from the Russian past, it is inscribed with an extract from the speech that Stalin made at the beginning of the war in which he reminded Russians of the bravery of ancestors like the princes Alexander Nevsky and Dmitri Donskoi, and Kutuzov, vanquisher of Napoleon. The box was Stalin's victory present to the Patriarch. Even the church which the Communists had done their best to destroy was brought briefly into this moment of reconciliation between the country's past and present.

The reconciliation had lasting effects for the army. The soldiers who emerged from the war were scarcely recognizable as the men who had retreated in front of Hitler's surprise attack. Stalin had brought back, just before the war began, the ranks of admiral and general that the young Red Army had done away with. The Guards units were revived, in a new Soviet form, within three months of the start of the fighting. After the decisive victory at Stalingrad the army was transformed, a gorgeous military moth bursting out of the drab revolutionary chrysalis. The old revolutionary slogan attacking Tsarist officers – 'Down with the gold shoulder-boards' – was forgotten. All ranks were issued with shoulder-boards that clearly distinguished officers from men. An uncomprehending British military mission was irritated to receive an urgent request for a large supply of gold thread to make the Soviet officer corps' new badges. Stalin brought back all the old ranks and invented some new ones, including that of marshal for himself and his most senior commanders. Though no one would have cared to comment on it at the time, the Soviet army looked at the war's end remarkably like the old Tsarist one that its founders had fought against. Its medals, too, now ignored the revolutionary divide. In the summer of 1942, as the battle around Stalingrad was developing, Stalin introduced three new military orders named after Suvorov (considered by some the greatest of all Russian soldiers), Kutuzov and Alexander Nevsky. A modern Soviet authority explained that 'with the creation of awards named after great Russian commanders the Motherland called upon Soviet soldiers to fight bravely and steadfastly against the hated enemy, to increase the glory of Russian arms, to follow the best examples of military art, valour, courage and heroism'.

The first order of Suvorov was given to Zhukov. The first knight of the order of Alexander Nevsky (members of orders were and still are called knights) was a young lieutenant who is said to have successfully imitated Nevsky's own tactics in an engagement round Stalingrad. Dmitri Ustinov was awarded both the Suvorov and Kutuzov orders. Two Tsarist admirals, Nakhimov and Ushakov, provided the names for decorations for sailors. It was only to be expected that Russians would with time come to regard some medals awarded by the Tsars as the legitimate ancestors of the new Soviet awards. Lenin had abolished the Tsarist orders but by the 1980s there was a popular, though incorrect, belief that this did not apply to the St. George's Cross, the most important Tsarist award for military valour. One magazine even printed a photograph of an old soldier with his soldier son in which the younger man wore his three Orders of Glory (the bravery award for other ranks, instituted in 1943) while his father was wearing his St. George's Cross, their pre-revolutionary equivalent. The army newspaper had to explain this was wrong but its arguments were tortured. 'We know, remember and honour the heroes and military commanders of the Russian army but we measure their services to the fatherland not according to favours bestowed by the Tsars.' Nevertheless the same newspaper would publish its own photographs of newly-decorated Soviet soldiers posing in the noblest apartment in the Great Kremlin Palace, the white St. George's Hall whose pillars were inscribed with the names of those who had won the order introduced by Catherine the Great. It was difficult to believe the obvious symbolism was unintended.

As for Soviet medals, citizens were expected to treat them as sacred objects. A long public debate in which many examples were given of the growing fashion for trading in and collecting medals (in one or two much-talked-of cases criminals had even killed to get them) ended in 1985 with a new law that banned outright their sale or exchange and brought in a one-year jail sentence as punishment for those who ignored it. The law applied not only to military awards, about which feelings could be expected to be strong, but to all the growing family of civilian decorations, which included such titles as Merited Machine-builder and Merited Technologist.

With uniforms and medals went an attention to military ritual that would have gladdened the hearts of sergeant-majors the world over. Military handbooks on ceremonies and parade-ground manoeuvres stressed their continuity with those of the old Russian army. The classics of ancient Russian literature were searched for references to military rites and traditions. Soldiers raided Pushkin for poetry which 'underlined the aesthetic side of the ritual of a parade'. Suvorov was particularly praised for having resisted Tsar Paul I's attempt to Prussianize the army and for preserving the Russian tradition of the big military band. The great commander who had 'put his hand on the heart of the Russian soldier and studied its beat' was quoted for his remark that music 'doubles, triples an army', an opinion, judging by modern Soviet military parades, that today's marshals entirely share. The discipline and endurance of the special regiments that stand duty on most of the big Moscow parades would have satisfied the soldier brother of Nicholas I who kept a regiment at the present arms for an hour and commented, 'Very good, only, *they breathe!*' He would certainly have recognized the barked-out greetings given by Soviet soldiers to their officers on parade. They now addressed a 'comrade marshal' rather than a royal highness but the drill chant was identical. No one was surprised any more if a political officer attached to the strategic rocket forces quoted a soldier's poem about the 'historical road' from the 'Russian bayonet to the ballistic missile' or when Marshal Tolubko, commander of the rocket forces, declared Soviet gunnery to be six hundred years old.

Links with the past and tradition – including the encouragement of 'military dynasties', families in which each generation served as soldiers – were more than a professional military foible. All young Soviet men were obliged to do two years' military service. In the spring and autumn they could be seen waiting at railway stations, shaven heads protected by knitted ski caps, joking, smoking, and a little nervous. A few tried to avoid conscription but surveys suggested that most eighteen-year-olds had a reasonably positive attitude to it, though enthusiasm diminished among those over twenty. The first few months' basic training were a shock. Soviet officers complained that modern society was producing recruits who were badly prepared physically and mentally for the army although there was, on paper at least, an elaborate system of both pre-conscription training and para-military activities which included technical sports like motor cycle racing or hang gliding.

But the army was for many young men a respected teacher in a society where other institutions, including the Communist party, were in danger of losing their authority. That it was also the one institution which could afford to ignore the break of 1917 and call on the emotional symbols and memories of the past added powerfully to that authority – at least for its Slav conscripts. Since 1983 the conscripts' course on Soviet military and political history had been filled out with another twelve hours on pre-revolutionary military history, beginning with the 'liberation struggle of the Russian people against the Tatars' in the thirteenth century. The Russianness of the Soviet army was reinforced by having Russian as its language of command and a predominantly Slav officer corps.

The armed forces were not perfect. The military press wrote about lazy officers, neglected drills and sloppy manoeuvres. Vodka claimed its victims among men serving in distant, drab garrisons and in more comfortable postings, too. Some soldiers stole from army stores. After Andropov started his war on corruption a particularly shocking story came to light about the commanding officer of a military hospital in the Moscow military district who built up a network of useful contacts by prescribing scarce medicines or allotting desirable hospital beds. The colonel managed to build himself a large villa with sauna, swimming pool, central heating and a big artificial pond before the military police caught up with him. Stories were told about some very senior officers grown greedy with age. More idealistic Russians disliked the way the armed forces were no longer recognizably revolutionary. 'A Thermidor has taken place in the army,' a Moscow intellectual complained, 'and now they are all in love with their medals and privileges.' But it remained the most potent mobilizing force in the country. The army's greatest triumph – the defeat of Hitler – provided the one public holiday that people seemed genuinely happy to celebrate. In a society grown cynical it was still possible to believe that self-sacrifice and a spirit of public service lived on among the soldiers. When the army produced a self-congratulatory song about the patience of officers' wives living on far-away posts ('Here of course it isn't Nevsky Prospect . . . next to the threatening, mighty rockets') it could not be entirely laughed off. The national memory of Russia as a country time and again unjustly invaded gave a gloss even to third-rate productions of the Soviet Tin Pan Alley.

Intellectuals were not slow to spot the glamour of a tested patriotic army in a country where glamour had ebbed out of public life. In the Brezhnev years Russian nationalism and the cult of the military produced exotic intellectual flowers of which the most striking example was a 'code of morals' drawn up by a young official in the propaganda department of the Moscow Komsomol, and circulated for a while among Komsomol officials. It was a programme for Russian romantic authoritarianism. The young were to be taught that life was a 'permanent mortal struggle'. Love of the motherland and a 'cult of ancestors' provided the only sure base for morality. Education should be harsh ('the whip is the best teacher') and punishments for deviant behaviour savage. The ideal man was to be found among soldiers: 'The intellectual is the slave of dead reason, and the soldier is the lord of life . . . it is necessary to resurrect and assert forever the cult which is health giving and leads to true immortality – the cult of the soldier.'

This was an old Russian voice, one that had been heard in arguments about the country's fate ever since Russia had come into contact with the West. But although some senior officials seem to have tolerated such philosophizing it was too heretical to be openly accepted, and met strong resistance from its old enemy, the rational and humane tradition of the Russian intelligentsia. What was needed to give such ideas a wider life was a

new demonstration of national heroism. This was provided in a way that no
one had foreseen by the Soviet invasion of Afghanistan.

The Soviet army liked to be shown in only the purest colours. It did not
appreciate attempts by some of the finest Soviet writers to suggest that even
a feat of national heroism like the war against Hitler had its dark side. The
case for heroes being nothing but absolutely heroic was put by Army
General Aleksei Lizichev, the new chief political commissar appointed by
Gorbachov. As far as he was concerned there could not be several truths
about the last world war. There was only one – 'the truth of Victory, the
truth of heroism and of the steadfastness of the Soviet people shown in the
years of their greatest trials.' The general was upset by attempts to write
about the 'tragic side' of the war, about its 'human sacrifices . . . and
destruction', when what was needed was to stress its 'epic' nature. It was
inevitable that once the government realized the war in Afghanistan could
not be fought in secrecy it would embrace as its theme the forging of new
Soviet heroes of the Lizichev sort.

With over a hundred thousand Soviet troops in Afghanistan, and the
conscripts among them not staying much longer than a year, every Soviet
family with a son of an age for military service had reason to think about the
war. Parents frightened themselves with terrifying stories about the cruelty
of the Afghan guerrillas and the matching response of Soviet troops. There
were tales of crazed officers, drugged soldiers and mutilated corpses, all the
more vivid because the government did not deign to deny them. Instead
Krasnaya Zvezda began to publish regular reports about the war under the
catchline 'Place of the heroic feat – Afghanistan'. These became more and
more detailed from 1983 onwards, usually describing the Soviet soldier
defending peaceful Afghans from the guerrillas' attacks or taking supplies
from Soviet Uzbekistan to Kabul via the Salang Pass. The journalists seldom
suggested that Soviet soldiers might take part in offensive operations. Soon
this very partial war-reporting began to strike another theme – that of young
Soviet people testing themselves in Afghanistan and proving to older
generations that they too were made of the right Soviet stuff.

It became a cliché that the boys in Afghanistan were different from the

lads who before joining the army think only how to dress as fashionably as
possible . . . and then turn up at the discothèque and slay the girls on the
spot; or the lads who hang around entrances [on housing estates] because
their parents didn't supervise them properly; or those with boss-fathers
and manager-mothers who get a place in college without having to try and
live much better than they could on just a student's allowance.

The boys in Afghanistan sang different songs, too, the good old songs. A
political officer explained that some young soldiers did try to play pop music
('mournful phrases shouted to the deafening strumming of a guitar') but it
never caught on. He would let the misguided soldier perform his pathetic

pieces and then walk over with his Russian accordion and sing something from the last war:

> If the Fatherland commands,
> He'll stand in rank again –
> The lad from the Urals,
> Or perhaps he's from Baikal,
> The private of the Guards.

Girls, too, could take part in this re-affirmation of old Soviet values. Nurses said they volunteered for Afghanistan because they 'wanted to test themselves in a difficult and important undertaking'. And as the years went by Soviet reporting seemed more confident that the younger generation had not, after all, been ruined. Writing five and a half years after the invasion a *Pravda* correspondent felt able to declare that 'Afghanistan has shown . . . that we have a very good youth. And yet, to be honest, many people had doubt. They said today's young people had been born in plenty, had lived without burdens, had never been hardened by trials . . . [but] the Soviet character, patriotism, and an inherited military pride are working.'

If the older generation was satisfied, there were signs that this younger generation which had just proved itself was not. Their fathers and grandfathers had had an obvious battle to fight. They had done what Russians had always done – beat back the invader. Doing what was called one's 'international duty' in Afghanistan was not so straightforward. In the first years, when so little was being said publicly about the army's exploits in Afghanistan, it was easy to feel you were engaged in something the rest of society preferred not to know about. For the first time since 1945 young Soviet citizens were truly having to fulfil the oath each new soldier swore to be 'honourable, brave, disciplined and watchful . . . and to be faithful to my last breath to my people, my Soviet motherland and the Soviet government'. Yet for five years there were no public ceremonies to greet them when they came home from the war. The first experimental welcome home with bands and girls and bouquets of flowers was organized only in the spring of 1986 at the airport of Tashkent, headquarters for operations in Afghanistan. 'Greetings, boys, we're proud of you,' said one newspaper headline, a bit late for the half million or so conscripts who had already done their 'international duty'.

Those who died in the war's early years were buried quietly, almost as though in disgrace. The wounded were at times treated as nuisances. It was the story of chilling disregard of a soldier crippled for life by a bullet in his spine that served to break some of the taboos surrounding the army in Afghanistan. Sasha Nemtsov returned home with the Order of the Red Banner and both legs paralysed after trying to save his commanding officer during a guerrilla ambush. None of the local authorities hurried to help him. The local Komsomol did not send anyone to see him for two years. Officials at the factory he had worked at would not allow him back when he wanted just to see the place again. The first article about Nemtsov was called 'Duty'. The soldier had done his. Now it was the turn of those who stayed at home to do theirs.

In a letter to his old school Nemtsov had written that it was important for people to understand 'at what price our happiness is achieved'. But if young men were admitted to be paying a terrible price in Afghanistan didn't this give them certain rights? One of the readers responding to the Nemtsov story sounded a note of warning for the future. The writer, a veteran of the 'great patriotic war', said that like the young soldier he had been through a lot, and it seemed that both of them at times had 'beaten our heads against the bureaucracy. But if we think even once that it was Soviet power that treated us in that way we're not worth a penny as Soviet people. The ones who behaved like that to us don't have the right to sit in their jobs. Soviet power will find in itself the strength to restore order.'

The strongest warning that unworthy men (in Stalin's day they might have been called 'wreckers') were sitting in positions of authority and making a mockery of the Afghan heroes' sacrifice was to come, appropriately, from the élite of the Soviet army, the paratroops. (The other super-tough troops, the marines, had no role in Afghanistan. Instead they provided Major Shatokhin, the macho hero of *Lonely Voyage*, the Soviet film hit of 1986. Much time was subsequently spent arguing that Shatokhin in no way resembled Rambo.)

Stories were told of young men who had set their hearts on joining the paras collapsing in tears when they were turned down. The airborne troops cultivated a reputation for bravery and toughness. Recruits were tall and brawny and dressed in uniforms that marked them out from other soldiers: a blue and white striped tee shirt beneath tightly cut battle dress and a light blue beret (an airborne song went 'the berets, the berets, we've put on light blue berets because that's the most peaceful colour in the world'). In spite of regulations the beret was usually worn on the back of the head and Afghanistan was the reason for that. One of the first heroes of the war was a paratroop sergeant called Nikolai Chepik. Wounded, he had blown himself up with grenades, killing thirty Afghan guerrillas at the same time. Chepik was made a Hero of the Soviet Union (on that occasion *Pravda* recorded with pride that Chepik's peasant grandfather had also been a hero who had won the Tsarist St. George's Cross). Political officers of airborne regiments gave Chepik's photo to the soldiers who performed best on manoeuvres. The photo albums troopers took home after service in Afghanistan invariably included a picture of him that showed a young man with a serious, big face, sticking-out ears and a neatly pressed blue beret right on the back of his head. That was how he had always worn it, and officers had been unable to prevent the fashion spreading.

The embarrassment of a government that did not want to say too much in public about the war; the country's potent military tradition and a thirst for heroes in a unheroic age made it very likely that one day a Chepik who survived would return home – and not want to stop fighting. There was not much that a crippled soldier could do to fight back against an indifferent officialdom. But in 1985 a young procurator in the town of Tolyatti discovered that some healthy Afghan veterans were decidedly impatient about the disorder they had returned home to. A tough young man turned up at his office and asked about a criminal case against a local official that had been dropped for lack of evidence. Why, the visitor asked, had he let off that 'reptile', that 'Contra'? He had been fighting for eighteen months against 'reptiles' and 'Contras' like that and if the procurator couldn't deal with him 'we'll settle accounts with him ourselves'. The young man explained that he had been demobilized from Afghanistan a few months earlier. He seemed, the procurator said later, 'a man from a different world'.

The soldier had been through terrible experiences in the war and he could not reconcile them with the life he had come back to. His old friends were chasing round after fashionable clothes or new discs. One of them was getting ready to buy a car and everyone else envied him. The soldier's parents had offended him by trying to put him in an easy job. His girl friend wore American jeans and wanted to dress him up in them too. He asked himself: 'What did my comrades die for? Surely it wasn't for these traffickers, for these well-fed thieves who are so pleased with everything? What's the war "over there" being fought for? So that afterwards we can live like this? So we can show off and steal and get drunk?'

That was when he first exploded and shouted at one of his old friends that he was a 'Contra'. Later he ran into some other 'Afghans' as he called soldiers like himself. They began to meet secretly, to train, and to polish their military skills. They decided there were too many 'Contras' around the place and that the government would only be grateful if they settled scores with them.

The authorities would not have given this alarming tale of a Soviet Rambo the publicity they did if it had been a unique incident. Evidence grew that the fashion was spreading for groups of 'Afghans' to club together in vigilante mood. Some newspaper readers wrote in support of the idea of lynchings. The official solution was to praise the veterans for their idealism, and to guide them into more acceptable ways of expressing it. It was probably not by chance that photographs of paratroopers dominated the newspaper stories of that first welcome home ceremony in 1986. Later, when six Soviet regiments were withdrawn from Afghanistan in the autumn of that year, the Central Committee sent the returning 'servicemen-internationalists' a message of fulsome thanks – the first occasion on which the leadership had collectively thanked its soldiers who were fighting a dirty war. The first tank regiment to cross the border on this occasion was revealed to have 'liquidated' five thousand Afghan guerrillas, and the feat was favourably compared to an earlier generation of soldiers who in 1942 had won the regiment the title of a Guards formation and fought all the way to Berlin.

The emergence of discontented national servicemen was a dramatic signal that the system was losing its moral authority over the very people who were most loyal to its old values. The soldier who divided the people into 'revolutionaries' and 'Contras' lived in the black and white world of classic Soviet mythology. Another soldier who died in Afghanistan left behind an essay he had written at school about his favourite books. They were *The Young Guard*, one of the most popular stories about heroism in the war against Hitler, and the 1930s novel *How the Steel was Tempered* whose hero, in the soldier's own words, 'went to fight the enemy at the age of sixteen and at eighteen was already a cripple, but in spite of that fought against the kulaks until his last drop of strength'.

It was not that the party's power was threatened by the army, though Polish events had set a precedent for a Communist country's army having to bail out a bankrupt party. The danger was loss of the power to influence the young, rather than just control them. Some writers had sensed this and were trying – more subtly than the young Komsomol official who had called for a 'cult of the soldier' – to associate the armed forces with all that was best in the country, while keeping quiet about the Communist party. The best known of them, who liked to call himself a 'son of the state', was capable of writing mystic hymns to nuclear missiles: 'The rocket is a part of nature and of the cosmos, the expression of ancient dreams, from the caves with their wall drawings, through error and darkness, through great sacrifices. In it is the soul of the fallen infantryman and of generations yet to come.'

Aleksandr Prokhanov was an expert on the real Contras. He had been to Nicaragua and to Afghanistan and had written novels about both. He expressed pleasure about the army coming to life in Afghanistan after years of boredom garrisoned at home. He saw the war there as a bracing influence not only on the soldiers but also on young civilians who were now able to listen to healthy songs about beating the Afghan guerrillas. Prokhanov thrilled to the modern military state and its power. Visiting the stricken Chernobyl nuclear power station he discovered soldiers there who had fought in Afghanistan. 'The army in peace time,' he reflected, 'acts in the zone of danger. It defends, saves, fights.' He wrote not a word about any party officials there.

Some people at the top of the party did seem aware of how weak the party's power to attract had become. Yegor Ligachov, brought to Moscow by Andropov, once quoted a letter from a young man about to join the army which plainly stated the conflict between the purity of military service in the 'defence of the Motherland' and the life he would come back to where 'petty bourgeois attitudes are creeping in everywhere'. The boy knew he could – as he put it – be 'true to himself' in the army but was not sure it would be possible as a civilian. But many in the party establishment were either unaware of these crises of young conscience that were a symptom of a country losing its way, or did not know what to do about it. All they knew was how to manoeuvre to keep power slipping from them, and that was to be the story of the last, undignified months in the life of Konstantin Chernenko.

13

The Bishop's Move

Whatever the intentions behind the September 1984 ceremony at which Dmitri Ustinov gave Chernenko his Order of Lenin, the affair struck an ambiguous note. Ustinov asserted Chernenko's authority by listing his titles as chairman of the defence council and supreme commander-in-chief. But he also made much of Chernenko as the leader of a collective. He spoke warmly of his skill at organizing 'really collective work', his 'respect and attention to comrades', his 'personal modesty'. To stress collectivity – as Chernenko himself had done, a little desperately, when he proposed Andropov as party leader in November 1982 – was to hint that the leader should not throw his weight around. And Chernenko's own speech contained an admission of a frankness not usually heard on great Kremlin occasions. Describing the award as encouragement for the 'collectively worked out' policies of the leadership he said it came at 'the most responsible and, frankly speaking, a very difficult period' in his career of fifty years in the Communist party.

The collectivity Ustinov referred to was not so much a brake on a would-be wilful leader as a compromise, or even stalemate, at the top of the party. Chernenko in his speech had paid tribute to both Brezhnev and Andropov as though the two men belonged to the same, unbroken tradition. This was purest Kremlin mythology as a glance at the picture of the other leaders present at the ceremony would, with hindsight, reveal. Tikhonov, the prime minister, stood at Chernenko's right, and a serious-faced Gorbachov on his left. The former represented the government created by Brezhnev, the administrators who for the most part could only prosper in an economic system that was Stalinism modified. Gorbachov, now second in the party hierarchy, believed that both had outlived their usefulness though the code of party discretion prevented him from saying so openly. There was no way the two men could profitably work together. The occasion was also unusual for the presence of Chernenko's six senior personal assistants. It was difficult to remember any other event at which all of a general secretary's staff of advisers had assembled like this, and it seemed to stress Chernenko's authority. But only two of the six were truly his men. Four had been inherited from Andropov and some believed Chernenko had been obliged by his colleagues to keep them on to make sure the work of his office stayed up to the mark. If this was another compromise it was also scarcely of the productive kind. It spoke of suspicion and tension at the top, and that was confirmed when Gorbachov came to power. He quickly got rid of the two Chernenko assistants, banishing them into shamingly insignificant jobs. Both were also made to resign the seats in Supreme Soviets they had been allocated when their patron became general secretary.

The happiest-looking man in the photographs in the Moscow papers the next day was Viktor Grishin, the bishop-like party leader of Moscow whose usual expression in public was one of impenetrable blandness. He was almost smiling. A stalemate suited him as it suited all other leading party officials who had neither the taste nor ability for changing the way they worked, and yet no intention of surrendering power. The Grishins in the party had had an unpleasant surprise in the summer. Chernenko had fallen ill during a holiday in the Caucasus and been hospitalized on his return to the capital. But he had recovered and from their point of view it was not necessary for him to be very active. As long as Chernenko kept the leadership, the old system would hold in place beneath him. The last years of Brezhnev had proved that. The question was how long he would last. At least one foreign embassy sat a doctor down in front of a video recording of Chernenko giving medals to three cosmonauts in early September after he had come back from the ill-fated holiday. It was plain he was short of breath even when not exerting himself. He was also troubled by a cough. But he still looked far sturdier than Brezhnev or Andropov during the last year of their lives. The Grishins had reason to be moderately hopeful.

In spite of this Gorbachov, helped by Yegor Ligachov as Central Committee secretary in charge of party appointments, was able to pick off some of the most vulnerable members of the old establishment. The Shcholokovs who had celebrated Chernenko's election as party leader were back in mourning by the end of 1984. First the ex-chief of police was publicly stripped of his general's rank; in December he died and was given a quiet burial. The story was put about that he had committed suicide rather than face trial. The Brezhnev family had also been disappointed after their triumphant reappearance at the Women's Day party in March. Galina retired to a clinic, and by the end of the year her husband Yuri Churbanov was removed from his job as first deputy minister of the interior. Names that had cropped up in 1982 when scandalous rumours were put to work to damage the Brezhnev clan made their last sad appearance. In September Anatoli Kolevatov, the genius behind the Moscow circus who was said to be linked with Boris 'the Gypsy' Buryata, received a thirteen-year sentence for bribery and other offences, though some of the best-known Soviet circus performers spoke in his defence. The execution was announced in late summer of Yuri Sokolov, Moscow's most fashionable grocer who numbered Galina Brezhnev among his clients. Friends had at first succeeded in delaying the death sentence imposed on Sokolov in late 1983 for fraud amounting to over one million pounds. What happened to Boris the Gypsy himself was never officially announced. Some Muscovites suspected he died in prison.

As 1984 went on pressure was also brought to bear on some of those local party leaders whom Andropov had tried, but failed, to replace. The first secretary of the troubled and much criticized Rostov region was removed in July, though the manner of his going observed all the face-saving and even dishonest fictions that had come to be thought proper on such occasions. Aged only fifty-eight he was said to have retired on grounds of health. He was thanked for his services. His replacement had been Gorbachov's neighbour when the latter was still in Stavropol, and was later to be appointed minister of internal affairs. An attack was also started on party leaders in Kazakhstan, home of Brezhnev and Chernenko's old friend Dinmukhamed Kunayev.

But none of this signified real change. That was only possible with continuous pressure and goading from the top which a coalition led by Chernenko was never going to provide. The conservatives showed lively form in the debate on how to improve (it was still not done to say 'reform') the economic and social system. At the end of the year *Kommunist* under its traditionalist editor Kosolapov extracted confessions of error from some of the radically-minded experts who had hinted at the need for thorough changes. As one of its own contributions to the discussion, the journal that was meant to set the party's ideological tone published a piece on the economy during the Second World War. Two wartime makers of tanks from Leningrad (the hint of a link with Grigori Romanov was of course noted) described how the country had managed to produce a huge number of excellent armoured vehicles in the giant factory set up in the Urals known as Tank City. This was presented as a vindication of the classic methods of the Stalin economy. Firm central planning, discipline and pronounced wage differentials had, they argued, made for high-quality economic production. The authors reminded readers that since quality and economy were what the country most needed from its industry in 1984 the experience of Tank City had not lost relevance. It was not an outlandish point to argue in Moscow where so many senior officials had begun their careers in the war economy. Among Politburo members, apart from the unmatchable Ustinov, the trio of Grishin, Tikhonov, and Kunayev had all done economic work during the war. Grishin's job was converting the industry of Serpukhov, just outside Moscow, to arms manufacturing. Many senior members of the council of ministers, starting with the head of Gosplan, Nikolai Baibakov (wartime commissar of the petroleum industry), had similar experiences. Anyone who had seen at first hand how the Stalin economy worked flat out under the appalling conditions of war would neither easily forget nor denigrate it.

Those who considered Chernenko's rule a waste of time the country could no longer afford were trapped by the system. One of the reasons for making so much of Chernenko's Order of Lenin was to show the best face possible to an outside world that had become chronically disrespectful of Moscow's sick and elderly leadership. The ceremony was held just before Andrei Gromyko met President Reagan in Washington and when the Russians were manoeuvring to return to the arms negotiations they had abandoned after the collision over nuclear missiles in Europe. The volume of praise for Chernenko increased and, inevitably, was ludicrously overdone. *Pravda* printed a message from the American Communist party that compared the general secretary to 'a light that disperses the shadow of war from every house in every town and village'. But no one in the Kremlin could with safety challenge this myth-making about the leader. It was the tradition, and considered necessary to the party's authority at home as well as abroad.

There was a solution: retirement. Chernenko could give up the party leadership but keep the presidency. In August the Mongolian leader Yumzhagiin Tsedenbal had retired after forty years in the job 'in consideration of the state of his health and with his consent', as the official announcement had warily explained. The Soviet Union was deeply involved in Mongolian affairs and the retired Tsedenbal was in fact brought to Moscow where Soviet sources insinuated that his problem had been drink. Was this meant to set a precedent for the Soviet bloc of a leader apparently giving up power voluntarily? Such a thing had never happened before. Retirement suggested the party leadership was no longer a Papal office whose sacred authority could sustain its holder until death, regardless of his physical or mental state. The Soviet capital was once again seized by a mood of rumour and speculation in which almost anything seemed possible. It was not surprising that when the pro-Andropov journalist Valentin Chikin published another of his musings about Lenin's life people jumped at a passing reference to the illness of Lenin's mother. 'At that age – seventy-three – any ailment can be worrying.' Chernenko, too, was seventy-three. It was getting to be like Brezhnev's last months all over again.

Who would benefit if Chernenko were to give up the party leadership? For all the signs that the campaign against miscreants in high places was continuing Gorbachov, the man believed to represent the new, did not seem to be making himself felt in other matters. At the October meeting of the Central Committee called to discuss irrigation and land improvement he did not even speak, although he was the Politburo member best qualified to talk about farming. The plenum confirmed the Brezhnev policy of beating the grain shortage by two vast irrigation schemes that would bring water from the north to the Ukraine, south Russia and Central Asia. The Asian water was to come from diverting part of the flow of rivers in Siberia and it promised to be extremely expensive. Many Soviet economists as well as a large part of the Russian intelligentsia considered both projects unnecessary and even dangerous. But premier Tikhonov gave his full blessing to the plans, saying that work should start on the first and plans for the Siberian diversion be quickly completed. Gorbachov, a man from south Russia, knew well the value of irrigation but he had doubts about both schemes. In the summer of 1986, after months during which opposition to the diversions was allowed its head, both plans would be indefinitely suspended. Gorbachov was obviously powerless to influence the decisions made at what was to be the last Central Committee meeting Chernenko attended. When an unusual session of the Politburo the following month discussed the plan for 1985 Gorbachov was again silent, as was another man advanced by Andropov, Vitali Vorotnikov, prime minister of the Russian federation. Gorbachov, it became plain later, had disagreed with the plan but again had been powerless to do anything about it.

Who, if not Gorbachov, was a candidate to succeed Chernenko? Many found it hard to believe, but the answer was Viktor Grishin, the man who had walked the Kremlin stage for years without ever speaking a memorable line. Since his appointment as Moscow party leader in 1967 he had been a prominent performer of the time-consuming Soviet liturgy, chairing meetings without number, fluent in the making of ritual speeches every bit as uninteresting as those he himself listened to without ever showing the least sign of boredom. He had the great prelate's skill of presenting an entirely public face to the public. He would arrive at some ceremony in his long black car, step out in the discreet dark clothes of a clergyman in mufti, offer a slight but knowing smile, perform his duties and vanish. It was the smile of a man grown plump on power. Of the politics he practised in his office next to the Central Committee building on Old Square there was never a hint. Grishin's candidacy was not fantastic because in all this he was merely a particularly accomplished representative of a generation and a tradition within the Soviet establishment.

Born in Serpukhov outside Moscow a few weeks after the outbreak of the First World War, Grishin was the son of a railway worker, and like Brezhnev and Chernenko had been swept into power by the Stalin whirlwind. With a limited technical education at best, the twenty-year-old Grishin was put to work that Stalin would not risk allowing better-qualified men to do. Grishin spent almost all his life in and around the capital. He ran the Soviet trade unions for over ten years before his appointment to head the Moscow party, a fine opportunity to learn how to manoeuvre along the gap between Soviet rhetoric and practice. Intellectuals, particularly older intellectuals who had survived Stalin, despised the likes of Grishin. They considered them men without ability, mere bureaucrats, corrupted by power and the gloomy privileges it brought of big dachas in pine forests and large heavily furnished apartments. But every state needs bureaucrats and it would be foolish to deny these men's abilities. They had endurance. They were canny. They could take punishment from superiors and mete it out to those below. What marked them out from great bureaucrats in other governments or big corporations was that, unless watched over by a driving leader like Stalin or Khrushchov, there was no check on them. As long as their colleagues supported them – which it was in their mutual interest to do – they were for ever blameless. No one could criticize them in public, let alone try to remove them from power. Whether from complacency or fatigue such men seemed unable to imagine a different way of conducting the state's business than the one they had been brought up and flourished in.

Grishin seems to have sensed the first threat to his position when Andropov was still alive. At the end of 1983, when Andropov was trying with only limited success to reshape the party leadership in the regions, he did manage one coup by changing almost a third of the district party secretaries in Moscow. Since these were all Grishin appointees it looked a clear insult to a leader whose party organization had for years been praised as a model. Andropov had also carried his campaign against officials' owning expensive private dachas to Grishin's subordinates in the Moscow party organization, some of whom were said to be unhappy at being told to choose between keeping their job or their private country cottage. Although Grishin had moved to support Andropov when he began his anti-dacha campaign the new focus on the Moscow party apparat was obviously uncomfortable for him, and all the more so because it came at a time when the drive against corruption was starting to reveal more and more horrors in the capital itself.

When Yuri Sokolov, manager of Gastronom No. 1, or Yeliseyev's as it was still known from Tsarist days, was arrested at the end of 1982 it had been spoken of as a singular case. In fact Sokolov's shop, with its one thousand employees and a trade turnover of almost ninety million pounds a year, was just part of a network of corruption that included the managers of the capital's most important food shops. By the spring of 1986 eight hundred people had been arrested, including N. P. Tregubov, the official who for many years had headed the whole Moscow trade network before seeking refuge in a senior post in the Soviet ministry of trade itself when he learned of the investigation of Sokolov. Tregubov was to be sentenced to fifteen years' imprisonment.

Investigators discovered that most of the capital's big shops cheated their customers most of the time. Assistants made money by giving short weight and overcharging. They paid a share to their superiors who used much, perhaps even most, of the money to purchase the favours and services needed to keep the business running. People lined their own pockets, too, but essentially it was an alternative system born out of the deficiencies of the official one. As one of the shop managers said later, 'you can't move a step without paying out money'. Everyone did it. For years there was no risk for no one was caught. The size of the pay-offs grew each year. One of the key figures had unwisely made out a list of people to whom he sent gift packages of delicacies on such holidays as New Year and May Day. They included party and government officials in the capital's districts, senior trade officials up to the Russian ministry of trade and the Moscow fraud squad itself. The distinction between a bribe and a present had become hard to perceive by the 1980s, so widespread was the custom of making regular presents to people who were useful in one's work or daily life. 'We're scooping and scooping but we still can't get to the bottom of this dirty well' was how Grishin's successor Boris Yeltsin described his battle with the Moscow shopkeepers.

The police were surprised to discover that the shops that stole most were also the shops most often rewarded for their work and whose directors won the most honours. And just as Gastronom No. 1 was supposed to be a model shop so was Moscow meant to be the model Soviet city. Capital of the Motherland, Hero City from the time of war – could it be that secrets as shaming as the great Gastronom's hid behind its famous façades? The answer was yes, as any Muscovite could have guessed. The famous buildings that were so prettily painted on special occasions; the main streets that were watered in summer and ceaselessly snow-ploughed in winter; the bridges hung thickly with red flags on every holiday concealed an ordinary Soviet city that went about an ordinarily sinful life – except that in the capital the opportunities for sin were much bigger than anywhere else.

Even while Grishin ruled some of these sins could not be hidden: black marketeering in foreign clothes and consumer goods, for example, though the blame for the most visible part of that could be put on the wicked West. Other Moscow rackets were revealed only after Grishin was pensioned off at the end of 1985. There was the racket in the mini-bus taxis which followed set routes all over the city. It began with drivers re-selling used tickets that passengers left behind and ended in a system of pay-offs that included almost everyone in the large taxi network. Anyone who refused to take part was frozen out of his job. The capital's car repair and servicing organization was home to another major racket. The growing number of private cars, an acute shortage of spare parts, and the backwardness of the too few service stations that existed were an irresistible invitation to corruption. Car owners had to bribe to get vehicles repaired. Mechanics plundered engines of cars they were servicing for parts that they could sell handsomely on the black market. Customer protests at best got nowhere, at worst could lead to a beating up. It was not just a matter of crooked bosses. The workers were involved too. No one wanted the system to change. A young manager from the ZIS car factory, a prestigious and decently run operation, who was drafted in to clean it up, said it had felt like arriving on 'another planet'.

When Grishin was gone it could also be said openly that he had not even done a good job preserving the city's famous façade. 'What has happened in these last twenty years?' a well-known painter asked. 'Why is it necessary to have some straight talking about how Moscow has lost its distinctive architectural face?' Under Grishin's eye much of the old city had been pulled down in the name of modernization without anyone being able to express an opinion about what was happening. The modernized Kalinin Prospect, down which one drove from the Kremlin to cross the river and on to the grandest dachas beyond Kutuzovsky Prospect, had been greeted as the brilliant future face of the world's greatest socialist city. Its glass and concrete blocks were the first big experiment in modern planning in the centre of Moscow. One can imagine the leaders driving down it and being flattered by its modern sweep, as Stalin had been by the new city of the 1930s that he, too, had only seen from a car window. The new Kalinin Prospects were so different from the old Moscow of wooden houses and little classical palaces of plastered wood which the Grishins perhaps associated with the hard, poor world they had grown up in. The painter described showing people round his studio with the drawings he had made of old Moscow buildings and streets. 'That's not there any more.' 'That's destroyed.' 'They're going to pull that down soon.' The casualties included streets and whole quarters that for many were Moscow. Arbat Square and much of the Arbat district beyond it with its hidden, village-like courtyards behind elegant but friendly Empire façades; Taganka Square; the Zaryadye, an old merchant quarter on the river near the Kremlin, pulled down during Grishin's rule and replaced by a hotel with the charm of a monster prison – none of them had survived. And in their place stood 'something new, but faceless and entirely unMuscovite'.

Moscow was not the only old European city bent on self-destruction in the 1960s and '70s. But it was the European city where the new buildings were least redeemed by the quality of their architecture. As with the other cities of Russia (some of the non-Slav republics did better) an old urban world was being destroyed and nothing remotely comparable put in its place. Even buildings of the greatest prestige, among them the new Tretyakov gallery that was to house Soviet painting, could end up looking like cheaply built factories. It became the custom to call in foreign firms for the biggest construction projects like tourist hotels and Moscow's new airport. Grishin's administration was not the only one to blame for the poor quality of architects and builders but it had never given a sign that it saw this as a problem. Particularly shocking was its carelessness towards the great monuments that remained, as shown by a sorry tale that was only told after Grishin's retirement. Moscow's underground, for ever extending its network, was given permission by the Moscow authorities to tunnel a new station almost directly beneath the Lenin Library, the country's greatest collection of books and manuscripts which is partly kept in a fine eighteenth-century palace overlooking the Kremlin. The metro men's tunnelling caused serious damage to the library's foundations. Both book stacks and reading rooms were threatened and the library had to curtail many of its services, to the grief of the scholarly community. The Moscow city council knew about the crisis. It could have intervened, but did not. Nor did Grishin and his own committee which was supposed to watch over the city council like a guiding angel. The newspaper that revealed the disaster concluded that 'the country's unique library, a priceless cultural monument, is trapped in the thick of indifference and irresponsibility'.

The city's plans for the future inspired no greater confidence. Work had begun on the great Victory monument on the hill at the end of Kutuzovsky Prospect where Napoleon had stood to survey the city. It was to consist of a huge red granite flag the height of a thirty-storey building. The country's leading poet Andrei Voznesensky was to call it (when Grishin had gone) 'one of the most boring and least talented monuments in the world . . . What a horror!' Was this the best the capital could do to remember the country's greatest battle ever? Evidently not, for in 1986 to the delight of many Muscovites the Politburo had the project halted.

Grishin had woven a cover of pleasing statistics and fine words over the city but wherever it was lifted up the real state of affairs looked different. Moscow's industry met its targets often because it had revised them downwards: what bureaucrats called 'correcting' the plan. In fact its industry was below the national average and some of its most famous factories shockingly out of date. The city fulfilled its housing plan (and its construction workers won their bonuses) by registering unfinished buildings as completed. The truth was that a quarter of the city's nine million inhabitants needed new housing. A million of them were still living in old communal apartments with shared bathrooms and kitchens. Complaints about housing and other city services were growing. The buses, Grishin's successor Boris Yeltsin was to say later, had become so bad they were a 'political problem', an unusual and alarming admission for a Soviet leader to make. Yeltsin had been on the buses himself 'to talk to people at the bus stops, and it is no longer an abstract matter to me. People have reason to be indignant.' One reason was that the buses were so old and so badly maintained that a third of them were out of action every day. Many other services were no better though Muscovites were particularly scathing about hospitals where nurses might have to be bribed to use a decent needle for an injection and where some famous specialists charged several hundred pounds to do an operation. There was a shortage of both doctors and nurses.

The main charge that was made later against Grishin (and by extension other party leaders like him throughout the country) was that they had grown complaisant and mistook the laborious operations of their own bureaucracies for real achievements. Moscow had started a country-wide campaign for labour discipline under the slogan 'Honour and praise – according to one's work' but the number of workdays lost in the capital by absenteeism was going up. The Moscow party had not maintained the necessary pressure to make the campaign effective. The capital had many of the country's most important scientific research institutes employing nearly a million specialists but only a fraction of them had any impact on what was going on in Moscow's factories. As for the Moscow party committee it produced so many decrees and other bits of paper that when Grishin's successor cut them by half no one apparently noticed any difference. Grishin was really accused of living in a world of fantasy. He and his subordinates (the charges would go) came to consider that carefully prepared meetings and conferences at which never an impromptu word was spoken fulfilled the Communist leader's duty of making contact with 'the masses'. They were to be particularly criticized for never being seen at a trouble spot like a queue or a breakdown of public transport where they might 'run into criticism'. At the same time they cultivated a myth of perfection which no one was allowed to challenge by criticizing either Muscovites or their leaders.

Grishin's sins were the sins of Brezhnev's Soviet Union, but the importance of Moscow in Soviet politics and the visibility of the city's leader meant he would be particularly vulnerable in any period of change. As far as can be gathered he never tried to join the bandwagon of change. The story was to be told that at a meeting of the Moscow party committee at which Yeltsin, the new first secretary, tore into the city's failures Grishin, who was present because he was still a Politburo member, tried to protest. 'What,' he is supposed to have cried in horror, 'will Muscovites say if you tell them all that?' Gorbachov, also present, chipped in that Muscovites knew it perfectly well already. True or not the anecdote suggested what was easily forgotten. The Grishins of the Soviet Union may have become complacent and incompetent but they also believed their way of running things was best. From the end of the summer he manoeuvred to improve his position. When Chernenko presented him with an Order of Lenin on his seventieth birthday in October he praised Grishin for his 'political and organizational abilities, his capacity to inspire and mobilize people in the solution of great and complicated tasks'. Moscow, Chernenko said, had 'always served as a good example for the rest of the country'. The number of nominations leaders received for elections to the Russian Supreme Soviet at the end of the year was a traditional way for the leadership to signal Politburo seniority to the rest of the country. Grishin was shown to be number four, coming after Chernenko, Tikhonov and Gorbachov; an advance for him since the year before.

Kremlin politics acquired a new urgency at the end of 1984. Dmitri Ustinov died on December 20, leaving a gap in the leadership no one could fill. Chernenko stood briefly in the honour guard around Ustinov's coffin but too, vanished from sight. All the old Brezhnev tricks were performed to show he was still in charge. His office despatched letters in his name to Argentinians and foreign clergymen and even to a Canadian student. Editions of his speeches were published in French, Polish, German and Vietnamese. Each time the Soviet press printed a preface said to have been written by the great man. Grishin led the way in bolstering the absent leader's authority, on one occasion describing him by the rarely-used but potent titles of chairman of the Defence Council and Supreme Commander-in-Chief (which he may have had no right to do for the next day *Pravda* cut this out of its report of his speech). By this time Moscow was seized by the rumour that Grishin would be Chernenko's successor. Gorbachov, during his visit to London in December, had been given unusually good coverage in the Soviet media and he had also started to make more striking speeches. But the Grishin rumour was put round so vigorously – to foreign embassies as well as among Russians – that it was taken seriously. The 'old men', it was said, were still not ready to give up.

Unable to deliver his own election speech (Grishin read it for him) Chernenko did at last reappear to vote in the Supreme Soviet elections in February 1984. Soviet television showed him, accompanied by none other than Grishin, in what seemed to be a specially furnished hospital room into which a ballot box and polling officials had been brought. The cameras only showed Chernenko sitting down or standing up. He looked hesitant and weak but managed to drop his voting paper in the box. A girl gave him flowers. Grishin gave him flowers. This strange, sad theatre was continued four days later when the leader was given his deputy's credentials. The cast was smaller: Chernenko, two solid young men from his Kuibyshev district constituency, and Grishin, this time smiling at the shaky old man as though he was a little child managing its first steps. Viewers of the nine o'clock TV news saw one of the solid young men give Chernenko more flowers. All four sat down.

[Grishin] We must express our satisfaction to you that you were elected unanimously in Kuibyshev district.

[Chernenko] Thank you, thank you.

[Grishin] I don't remember exactly, but roughly one hundred and thirty thousand voters . . .

[Solid constituency man] One hundred and thirty-six thousand.

[Grishin] One hundred and thirty-six thousand voted precisely for you. This testifies to your tremendous prestige among the working people, all the working people of course. Any other constituency would certainly have voted the same way. We are glad that Kuibyshev constituency, so to speak, rose to the occasion. Now they have prepared a souvenir, Konstantin Ustinovich. And they've written here: to Konstantin Ustinovich Chernenko, from the electorate of the Kuibyshev constituency.

And Grishin pointed to the present, a model of a sailing boat in a glass case.

It was fitting that the last sight Soviet people had of Chernenko was a ceremony that summed up all the make-believe and self-delusion of recent years. Grishin was the right person to stage-manage it. It is a fair guess that he believed he was advancing his own cause by being present at these ceremonies. That his own cause was under threat there is no doubt at all.

On the evening of March 10 Moscow radio started to play classical music and soon the telephones were ringing.

'Are you listening to the radio?' one friend would ask another, 'Yes', came the answer. 'It must be one of them.'

'Yes. I think it must be Him.'

It was. Chernenko had died but his death marked the country no more than a small stone marks the great, dark lake into which it is dropped.

14

A Hero Appears

If the history of the Soviet Union from the last painful year of Brezhnev's reign to the crowning of Mikhail Gorbachov at the party congress in March 1986 had been written as drama, its author would be criticized for preparing the entry of his hero badly. It is easy to forget how little was known about Gorbachov when the Central Committee elected him the party's new leader the day after Konstantin Chernenko's death. Thanks to his visit to Britain in December he had begun to win attention in the West as a different sort of Soviet leader, though less because of what he said than the manner in which he said it. Inside the Soviet Union few people beyond the Central Committee seemed to have any strong impression of him at all. This was partly because of the secretive way in which real politics were conducted in Moscow, but Gorbachov's skill as an actor also had much to do with it.

A useful talent for a politician anywhere, in the Soviet Union it was impossible to survive without it. A Russian communist would object this was discipline, not acting, and there was something in that. Andropov had said that 'for communists the "necessary" has always taken first place'. Anyone making a career in the Soviet Communist party had to do as he was told. The successful party official was the scrupulous executor of the leadership's policies. But to rise a man had to attract the attention of superiors, and the known meagre outlines of Gorbachov's career suggested considerable skill at satisfying the right people at the right time. His first patron had been Fyodor Kulakov, party leader in Gorbachov's home in Stavropol and then his energetic and ambitious predecessor as Central Committee secretary in charge of agriculture. The two men seemed to have been close; certainly Gorbachov's wife Raisa had been known to remember Kulakov with affection. But Gorbachov's career did not suffer in the least after Kulakov's somewhat mysterious death in 1978, when there were rumours (never substantiated) of suicide, and neither Brezhnev, nor prime minister Kosygin, nor Mikhail Suslov attended his funeral. It was widely assumed that Gorbachov by then had an even more powerful protector in Suslov himself, who had been party leader in Stavropol before and during the war. Like the ill-fated Sergei Medunov in Krasnodar, Gorbachov had the advantage of having holiday resorts on his territory, and one of them, the mountain spa at Kislovodsk, attracted several members of the leadership who needed to cosset bodies worn out by relentless careers. Suslov went there, so did Kosygin and Andropov. Without a champion in the Politburo it was hard to see why Gorbachov should have been chosen at once to replace Kulakov as farming's overlord in the Central Committee: there were other party leaders from agricultural regions with, on paper, as good or better qualifications for the job. It was plain, too, that Gorbachov had known how to please Brezhnev, otherwise he would scarcely have become a full member of the Politburo in 1980 at the almost shockingly young age, for the Brezhnev leadership, of forty-nine.

These patrons were very different men, and Gorbachov was not a replica of any one of them. It is hard to believe that Gorbachov did not find Suslov's approach to ideology stifling. He cannot have served long in the ageing Brezhnev Politburo without becoming aware of its lack of new ideas and political will. It is debatable how much he agreed with the farming policy he had to carry out as Central Committee secretary under Brezhnev and which was to prove such an expensive failure. Plans for the farms introduced after he became party leader were much more imaginative. The evidence is that Andropov, with whom he worked so closely, was much more cautious about changing the Soviet system than his young protégé. Yet Gorbachov apparently won each of these very different men's confidence. He also behaved impeccably during the difficult months when he had to serve as number two under Chernenko, a man for whom he can have had little respect. This was much more than just proving he was a loyal practitioner of the current party line. It was also a nimble performance by a political actor blessed with great patience and self-control.

Little of this could be guessed in March 1985. Regional party leaders did not usually have any impact on the rest of the country, and Gorbachov in Stavropol, the smallest of the three north Caucasus territories, had been no exception. If he had made a particularly good or bad impression on the people of Stavropol during the twenty-three years he worked there, first as a Komsomol and then party official, it certainly was not widely known in Moscow. Gorbachov's years in the capital had been as private as only a Soviet leader's life can be. That he had been seen with his wife in a box at the Bolshoi on a few occasions was considered unusual. Equally unconventional were his appearances at the annual class reunion of the Moscow University law faculty, though after reaching the Kremlin heights he is said to have excused himself from the dinner held afterwards, saying Politburo permission was needed for that. He had also shown a liking for doing his job without the pomp and security precautions that usually surrounded a Politburo member. But Gorbachov would have offended his colleagues, and damaged himself, if he had broken the rule, set by Stalin, that leaders should live apart from Soviet society, not within it. Though once elected leader he was to show an impatience with the Kremlin's interminable public rituals, he had sat through them year after year as impassively as that master of the uncommunicative public face Viktor Grishin. Of medium height and stockily built Gorbachov even looked like most of the other leaders, and like them wore clothes that could only have delighted a conservative businessman.

Yet even then there were those who felt, or hoped, that he might be different. In an elderly leadership he was the one person younger party members could pin hopes on. That he had studied law at Moscow University intrigued the better-educated for this made him the only member of the Politburo with a first-rate education in the humanities. (Gorbachov later took a degree by correspondence at Stavropol Agricultural Institute which led to the first punning joke about him after he became leader: that as an agronomist and lawyer he knew both 'when to plant and whom to plant'). Enough was known of his wife for people to talk of her striking auburn hair as well as her own philosophy degree from the same university. And though Gorbachov was one of the few leaders never to have published a collection of his speeches and articles it was not quite true that he had never said anything in public to give hope to those people who believed the country had to change its ways. Just before he went to Britain in December he made a speech in which for the first time he hinted at some of the themes he would pursue as party leader. A younger educated Russian might have been encouraged by this unusual passage in spite of the wooden language:

> Our contemporary is a person of increasing culture and education, with a wide range of spiritual interests, and who has seen and experienced much. The present generations have behind them the October Revolution, industrialization and collectivization, the patriotic war, the difficult postwar decades. A person living and working in [such] a society . . . will not accept simplified answers to his questions; he senses any hint of falseness that is the result of an inability or fear to reveal the true contradictoriness of social development and the origins of those problems that concern and worry him. We must speak to him only in the language of truth . . .

Gorbachov was partly talking about himself. On the trips he had made abroad before March 1985 he had given the impression of a man who was confident about himself and his country and could therefore afford to be relaxed. He was not afraid to show he was human. He could be charming. He had a sense of humour. In London he was ready to joke that the creator of Parkinson's Law was alive and well and living in Moscow. He did not mind when a seventy-three-year-old British peer suggested he was the right age to join the Soviet Politburo. It was not so much that Gorbachov was a new kind of Russian as a Russian in a new sort of situation. The vulnerability of the young Soviet Union had been a powerful element in Stalin's paranoia about the outside world. The complex about Soviet weaknesses that Khrushchov took with him on his first trip to London and the West in 1956 would have paralysed a less vivid personality. As it was, Khrushchov's suspicions of his British hosts were so great that he stopped his son Sergei, a member of the official party, from going on a visit to Oxford for fear he might be kidnapped.

The almost thirty years since Khrushchov's London visit were the years of Gorbachov's mature political life. They had seen the Soviet Union match America in military strength. They had seen the political system developed by Stalin survive without tipping into the extremes either of a new dictatorship or of ungovernability, and at the same time bring the country for the first time to the threshold of the modern industrial world. Gorbachov's adult life had coincided with the years when Soviet society had become better educated; when cities that had grown up as agglomerations of peasants without roots were edging towards a more civilized way of life; when some of the links with both the Russian past and the outside world that the Revolution and Stalin had almost succeeded in cutting were starting to revive. Before going to Moscow as Central Committee secretary Gorbachov had made at least two unofficial visits to West Europe, one to Italy, one to France. On both occasions he had hired a car and driven himself round the country, making on French roads a journey of a full five thousand kilometres. It was an experience far beyond the dreams of a Khrushchov or a Brezhnev as they had worked their way up the ladder of power. When a British intellectual invited to meet Gorbachov remarked that he seemed the sort of man it would be enjoyable to have dinner with it was only partly a judgement on the man. It also reflected the growing confidence of the Soviet ruling class to look out of the castle to which Stalin had confined it. Gorbachov had had chances to prepare himself to be an agreeable dinner guest that his predecessors had not had.

In one respect Gorbachov was a child of Stalin's Russia. He came from a special kind of peasant family, one that had supported Stalin's revolution in the countryside and prospered under it. Collectivization and the famine that followed struck particularly hard in the North Caucasus and the Kuban. Hunger was reported to have killed 50,000 people in the town of Stavropol alone. Gorbachov's peasant grandfather had been on the side of the collectives from the start. A party member, he was founder-chairman of the first collective farm in the Gorbachovs' home village of Privolnoye. His father had become that supposedly glamorous symbol of revolutionary agriculture, a tractor driver. Sergei Gorbachov was to fight in the war and later become a local party official, dying while his son was still first secretary in Stavropol. Gorbachov remained close to his family and even as a Politburo member returned to his village each year to celebrate his birthday with his mother and other relations.

The family's exemplary political credentials may explain how Gorbachov managed to get into Moscow University in 1950 at the age of nineteen. That he had won an important decoration, the Order of the Red Banner of Labour, the year before while working as a tractor driver like his father and was already a candidate member of the party must have helped too. Both qualifications were unusual for someone so young. He had started working on his home farm when only thirteen and would later say he got his first 'tempering' from the older tractor drivers (this echo of *How the Steel was Tempered*, the famous Stalin-era novel of the forging of a young Communist's character, was, one suspects, intentional). His strongly 'party' family background, his own early application to join the party and the fact that he chose to study law all suggest (as do even the brief official biographies) that he had already decided to make a career in the Communist party. He went back to Stavropol after graduation in 1956 to become at once a Komsomol official, a common first step towards joining the party apparatus. But to have taken it immediately after finishing his formal education was unusual: all the other members of the 'Gorbachov Politburo' elected at the party congress in 1986 had done a spell at an ordinary job, and sometimes a long one, before switching to a party post. Only two of them, Chebrikov and Vorotnikov, had been as young as Gorbachov when they joined the party.

None of this was obvious when Gorbachov was declared to be Chernenko's successor as general secretary. If it had been, some difficult questions might have been asked. What sort of a young man would have wanted to make a career in the party in 1950, the year Gorbachov went to Moscow University? There were two more hard years under Stalin ahead. No one knew that Nikita Khrushchov, of all people, would become the country's leader and dare to turn against the terrifying dictator who had made him. A very young man from the provinces had no reason to suppose that the country's future did not lie with a prolongation of Stalinism. But to ask the question is to risk getting bad history as an answer. Reminiscences of Gorbachov at university are contradictory. In some he appears as a bossy Komsomol activist, and he certainly was an activist. The romantic challenge for his generation was reconstruction of a war-shattered country. He once talked of how this affected him.

I went to study at Moscow University and I travelled through Stalingrad which had been destroyed, through Voronezh which had been destroyed, Rostov was destroyed, Kharkov was destroyed, nothing but ruins everywhere. The whole country was in ruins. But I shall tell you it was a militant Komsomol then. It was Komsomol with teeth . . . I talked directly about everything I thought about, the Komsomol meetings were such militant events.

Zdenek Mlynar, a young Czech Communist who shared a room with Gorbachov at Moscow University and later became one of the leaders of the 1968 Prague Spring, has described the student Gorbachov as intelligent, self-confident, and also showing some sign of questioning the harsh Stalinist doctrines they were taught. But Stalin's prestige, not least as organizer of the victory over Germany, was at that time immense. There were many people far more experienced and who had suffered and even been imprisoned under Stalin who did not, yet, question him. A near-contemporary of Gorbachov's, the writer Yuri Trifonov, won a Stalin prize for a first novel about students published the year Gorbachov went to Moscow. Trifonov was a well-educated Muscovite who belonged to the Revolution's aristocracy. The family of his Bolshevik mother had hidden Stalin when he was on the run from the Tsarist police. His Bolshevik father and uncle, both prominent in the Revolution and Civil War, died in the purges of the 1930s. Typically, though, Trifonov, with far more knowledge and reason to fuel his doubts, would only set out on the painful road to reassessment of the Soviet past after Stalin's death.

A peasant boy from distant south Russia whose family had benefited by collectivization and himself got to Moscow State University had less reason than most to be critical of Stalin. Gorbachov's wife to be, a Stavropol girl who also had the unusual good luck to go to Moscow University, seems to have come from the same background. They were Stalin's people, the new middle class whom he needed to rebuild the post-war Soviet Union. He offered them what has been called the 'Big Deal'. They gave him their obedience and competence. He gave them responsibility, privilege and the chance of regular advancement for themselves and their families. The Revolution could now be served without complete self-sacrifice. Decent clothes, pink lampshades, expensive china – such bourgeois comforts could again accompany a successful career. The young Gorbachov was already sharing in the deal at university. Perhaps the best proof of his reliability was that he was chosen to share rooms with a young student from Czechoslovakia, a communist to be sure but a foreign one and therefore only to be entrusted to safe hands. It was typical of the apartness of Stalin's Soviet Union that it had such little confidence even in those who were supposed to be its allies in world revolution. Mlynar once sent Gorbachov a postcard while on vacation in Prague. This was so unusual that the local chief of militia felt it necessary to deliver it himself to Gorbachov while he was in the fields helping with the harvest.

There was no way of knowing how Gorbachov's ideas had developed since those days when a postcard from a friendly neighbour country was treated as potentially incriminating material. He had returned to Stavropol only a year after Stalin's death. He worked there throughout the Khrushchov period and the years of a political and intellectual thaw during which it was possible to debate some of the most painful problems of the Soviet past and present. Gorbachov was far away from the excitement that seized Moscow in those years. There was also no way of assessing how able the new leader was. The country's agricultural performance was scarcely a recommendation but that apart the leadership's secretive habits made it very hard to judge a Politburo member's competence. Andrei Gromyko, who for years had read from predictable texts in public, only towards the end of his long career revealed himself as a master of the international press conference. It was said that when Aleksei Kosygin was prime minister he would never allow members of his council of ministers to read out prepared speeches. His attitude was that a man who knew his subject should not need notes. But stick to a prepared text was what Soviet ministers invariably did in public.

The first hint that Gorbachov might have impressive political talents was itself shocking because of the unusual form it took. The Politburo delegated Gromyko to propose Gorbachov as the new general secretary when the Central Committee met on March 11. The meeting had been hurriedly called – Chernenko had died only the day before – and whether for that reason or some other Gromyko spoke impromptu. His short speech was different in tone, language and shape from anything the leaders were ever printed as saying. Perhaps because it was so unusual the Soviet papers did not publish it in their first reports on the meeting that gave the country its new leader. Gromyko's speech was a fascinating document, unique in that it was the first hint for many years of how the Soviet leadership discussed matters among themselves. As a text it demanded some caution. It was possibly incomplete. Gromyko, who himself had apparently preferred Chernenko over his younger rival only the year before, was intent on forcing the hand of a Central Committee that included opponents of Gorbachov. Nevertheless it was, and remains, the most authoritative report on the public character and ability of Mikhail Gorbachov at that time.

Gromyko announced that Gorbachov had chaired the meetings of the Politburo during the weeks of Chernenko's last illness. He had done it 'without any exaggeration, brilliantly'. Gorbachov, he went on, was a man of strong convictions who said what he thought regardless of whether it pleased the person he was talking to. His mind was 'sharp and deep . . . anyone who knows him, who has even met him only once, will confirm that'. Gorbachov did not insist on seeing everything in terms of black and white. He knew how to take 'in-between' decisions. Gromyko then gave his approval to Gorbachov's grasp of world affairs:

> Perhaps it is somewhat clearer to me because of my long service than to some other comrades. He grasps very well and quickly the essence of the processes that are taking place outside our country . . . I myself am often

struck by his ability to grasp the heart of the matter quickly and accurately
and to draw conclusions, the correct party-spirited conclusions.

Gromyko several times praised the analytical strength of Gorbachov's
mind. 'He has brilliant ability in this respect.' He praised his talent for
knowing how to find 'a common language' with people. 'This is not given to
everyone.' And he ended with a last tribute to the younger man's unfailing
ability to spot what was important in a problem or situation and to
subordinate everything else to that. It was 'a virtue, a great virtue'.
This curious speech also contained a warning about unity.

Figuratively speaking there are various telescopes trained on the Soviet
Union . . . some from near but possibly more from afar . . . And they are
looking to see if at last they can find some cracks in the Soviet leadership. I
assure you that we've become acquainted with such facts dozens and
dozens of times . . . We have been witnesses, if you like, to conversations, to whispered and half-whispered predictions: somewhere abroad
they are hungry for a glimpse of disagreements in the Soviet
leadership . . .

Both the unorthodox style of Gromyko's speech and his warning about
enemies searching Moscow for evidence of cracks confirmed suspicions that
Gorbachov's election was no straightforward matter. It was difficult to
identify a majority for Gorbachov in a Politburo reduced to ten members by
the deaths of Ustinov and Chernenko. Gorbachov was to get rid of three of
these – Grishin, Romanov and Tikhonov – within a year, and they had every
reason to be wary of him. The Ukrainian Shcherbitsky and the Kazakh
Kunayev had cause to be suspicious too. As for the Central Committee
which would be asked to vote for the Politburo's nominee, its average
member in his sixties had more in common with someone like Grishin than
with the less predictable younger man. It soon became part of Moscow lore
that Gromyko had also said that Gorbachov had a nice smile but teeth of
steel. Perhaps this was meant to reassure those who wondered whether
Gorbachov was tough enough to stand up to the country's enemies abroad.
But the prospect of a sharp-toothed young leader who had already shown his
colours by his close cooperation with the puritan Andropov cannot have
reassured the old Brezhnev establishment.

What happened when the Politburo met the night of Chernenko's death
and the Central Committee gathered the next day was never officially
revealed. It was obvious both meetings had been called in unusual haste.
Three members were unable to attend the session of the Politburo.
Shcherbitsky was in America; Vorotnikov in Yugoslavia; and Kunayev
could not get to the capital in time from distant Kazakhstan. One unofficial
version, though, did emerge of what happened among the seven who were
present (Aliyev, Gorbachov, Grishin, Gromyko, Romanov, Tikhonov,

Solomentsev). Not surprisingly it showed Gorbachov in a good light and his competitors in a bad one, for like most Moscow rumours it supported the man who was making the running. But it was a not incredible script for such a meeting. It had Gromyko proposing Gorbachov as general secretary and Grigori Romanov counter-proposing the candidacy of Grishin. But, this version went, Grishin's candidacy was hopelessly muddied by a dossier submitted to Politburo members by the KGB. This listed the investigations going on into the wide-spread corruption and misgovernment in Moscow, and may also have included personal files on both Grishin and his son Aleksandr. The summoning of the Central Committee the next day meant that Shcherbitsky missed that too (it was even said that steps were taken to delay his plane), leaving its large contingent of Ukrainian members without a leader. Chebrikov, the KGB chief, was again in evidence and was even said to have left the meeting in the same car with Gorbachov.

Such stories have something in common with myths. Their details may not be correct but they can contain a general truth. In this case the identification of Grishin with the dubious past was accurate. The picking out of Chebrikov as one of Gorbachov's knights was also accurate enough. Later that year, when he had already been promoted to full Politburo membership, he was to deliver one of the strongest calls for change to come from any of the leaders other than Gorbachov. As far as was known the KGB was not affected by the personnel changes that would sweep almost every other branch of the Soviet government in the year to come. The story also made it plain that the fight between the forces of good and evil had been a close run thing. Whether Grishin really had a chance of beating Gorbachov is debatable. One knowledgeable Russian commented at the time that if the Central Committee had conducted a secret ballot on the two men Grishin might have won. But that was not the practice. Gromyko, on the Politburo's authority, proposed just one name to the Committee – Gorbachov's. Even so, though the Central Committee was officially said to have elected Gorbachov 'unanimously', the Russian word picked was the less precise of the two that could have been used. It was possible to interpret this as meaning that not everyone had raised his hand in support of Gorbachov. In the atmosphere of rumour and uncertainty that surrounded the choice of a new leader this was bound to be seen as evidence that there had been opposition to Gorbachov. True or false, the speculation served to make the point that there had been a struggle among the gods on the mountain top of the Kremlin, and that the new order was experiencing a difficult birth.

Gorbachov was beset with all the disadvantages a new Soviet leader had to expect. His senior colleagues were there by their own right, not by his choice. Remodelling the most important organs of party and government was like altering a house already built by other hands: a slow and not very satisfactory business. When in April he was able to make his first promotions to the Politburo the three men he chose to advance to full membership

(Chebrikov, the party organization man Yegor Ligachov, and the industrial expert Nikolai Ryzhkov) were among those who had first been spotted by Andropov. They might agree with most of what Gorbachov wanted to do but they were not his men. Gorbachov needed somehow to surprise and even shock the country. The days had gone when a Stalin could force a passive population, ill-educated and poor, to do what he wanted. As Gorbachov had said in his speech in December, today's Soviet people were different. They had to be reasoned with. The knack was showing a readiness to do this without destroying the image of a strong leader. That at least was Gorbachov's formula. In one of his first speeches as general secretary he was to say that people disliked immodesty and ostentation in their leaders. It was necessary 'to get closer to people, to have more trust in them', but this did not mean 'playing up to them. People don't like leaders like that. People like strict leaders, who are organized, demanding, caring and who show by their personal example a conscientious attitude to the business of the state.'

Leaders of this kind, Gorbachov said, would always find support. Many Russians would probably have agreed. A more cynical version of the Gorbachov formula was offered by a shrewd Muscovite. People wanted a strong leader who would frighten the little bosses they had to deal with in their everyday life. As long as they felt a leader could make the lower bureaucracy tremble and behave better they would not bother much about what else went on at the very top. It was not so different from the attitude expressed in the old proverb: 'Oppression comes not from the Tsars but from the Tsars' favourites.'

The least of Gorbachov's problems was dissociating himself from the previous leadership. The unusual speed with which he had been chosen to head the party meant that the news of his appointment could appear on the front pages of the papers while the announcement of Chernenko's death was pushed onto the second page. Chernenko's funeral was not allowed to interfere with the business of the state. And the late leader's diminution in death was made shamingly plain when the list of places and organizations to be re-named in his honour was published. Brezhnev's name had been given to a big new town where the most modern Soviet truck, the Kamaz, was built. The old Volga River town of Rybinsk lost its name to Andropov who had studied there as a young man. Chernenko's name was to be perpetuated by a town no one seemed to have heard of called Sharypovo. It turned out to be a small place in his home territory of Krasnoyarsk. The army apparently objected to having his name attached to anything to do with it though military units had been called after both his predecessors. Chernenko only got the KGB frontier unit where he had served as a young man. The habit of changing the names of old towns to accommodate dead politicians was becoming increasingly unpopular, particularly with the Russian intelligentsia, and it would not be long before it was possible to criticize it publicly. The unpopularity of calling a well-known place after Chernenko would have been immense when people were already preparing to question the desirability of sacrificing old Russian place names even for much more respected leaders like Dmitri Ustinov and Yuri Andropov.

Gorbachov hit upon two ways to project the image of the strong leader who cared. The first was in the style of Andropov, the second was pure Gorbachov. Rumours of the first move began as soon as it was learned that the Politburo at its meeting in the beginning of April had agreed on a new set of measures to combat drunkenness and alcoholism. The official announcement gave no idea how far-reaching these measures would be, but male Muscovite drinkers, which meant most Moscow men, needed no help in imagining the horrors that were being prepared. Some swore there would be complete prohibition, recalling the partial prohibition introduced by the Tsarist government at the beginning of the First World War, and whose abolition in the twenties earned the Soviet prime minister of the day the honour of having vodka christened 'Rykovka' after him. Others insisted vodka would be rationed, or its price doubled. Everyone expected that the punishments for drunkenness would be made much more severe.

The rumours were most likely officially encouraged for they exaggerated the severity of the measures eventually published in May and thus softened the blow. A curious *samizdat* document claiming to be a report from the Siberian branch of the Academy of Sciences had the same effect. Leaked to foreign journalists in the winter, quite ordinary Muscovites had got to know about it by the spring. It was dramatic stuff, claiming the country already had forty million 'alcoholics and drunkards' and forecasting that two thirds of all adults would belong in that category by the end of the century unless drastic measures were taken.

'Why should anyone wage war on us,' its anonymous author asked, 'if in twelve to fifteen years we will disappear as a sovereign state – a state in which more than half the adult population consists of alcoholics and drunkards is neither competent nor capable of defending itself?'

The writer kept his most chilling forecast for the Russian nation which he claimed was doing by far the most damage to itself. He gave details of the growing number of Russian children born with defects because of alcoholic parents, and predicted that by 1990 fifteen per cent of all children would have to be in schools for the handicapped. 'This degeneration of our people is a process that will wipe us as a nation from the face of the earth.' Alcohol was destroying the Russians. It was what Hitler had ordered for the Slavs in *Mein Kampf* – no hygiene, just vodka and tobacco. 'This mandate of Hitler is now being fulfilled.'

The document was obviously no scientific report. It is not out of the question that the KGB had a hand either in its preparation or dissemination for its exaggerations – foreign experts doubted the figure of forty million alcoholics and a good deal else – were a much more powerful justification of the planned new measures than the guarded and bitty reporting of the official press. It was not the first time that official reluctance to allow a full picture to be given of social problems made it harder to prepare people to fight them. The full impact of alcohol on Soviet society was, at that time, hidden by the unwillingness of the government to publish figures for life expectancy of men (which foreign experts calculated had fallen) and infant mortality (believed to have risen). Drug addiction was another growing problem for which society was unprepared because until 1986 almost nothing was allowed to be written about it.

The report on alcohol reflected a very real alarm among part of the intelligentsia which had been expressed by, among others, the writer Rasputin in his story *The Fire*. Women who learned of it were easily impressed since vodka caused them so much suffering. Drinking husbands were a major cause of the rising divorce rate, and only forty per cent of marriages now lasted more than three years. The measures, when they were announced in May, were more moderate than the alarmists had forecast. They included a ban on sale of alcohol to those under twenty-one; fewer liquor shops and those to open only at two o'clock in the afternoon; no sale of liquor near schools, factories and other public places. Fines for drunkenness were increased. A man caught drunk in public twice in one year could be condemned to up to two months' corrective labour with a fifth of his wages withheld.

The campaign bore the new leader's mark. It did not try, in what was to be only its first stage, to do too much – Gorbachov argued that complete prohibition did not work – but even so it made a sharp impact on Soviet life. To see Russians standing in the long queues that became common at most liquor stores regardless of the weather was to realize that the whip of government was once again in a firm hand. It was a striking example of how new laws that affected most Soviet citizens could be introduced with almost no warning and no public discussion whatsoever. It was an example, too, of how a determined leader could expect to make a large part of the government and party machine jump at his command, even in matters that might be thought to concern their private lives. Apart from the new penalties and administrative measures the Central Committee issued a decree which declared any drinking – not just drunkenness – in any organization or on any official occasion to be 'absolutely impermissible'. Anyone in a position of authority in the party, government and the economy would be sacked if he showed a weakness for drink or allowed subordinates to hold 'drinking parties'.

People joked about the new rules. The rough beer bars where serious drinkers gathered were christened 'the last hotbeds of resistance'. Gorbachov was referred to not as the general, but the mineral, secretary. But the evidence in Moscow was that many white-collar workers and officials did try to change old habits. It was partly because they knew the problem had reached such alarming national proportions. But it was also because they were afraid. The government had made its weight felt in a way that had not happened since Andropov sent the militia out to scour the shops and cinemas of Moscow for people who ought to have been at work. Gorbachov set an example himself. It had been noted that when travelling abroad neither he nor his wife had touched alcohol. Her influence in this matter was thought to be particularly strong. His home village was one of the first districts to ban the sale of alcohol. Stories were soon circulating which, whether true or false, painted Gorbachov as a leader of a new and more demanding type. A well-known writer was fascinated by an account he had heard of how when the Central Committee, after Gorbachov's election, sat down to a meal together the new general secretary had declined to join them. He had no time, he said, and he advised the Committee members also to return to their duties as soon as possible. But it was not enough to rely on anecdotes to publicize the example of brisk responsibility that Gorbachov obviously wanted to set. The method he picked was both traditional and new: he showed himself to the people, but he used television to make sure that the novelty of his style and message got across to as much of the population as possible.

The campaign to project the new leader was carefully prepared. At first it seemed that he was avoiding publicity rather than seeking it. Like Andropov before him, Gorbachov stopped the practice of quotations from his speeches being used as an authority in any newspaper article of weight (the story about Andropov ringing up the editor of *Pravda* to suggest he quote Lenin instead was soon being told about Gorbachov). The press no longer published pictures of the leader's meetings with important foreign visitors as a matter of course. Even when in April Gorbachov spent two days touring Moscow not a single photograph appeared in the press. Television news carried only still photographs of the tour, although Soviet television cameramen were said to have filmed all of it. This near-secrecy about a visit which was apparently meant to show Gorbachov's concern about the living and working conditions of ordinary people was puzzling for it was not so obvious then that his relations with Grishin, who as Moscow party leader had to accompany him, were deteriorating rapidly. It is also possible that Grishin had tried to make sure that Gorbachov saw only a Potyomkin or counterfeit Moscow. That was the tradition which under Brezhnev the leaders had come to put up with quite knowingly. It was said that Gorbachov managed to have some revealing conversations nevertheless. Muscovites particularly enjoyed what the head surgeon of the hospital he visited was supposed to have told him. Grishin had sent men the day before to prepare the hospital but the surgeon nevertheless complained that he had to do most of the operations because one of his colleagues was too young and the other usually drunk. He added that he was paid only five roubles (about four pounds) for each operation while some of his nurses were earning under half the average wage.

It was only when Gorbachov flew with his wife to Leningrad in the middle of May that he was seen to break with the liturgical style of leadership that had suited a leadership of old men. That the visit would be unusual was obvious the moment the Gorbachovs landed. After suggesting that the customary flowers with which he was presented ought rather to be given to women, Gorbachov took the Leningrad leader Lev Zaikov aside and rearranged the programme for the visit. Even so, he was to break away from the new schedule on several occasions, going to look around ordinary food shops that the local authorities had not smartened up for his visit. After laying a wreath at a new war memorial he went into a crowd that included many old soldiers, to shake hands and talk. Walkabouts were not new in Soviet politics. Khrushchov had done them compulsively. Brezhnev also enjoyed walkabouts of a more decorous and self-congratulatory kind as long as he was fit enough. Gorbachov said he had done the same thing in Stavropol. But he was the first Soviet leader to understand television's power to turn these occasions into political propaganda. Attempts to teach Brezhnev to learn a modern television technique were not successful. He had been offended by the suggestion that he had anything to learn. Television had been too primitive in Khrushchov's time to be of much use to him. Only one in four families had a set by the time he fell from power. In 1985 almost every family had one. The nine o'clock evening news was watched by over half the population and was probably the most important moulder of public attitudes to both Soviet and foreign affairs. Television was at last ready for a Soviet leader who knew how to exploit the camera. Gorbachov, in Leningrad, showed that he meant to seize the chance.

The first Leningrad pictures were shown the day after his arrival. The evening news ran twenty minutes of his visits to factories and exhibitions, on one occasion accompanied by his wife, on whom the camera lingered. Gorbachov seemed lively, informal, and in complete control. The contrast with his predecessors could not have been greater. The biggest surprise that evening was film of him talking to people on one of Leningrad's squares. Although security men were present the conversation did not seem rehearsed. Gorbachov was shown surrounded by people, his south Russian accent sounding much stronger than when he was reading from a text. This was the man who had appeared on British television screens in December: a mobile, expressive face; gesturing hands; someone who knew he knew how to handle a crowd. Very few Soviet citizens had seen this Gorbachov before.

He told the crowd he had come to Leningrad to talk and to listen. A man called out that he should go on as he had started. Gorbachov then seemed to start to speak his mind, just as Khrushchov had so often done when talking informally in public. 'There is . . . one thing you should bear in mind. We are always obliged to keep accounts, just as you keep accounts in your families. [Murmurs of 'of course' from the crowd.] We have to live within our means. As they say: what we produce we will share . . .'

171

Perhaps not many Soviet viewers understood what he was getting at, but the idea that the country and each economic unit and worker within it should somehow be made fully to pay its way was to emerge as one of his strongest obsessions. He also told the little crowd pressed close around him about the new anti-alcohol measures that were on the point of being published. A woman called out, 'You should be closer to the people. We won't let you down;' to which he grinned and replied, amid laughter, 'How can I be any closer?'

That these few minutes of television film should have made such a strong impression said as much about the vast distance that had grown between the rulers and the ruled in the Soviet Union as they did about Gorbachov. That a leader was ready to let television show him being told to get 'closer to the people' was astonishing, but for many of those watching it must have been extremely satisfying too. It was during this visit to Leningrad that Gorbachov was supposed to have condemned officials who set off to work in grand columns of fast-moving cars that 'not even the Tsars would have allowed themselves'. The remark showed an awareness of the resentment that the leadership's grand remoteness had caused. 'To deserve an Order of Lenin,' a bitter Muscovite had said during the last days of Chernenko, 'you should walk around on your own two feet.' It was true that virtue had usually gone on foot in Russia: Jesus Christ (according to Russian poets), holy men, and the tormented Lev Tolstoi had all *walked* through its sad villages. One of the most curious stories about Gorbachov was that he had once got out of his car in Moscow to help an old woman across the street. A Soviet leader who went walkabout was showing his virtue in a way people understood and in Leningrad the response was also traditional. Men and women pressed letters and petitions on him. It was even said that 'among simple people' there had been half-whispers, half-prayers, of 'if only they don't kill him' – a reference to the assassination in 1934 of Sergei Kirov, the most popular leader Leningrad had ever known.

It may be imagined that the most important members of the Leningrad party gathered to hear Gorbachov speak on the last day of his visit in a mood of excitement and anxiety. Gorbachov's remark about leaders in fast cars was inevitably taken by Leningraders as a dig at their previous party chief Grigori Romanov. It was also seen as a slight that Romanov had not been asked to accompany Gorbachov to Leningrad, though he had been back there several times since his promotion to Moscow and on each occasion treated with greatest deference by the city authorities. The general secretary was to speak to the party in the Revolution's birthplace, in the very building, the Smolny, from which Lenin had masterminded its first stages. There was no better setting in the country for a leader who wanted to claim his place as heir to the 'best' Soviet traditions, the ones supposedly undefiled by both the publicized errors of the recent past and the still mostly unmentionable ones of the Stalin years. The impact of the speech can be guessed from the media's bewilderment about how to handle it. Television that evening showed Gorbachov talking but without any live sound. The papers the next day carried only a short and safe résumé of what he had said. The recording of Gorbachov speaking live was only broadcast after a delay of several days. People who saw it had their first glimpse of a party leader talking mostly without text and with unusual emotion and frankness about the country's problems.

Although Gorbachov used the speech to make points that were to prove fundamental in his thinking about new economic and social policies, its main impact was psychological. The strong, direct style was as important as the ideas about policy. An audience grown used to hearing speeches as predictable as the prayers its great-grandfathers listened to in church instead heard this:

It is obvious that all of us must restructure ourselves, all of us. I would even say everyone from worker to minister, to secretary of the party Central Committee, to the head of the government. Everyone has to master new methods and to understand there is no other way for us . . . The hardest stage is the stage of psychologically restructuring officials in the spirit of [these] new demands . . . You remember that before the war the older generations solved the problem of how to achieve in decades what other countries had taken centuries to do . . . We too have to do a great deal in a little time . . . Why can't we have a quiet life? . . . It's been almost seventy years of effort, so to speak, since [the] October [Revolution]. It would seem that it's possible to relax. No, comrades, history isn't giving us the chance, at least not now. And I don't know if it will . . . [The economy was growing at around only three per cent a year but] calculations show we need a minimum of four per cent. If we don't get four per cent – and really we need more – the question is – what do we do? Cut the rate of growth of the standard of living? . . . We can't go down that road . . . We are swimming in resources in the sense that we possess huge natural riches. These riches – forgive me for the sharp language – have corrupted us . . . [Factories work badly] but no one is ruined by it. True, comrades, it only seems like that. In a family you feel it when something is taken from your pocket, but if it's the state pocket then nobody feels it directly . . . We have a plan for housing repairs but try to repair your flat yourself, with your own means, and you'll certainly have to find a moonlighter. And he will steal the materials from a construction site so they are coming from the state funds anyway . . . Of course we must, as it were, give all our officials a chance to understand the demands of the moment and to restructure themselves. But he who doesn't want to restructure himself, more than that, puts a brake on the solution of new tasks, has simply got to get out of the way and not be a hindrance. We cannot put the interests of one man above the interests of the whole society . . . [Those] who are not capable of ensuring discipline and order . . . cannot occupy a leading post . . . Questions of moral order and social justice are being raised ever more sharply and persistently in every layer of our society. We in the Central Committee are aware of the acuteness of this . . .

It was here, at the end of his Smolny speech, that Gorbachov urged the Leningrad party to 'get closer to people, have more trust in them' and offered his definition of the 'strict' but just leader referred to above.

The trip to Leningrad was the first of four that Gorbachov made in the course of the summer, taking him to the Ukraine, Belorussia, and a double dash that included the Siberian oilfields and the grain lands of Kazakhstan. Speaking to steel men in Brezhnev's old base of Dnepropetrovsk he asked them whether they thought that the leadership's policy meant the country was 'turning too sharply'. When they called back that the policy was correct, he said he was glad because the Politburo had discussed the matter more than once and 'come to the final and irrevocable conclusion . . . that a different approach, a calmer one, will not do for us'. He repeated that people would be given time to understand the new demands being made on them 'but this in no way means we shall step back if anyone is not prepared or does not want to take part in this struggle'. In Siberia the oilfields were the perfect illustration of his point that the country had been corrupted by its wealth. The huge resources of oil and natural gas had encouraged wasteful exploitations for which a heavy price in unmet production targets was now being paid.

The visits allowed Gorbachov to dramatize problems and to demonstrate the party's concern for ordinary people's life and problems. Speaking in the Siberian oil capital of Tyumen he showed real anger recalling a conversation with a worker in Surgut in which he had learnt that the town of two hundred thousand people still had no cinema. 'What are the leaders thinking of?' he asked. He returned several times to the theme of truth, excoriating the ingrained habit (which some would say was Russian as much as Soviet Communist) of bragging and boasting to cover up mediocre results. Lenin, he told the oil workers, had said that 'in everything and always we must follow the truth, whatever it might be'. When the head of any great state talks about the need for truthfulness the prudent man tempers his pleasure with scepticism. But Gorbachov was showing by his travels and his determination to have some encounters, however limited, with ordinary citizens, that he understood how damaging the apartness and secretiveness of the system had become. At times he seemed to be searching for that elusive piece of gold every autocrat seeks – a sign of support for what he was doing. He said to a group of workers in Siberia: 'Without the workers' support no policy is worth anything. If it is not supported by the . . . working people, it is no policy, it is some far-fetched thing. Policy is policy when it expresses these pressing requirements and finds support among the people. That is policy. If the support is there . . . I ask this question everywhere.'

The men he was talking to of course said they supported him but incontestable proof of that was the one thing the Soviet system could not easily give him. The American industrialist Armand Hammer, who talked with Gorbachov after the disaster at the Chernobyl nuclear power plant had drawn Western criticism, reported the Soviet leader as asking: 'What are [Reagan and Shultz] trying to do to me? Create a breach between me and the Russian people?' It did not sound the question of a man who was absolutely sure of his popular support.

By the time Gorbachov got to Kazakhstan the trips had begun to have less impact and he made no more till the following spring. Perhaps he was aware that the interest in his style provoked by the days in Leningrad could in the long run only be sustained by an obvious improvement in people's daily life. But possibly there were other considerations. The media still seemed unsure how to handle the trips. The broadcasts of live speeches with the many impromptu passages were shortened and toned down by the newspapers. And Gorbachov, though obviously a man who could talk for an hour at the drop of a hat, did not want to look like the garrulous Khrushchov. Comment was not altogether favourable after a meeting he held with old Stakhanovite workers in Moscow in late summer and in which he continuously, though in a friendly way, interrupted the speeches of others. And in the longer run his solo virtuoso performances were pointless unless he could re-make that unique tool of government, the Soviet Communist party, somewhat in his image. That was the thought with which he had ended his speech in the Smolny.

As you will see from whatever the questions we have been touching on, to accelerate our movement, the movement of our locomotive, our great state, we have to start with improving every activity of our party, of all our officials. This is the main condition.

One new Soviet hero was not enough. Gorbachov needed hundreds of thousands.

15

Party Man

The party leadership of a great region along the Soviet coast is in crisis. It has sent off a merchant ship to collect expensive foreign equipment for a new port but one of the ship's engines has caught fire in a storm. What should be done? They can leave the captain to make his own decisions; or they can order him to declare an SOS with the chance that he might be rescued by a foreign ship which could claim part of the valuable cargo as salvage money. The region's first secretary supports the tougher choice: leave it to the captain. His number two, an older man, insists on the apparently more humane solution of ordering the SOS and saving the ship and crew at whatever the cost.

Shakhmatov, the first secretary, is an intellectual, a Ph.D who speaks three foreign languages. It is said of him that 'he's the first to spot the mistake in any plan or model. And he's also the first to find a solution'. His refusal to order the ship's captain to ask for help turns out to be the reverse of callous. He believes that times have changed. He says people have become mature and want to lead their own lives. They are fed up with constant interference. They should be allowed to feel themselves strong and independent. That is why he wants the captain to decide what he thinks best. His number two, Serebrennikov, has no time for such liberalism. He thinks people should do what they are told as they have always done in Russia. He mourns for the 'men of flint' who were the party leaders of the past. He tells Shakhmatov that he and his like are ruining the country. After they have been arguing he looks at his first secretary and says, 'I'm frightened for you'; to which Shakhmatov replies that it is necessary to love the people, 'not command them, but love them'.

The first secretary is vindicated when the captain saves the ship by his own efforts. Serebrennikov is shown to have had his own reasons for wanting to salvage the vessel whatever the cost: he had forced it to sail before full repairs had been carried out. Had it sunk he would have been held responsible. But Shakhmatov's victory is a close run thing. Had he been proved wrong his number two would have ruined him. The strain is too much for the first secretary. On the eve of going to Moscow where he is to take up an even more important appointment he dies of a heart attack.

The future nevertheless belongs to the Shakhmatovs. His type can be recognized in a new first secretary who returns to Siberia to run the region he was born in. Anton Sobolev is also well educated. He has worked abroad and knows how to drink bourbon on the rocks. Sobolev's behaviour in his first weeks in the job shocks most of his colleagues on the regional party committee. They do not like the way he insists on walking round the peasant market to check up on the prices and find out why some are so high. He horrifies his chauffeur by getting out of his official car to talk to people at the bus queues during the morning rush hour. His colleagues do not like his suggestion that they too should travel to work by bus. He is furious when one of his district first secretaries welcomes him with a pompous reception for which she has dragged schoolchildren out of their summer camp. He dazzles a peasant boy with his skill at solving Rubik's cube, not to show off but to make him realize that modern farmers must understand modern techniques. But above all he broods on the waste, and the sloppy, feckless management that has dragged down his Siberian homeland. 'Yes,' he's heard say to himself, 'yes, we live richly. We're trampling gold into the ground with our feet.'

Sadly these two competent, modest and trusting party leaders did not exist in real life. Shakhmatov was the hero of the play *Four times the size of France*, first performed in Moscow in 1982; Anton Sobolev appeared in a 1985 television drama based on a novel by the first secretary of the Soviet Writers' Union that was also later adapted for the stage. Nevertheless both fictional heroes were treated as though they were men of flesh and blood. 'Sobolev for me,' a party member said after seeing the stage version of his story, 'isn't just a literary or theatrical personage, he is my support, my close comrade.' *Pravda* ruled that Sobolev typified the 'party leader of the end of the twentieth century'. As for Shakhmatov, a powerful literary critic declared that he too personified 'the new type of party leader who has been formed in the very last years'. Shakhmatov's opponent, on the other hand, was judged to be a tragic figure, once a good public servant no doubt, but the product of earlier times whose harsh, wilful style no longer suited the present day.

The party was always badgering Soviet writers to produce role models, or 'positive heroes' as they were called in Moscow. But though the best writers (best, that is, in the judgement of the intelligentsia) paid little attention there were always some writers who tried to oblige. They did not draw types like Shakhmatov and Sobolev out of thin air. The latter's education and professional skills (though not, perhaps, their knowledge of foreign languages) were typical enough of the senior party officials of the 1980s. Almost all of their real-life counterparts, the secretaries of party committees at regional level, had higher education, compared to only two out of three thirty years earlier. The educational advance of officials on the party's next level down, the districts and towns, had been even greater. In the mid-fifties only a quarter of them had managed to get full higher education. By Gorbachov's day almost all of them had it. The party rank and file were better educated, too. In 1952, on the eve of Stalin's death, half of the party's membership had not even completed secondary school. Only one in ten had been to university. By 1983 three-quarters of the party had full secondary schooling and almost a third some kind of university degree.

The older Serebrennikovs who believed it was their duty to command and others' to obey were the product of a still-developing society ruled over by officials scarcely better qualified than the people they governed. They were a consequence of the joke played by history when it brought the world's first proletarian revolution to a country where most of the population were still illiterate peasants. But were not the party's own policies also partly responsible for its under-development? The self-imposed exclusiveness of the Bolsheviks in the 1920s had meant that educated left-wingers who did not subscribe to Lenin and then Stalin's line were pushed to the margins of Soviet life, if not eventually killed or put in prison. Stalin's purge in the 1930s destroyed many if not most of the party's best-qualified men and women. Official Soviet figures show the number of full party members declining from 2.2 million in 1933 to a low of 1.4 million after the purge's climax five years later. The war was another awful wound, though this time not self-inflicted. Party membership was higher at the end of it than at the beginning but that was because so many people joined during it. The best soldiers were allowed to become full members after only three months as a candidate and by the end of 1943 over half of both members and candidates were wearing uniform. Much of the party was thus directly exposed to the terrible casualties inflicted by the war. When it was over Stalin had to start re-building it again.

The Shakhmatovs and Sobolevs – and Mikhail Gorbachov, too – belonged to the first generation of party officials who had joined as young men and come to maturity in its service without some appalling interruption either from outside or from their own leadership. By the mid-1980s this was the experience of almost all party members: nine out of ten had joined since the end of the war. But it was doubtful that even this much more stable contemporary party had tapped all the talent of the country. Although the young Gorbachov could set off on a party career in the early fifties as though it were the natural thing to do, much of the intelligentsia would have nothing to do with the party while Stalin was still alive. Some were won over after the twentieth Party Congress in 1956 had begun to admit Stalin's crimes. Many, while not thinking of themselves as dissidents, still remained as alienated from the sour, bureaucratic face it acquired under Brezhnev as they were from the selective truths of official Marxism-Leninism.

The party's history, quite as tormented as the history of modern Russia itself, explained why it was so hard to find heroes there. Lenin was unmatchable perfection. What was needed were Communist apostles, saints and martyrs whom each new generation could look to as their 'support', their 'true comrade'. But, even when they existed, were they relevant? After Gorbachov came to power *Kommunist* printed a fiery editorial headlined: 'The good and pure name of a party member.' The model it proposed was Feliks Dzerzhinsky, founder of the Cheka and acknowledged inspiration to Yuri Andropov. *Kommunist* used the words of the German Communist Klara Zetkin to characterize 'Iron Feliks':

One thing was decisive: the revolutionary convictions in whose blazing fire all [his] outstanding characteristics reached full flower. For him these convictions were something holy, inviolable, a duty. In their name this man who was by nature kind and sympathetic could and even had to be strict, hard and implacable to others because in their service he was incomparably stricter, harder and more implacable towards himself. He worked passionately but absolutely methodically according to his conviction, free from the slightest sign of personal ambition . . . He never tried to seem what he was not. Everything was true and good in this revolutionary: his love and his hate; his inspiration and his anger; his words and his deeds.

The characterization rang true. It fitted the Communists' justification of what they had done. It flattered their view of themselves as rare and noble people. But did the modern Soviet Union need to be run by ascetics who suffered as they administered the most dreadful punishments in the name of the Revolution and died, exhausted, as Dzerzhinsky had, before reaching the age of fifty? Gorbachov and his right-hand man for party affairs Yegor Ligachov both had a puritan streak, not least where alcohol was concerned, but they did not come close to the image of men destroying themselves in the good of the cause, nor did it seem desirable that they should. The new party leader of Moscow, Boris Yeltsin, claimed to work from six in the morning till midnight, and sleep for only four hours. But he also claimed to be in excellent health, and certainly did not look as though he was wasting away. The problem was to transpose revolutionary fervour and glamour to the business of running a great modern state. In the spring of 1986 the Soviet media celebrated with unexpected enthusiasm the hundredth anniversary of the birth of Sergei Kirov. This was a very different character from Dzerzhinsky: handsome, popular, and lively. 'The devil take it' (one of the papers printed this remark of his under a photograph of a boyish, smiling

Kirov) 'but, speaking as a human being, one just wants to live and live.' Was Kirov a better model for the present? 'It is hard today for us to believe,' a modern Leningrad worker was quoted as saying, 'but that's how it was: every working man in Leningrad used to know Kirov. Informal, friendly relations linked him to dozens of people who worked at factory benches. Today our leaders and engineers consult with their computers rather than with flesh and blood workers – what a retreat from Kirov's style!'

Kirov sounded suspiciously like the Gorbachov who had amazed Leningraders by going out to talk with them during his visit in 1985. Kirov, too, delivered his speeches from notes, as Gorbachov had done at the Smolny. Both men could be charmers. An old Bolshevik who had known Kirov confirmed that he had been 'a big-hearted, charming man'. But it should not be forgotten, he added, that he was not just a 'nice fellow'. Kirov could also be 'stern and even severe'. That, too, sounded like the man whose winning smile was said to conceal teeth of steel.

But there was a problem about any model taken from the Stalin era. It was uncomfortable to make too much of either its villains or its victims. Kirov was generally supposed (though not officially acknowledged) to have been one of the latter. Nothing had come of the enquiry promised by Khrushchov into his assassination, probably because it would have been too embarrassing. Finding heroes in recent history was not easier. It was strongly rumoured that an article would be published in April 1984 on the ninetieth anniversary of Khrushchov's birth – his family seemed to have expected it – but nothing appeared. Chernenko's unexpected succession may have been the cause. But perhaps it was because Khrushchov's career was still too controversial. It would have been impossible to approve of everything he had done, and official history was not ready for mixed assessments, even though some party intellectuals would have liked to make it so, and by 1986 were saying it in the pages of *Pravda*. By far the safest heroes that could be salvaged from earlier times were the predecessors of Serebrennikov and Shakhmatov, fictional ones, though many of those were only likely to appeal to adolescents in the first ecstasy of political romanticism.

The truth was that the men whom Gorbachov wanted to see running the Communist party no longer had much in common with their predecessors. They were incomparably better qualified and much more secure. They belonged to a meritocracy in some ways like that of any other modern state, and no longer had either the need or the taste to live on the edge of risk. But the casting back for models from the old days pointed to an important truth. The people who ran the party might be different. The pretensions of the party were not. They had even grown: from being the mastermind of a revolution that might easily have failed it had become the mastermind of a nuclear super-power. The small but tough machine that Lenin devised to make and run a revolution, and which Stalin hi-jacked to build the foundations of a modern state, had grown so richly into every corner of the country's life that, like some giant sea creature fastened round a great rock, it now seemed impossible to tear the two apart.

There were different opinions as to the nature of the creature for, like many large beasts, it was shy of strangers. Foreigners were seldom allowed near it. Its lair could easily be spotted travelling round the country. It was usually the most solid, and sometimes the best designed, building in any town or village, and with a red and gold sign on the door. The party's own household invariably looked clean and orderly, whatever the confusion around it. The senior inhabitants of these lairs that did present themselves to foreign eyes usually smelled of authority. Self-assured, well-groomed, glowing from that rare tonic power gives men particularly as they grow older, they were at once recognizable as politicians – a species not normally admitted to exist in the Soviet Union. They were often impressive. When one of the great barons like the first secretary of the Siberian region of Tyumen, home of the world's greatest oilfield of Samotlor, was allowed to meet foreigners the latter might go away very impressed indeed.

A foreigner also sensed the party's watchfulness. When a much-decorated chairman of a prize collective farm showed a visitor round his fields he was accompanied by a silent young man with beautiful cow's eyes – the emissary of the district party committee. The young man said almost nothing, but he watched and listened all the time. There were occasions when one could feel this watchfulness making others wary. A junior official from the Central Committee in Moscow sat in on a meeting of Soviet and foreign academics and journalists. He would have passed unnoticed in the street, for this was a man who did not have the superficial polish of power. He could have been any stocky Russian at the onset of stoutness and middle age. But his unremarkable face was shrewd. He smoked without end and like the squire's wife at a tenants' tea party knew how to keep his distance even when socializing. He was watching too. At the end of the meeting he drove off in a black Volga. Everyone else climbed into a bus.

Such impressions may even have underestimated the party's 'apartness' at the end of Brezhnev's rule. Viktor Grishin, later excoriated for allowing fine old buildings to be destroyed, had new headquarters put up for Moscow's district parties and, appropriately though surely unintentionally, they mostly looked like little fortresses. It was not only foreigners who found it difficult to get into them. An agronomist who wanted to talk to his regional party about a technical problem in local farming was barred by the doorman from entering its headquarters. The doorman explained that a party card did not give the visitor an automatic right of entry. The agronomist telephoned the first secretary's office and was told that he had to apply in writing for an appointment. He dashed off a postcard, only to get a telephone call instructing him to lay out the matter fully in writing. The last telephone call from the party leader's office informed him that he could not have an appointment with anyone, and that was that. It even happened that secretaries of primary party organizations (the lowest level elected party official) could not manage to see the men in regional headquarters. And those that did get inside party headquarters risked a painful rap on the knuckles if their opinions were unwelcome, as Gorbachov himself once explained: 'A Communist speaks his mind or tries to share his doubts in a town or district party committee and instead of answering his point they say "Don't forget where you are". And where in point of fact is he? In his own home. Where should he go with his worries and problems if not to his own party committee?'

The problem lay in the party committees and their staffs, starting with the Central Committee in Moscow (whose main old building was known before the Revolution as Nobleman's Court) and spreading down the pyramid of command to the districts. What exactly went on in these Committee headquarters? Theirs was a complicated secrecy. They were sanctuaries of the Revolution, accessible only to the most highly initiated. They were old-fashioned smoke-filled rooms where politics was done on the quiet according to principles established by man long before 1917. For that reason, too, they had to be closed to outsiders. And they were centres of bureaucratic power which, like all bureaucracies, could only be inconvenienced by publicity. In turns servile and obstructive to those above them, it sometimes seemed there was nothing a party committee would not do to put tiresome subordinates in their place. A scientist called Chabanov who had designed a new and much-acclaimed machine tool was appointed to run a factory where he was able to put his new model into production. The local party committee (and the ministry in Moscow) decided he had exceeded his instructions, sacked him and ordered a criminal enquiry into his behaviour. The Central Committee in Moscow intervened to help him. The regional committee, unabashed, proceeded to expel him from the party. When a letter protesting this was sent to the party congress then about to meet in the capital the local leaders had it removed from the post. And this took place not in the 'dark' Brezhnev years but after Gorbachov had come to power.

What the French call *déformation professionelle* was at work. The party was organized in such a way as to leave its officials at the mercy of superiors but with the power to terrorize their own inferiors. The key lay in the system of appointments, with Moscow making the most important (such as regional party and government leaders) while the least important (like directors of a state farm or the chairman of a village council) were left to party district chiefs. We have seen how this could result in the sort of mafia that was discovered in Sergei Medunov's Krasnodar. What it most ordinarily resulted in was constant interference in the local economy by party officials whose advancement depended on satisfying those above. The party official who prospered was the one who got good economic results. Other matters, like housing, social services, even food supplies, were of minor importance as long as the production figures were right. Here was an explanation of the dreary and uncomfortable life of so many Soviet cities, and which Gorbachov and his advisers eventually spotted as a problem that affected production through people's morale. Running the economy was not meant to be the party's business. There was a government and a corps of industrial and agricultural managers for that. But since the latter were appointed by the party, and since the latter's success also determined the success of their party masters, it was not surprising that the party had become a sort of super-government. Even the Central Committee department that was supposed to watch over the most important personnel appointments – the essence of party work, in Gorbachov's view – had ended up worrying about 'railways trucks and cattle feed and fuel'.

Everyone knew this was wrong. The papers wrote many a cautionary tale about the phenomenon. Party leaders regularly attacked it: it was even one of Chernenko's hobby horses. But none of it had much effect because the defect was built into the system. The chairman of the collective farm mentioned earlier took it for granted that men from regional party headquarters would call by with instructions. One of them told him to increase his acreage under clover. Why, asked the chairman. 'Because there's an order from above.' The chairman protested he already had several hundred acres of clover. 'Make it fifteen hundred for a round figure' he was told, and advised to 'trim back' his maize to make space. The chairman explained he could not do this because he needed the maize to feed his dairy herd. 'Luckily,' he commented later, 'this chap was sensible and we managed to convince him.' If this was the way one of the most successful farmers in the Soviet Union (and a two-times Hero of Socialist Labour) was treated it can be imagined what happened with the average ones. What happened was that they were constantly sacked. It was not uncommon even in parts of the country where the farming was good for four out of five farm chiefs to be replaced every five years or so. If a party official could not present his superiors with the figures of a bumper crop he could always give him the supposedly guilty men's heads. Not surprisingly industrial and farm managers who lacked confidence preferred to let others, and above all the party, make decisions for them. It was not unknown for a farmer to have fields full of ripe barley but only to harvest them when he was told to. If farms and factories got into difficulty they naturally ran to their party superiors for help, rather than look for a solution themselves. It was the safest thing to do.

Party organizations bossed their party inferiors just as busily as they bossed the government and economic managers. This was the plaint of a district party secretary:

It's easy to work out in the sticks nowadays, you don't have to think or guess anything for yourself. You sometimes even ask yourself why you and your comrades are in the district. After all, everything's foreseen for you. They tell you by special letter or telegram or telephone when to put fertiliser on the fields, or to begin collecting scrap metal, when to start the harvest, how . . . to work the fields, when and which cattle to sell, even what the copper content of the scrap metal must be . . .

Instructions to those outside the party apparatus were most conveniently given by telephone which left no bureaucratic trace and was thus excellently matched to the party's ghostly but unchallengeable role. The telephone lent itself to misuse but it was essentially a routine instrument of party rule. At the time of Khrushchov's fall a Moscow publishing house received an urgent call from the Central Committee. The voice, which as usual expected to be recognized without identifying itself, enquired about a new history textbook soon to be released that unfortunately included the deposed leader's picture. On learning it had already been distributed the voice ordered the book's instant recall and the offending photograph removed. It ignored a question about the cost of such an operation. 'This is a political decision.' Sometimes the voice, at the start of a conversation, commanded 'write this down'. The Central Committee did not have to commit anything to paper.

The ghostliness of the party's movements just as often led to the other extreme – a fantasy world in which the holding of meetings and issuing of decrees (even on such matters as how to hold a brass band festival) passed for real work. Over seven months the agricultural department of one district headquarters received from its regional superior five hundred and seventy-two instructions by letter, eighty-two 'radiograms' and thirty-two telegrams, most of them urging the district to show 'initiative and independence'. Little time was left for anything else, and certainly not for getting about the town or countryside to see what was going on. The fantasy was usually maintained even in the closed party gatherings where rank-and-file members were meant to be able to speak their mind. It was common practice for all speeches to be vetted before delivery and critical remarks removed. Party members who could not be trusted to be discreet were simply not given the floor. A veteran of such gatherings passed on the advice that 'criticising the powers-that-be is like kissing a tiger'. It was scarcely an exaggeration. In some regions it had become taken for granted that rank-and-file members who tried to criticize the leadership risked punishment and even expulsion from the party. The party's secretiveness helped those of its members who were rascals. But it also seemed proper to the virtuous who, like the members of large organizations anywhere, preferred their public image to be spotless. They argued that any discussion about an unsatisfactory or dishonest official, and also any punishment inflicted on him, was best kept a private party matter. Silence about such matters had been almost absolute for years, from the top of the party down to the bottom.

If it were plain what the party ought not to be, what was its proper role? What, for example, did a good regional secretary actually do? A rare Soviet account described some days in the life of Vladislav Mysnichenko, first secretary of the Kharkov region, an aviation engineer appointed to the job in 1980 at the age of fifty-one after working for the famous aeroplane designer Tupolev. A Soviet journalist accompanied Mysnichenko to a three-hour meeting at the Kharkov tractor factory which had been criticized for under-using its machinery (a common failing). Other participants were the factory director, the head of the regional party committee's agricultural machinery department, and the head of the factory's own party organization. The four men had 'a complicated discussion' about people: who should be put in what job, how production units in difficulty might be helped, and 'especially' about the education of the younger workers. Mysnichenko promised to be back in two months to check up on what had been done. Before leaving he ticked off the factory party secretary for having recently made a speech in Kharkov rather than take a tour of a similar factory in a nearby city that was getting better results.

The next day Mysnichenko had a two-hour meeting with a minister from Moscow whose visits usually meant he wanted to expand one of his factories in the city. The two ended up talking all day, filling the first secretary's office with their cigarette smoke. The minister, as expected, wanted to enlarge one of his plants. The dispute had been about his reluctance to pay for the additional housing and social infrastructure that would be necessary. He hoped to leave that to the city. It was an attitude, Mysnichenko complained, that 'created very acute social problems', meaning discontented workers without proper housing, shops, and schools. In the end the first secretary got his way.

Later that day he spoke to a conference of the secretaries of the so-called primary party organizations in farms and factories. These were the most junior of all party organizations, whose secretaries were not yet and might never become professional apparatchiks. He spoke for an hour without referring to his notes and 'without sounding didactic'. He talked about the need for farms to economize on fuel. He criticized those in the audience who were reluctant to report the mistakes of their farm or factory management. It was understandable, he said, because if the party secretary failed to be re-elected to the job he might find himself at the mercy of a revengeful boss. But they shouldn't worry. The party would not abandon them. They were, after all, the regional committee's 'main assistants', its point men in the party's endless struggle. A day or two later Mysnichenko convened for the first time a joint meeting of the region's senior party officials with the committee members of its subordinate towns and districts. There had been a scandal in one of the districts: two top members of the district government, both party members, had used their influence to build big houses for themselves. The sense of the meeting was that it would be enough to give them a warning. Mysnichenko insisted they be expelled from the party and that the district first secretary himself be removed from his job. Mysnichenko said he did not doubt the latter's personal honesty, but as party secretary he had to answer for others too. 'This is our chief concern in the party. And he forgot about it.'

As an aviation expert Mysnichenko had an educated interest in science and technology and he chaired a regular meeting of academics and party and government officials to monitor their progress in Kharkov. He was in his element, guiding the meeting with expert skill. The journalist noted approvingly that the first secretary only allowed meetings of this kind to start after five o'clock in the evening, when the participants' ordinary work day was over. The journalist last saw Mysnichenko at the funeral of a war-time hero who had fought in a famous battle just outside Kharkov. When the first secretary was told that the coffin would be one and a half hours late 'the expression on his face changed for the first time' – until he understood the reason. The old soldier's neighbours had insisted on carrying him all the way down the long street he lived on because it was named after the unit he had fought in. The first secretary was silent for a moment and then said quietly, 'Yes, the veterans are leaving us . . . Now it's up to us not to delay with help, attention and care for the living.'

This was party man as Gorbachov might have described him: chastising yet caring, inspiring yet watchful, and never doing other people's jobs for them. Put in heavier, more official but carefully chosen words (they are taken from Gorbachov's report to the party congress in February 1986) the recipe sounded like this:

> The party carries out political leadership and determines the overall perspective of development. It formulates the chief tasks in the socio-economic and spiritual spheres of life, and engages in the selection and deployment of personnel and their overall supervision. As for the ways and means of solving specific economic and socio-cultural questions, every unit of management, every work collective and all economic cadres have here a wide freedom of choice.

The system was familiar to anyone acquainted with a mildly progressive English school. The headmaster (or general secretary), his housemasters (the regional secretaries) and the rest of the staff (the lesser party officials) tried to prepare the pupils to accept as much responsibility as possible. They chose the senior pupils who were to be charged with running much of the school's daily life. They picked the captains of the sports teams and the heads of the various school societies but then, while keeping an eye on them, left them as much as possible on their own. The aim of the school's programme of intellectual and moral education was to make the boys and girls do voluntarily what the headmaster and his senior colleagues had already decided was best for them. Every technique was pressed into service. There were inspirational lectures and learning by rote. The pupils were encouraged to compete among themselves. Group pressures were brought to bear on the lazy and uninterested. The masters were proud of their pupils – they insisted they were the best in the world – but they never seemed to imagine that one day they might wish to leave school. Indeed the punishment of last resort was expulsion, for the school did not accept that it had a responsibility towards those who remained completely indifferent to its goals (the Russian-born philosopher Isaiah Berlin liked to compare the Soviet press to British school magazines: 'There's a lot about the matches we won, not very much about the matches we lost and of course no criticism of the masters').

If Gorbachov ever had doubts about the system he had been brought up in and in which his family had prospered he never showed it. On the contrary, he spoke as a man who had inherited a marvellous machine, which if properly overhauled would work wonders. 'We have a powerful economy,' he said in an impromptu passage in a speech in 1985, 'the most powerful advanced science, a qualified working class and educated people – a people possessing ample love of the homeland. Finally, we have such a powerful force as the party, which is capable of skilfully holding on course our socialist ship and our Soviet society.'

And the party, on paper, was a powerful force. It had nineteen million members by 1986, some seven per cent of the Soviet population. The biggest group were workers (over forty-four per cent in 1983) but white-collar workers and professionals followed only a percentage point behind. Collective farm peasants made up the remainder. The party's officer corps was headed by the Central Committee in Moscow with its staff of a few thousand career apparatchiks. At the lower levels it included over 400,000 members who served on the party committees of the republics down to the district and town committees (all of these were also serviced by permanent staffs whose numbers were not revealed). But the party's power – and it was this that sometimes seemed most to excite Gorbachov – lay in its ability to permeate all parts of Soviet society from the bottom up as well as from the top down. The Central Committee had its departments that watched over the country's scientific and cultural intelligentsia: more important was its very high membership in those groups. One out of three specialists with higher or special secondary education belonged to the party. So did every other writer, one out of three composers, one out of five painters and sculptors, and three-quarters of all journalists. The party penetrated every Soviet institution. Two and a half million men and women sat on party committees in factory workshops. There were over two million members on the committees of the primary party organizations that were set up at every workplace, from ministries in Moscow to the most distant collective farm lost down roads that turned to mud each spring and autumn.

If only this huge army could be mobilized to make sure that everyone did what the leadership in Moscow wanted. Gorbachov imagined every party member playing the schoolmaster. He would set an irreproachable example in everything, including his private life ('daily life is also party work,' Yegor Ligachov liked to say). He would advise, encourage and keep others up to the mark. Ideally the inadequate collective farm chairman would be assisted by the farm's party committee just as the greatest minister in Moscow – or marshal in the army, for that matter – would be kept on virtue's path by an alert party organization that could neither be suborned nor intimidated (Gorbachov complained these committees especially in ministries had lost their 'political acumen' and usually 'backed away' from their right to monitor their ministers' performance). As for those leaders who turned out to be corrupt or hopelessly incompetent, it was the duty of ordinary party members to blow the whistle on them first. The party was designed to be as deadly to the bad official as the boulevards of nineteenth-century Paris to the insurrectionary: fire was to be poured on the quarry from all directions. It should have given Moscow a power of control over the execution of its policies that no government in the West could hope to match. But as everyone knew, and as it began to be admitted publicly after Brezhnev's death, the party did not work like this and had never really had a chance to. Far from being a disciplined brotherhood of equals in which each member had the right to speak his mind, it had become over the last two decades a federation of power groups, often no more enlightened than a great oriental bureaucracy and on occasions almost as crooked as any mafiadom.

There were precedents for how to re-make a party to the leader's wishes. Stalin had destroyed the large part of it he distrusted. An impatient Khrushchov had in the end broken all party principles by dividing it into agricultural and industrial sections and trying to make it a tool of economic management. In China a restless Mao Zedong had let the Cultural Revolution loose on a party he thought had become bureaucratized. It was a measure of the development of the Soviet Union that such drastic options were not available to Gorbachov. His choice, perhaps the only realistic one, was to make use of the greater sophistication of the party's membership by giving them more say in how it was run. That the idea appealed to a good many party members was shown in the weeks before the 1986 congress during a discussion on amendments to the party's rules. In letters published in the party press Soviet Communists argued that the time had come for recognizably democratic elections at least in the primary party organizations.

The old rules had provided for secret elections to party committees at all levels, but the candidates, one for each post to be filled, were chosen by the party organization above. Anton Sobolev may have been an ideal leader of the new type but the television drama he appeared in plainly showed that he was picked by Moscow while his Siberian region remained in ignorance about it until he stepped off the plane. The usual practice was for a representative of the superior party organization to arrive at the election meeting and announce the nominee without informing anyone else. Sometimes, though rarely, a question or two was asked about the new man. Then the meeting was asked to vote for him, even though the candidate might be an unknown quantity to all those taking part. There were cases when the officially chosen candidates in elections in primary organizations failed to get the necessary fifty-one per cent of the votes, but it was not easy to vote against the selected candidate. Voting took place under the eyes of the local party leaders and there was no way to cross out the name without it being seen. Some party members would have liked the ballot papers to be marked with 'for' and 'against' boxes that had to be checked. Others wanted closed voting booths like the ones used in local government elections. But that was not the practice and as a rule the party leadership appointed whom it wanted where it wanted.

The principle was so central to the Soviet system that none of the pre-congress letters tackled it head on. But there was evidence that perhaps a half of party members thought there should at least be multiple candidacies in elections to the leadership of primary party organizations. Several letter-writers stated the obvious truth that people could not be expected to be interested in elections that offered no choice. It was also argued that a competitively elected party secretary of a factory committee had a much better chance of doing a good job than one whose election had been uncontested and perhaps even influenced by the management, which was easy enough if the management was on good terms with the local party leadership. A university professor made the point that officials who had never had to submit to a real election easily came to feel they were 'beyond punishment'. If anyone dared suggest something similar for elections to district party committees, let alone more august bodies, their ideas were not published.

There was, though, strong feeling that something should be done to stop men doing the same job year after year, as had become the practice under Brezhnev. A party member of forty years' standing declared this led only to trying to solve problems with the same old methods and to the 'servility' of subordinates towards the supposedly immortal 'irreplaceable one'. The strongest remedy proposed was to put a limit of two terms in a row on any elected post, with a third term granted only in special cases and on condition that three-quarters of the votes were cast in favour of it. This would have meant that Gorbachov, to serve another five years as general secretary beyond 1996, would have had to win the support of a large majority of the Soviet Central Committee. It was also proposed that a third of all elected bodies, from the Central Committee in Moscow down, be renewed at each election, in order to prevent their membership becoming too old. An old-age pensioner who had joined the party in 1931 tactfully explained that under present practice there were many senior officials 'of a rather solid age which undoubtedly affects their ability to work and must hamper the conduct of business'. There were also suggestions that an age limit be put on party appointments at all levels.

The other major theme in these unusual letters was the insistence that party members be guaranteed the right to speak their mind even to the point of criticizing their leaders. This protection was in theory written into not only the party rules but also the Soviet constitution which declared: 'Persecution for criticism is prohibited. Persons guilty of such persecution shall be called to account.' The letter-writers complained that while the press often reported cases of senior officials suppressing criticism no one had been expelled from the party. It was also true that very few people had been brought to court, though it was also an offence under criminal law. There were suggestions that an official guilty of persecuting his critics should automatically be expelled from the party. By far the most far-reaching and considered argument in favour of greater freedom of expression within the party came from an economist at Moscow University. A minority in today's party, he wrote, was quite different from the 'minority men', the Mensheviks, against whom Lenin had battled before and during the Revolution and about whom not a good word could be said in official Soviet histories. 'They are those members of the party who have different views on solutions . . . in their organizations and on the people heading them. In a party of like-minded people it makes sense to have a mechanism that obliges the chosen leaders to pay the maximum attention to all opinions.'

The economist argued this would make it harder for leaders to pursue their favourite policies long after they had been proved ineffective. Even more important was the need, at a time of rapid scientific change and experiment in economic management, to consider every alternative view and possible solution. 'What is new and progressive can in the early stages find itself more than once in a minority.' Soviet society was becoming more homogeneous from the point of view of class (this was a touch of the cap to official ideology) but at the same time people were more independent-minded and there were bound to be more and more different approaches to various problems. Embracing this growing variety of views would encourage members to take a more active part in public life. The economist proposed that party newspapers should be obliged to print any letter supported by a sufficient number of party members, a hundred signatures to ensure publication in *Pravda*, less for local papers. To the extent that there was a 'liberal' wing in the Soviet Communist party this was its voice.

None of these proposals was written into the revised party rules accepted by the 1986 congress, though an article was added to the criminal code on the persecution of citizens for criticism. An official found guilty of this risked a £250 fine or losing his job, and in the gravest cases a two-year prison sentence (Soviet lawyers pointed out, though, that it would be difficult to prove that someone had been punished for being too critical rather than for a real offence). In one respect the documents accepted by the congress were less democratic than the old ones. The party programme adopted under Khrushchov laid down that a quarter of the Central Committee and all subordinate bodies be replaced at each election and that the Politburo members be normally limited to three consecutive terms. Brezhnev had managed to remove similar provisions from the party rules but they remained, embarrassingly indelible, in the party programme. The revision of the programme for the 1986 congress allowed them at last to be removed from there too.

What was the point of allowing the suggestions to be made only to ignore them? No explanation was given. There were rumours, but no evidence, that Gorbachov broadly supported such changes but had been overruled by more cautious colleagues. Perhaps it was thought a useful safety valve to let a debate like this take place in publications as impeccable as *Kommunist*. Gorbachov said that the far less daring official amendments to the party rules that were made would increase the power of the primary organizations. They would have more chance to vet new leaders, to monitor the performance of the factories, farms and government organizations they worked in, and to check up on the performance of senior officials, especially those found guilty of negligence or wrongdoing. But Moscow's power to make, directly or indirectly, all appointments within the party and the traditional discipline which made Moscow's word unchallengeable were the keys to the general secretary's power. To allow real elections even in the primary organizations might set an embarrassing precedent. And how many leaders have been ready to limit their own time in power?

Gorbachov was involved in a delicate operation. He was searching for ways to bring pressure to bear on the inadequate, lazy and dishonest party leaders without diminishing the party's power and his own control over it. He seemed to feel he could deploy the rank-and-file party members as a discreet sort of Red Guard who would make life uncomfortable for those leaders who did not go along with Gorbachov's cautious version of a Cultural Revolution. His unwillingness or inability to make more dramatic changes to the party's rules was partly compensated for by his campaign for *glasnost*, openness, in Soviet, and particularly party, life. This was to be the weapon with which the virtuous Communist and citizen would slay injustice and incompetence. And it was also to be the miracle drug that would turn them into enthusiastic executors of the leadership's policies. Every party member, Gorbachov said, should use to the full his 'constitutional right to make proposals and criticisms', while 'the better informed people are the more conscientiously they behave, and the more actively they support the party and its plans . . .' On another occasion he linked openness with the need to overcome 'the complex of infallibility', an unusual dig at the old

191

Soviet habit of always claiming to be nothing less than perfect. His most vigorous defence of openness came in the summer of 1986, after the accident at the Chernobyl nuclear power station. 'Recent events' had proved the correctness of Lenin's words that self-deception was terrible and the fear of truth destructive.

The party and the people need all the truth – in big things and in small. Only it can educate people with a developed sense of civic duty, while lies and half-truths corrupt the consciousness, deform the personality, and prevent people making realistic . . . assessments.

The campaign for openness was pressed particularly hard in personnel matters: the most sensitive of all party business. Gorbachov and his like-minded colleagues were convinced that bad party and government officials were saved time and again by their ability to work in secret. Much was made of the need to tell people why senior officials got which jobs and, most important, why they lost them. Such things were seldom mentioned except by gossip which was plentiful but often inaccurate. In this new spirit the first secretary of the Perm region published a book giving the names of all officials he had sacked and why.

It was also said that Soviet people had lost the habit of criticizing and would have to re-learn it. Soviet Marxism, a writer in *Kommunist* complained, seemed to have been expurgated to make it suitable for the daughters of gentlefolk. The atmosphere of mutual admiration had to be destroyed. 'None of us can pretend to a monopoly of the truth . . . to papal infallibility.' Mikhail Nenashev, the editor who had made so much of Andropov in his paper *Sovietskaya Rossiya*, attacked party leaders' habit of preventing local newspapers publishing anything critical about their organizations. He poured scorn on journalists who said to their editor, 'I will write something critical but you must ask for the approval of the district party secretary.' This, he said – surely to the surprise of many journalists – was not good journalistic ethics. Party officials who declared journalists to be people of 'little competence' who did not 'understand the essence of the problems about which they write' found themselves being taken to task by – journalists. Boris Yeltsin who had succeeded Grishin as Moscow party leader in December 1985 was put forward as a model of openness. He was described at a meeting of the capital's corps of propagandists answering everything, even questions that were 'complicated, quarrelsome, angry and prickly'. He did not select the ones he liked, *Pravda*'s chief specialist on party affairs wrote admiringly, 'he answered them all'. Notes taken at this meeting that found their way abroad showed this was not an overstatement. It was Yeltsin who had said at the party congress that fear of openness was one of the main obstacles to change. Too many leaders did not have the 'courage' to admit the true state of affairs or to speak the truth when it was bitter.

The press had to work hard to persuade a doubtful public that truth-telling would still not be selective. 'Our trouble is,' one of these doubters wrote to a journalist, 'that you and I can only talk about real openness in all quarters in a private chat over a bottle of brandy in your comfortable kitchen and on condition that we absolutely trust each other. After all you too are only a cog in this machine. You only have to start slipping and the big gears will grind you to powder.'

Others were convinced that critical letters addressed to higher authorities would never arrive at their destination and that if you wanted to be sure that the Central Committee or some other office in the capital got your complaint you had better go to Moscow to post it. The fear was not unfounded, as we have seen, and in general junior party members, let alone ordinary citizens, still had reason to be cautious. The editor of an important Ukrainian newspaper had proposed that the party rules be amended to oblige party leaders 'at all levels' to answer criticism from the press and any other quarter. This was not done. Openness remained selective. Sometimes it was local newspapers that could not bring themselves to publish the full text of a new-style speech. Even several months after the party congress Gorbachov came across an editor who had made thirty cuts in an address delivered by none other than his regional party first secretary. But it was often the local leaders themselves who found it objectionable to read criticism in their own press. Even in Moscow, however, where the taste for journalistic adventure was strongest, the central press did not demand to be told the full truth of such matters as why Romanov left the Politburo or why Grishin had to be removed from the Moscow leadership. Only the most naive Soviet citizen believed that the new policy allowed any party official to be publicly criticized. As the conduct of the local party election campaigns in 1983 and again before the 1986 congress showed, the leaders most heavily criticized were those the general secretary wanted out of the way. It was only through rumour that the abolition or cutting back of censorship was made widely known in the summer of 1986.

Limited though it was, openness had become an essential piece of party man's equipment. Gorbachov seldom lost an opportunity to remind him of the need for what he called 'Bolshevik frankness', that 'today we call things by their proper names: successes are referred to as successes, and mistakes as mistakes'. The full Soviet report on the Chernobyl disaster showed that he meant that. It was also in keeping with a remark of his about the absence of 'opposition parties' in the Soviet Union making it more important to practice self-criticism and analysis. It suggested he understood the argument of the Moscow economist who wanted the party to be more tolerant of minority views that might prove correct in the future. During Gorbachov's trips round the country apprehensive officials found themselves urging each other to answer the general secretary's questions 'honestly' even though they were being televised. It was in general a painful business. A group of district officials accused of favouritism and corruption had to give a public explanation. 'This wasn't in secret, a matter of crying on someone's shoulder in a dark corner as it used to be before, but explaining to the people in the bright light of day, in the light of openness, how and why this became possible. How it was they failed to see the birth of evil. How their lordly carelessness and negligence planted and nurtured this evil.'

The melodramatic vocabulary of a *Pravda* correspondent was suited to the many little dramas of repentance and retribution for which Gorbachov had drafted the script. The mood was that of a staid church whose membership had for years attended out of conformism, social ambition, and a moderate degree of belief, but which had now fallen into the hands of evangelists.

The lordly party leader, turning aside inconvenient questions as 'improper', had to give way to the man who did not sit in his office drafting decrees but got out among the people, and answered everything they cared to ask. Regional first secretaries began to boast how they and all their staff went down mines, walked the streets and toured the shops, listening 'to what people are saying and what worries them'. A new sort of statistic became fashionable – the amount by which a party office had managed to cut its paper work. Officials whose job it had been to supervise industry and farming underwent a conversion to the need to concentrate on personnel matters. The worst sin now for a party secretary was to sit at a table surrounded by factory managers and government officials and tell them exactly what to do. Everyone became concerned with the 'human factor', an expression Gorbachov was particularly fond of. Leaders had to learn how to conduct informal meetings that made for 'a free, unforced exchange of opinions'. When the disaster struck at Chernobyl it was reported that several of the rescue workers at once applied to join the party. A police captain declared: 'I wish to perform my professional and civic duty in clearing up the consequences of the accident . . . as a Communist.' It was a fine example of the new evangelical spirit at work. (But the Politburo also decided to increase its control by appointing representatives of the Central Committee to the party groups of all nuclear power stations. This was a well-tried method, going back to the 1930s, of control from the centre.)

The title of a play put on in 1986 at one of the most popular Moscow theatres might have provided the party's new slogan – *The Dictatorship of Conscience*. Its message was that when all Communists (and all Soviet people) learned to 'act in everything according to Lenin's precepts', only 'one dictatorship will remain – the dictatorship of conscience'. During Stalin's time, the reform-minded economists had explained to Gorbachov, Moscow had been obliged to tighten up the human nuts to keep the great Soviet machine moving. Now Gorbachov wanted people to do it for themselves. On his tour of the Soviet Far East in the summer of 1986 he urged a crowd in Vladivostok: 'We have to put in order all of society, and start, start with ourselves: I will keep order, I will maintain discipline, I will, you understand, tighten the nut completely . . . That is what one has to say.'

It was new, but again not so new. There were echoes of the young Komsomol official inspired to militancy by the ruins of post-war Russia. There was a strong trace of the headmaster who encouraged his students to pick virtue of their own accord, and wanted to believe they were at last mature enough to do so. But there was never a suggestion that the party should relinquish its control. The dictatorship of conscience was still underpinned by the unchallengeable power of the party's leadership, the dictatorship enforced in the name of the proletariat. There was nothing new about the idea of a party of the virtuous 'dominated by one ambition, one passionate idea: to make the majority of men happy and to invite as many as possible to the banquet of life. The bringing about of this idea becomes the only purpose of their activity, because this idea is completely fused into their conception of personal happiness. Everything is subordinated to this idea, everything sacrificed.'

This was the credo of nineteenth-century Russian revolutionaries who had paved the way for Lenin's party. There was no evidence that Gorbachov would have been any the less amazed than they were by the suggestion that such a party, if properly run (an important proviso for him), might be corrupted by absolute power. 'What are you frightened of? What right have you to think that this minority – partly through its own social position, partly through its ideas, and totally devoted to the people's interests – by taking power into its hands will suddenly turn itself into a tyrant?'

Most people brought up in the tradition of Western democracy would find it natural to ask that question. Little if anything in Gorbachov's education and experience prompted him to do so, and just as little in Russian history. He was urging that the party no longer try to do everything itself. He believed, or wanted to believe, that in the past it had been that way 'out of need, as a sort of compensation for the failings of the economic mechanism'. But he held tight to the real source of the party's power – its control over the *nomenklatura*, the key appointments throughout the whole of Soviet society; in the party itself, of course, but also in government and industry, education and science, the armed forces. These appointees were only as responsive to the millions they led as the Politburo and Central Committee thought right. Gorbachov wanted more control, not less, and meant to get it by calling on the rank-and-file to check on their superiors without the latter letting up on their supervision of subordinates. 'Not a single party organization and not a single worker should be left outside the system of control.'

This was still a recognizable Soviet Communist voice. He was adapting old traditions to new circumstances, and it was there, not in any threat of 'liberalization', that the pain was first felt. Gorbachov admitted almost as soon as he was elected general secretary that there would be opposition. But as the months went by he talked of it with increasing impatience, as though even he had underestimated its strength and stubbornness.

16

Opposition

Russian history was at its most repetitious whenever a new leader came to power. He could count on respect bordering on servility. But he would also be silently opposed by the conservatism natural to a great bureaucratic state, and the no less frustrating passivity of a people who had learned over centuries how to protect itself against powerful leaders. 'The Tsar wishes,' the old saying went, 'but the boyars will not allow.' As the months went by and many of the most fractious boyars were manoeuvred out of office it was this uncoordinated, almost unthinking resistance to new ways that would often seem the greatest threat to Gorbachov's plans.

His emergence as general secretary from the Central Committee meeting in March was reminiscent of a long-awaited cast change in one of those old-fashioned Moscow theatres where the roles were assigned according to seniority. The last of the elderly stars had died and Hamlet could now be played by an actor of the appropriate age. Gorbachov at fifty-four was not the youngest man to become party leader. Stalin had only been in his mid-forties when Lenin died. But Gorbachov was at a good age, and with luck had two decades of power ahead of him, as a slightly older Brezhnev had when he succeeded Khrushchov in 1964. Gorbachov's years as understudy that had begun during Andropov's rule may have been frustrating but they served him in good stead. Whereas his older patron had been hesitant about the nature of the country's problems and possible solutions Gorbachov showed from his first speeches as general secretary that he had reached broad conclusions about both. His speech to the Central Committee plenum in April sounded almost all of what were to become his major themes: the gravity of the country's situation; the need to re-model the economy so as to extract greater effort from both workers and management; the danger of the

197

technological lag behind the West; the party to work in a more open, less bureaucratic way, and the Soviet people to be more involved in the business of government. Shortly afterwards he would underline his sense of urgency by coining the slogan 'acceleration'.

The most important first impressions were emotional, atmospheric and even irrational. It counted for much that Gorbachov knew how to hold himself as a leader. The welcome readiness to go among the public was balanced by a politician's skill at controlling the encounters he had during his walkabouts ('Wait a minute, I listened to you, you listen to me'), and of turning the tables on mild heckling (to a man who complained about the queues outside liquor shops, 'Well, don't stand in them, why torment yourself?'). He had the build and the voice that many Russians thought proper for leadership. 'He's not bad,' a Moscow housewife said soon after his election. She shook her fist and grinned: 'He looks solid.'

Gorbachov took naturally to the ceremonies of power and even added to their gloss. His predecessors had usually received foreign dignitaries in the colourless offices of the Kremlin's Senate building, where the Politburo held its weekly meeting. On the outside a fine three-sided classical building by one of Russia's greatest architects, its rooms had been re-modelled to suit the bland tastes of the party's rulers. There was wood panelling, beige wallpapers, conference tables you could have played cricket on, and the routine ikons of Marx, Engels and Lenin for decoration. Gorbachov showed he had a sense of theatre by preferring to meet some of his guests in the far more glamorous rooms of the Great Kremlin Palace, built in the early nineteenth century as the Tsars' Moscow residence. After only two months in power he greeted President Husak of Czechoslovakia there, the two men advancing towards each other like duellists from opposite ends of the sixty-yard length of the St. George's Hall. Before going to France in October 1985 Gorbachov gave his first interview to Western television from a small room in the Palace that was of almost Parisian elegance. He looked quite at home in it. Kremlin dinners for foreign visitors had become gloomy feasts in which indifferent courses followed rapidly one after the other. When Gorbachov entertained President Mitterand to dinner in the Kremlin in 1986 it was much more lively, with the guests divided between small tables; and for the first time television cameras were allowed in. Gorbachov was not bothered by the theoretical problems of fitting a general secretary into the protocol of presidents and prime ministers. If there were documents to be signed with another head of state or government he signed them. By the time he went to Geneva in November for the summit meeting with President Reagan the fact that the American was a head of state and the Russian technically a constitutional ghost did not worry anyone.

There was self-confidence, too, in the way Gorbachov advanced his wife into Soviet public life. Starting with the first brief television pictures of her accompanying him in Leningrad in April, Raisa Gorbachov was to break away more and more from the old pattern of the Kremlin wife who remained in the *terem* on all but a few special occasions. After a few tours with her husband she began to step out of the background, to ask her own questions and to hug a child or two in the crowd. It became the custom for Soviet television to show her at least once if she was in the audience while her husband was making a speech. Few Russians seemed to notice it but at times she looked remarkably like another determined first lady, the young Eleanor Roosevelt, wife of the American president whom Moscow had turned into one of its rare heroes in modern American history. Mrs. Gorbachov appeared with her daughter and grand-daughter at the great Red Square parades, apparently keen to be seen. Showing Moscow to wives of visiting leaders, she proved as knowledgeable about the Russian past and culture as official guides. In the summer of 1986 she earned a footnote in history when her meeting with the vice-president of the Red Cross, the wife of ex-premier Fanfani of Italy, was reported by the Soviet news agency: the first time in memory that the Soviet media had recorded a home public engagement by the leader's wife. Other engagements followed and in 1986 she became a founding member of a committee for the promotion of Soviet culture.

Not everyone approved. Women were heard to murmur after the Leningrad visit: 'Who's running the country, the wife or the husband?' The authorities seemed nervous about gossip that she had visited grand shops while in London, for it was no secret that people grumbled about the leadership's access to foreign luxuries. There were reports that some party meetings were told Mrs. Gorbachov wore Russian clothes when she travelled abroad and looked very smart in them. Later her Moscow dress designer would be introduced to the foreign press. One purpose of her advancement seemed to be to break down old ideas about a woman's place, ideas that many Russian women defended as fervently as most men. Raisa Gorbachov, with her own professional career and strong ideas about Soviet society, above all the need to curb the drinking that was destroying family life, was typical of a new, more 'Western' Soviet woman. But most women were still far from having a fair share of power or social influence. They made up little more than a quarter of the party, the average hiding a share of up to forty per cent in some parts of Russia but a much lower one in Soviet Central Asia. Women were rare at the senior levels of party and government. The general secretary and his wife seemed keen to change this. Gorbachov talked of the need to promote women, and set an example himself when he appointed the trade union official Aleksandra Biryukova to be one of the eleven Central Committee secretaries. It was the first time in a quarter of a century that a woman had held such a senior position in the party.

'You have to remember,' an impressed Soviet official said only a few months after Gorbachov's election, 'that we now have a new *Vozhd*' – using the Russian word for Leader that had been applied to Stalin and which

Brezhnev showed signs of coveting but never managed to acquire. Gorbachov understood the need to make an impact as leader as soon as possible. Two measures announced in May showed him as strong but concerned: the campaign against alcohol balanced by increased benefits for pensioners and single-parent families. Pensions and benefit payments for most people in these categories were to be raised to a minimum fifty roubles a month, which the government recognized as the lowest tenable income for one person. Even though the cost of living figures on which that calculation had been made were out of date the change was a signal of Gorbachov's belief that years of neglect of the whole array of social services were now damaging the country's efficiency as much as its well-being.

He also had to make his mark by showing who his team was and getting it into place. The nature of Soviet politics made this difficult but Gorbachov was lucky. There was soon to be a party congress (whose date he put back a few weeks till the end of February 1986). Before the congress there had to be elections for new leaderships in every party organization. The congress itself would vote in a new Central Committee. Gorbachov's chance to use these carefully guided elections to remake the party's officer class was improved even more by his other piece of good fortune. Many of the men who had been allowed to grow old in office were now too decrepit to resist pressures to retire. Some were even being claimed by the grim reaper whose existence they had for so long ignored.

'To be close to the Tsar,' the proverb said, 'is to be close to death. To be close to the Tsar is to be close to honour.' A first glance at the thorough changes Gorbachov managed to make in his first year of power suggested it was still true. Of the fourteen Politburo members elected at the last Brezhnev congress in 1981 only four (Gorbachov, Gromyko, and the two out-of-town members Kunayev and Shcherbitsky) were in the Politburo chosen in March 1986. Five of its twelve members (Chebrikov, Ligachov, Ryzhkov, Shevardnadze and Zaikov) were elected under Gorbachov's leadership. Only two Brezhnev appointees remained among the Politburo's candidate members. Only one of the Central Committee secretaries (Gorbachov himself excepted) survived from 1981. Almost a third of the full members of the Central Committee elected in 1986 were entirely new, not even having served before as candidates. Two thirds of its candidate members were newcomers, and almost three-quarters of the auditing commission, which served as a waiting room for membership in the Committee proper. If Brezhnev's ghost had walked round the offices of the Central Committee it would have recognized only two of the heads of its departments, officials more powerful than the greatest government minister. When the twenty-seventh party Congress opened on February 25 half of the regional first secretaries appointed in the Brezhnev days had disappeared, the majority of the new men having been chosen under Gorbachov's supervision. As for the government, sixty new ministers were appointed in

Gorbachov's first year, more than twice as many as had changed under Andropov and Chernenko together. Three-quarters of the government's senior members, the dozen deputy prime ministers, had been appointed over the previous two years.

No other Soviet leader had been able to shift around so many of the men of power so quickly. Brezhnev, Khrushchov, and even Stalin had to wait much longer to get the people they wanted into place. It was not, however, as easy as it looked. Gorbachov had luck. But the battles he had to fight to make these changes demanded all his cunning and patience. There must have been times when he wished he was the almighty autocrat that some foreigners believed him to be.

The man who looked a model of Soviet toughness proved the easiest to pick off. In July Grigori Romanov was retired from the Politburo, ostensibly for reasons of health. Romanov had never had either Gorbachov's luck or his sure feet. He had allowed himself to be used by Andropov when the latter was manoeuvring for power. Even if it was not true that Romanov supported Grishhin to succeed Chernenko, Gorbachov had to see him as a rival, and one whose style he found distasteful. Romanov's fondness for alcohol seems to have given Gorbachov the weapon he needed. The Central Committee decree announcing the measures had said that party and government leaders with 'a weakness for alcoholic drinks' should be removed from their jobs and possibly expelled from the party. Romanov was known to be a hard drinker. His drunkenness during a visit to Finland the previous winter had been widely talked about. Finnish officials, themselves not inexperienced in drinking matters, were surprised when the Soviet embassy doctor had to be summoned to restore him to a state fit to deliver a speech. There was no hint that any of Romanov's colleagues came to his support, though it was in the interest of Grishin and Tikhonov (and arguably Kunayev and Shcherbitsky too) not to let anyone be thrown overboard at that stage for fear of being made to follow themselves. Romanov was eventually given a minor job in Moscow and appeared at the party congress as a member of the Leningrad delegation – a bitter pleasure for a man who had once been talked about as a possible leader of the Communist party.

The next to go was Tikhonov, the Ukrainian whom Brezhnev had made a deputy prime minister in 1965 and prime minister in 1979. What was interesting about Tikhonov's departure was the time it took to arrange. The prime minister, eighty in May, was remarkably spry for his age, wore some of the best-cut suits in the Politburo and cultivated an agreeable manner. No one would have been surprised if he had gone sooner. He was irredeemably identified with the economic policies whose failure had been the main topic of public debate for the last three years. If he had any ideas for a new economic strategy they were an excellently kept secret. He had never acquired the stature of his predecessor, Aleksei Kosygin, who had been a hero for the great bureaucrats. Gorbachov was impatient to make the personnel changes he believed long overdue, and would later claim publicly that the delay in doing so was the cause of considerable discontent in the party and country at large. But as long as Tikhonov remained prime minister he managed to hold back change in the government beneath him. The amalgamation of five ministries dealing with different parts of agriculture – a bureaucratic revolution by Moscow's standards – only took place after he had gone. It proved difficult to pension off his deputies and some of the other ministers Gorbachov badly needed to replace while Tikhonov was still prime minister. High on this list of men who had to go was the seventy-four-year-old head of the state planning committee, Nikolai Baibakov, who had been in the job for twenty years. Gosplan had to play a central role in any economic reform, and Gorbachov needed a younger man there who could see it through. (Baibakov retired a month after Tikhonov. His replacement, Nikolai Talyzin, was brought into the Politburo, which underlined his importance.) The longer the Tikhonov team stayed in place the more complicated was the business of revising the five year plan due to start in 1986, and which was to be the stepping stone to Gorbachov's longer-term plans and economic reform.

And yet Tikhonov did not give up the premiership until the end of September, less than five months before the new long-term economic strategy had to be presented to the party congress (he resigned from the Politburo a month later). The manner in which Tikhonov went was unusually dignified. He addressed a short letter to Gorbachov explaining that his health had worsened and that his doctors insisted he stop working. He had no choice, he said, but to ask to retire. In conclusion, he wrote, he wanted 'particularly to mention the warm, comradely atmosphere that has been created in the Politburo in recent time. How one would now like just to work and go on working.'

It was a very odd document for the Kremlin. Could it possibly have meant what it said? That Tikhonov was not well was obvious. He had started to show his age soon after Chernenko's death. It cannot have been easy for him to keep up with the quicker pace of the Gorbachov Politburo, and at times it was hard not to wonder if he was being intentionally worn out by the many public duties he was made to perform. But no one believed that the prime minister left just because of poor health. As for his remark about the pleasant new atmosphere in the Politburo, this was the very moment of the final campaign of innuendo against Viktor Grishin, about which there was nothing the least bit warm or comradely.

There is no way of knowing whether Gorbachov tried to get Tikhonov out sooner, or whether he was patient enough to wait for age and stress to do his work for him. He had the replacement ready. Nikolai Ryzhkov, brought into the Central Committee secretariat by Andropov, had been promoted to full membership of the Politburo in April. But it looked as though

Gorbachov made the best of a difficult situation by turning the prime minister's retirement, when it came, into an example for the country's other elderly leaders and their dependants. It was not just the old men themselves who had to be pacified. No Soviet official of importance wished to see retirement made too easy, just as no member of the Politburo believed his status should be put aside any more lightly than a good Christian marriage. The tradition of the last twenty years, that powerful men did not retire, and the accompanying suspicion that if they did it meant they had been disgraced, had to be broken. The manner of Tikhonov's going helped. Gorbachov had nothing to gain by vindictiveness towards older colleagues with whom he had worked (without a public murmur) for seven years, as long as their only crime was lack of brilliance and an elderly person's distaste for change. The new general secretary made a last bow to the old generation when the party congress elected three retired elder statesmen – Tikhonov, Baibakov, and Boris Ponomaryov (eighty-one, and head of the Central Committee's international department for thirty years) – to the new Central Committee. This had never happened before, and it looked like another deft, and perhaps unavoidable, gesture to the departing generation.

The anxiety of the party and government élite about its future can only have been increased by an editorial published by *Kommunist* in June. Beginning with some poetry ('And do you know what it means to be free?/It means to be responsible for everything') it declared that the time for 'petty improvements' had gone, while that of straight and critical talk had arrived. It made it plain that many senior officials were showing they could not or did not want to adapt to the new times. If it was bad to be the 'unthinking executor of the commands of others' it was no better to enforce one's will by dressing people down over the telephone and delivering threatening commands. This was not the meaning of discipline as Lenin defined it. *Kommunist* concluded with some ominous words from the master. The proletariat 'supports officially and openly the candidacy of the good worker Ivan, proposes that the bad Pyotr be replaced, takes action – energetically, toughly and to the finish – against the rascal Sidor . . . against the criminal transactions of Miron.'

The trouble with the formula was that it made no mention of the decent if unbrilliant Yuri who had worn himself out serving a system he had no hope of changing by his own efforts. Yet it was easy to imagine the resentment that one of the usual clipped announcements of retirement would provoke if the leader in question, while no doubt unsuited to the demands of the new age, had done an honest job and earned the gratitude of subordinates whose careers he had advanced. In such circumstances the meeting of a regional committee to elect – on instructions from the Central Committee, whose representative would be present – the successor to the respected old chief might be a tricky occasion. Just such a problem occurred in the northern region of Vologda, part of the old Russian heartland and home to the writer

Vasili Belov, one of the leading champions of old rural values and customs and a friend of the hero of this story.

Anatoli Drygin was seventy-one and had been head of the Vologda region party since 1961. His friends and colleagues could not believe it when he told them in July that he was going to retire. He looked the same 'rock of a man' they had always known. His voice was as loud and commanding as ever, his mind as capacious, his shoulders as straight. As far as they could see he was still the tireless first secretary who visited every district in his kingdom of 145,000 square kilometres at least twice a year, always travelling with top boots that came above his knees so he could get down the dirt roads to the furthest villages. Things were improving in Vologda, too, which made it all the harder to understand why he was giving up now. Drygin's explanation was simple but, to his acquaintances, shocking. Life was getting more complicated, problems more difficult. It needed a surge of strength to solve them and that could not be counted on at his age. His batteries were running out. The correspondent of *Pravda* who told this story made it plain it was meant as a moral tale for other elderly leaders and their supporters. Drygin knew his strength was failing and that it would be wrong to slow down his style of work. The demands of the time were what counted, and these were 'indifferent to the fact that you are used to your position, to the interests of your household, and to your desire to go on working'. A hero in his work, Drygin showed how to become a hero in retirement:

Anatoli Semyonovich Drygin stepped aside. Like a soldier on duty, making way for his replacement. At the [annual parade on] Victory Day Vologda was used to seeing the regional first secretary marching in the ranks of the war veterans. In a colonel's uniform, with four battle decorations and flashes awarded for three wounds. Vologda knew it: Drygin was a brave man. But his last step demanded courage of a special kind for which they don't give medals, but which never loses its value.

Drygin was replaced by the younger man he had nurtured as his successor. He did not move away from the region and took a job in a local factory. The locals were pleased about that. 'Anatoli Semyonovich knows he can go about Vologda with his head raised high.'

It was a rare glimpse into the private dramas of a generation of Soviet leadership that had inherited great power and used it to confer the illusion of immortality on themselves. If voluntary retirement was so painful, and needed such heroic determination, it was not surprising that most people preferred not to contemplate it. Perhaps there were others who followed Drygin's example but the press did not write about them.

Viktor Grishin certainly did not feel tempted to retire. The need for Gorbachov to fight to get Grishin removed was proof of the limitations on the power of a newly-chosen leader. The Moscow party leader had opposed Gorbachov's election. He was, in the eyes of the new men, the essence of what was wrong in the party leadership. He was vulnerable to charges that he had been a poor steward of the capital, and had compounded his failures by declaring them to be great successes. But, in spite of the mass of damaging rumours hinting to the contrary, he was never officially accused of being guilty of anything deserving expulsion from the party, let alone criminal prosecution. His successor in Moscow said he had been removed from the Politburo only for 'mistakes in his work'. Grishin probably benefited from the traditional reluctance of the Politburo to let any member go easily for fear of setting an unwelcome precedent. Some Politburo members who had worked with him for many years, including Tikhonov and Andrei Gromyko, may have supported him. When Grishin did at last leave the Politburo in February 1986 it was Gromyko's new office, the Presidium of the Supreme Soviet, that gave him a sinecure job as a consultant.

The public attack on Grishin began with an article in July in *Sovietskaya Rossiya* whose editor Gorbachov was soon to promote. It asserted that new housing estates in the capital were being accepted as completed and ready for occupation when in truth they needed another twelve months' more work. Everyone benefited from this subterfuge. The city was made to look as though it had fulfilled its housing target. The building organizations got their bonuses. The sufferers were the Muscovites who needed new flats. The paper admitted this sort of thing went on all over the country but suggested ominously that 'negative phenomena are particularly intolerable in the capital'. The following month Vladimir Promyslov, the Moscow mayor who was closely connected to Grishin, sent a soothing reply. It seems that, like many other officials soon to lose their jobs, he could not understand what all this talk of a need for change meant for he was asking to be given another five years in office up to the moment of his removal in January 1986. Within a month the mayor's reply was torn to pieces by a senior procurator of the Russian Republic. He accused the city authorities of still ignoring a problem that was now a criminal matter. The law, said the menacing headline in the newspaper, is the same for everyone.

The same month the poet Yevgeni Yevtushenko published a long poem which among other intriguing political references alluded to the notoriously savage sex life of Stalin's last secret police chief, Lavrenti Beria. Yevtushenko liked to say that 'a poet in Russia is more than a poet' which was certainly true of himself, for he had many times proved himself an agile laureate of change who knew how to avoid serious trouble with the authorities. Yevtushenko's allusion to Beria revived old gossip about the latter's link to the Grishin family. Grishin's son Aleksandr had married Marta Galperina, who was Beria's daughter by his favourite mistress Lyalya Galperina. The two had divorced in early 1985 but the connection was obviously controversial, and had already been gossiped about at the time of the skirmishing before Chernenko's death. Such talk could only add to the impression of Grishin's unsuitability.

This was the old-fashioned Kremlin politics of intrigue and innuendo: evidence enough of the difficulty Gorbachov was having in prising Grishin out of Moscow. The latter behaved as though nothing had changed, and it was impressive to watch, like a ship that is already taking in water but ignores the storm it is sailing into. Grishin propagated the new party line ('See the perspective, act energetically' was the headline to one of his speeches). He attended the usual public functions with his usual knowing smile. There was no sign that his health was cracking. And then it was over. He resigned at a plenum of the Moscow city party on December 24 at which, though it was attended by Gorbachov himself, there may have been a last, hopeless fight. Grishin had had years in which to put trusted people into the Moscow party. These men and women knew that if he went many of them would go too (most of the Moscow party leadership was changed within a month of Grishin's retirement). They had nothing to lose by voting against his resignation, as party rules gave them every right to do. Grishin's successor Boris Yeltsin, the party chief of Sverdlovsk who had been made a Central Committee secretary in July, was later to reveal the anger some people felt at Grishin's removal. During a meeting with Moscow propagandists the next spring he read out a letter, which scandalized his audience but Yeltsin dismissed as coming from a madman, accusing him of having 'Napoleonic plans. What are you interfering for? Gorbachov just needed one of his own men in the job. Go back to Sverdlovsk before it's too late.'

Grishin's humiliation was not over. The next month he had to attend a meeting of the Moscow party under its new leader. Gorbachov and six other members of the Politburo were also present. Yeltsin's speech blew to pieces the carefully polished façade of Moscow as a model city. 'Perhaps some people will think these judgements too harsh,' he said, 'but sooner or later they had to be spoken.' It was apparently then that Grishin asked his uncomprehending question: 'What will happen if you tell all that to the Muscovites?'

There was one other member of the Politburo who threatened to be an obstacle to the new leader. Andrei Gromyko, who had supported Gorbachov's appointment as general secretary and become the venerable talisman of the new régime, sat like Cerberus at the gates of Soviet foreign policy. As long as he was there it would be difficult, if not impossible, to change the manner of Soviet diplomacy, let alone its tactics or strategy. Gorbachov made Gromyko a proposal that was flattering and hard to turn down. Instead of the general secretary becoming president, as his three predecessors had done, the office should go to Gromyko. Did Gromyko resist? Or did he, like the heroic Drygin of Vologda, accept that it was his duty to make way for another man? Great bureaucrat that he was, and knowing by heart the channels along which power flowed in Moscow, he must have understood that giving up the foreign ministry meant losing control of Soviet foreign policy. He would keep his voice in the Politburo.

But even his voice would eventually count for much less without the ministry files, the embassy telegrams, and the power over diplomatic appointments (all of which was indeed to happen).

Gromyko's election in June as chairman of the Presidium of the Supreme Soviet showed the limits of the new policy of openness. No Soviet expert on foreign affairs was allowed to discuss the implications of Gromyko's new appointment for the country's foreign policy. No one tried to explain why Eduard Shevardnadze, a Georgian policeman turned party leader, was the right man to succeed him as foreign minister. It also showed that there were few if any precedents in Soviet politics that could not be broken. When Gorbachov had proposed Chernenko for the presidency just over a year before he said Soviet practice and experience showed the need to unite the posts of president and party leader in one man. This reflected 'the leading role of the Communist party' in all aspects of Soviet life but especially the government. It also had 'immense significance' for Soviet foreign policy. These arguments were forgotten when he came to propose Gromyko for president. He now said that the general secretary needed to devote most of his time to the party whose work was to be intensified.

There was no evidence that Gorbachov desired the presidency for himself but was frustrated by his colleagues. Brezhnev had wanted the job out of vanity, to show he at last was undisputed leader of the Politburo. East European leaders had imitated him. It was an easy way to flatter Brezhnev and themselves at the same time. Pushing Gromyko into the presidency brought Gorbachov much more power than if he had left the older man in control of the foreign ministry and taken the honours of head of state for himself.

A Soviet party congress cries out for a star and Gorbachov did not disappoint the five thousand delegates gathered in the Palace of Congresses that Nikita Khrushchov had built in the Kremlin in time for his last congress in 1961. The delegates were unusually young (one in three was under forty) and three-quarters of them had never been to a congress before. To them especially Gorbachov must have seemed a commanding figure, making a joke of it when his voice grew husky towards the end of the five-hour report with which he opened proceedings, and on several occasions interrupting other speakers. He gave a brutal lesson in the 'new style' to the head of the film makers' union who was unwise enough to start his speech by saying he had so enjoyed Mikhail Sergeyevich's report that he was sorry when it ended. 'Let's not start declining Mikhail Sergeyevich,' Gorbachov broke in, to which the astonished film director, with a verbal click of the heels, replied, 'This is a lesson that we must put into practice.'

Even the sentimental ceremonies usual on these occasions were adapted to the demands of the new. When the time came for the young Pioneers (the children's pre-Komsomol organization) to deliver their squeaky greetings to the delegates they sang a song about how every child needed special textbooks for the coming age of high-tech.

Let us please have quicker
Computers and displays!
If only in our schools
We could get to touch them!

Even under Brezhnev a party congress provided a few rare glimpses into the mind of the Soviet leadership. The gathering gave important officials the chance to express, even if in guarded language, their special concerns and regional interests. This congress inevitably showed differences of emphasis. Some of the surviving old members of Brezhnev's team, like the Ukrainian Shcherbitsky and the Kazakh Kunayev, were much less forthcoming about the errors of the past than prime minister Ryzhkov or the Russian Federation's premier Vitali Vorotnikov. Some of the party and government leaders stood out from their colleagues by their enthusiasm for pursuing to their logical end the economic changes that were only just beginning to take shape. Prime minister Ryzhkov did not seem to be among them. Alarm about the consequences of ignoring housing and other social services was a strong new theme that no one cared to challenge. An unusual admission of the seriousness of popular discontent with living conditions came from Yegor Ligachov who said that no less than the 'political stability of Soviet society' was at stake. Many of the regional party first secretaries described the different forms that opposition to the party's new policies had taken. There were those who 'approved on the outside, and resisted on the inside'. There were those who did not understand how to change, and others who were simply unable to. 'Some leaders' psychology,' complained the first secretary from Lenin's native region Ulyanovsk, 'is not geared to revolutionary changes in the conduct of affairs, but towards the old stereotypes that guarantee . . . a quiet life and the superficial signs of well-being. So some of them are adapting to the new demands . . . like fashionable society ladies to a new fashion.'

The party leaders seemed to think the government ministries were the biggest obstacle. Many of their workers had 'ossified' and were impervious to change. The newly-elected Georgian party leader Dzhumber Patiashvili called those who falsely made themselves out to be 'new' men 'traitors in the literal sense of the word'.

These remarks scarcely did the problem justice. They were not much more revealing than another Yevtushenko poem published before the congress called 'The what if it doesn't work men'. The poet's target were officials similar to those whom the humorous magazine *Krokodil* had been satirizing for years. He called them 'alcoholics of fear'.

Instead of worrying about bread,
about meat,
about iron
you hear the gluey mutters
'What . . . if it . . . doesn't'

This was the most important assembly of the world's premier Marxist-Leninist party. The Soviet Union had begun on what its leaders claimed to be a thorough remaking of its way of life. It was surely inadequate to explain the gathering signs of resistance by references to incorrect psychology, or stupidity, or even criminal ill-will. Might there not be more profound social and institutional reasons for resistance to change that went far beyond disposition? The one attempt to identify a group with an interest in resistance led to an argument that must have puzzled some of the delegates. Yeltsin of Moscow, in the most outspoken speech the congress heard, admitted that many questions needed answering. Why was it that congress after congress found itself discussing the same old problems? How could it be that a totally unsuitable word such as 'stagnation' had become part of the party's vocabulary? 'Why for so many years have we been unable to tear out of our life the roots of bureaucracy, social injustice and other abuses? Why even now is the demand for radical changes getting stuck in an inert stratum of time-servers with party tickets?'

Yeltsin went on to say he thought one reason was some leaders' lack of courage when it came to assessing the situation and their own role objectively. They had been scared of the 'bitter truth'. While this was yet another explanation rooted in the weaknesses of the individual his mention of an 'inert stratum . . . with party tickets' made knowing ears prick up. The expression was used again, but this time indignantly, by Vladimir Kalashnikov, the newly-appointed first secretary of Volgograd region who had worked for many years with Gorbachov in Stavropol. 'One should not for the sake of sensation or under the pretext of "frank discussion" blacken the officials of a certain "slow-moving, inert and sticky party and administrative stratum".' Applauded at this point he went on, 'It is not difficult to understand whom such authors have in mind.'

The clumsy phrase about an inert and sticky stratum had appeared in an article in *Pravda* two weeks before the congress opened. It quoted a letter from a worker which defined this 'stratum' as 'lying between the Central Committee and the working class' and having no eagerness for 'radical change'. Some, perhaps all, of its members were people who 'merely carry party cards but have long ceased to be Communists'. As far as the party went, that seemed to mean the middle level party officials in the regions and districts. The complaint had a traditional ring to it: a modern variation on the old saying that 'the tsar's kindnesses only trickle through the boyars' sieve'. It was not surprising that many at the congress found the idea offensive in the extreme and applauded Kalashnikov. The congress had already heard Yegor Ligachov take *Pravda* to task for carrying criticism too far. It was assumed he meant this article, for it had gone on to print an unprecedented attack on the privileges enjoyed by party and government officials. Taken together, this seemed to some important delegates to be an intolerable attack by journalists on the party. N. S. Yermakov, party leader of the Siberian region of Kemerovo, developed Ligachov's criticism of the press. Again to the applause of delegates, he said it was wrong for journalists who had 'neither experience nor professional knowledge of party work' to give their 'subjective assessments' of the party's great undertakings. It was not surprising that there was talk of the danger of too much democracy and 'rocking the ship of state'.

Voices outside the party establishment would try to counter this mood. 'It all depends,' Yevtushenko argued later, 'who is holding the ship's wheel and it is now in reliable hands.' Boris Yeltsin seemed inclined to agree with that. He had said at the congress that the time had come for there to be neither positions nor people 'beyond criticism'. And he also seemed, by his use of those words 'inert stratum', to have a more methodical understanding of the problem of bringing change to the Soviet Union than he admitted to in his speech. It was an idea that might have come out of the study paper produced in the spring of 1983 by Academician Zaslavskaya. She had warned that opposition had to be expected to any significant change in Soviet society – an opposition not just from lazy and irresponsible individuals but from social groups who stood to lose from change. The party's theoreticians had been wrong, she argued then, to suppose that changes could be made in Soviet society without touching off conflict. The truth was that a 'radical reconstruction of economic management considerably affects the interests of many social groups'. They included the most senior planners, who feared that bringing economic pressures to bear on Soviet society would lessen the importance of the plan. At the lowest level there were the factory managers and workers who were not sure of their own abilities to do well under new rules, and were frightened of having more responsibility. They preferred to be passive, as the old system allowed them to be.

Zaslavskaya, keen reformer that she was, considered the opposition of these two groups to be of secondary importance. She believed their fears to be exaggerated, and that they would find the water of economic reform quite tolerable once they were in. She predicted that the toughest opposition would come from the men in the middle, the officials of the ministries and sub-ministries and the whole immense bureaucratic world that had grown up between the few who made the decisions in Moscow and the many who had to execute them on the ground. These people were right to be scared of change. Their organizations had multiplied 'like mushrooms' and turned into 'cosy little places' where obscure duties were performed in exchange for 'a very decent salary'.

Zaslavskaya was ostensibly only writing about officials in government and the economy. It was not her place, even in a paper never supposed to be published, to attack the party bureaucracy. But the logic of her argument was that the party's middle level officials also had every reason to resist change which, if successful, must cut back their power and privileges. If the leadership saw the need for change which promised more say for the party rank-and-file, it was the men in the middle, in the regional and district committees, who had reason to be worried. The Academician was able to put some of this argument in more guarded language in articles that were published in 1985. And three months after the congress was over her point was admitted, in almost Zaslavskayan language, by the man who as much as anyone represented the word of the party, the editor of *Pravda*, Viktor Afanasyev:

What is going on in our country is a struggle, a momentous struggle. People are different. By and large they support party policy, especially those in the broad masses of the people, but there is one section of the people, *especially the members of the middle segments of the party and state apparatus* [author's italics], who sit back and play a waiting game. What, they ask, if this is just some new campaign? They will rant and rave for a little while, and then it will blow over! So they sit back and wait. Then there are those who either directly or indirectly put spokes in the wheels of our new initiatives and party resolutions. So the situation is complicated and we cannot say that everything is going ahead smoothly.

This was daring talk, and perhaps significantly it was delivered to an East European rather than a Russian audience. The idea that Soviet communism had produced a new bureaucratic class unforeseen by Marx was scarcely new. But it was one of those ideas of Trotskyists and others on the heretical left that stout Soviet Marxist-Leninists were supposed to put behind them. Neither Afanasyev nor Zaslavskaya had gone as far as that, but they were arguing that the Soviet system had thrown up whole social groups with an interest in resisting change. Afanasyev was known to have Gorbachov's confidence. Zaslavskaya was a Siberian colleague of the reform-minded economist Abel Aganbegyan whom Gorbachov had picked to be a senior adviser. And it was striking that one of the first public remarks Gorbachov made after the congress was about the need 'to fight, literally to fight, for every line of the decisions' taken by the congress. By the end of 1986 he was talking of an 'acute struggle of ideas' going on in the country, a struggle between different psychologies and ways of thought. 'The old ways,' he warned, 'will not give in without a fight.'

He himself may have fought unsuccessfully to get his Politburo colleagues to agree to release information promptly about the accident at Chernobyl. Only two weeks before it occurred he had been ridiculing people who asked, 'Why are we criticising everything so much, why are we saying everything – after all, our enemies . . . will make use of it to harm socialism.' This sort of thinking was common. People would even argue that it was wrong to publish such things as the percentage of the labour force still engaged in manual labour. ('The truth is the truth,' they said, 'but it is not every truth that does us good'.) It was not surprising that the first reaction of most of Gorbachov's colleagues was to treat the nuclear tragedy as a secret.

Fighting the state and party bureaucracy was not only difficult: it could be dangerous. Khrushchov had fallen partly because the regional barons had lost patience with the endless interfering and reorganizing which made their lives so uncomfortable. Gorbachov chose a different strategy. He would try to squeeze the famous 'inert stratum' between Moscow's new vigour and the discontent of ordinary people. It was to be an experiment in guided democracy, Soviet style; a combination of dramatic remarks and gestures by Gorbachov and other leaders with cautious movement towards more public influence over those who governed them.

The general secretary's speeches and impromptu conversations during travels round the country came back time and again to the theme of resistance to change and how it should be overcome. He attacked party organizations that behaved as though reform was Moscow's business and went on in the same old way themselves. He said that attempts to make changes were coming up against 'a wall of indifference and sometimes even open opposition'. He referred to people 'who feel we are pushing things too far'. He came closest to the bone when he criticized the timidness of many local newspapers. Judging by a lot of them there was nothing but 'peace and quiet and plenty' in the land. The reason, he said, was that party leaders, from the regions down, were not allowing critically-minded journalists to get into print. 'What kind of socialism is it if things are kept from the people? Is this some private concern of entrepreneurs?' Leaders had responsibilities. They should not behave like feudal 'princelings' to whom the people had to say their prayers. Too many leaders had 'responded with dismay' to people's attempts to have a greater say in affairs. It was time for them to learn to live in conditions of 'a widening democracy'. Too many leaders and officials had a 'pathological reaction to criticism from the working people'.

It was not only Gorbachov who spoke like this. The much more outspoken Moscow-based press continued to report on hair-raising scandals whose protagonists appeared unaware of the changed mood in the capital. The police in a town in Krasnoyarsk, Konstantin Chernenko's Siberian home, uncovered what sounded like a typical conspiracy by the officials in charge of housing and food supplies. But in the end it was the head of the police investigation team who was sacked and expelled from the party. A local journalist who had written about the case found it prudent to re-settle on the Far Eastern island of Sakhalin. He explained that he had been summoned to regional party headquarters and told that if he did not go away he too would be kicked out of the party (local journalists were notoriously vulnerable to their party superiors and even some correspondents of the best-known central newspapers found themselves coming under attack in the summer of 1986 from the Soviet procurator general for alleged sensationalism). Officials still practised the traditional art of constructing Potyomkin villages. A district outside the old city of Pskov, host to a conference on public catering, filled its foodshops with special supplies to impress the delegates: a simple trick regularly performed in the past by all levels of the government. When the local paper tried to expose this in the spirit of the new age the district first secretary had the whole issue destroyed.

Even Boris Yeltsin in Moscow found it difficult to make his weekly inspection tour of the shops without word getting out and the assistants putting on clean white coats and bringing out the under-the-counter goods. Innocents who believed that the party congress automatically meant greater freedom for new ideas quickly discovered that it was not as simple as that. A timid but potentially significant experiment in the north Caucasus town of Groznyy to allow private car owners to license their cars as part-time taxis had barely begun when the local finance authorities stopped it.

It was also obvious that the changes Moscow had managed to force on the provinces sometimes caused bitterness without achieving total submission. In Kazakhstan, some of the five hundred senior officials who had been removed by the time the Soviet party congress met fought back with anonymous letters against the men who had accused and then replaced them. A newly-elected regional party chief who ridiculed his predecessor's achievements was in turn publicly attacked for being a time-server. People were offended by the new line that almost everything in the past was bad, to the point that it had become 'indecent . . . to mention successes'. The best explanation why Brezhnev's old colleague Kunayev remained Kazakhstan's leader seemed that under these circumstances no one could be found who was both suitable and willing to replace him. Reports from other regions spoke of sacked officials hatching 'dirty tricks' and spreading 'mean slanders'. When Kunayev was at last prised out of Kazakhstan in December 1986, Kazakh students rioted in Alma-Ata, not least perhaps because the new first secretary was a Russian.

When in midsummer a small news story was published about Vyacheslav Molotov, now ninety-six but still making notes in his copy of Engels' *Anti-Duehring*, it was hard not to wonder if the impenitent old Stalinist was being used to awe the leadership's hidden enemies. Molotov told the reporter who interviewed him that he was 'up to date with all events' and felt 'inspired by the changes which are taking place in our life'. His only regret was that he was too old to play an active part in them himself. It was the first favourable public mention of him, references to his wartime role excepted, since he had been driven from power by Khrushchov.

Gorbachov appeared to have no illusions that he could mould the vast party and state apparatus to his liking by his own efforts. It was while he was in the Far East, and closer to Tokyo and Peking than he was to Moscow, that he stopped a man who was urging him to apply greater control and asked him to consider the problems of governing the vast Soviet continent. His solution lay in his interpretation of 'democracy'. He had called on the party rank-and-file to put pressure on party officials. Now he was campaigning for ordinary citizens to use their rights to agitate for better service from the bureaucrats who governed them. 'This is the way things should be today,' he explained, 'every working man . . . should be involved in everything. He has a right to have and should have real opportunities to make criticisms if they need to be made, about production, as well as about consumer issues, educational issues and matters concerning discipline, and about the way things are done in general, both in the enterprise and in the town . . . and when it is not possible [to settle things quickly] then people must be told precisely and clearly why this is not possible.'

As he developed this message he must have seemed like a trouble-maker to part of Soviet officialdom. 'Don't be embarrassed,' he told a crowd of factory workers, 'tell the truth, honestly. There's no need to lose your composure, your confidence. But don't give in to boorish people, thieves, impudent individuals, you understand, those who try to humiliate and insult people, don't give in to them.'

The ideas and the language were a measure of Gorbachov's recognition of the gulf between people and government. Like his predecessors he was an actor condemned to play a great role in front of an audience that could not clap. The Soviet system did not allow its people to pass open judgement on its leader, and that at least Gorbachov showed no sign of wishing to change. Stalin did not need to be applauded: he had the means to enforce his will. Grudging obedience was enough. But Gorbachov's success depended on the cooperation of his audience. On his travels round the country he seemed to solicit approval from the crowds and one can imagine that a woman's cry of 'Mikhail Sergeyevich, you are a good *muzhik*' had almost the value for him of a great ovation. But he wanted more than applause. 'If you think that the general secretary is the only one who should take steps nothing is going to happen.' The only solution was 'bringing the whole of society to bear'.

The leadership's ideas for involving citizens in the affairs of government were not new. Since the debate that preceded the adoption of the new constitution in 1977 scholars and experts had offered quiet hints of ways to lessen the weight of government on the citizen. There was always more variety in attitudes and thought than the official portrait of the country suggested. From the outside the Soviet Union might seem like a great well-ordered factory, everything in its place and functioning according to rules made in the managing director's office. In reality it was more like a vast, rambling house, whose rooms were decorated in a puzzling number of styles; where antique chairs sat oddly in front of modern tables; and where all sorts of treasures from the past were hidden at the back of drawers while new ideas might be found scribbled on pieces of what looked like waste paper.

The constitution of 1977, by declaring the Soviet Union had progressed beyond the 'dictatorship of the proletariat', encouraged a number of party intellectuals to develop cautious ideas of how substance might be given to

Soviet 'socialist democracy'. Some lawyers tried to teach legal rights to a population that for obvious reasons was for the most part extremely ignorant about them. They fought, with some success, to establish the principle that a man was innocent until proved guilty; that defence lawyers should actually defend their client rather than echo the prosecution; that citizens had rights as consumers. The planned publication of the first full collection of Soviet laws was considered by reformers an important step towards a legal system accessible to all, and a break with the traditional Soviet and Tsarist attitude that many laws were best kept secret from the people they concerned. There were areas into which these 'reformers' did not venture. Anything 'political' remained beyond reach. The day when a dissident, brought to trial under the criminal code (as they invariably were), could face a court knowing he or she stood a decent chance of acquittal was not in sight. The power of the feudal 'princelings' over their territories certainly included influence over local courts. And the more general principle that the party should guide the law as it guided every other part of Soviet life remained beyond challenge. But the small changes were important and encouraged people to bid for more.

There had been a little progress, too, in putting life into the soviets, the nominally elected councils that began at the village and went up to the Supreme Soviet of the Soviet Union. Though they met for only a few days each year at least their standing commissions had been given more substantial supervisory work. People did not expect much from their deputies. Since the latter were nominated by the party and 'elected' without contest it would have been surprising if they had. The deputies' value was further diminished by the attitude of many government and party authorities towards them. Mayors who were both party members and party appointees could talk as though the title of deputy was bestowed as an honour badge for good behaviour: 'we seldom find a deputy who behaves badly or fails to fulfil the plan.' After Gorbachov began speaking about the problem it became fashionable for newspapers to reveal just how little many deputies really did; how they were given wretchedly ill-equipped rooms for the surgeries they were supposed to hold, and how few if any constituents bothered to come to them. These reports made it plain that the real masters of local government were still the permanent officials.

Experiments had been conducted in Georgia and other parts of the country to give local councils more power over factories and offices which belonged to ministries in republican capitals or in Moscow and which were powerful enough to ignore any town council. The party congress approved of this, just as it urged councils to use more energetically their theoretical right to oversee local services like food supplies, health, education and housing. They were told that they now had 'full responsibility for all aspects of life on their territory', and this was spelt out in a decree issued in the summer. The puzzle – tacitly acknowledged by the party congress – was how to make people feel the deputies spoke for them. It was agreed that the electoral system needed 'perfecting', a point that some 'democrats' had been quietly making for years, deploying powerful quotes from Lenin in their own support: 'The masses must have the right to choose its responsible leaders. The masses must have the right to replace them. The masses must have the right to know and check each smallest step they take.' That was still too bold but at last it seemed as though it might be possible to have more than one candidate for each seat in local elections (Soviet experts had watched the Hungarians try this without causing panic). There was also a move towards consultations before local government leaders and factory managers were appointed, and to bringing an element of competition to such appointments. Some regions were already trying out a system of regular public inquisition on the performance of officials (including the often unpopular permanent staff of the soviets) and industrial managers.

The purpose of these schemes was to add public pressure to the party's power to control. The party was present as a guiding hand in all these schemes, its right to the final word intact. If there were ever to be two candidates for each seat in Supreme Soviet elections, both would have the party's approval ('the party will continue to see to it,' Gorbachov told the congress, 'that the most worthy people are elected deputies'). The same was true for any other process of election or consultation, whether for leaders of work brigades or the director of a nuclear power station. And once chosen the leaders would be watched over by the local party faction. Who was head of the group of party deputies in the Moscow city council that was supposed to be its inspiration? The Moscow first secretary, Boris Yeltsin.

For a westerner to say that this was not democracy was to miss the point. Democracy in the Sixth Continent was not meant to be like democracy anywhere else. Soviet elections were not likely to become the moment when a government put itself in the power of its people. They would remain what they had long been – a chance for the government to demonstrate its power over the people. If the people could not be allowed to applaud for themselves the government would clap itself. There was no sign that Gorbachov wanted to or could change that. To suppose otherwise was to ignore the mentality and values of a leadership born out of a special brand of revolutionary Marxism and a country whose culture and history was a source both of pride in strong leadership, and of prejudice against classic ideas of freedom. But Gorbachov needed people's help to improve the way power was exercised on their behalf, and to make life uncomfortable for those who opposed change. His bid for that support was unusual, his manner often persuasive. It was perhaps the start of the making of a new deal between rulers and ruled.

By the autumn of 1986 the battle lines were sufficiently clear for the shrewd political scientist Fyodor Burlatsky (the man who had used Mao's China to make wounding points about Brezhnev's Russia) to draw a prose picture of a party oppositionist in an imaginary dialogue between a

Gorbachov-style regional first secretary and his unreconstructed number two. The latter's objections to the changes in the country made a long list. He considered the new ideas on economics were becoming dangerous, with too much emphasis on such dubious things as market forces and competition. Was it right to talk about new cooperative and individual forms of labour and to encourage people 'to get rich'? Was this what socialism was about, or was it a retreat from socialism, a 'step back from what we have won'? He worried that too many promises were being given about improving the standard of living. He did not like officials who would or could not 'restructure' themselves being threatened with the sack. The trouble was that many people simply did not understand what this 'new style' that was expected of them meant. The very word 'restructuring' sounded 'foggy, like some idea out of Dostoyevsky'. And, in the end, where would all this change leave the party? If there was to be 'self-management' and independence of decision-making in factories and local government 'what will there be for us to do?' The second secretary shook his head. 'Nothing will come of it.'

But the struggle to change the party was only part of Gorbachov's problem. He had another redoubtable foe to defeat – the attitudes and values that had been formed by the Soviet people as they were dragged into a vast social experiment and learned to set up their own moral landmarks on its often inhospitable and uncharted spaces.

17

Is Making Money Right?

Like a sick man who has for years dragged himself from doctor to doctor the Soviet economy had come to accept talking about its illness as a substitute for a drastic cure. It had been auscultated, pummelled, and submitted to tests and experiments without number. Faith-healers had been called in. There had been provocative advice from medical men abroad. The one thing always beyond serious contemplation was an operation. The surgeon's scalpel might work a cure but what sort of body would emerge from under it? Better the invalid's life one knew: there was always the hope that the new course of pills might do the trick that all the previous ones had not.

It had become the fashion after 1982 to blame this state of affairs on the previous incompetent leadership that had failed to react in time to new circumstances. It had also become possible to suggest that there were social groups in the country whose position and privileges depended on nothing changing in the way the country conducted its business. But the blame for the reluctance to go to the operating table deserved to be more widely shared than that. It went back in time to the myths of the Revolution and forward to the ideals of the communist society that was still promised for the future. And it belonged, too, on the shoulders of most Soviet citizens for whom the economy that so puzzled the economists had become part of the natural order of things, protective and troublesome in almost equal measure. That was something Mikhail Gorbachov seemed to understand. Almost from the day he became leader he started to make the point that the connection had been broken between how well people worked and how

218

much money they earned. It might sound common sense abroad: inside the Sixth Continent it was revolutionary.

> The most important thing . . . is to pay everyone for work, for the real result: at the coal face, at the machine tool, at the open hearth furnace, at the drawing board, at the scientific installation, everyone must receive pay for work . . . Everyone, management, workers . . . all must . . . receive their pay according to their final product. If you do not get the final product, if profit is not created, then it means you cannot get paid.

When he said something similar at the twenty-seventh Party Congress he had to make a joke of the fact that no one applauded him. It was radical talk because it suggested there could be no progress without a new approach to the problems of money and economic value, both of them uncomfortable subjects in the Soviet Union. The revolution had been made in the name of man against money. Modern Soviet Communists disliked the suggestion that they had anything in common with what they considered primitive revolutionaries like the Khmers Rouges who blew up the vault of the old Cambodian national bank and left the prettily engraved banknotes scattered over the street to prove that their evil power had been destroyed. But these Russians were forgetting their own past. 'We are moving towards the *complete abolition of money*. We pay wages in kind, we introduce free trams, we have free schooling, free (though at present bad) dinners, free lodging, lighting . . .' This was the Bolshevik Zinovyev speaking at the beginning of the 1920s, when serious inflation made the promise of a money-less society already written into the Bolshevik programme particularly attractive. There was serious discussion at that time about an alternative unit of accounting which, true to Marxist theory, would be based on a calculation of labour time (the wages of peasants on collective farms created in the 1930s would for many years be calculated in 'work days'). Lenin's New Economic Policy, with its call for classic financial incentives, put an end to these theories but they never went away entirely. No one was surprised when the new Communist party programme drawn up in 1961 sounded in places much like Zinovyev in 1920. It promised that within twenty years state spending on social programmes – the 'social consumption funds' – would make up over half of people's real income. There would be free health care and education; free medicines; free housing and utilities; free public transport; a range of free consumer services; and a step towards free lunches for all workers. While most of this had not come about, conventional Soviet wisdom still maintained that one of the greatest strengths of the Soviet way of life lay in its disregard of economic reality in the name of social justice. Rents that took a fraction of a worker's wages and did not cover the cost of apartment buildings' upkeep; the unchanging five kopek ride that meant the great Moscow underground was by 1985 running at a loss; food prices that had not gone up (in the state shops) for two decades while many farms lived in bankruptcy – all this only made sense as a step towards the abundant communist society of the future in which each would receive what he needed and nothing had a price any more.

The feeling that money was a dangerous animal which, if impossible to destroy, had to be kept on a strong, short leash was reinforced by changes in Soviet society. The 1970s, for all the leadership's alleged mistakes, had brought a rise in the standard of living for many. People had money. At the beginning of the '60s, shortly before Brezhnev became leader, there had been fifty-two million accounts in the state savings bank. When he died there were three times as many in a population of under two hundred and seventy million. The size of the average deposit had grown five times to reach over a thousand pounds. This money was of variable value. It was worthless in shops that had nothing one wanted to buy. Money only assumed its traditional economic role when it moved into the borderline of legality and across it. Shop assistants would produce well-made clothes or decent meat if the customer paid some more roubles 'on top' of the official price. And it was possible to buy anything from ball-point pens to personal computers on the black market.

This state of affairs confirmed old prejudices about money and people who were good at making it, a point made unusually sharply by a play called *Look who's arrived!* put on at the Mayakovsky Theatre in Moscow in 1983. The wife of a famous writer who has just died wants to sell their old dacha outside Moscow. Her intelligentsia family are horrified when the prospective buyer turns out to be a fashionable young hairdresser who charges thirty pounds an appointment. Nicknamed 'King', and dressed in white jeans, a black leather jacket, a suede cap, and a sports shirt decorated with a little Union Jack he is a fine example of a Moscow *nouveau riche*. His friends, a barman and an attendant at one of Moscow's fashionable baths, are also members of the new breed of people with scarce goods and services to offer. Their tastes are Soviet Hollywood. The barman (played in this production by Yuri Andropov's actor son-in-law) dreams of a beautiful park in which a coachman and carriage appear. He opens the carriage door to find a fully-equipped modern bar. It is the most splendid thing he can imagine. 'King' is more intelligent. He knows he has something to learn from this family who are so contemptuous of him. In return he wants their respect. He tries to convince them that his work is as worthy as their's. 'My work makes man feel better – does yours? I am like a creator; I remove what is not essential – and you? I know the consequences of what I do – do you?'

In the play as in real life the traditional élite remained unmoved. Their judgement was delivered by two elderly members of the dacha-owning family. After hearing 'King' talk about the need for 'commerce', the world's oldest profession as he calls it, they look at each other uncomprehendingly. 'Commerce? But I thought we did away with that sixty years ago.'

The money-lessness of Soviet life seemed to suit the temperament of the

Russian intelligentsia. To a West European they were at times almost child-like in their freedom from material concerns. They knew nothing of cheque books or bank managers, overdrafts or mortgages. They were for the most part under pressure neither to work hard nor to save. Their ancestors had been suspicious of the commercial class that grew up before the Revolution. They despised the 'Kings' of the new commercial class. They seemed to have forgotten that some of the most important figures in pre-Revolutionary Russian culture – like Tretyakov, founder of the great Moscow art gallery of the same name – had been merchants and businessmen. In this, at least, their attitudes reinforced the party's prejudices against money, against trade, and indeed against almost everything that in the non-communist world is regarded as part of normal business life. Money meant 'mine'. Soviet citizens had to be taught to think 'ours'. Few questioned the propriety of the article in the Soviet criminal code defining the 'sale and re-sale of goods for profit' as speculation, a crime that carried a minimum two-year sentence.

When Gorbachov warned workers that they should not be paid if they could not make profits he was talking about an economic system that did not exist. He was preparing the ground for changes, but they needed time to be worked out and could scarcely be put into practice before the end of the 1980s. But the enthusiasts of change already knew the shape they wanted it to take. The ideal, according to an experienced Soviet economic journalist, was to impose discipline and efficiency by obliging industry to make real profits: 'Economic responsibility will work more effectively than any directive.' A factory would pay taxes to the state but otherwise it would conduct its business as it thought best. Moscow would not tell it where to get its supplies or to whom its product had to be delivered. It would buy where it wanted and sell where it wanted. The planners would no longer have to toil away at the Soviet equivalent of Sisyphus's labours – hunting for the perfect 'indicator', the elusive measurement that gave a true picture of a factory's performance. 'In principle such a universal measurement already exists – it is profit.' If a factory could not sell its goods it would have to make something else (the journalist ruled out from his ideal world the possibility that an unsuccessful factory might have to close down). The work force would for the first time have a real interest in having managers who were skilful, for their wages would depend on it. They would also understand the advantage of getting rid of unnecessary labour. The smaller the work force, the bigger its remaining members' share of the profits.

To make such drastic changes would be to kill most of the sacred cows of the Soviet economic system. It would have to become money-conscious. Prices would have to reflect costs which as things stood they seldom did. There was uncertainty about what the true cost of many goods and materials was. It would end the planners' power to determine what made a factory successful. It would ensure that industries could trade among themselves, instead of having their supplies issued to them by the equivalent of a military

221

quartermaster's stores. It would take power from the producer and give it to the consumer, be it an enterprise looking for cement or a mother searching for baby clothes. People might even have to acquire some of the commercial skills of the old bourgeoisie. In other words it would amount to a revolution in the Soviet economic system and would therefore be difficult to achieve.

Gorbachov admitted that some economists and theorists considered almost any change in the existing system to be a 'departure from socialist principles'. He would have none of that. 'Dogmas' would not be allowed to pose as the 'eternal truths of socialism'. There would also be institutional resistance from the economic bureaucracy. It ought to be much less important in a reformed system and there would be fewer jobs for its members. What would they do? And what about the party? Gorbachov said its chief job should be to see that the right people were in the right jobs. But if it was true, as the reform-minded journalists pointed out, that workers under the new system would want control over who their boss was, what price the party's role as the executives' employment agency?

There was also doubt about how far Gorbachov himself wanted to push change. He was believed to have warned his East European allies only a few months after his election to be careful about reforms and not to abandon centralization in favour of a market system which he hinted some of them were looking to as a 'life-saver' for their economies. 'Comrades, you should not think about life-savers but about the ship, and the ship is socialism.' But he was, one of his advisers remarked, interested in practical ideas, not theories. He wanted an efficient, modern economy. And as the months went by the language he used about the need for change grew more dramatic. What had at first been called a need to 'improve the economic mechanism' became, by the time the party congress met, a need for 'profound transformation', even for 'radical reform'. A few months later he was using the word revolution himself. 'Restructuring', he told an audience of party officials in the Soviet Far East, should be understood as 'revolution'. What he seemed to mean by that was not a denial of the past but a new stage in Soviet history as important as such 'heroic' epochs as Stalin's industrialization and the reconstruction after the war.

The best proof that Gorbachov was earnest about change came in his attempts to explain to workers that, though it would make great demands of them, its burden would be fairly shared and social justice maintained. His economic advisers were recommending a system that 'confronted labour collectives with a tough dilemma: either work better and live better, or work in the old way and live badly'. The problem with the economic experiment begun under Andropov and enlarged by Gorbachov, the reformers were saying, was that so far the incentive system had not been taken to the 'threshold of sensibility' – an ominous phrase that meant if good workers were not being sufficiently rewarded bad ones were still not feeling enough pain. The new leader was not proposing to be egalitarian. Quite the reverse:

he was suggesting that the truly talented and hard-working should be truly well rewarded. He was enlarging the opportunities for inequality with a purpose. The greater prosperity of the virtuous workers of a profitable factory or farm would spur the lazy and incompetent to improve their ways. The theoretical justification was that this was in keeping with socialism's principle of to each according to his work. It was only in the distant communist future, now indefinitely postponed, that this could become to each according to his need.

Gorbachov seemed to understand that this sort of system stood no chance of being accepted unless there were changes in the way privileges and rewards were distributed throughout Soviet society. This promised to be a difficult business. The *Pravda* article that had so offended some speakers at the party congress had referred to a letter from a party member of forty years' standing which had angrily attacked the privileges of the party and government élite.

One cannot close one's eyes to the fact that party, government, trade union, industrial and even Komsomol leaders sometimes . . . deepen social inequality by making use of all kinds of special cafeterias, special shops, special hospitals, etc. Yes, we have socialism, and everyone should receive according to his work. Let . . . every leader get a higher money salary. But there should be no privileges in anything else. Let the boss go to an ordinary shop together with everyone else and stand in the queue on equal terms – perhaps then it will be possible to do away sooner with the queues that everyone is so fed up with.

The old Communist was revealing no secrets, but it was odd that his comment had been published. Privileges for officials had been introduced soon after the Revolution and were justified then by the need to keep key personnel provided with the necessities of life. The poverty and shortages with which the country struggled for another fifty years meant that this system of secret, privileged distribution of scarce goods and services continued and expanded. Even during the war the canteen of a scientific research institute might have six different menus, the best for those with Doctor of Science degrees, the least nourishing for humble service personnel. Ordinary people might not know all the system's details but they were well aware that it existed. Khrushchov had tried to cut such privileges back a little, but the system gathered force again under Brezhnev and the suspicion grew that many privileges had become luxuries rather than functional necessities. A popular joke about Brezhnev had his mother coming to stay at his dacha outside Moscow and her face falling as he showed her more and more luxurious gadgets. 'Don't you like it, mother?' a disappointed Brezhnev asks. 'But, Lyonya, what will you do when the Revolution comes?' It was an apprehension others shared in real life. A famous writer, asked why he had no flat in central Moscow as his fame entitled him to, explained that he did not want to be in one of the privileged parts of the city on the day the workers finally lost patience. He did not live to see a letter printed in the press which suggested such fears were not fantastic.

Take your academicians, and professors, the great writers and poets, actors and producers, the factory directors and bosses – that is, all the people who are well paid. From time to time they should be 'relieved' of what they've amassed. What's more it ought to be done periodically, every seven to eight years, until they show some shame . . . By the way, that's why a lot of people are delighted when they hear that burglars have well and truly 'relieved' some academician or famous singer. Of course, they don't say it openly, but my, how the soul sings!

The lawyer commenting on the letter naturally expressed horror. This was 'social demagogy, the psychology of lynching'. But that a leading newspaper should have printed anything so shocking suggested that something approaching a lynching mood (reminiscent of the discontented paratroopers back from Afghanistan) did exist among parts of the population where privilege was concerned. A leading sociologist summed up the public mood more broadly: 'frequent encounters' with social injustice had become 'one of the major causes of alienation of part of the workers from society's aims and values'.

It was seldom admitted that the party might be part of these problems of social justice and equality. A party member, it was always said, 'has no privileges, he has only increased duties': a revealing formulation for it suggested a genuine inability to see inequality of power as a source of public discontent. Even so, the explanation had worn thin. The feeling that party leaders had unnecessary privileges was common enough. It was shown in the admiring myth about Andropov living only on his salary. It was there in the stories about the special buildings reserved for the Central Committee and its staff ('Keep out, these are Committee lands!' a watchman told a little boy who had wandered into the conspicuously well-kept grounds of a Central Committee apartment house in Moscow). The first thing a Muscovite would do if he ever got into the Central Committee offices was most likely go to one of its snackbars or cafeterias where food of a quality seldom seen in the ordinary shops was sold at very low prices. 'They live in a different world there,' said a woman who considered herself lucky to have filled her shopping bag with Central Committee sausage. Other institutions followed this example. A leading design bureau in Moscow had four carefully graded dining rooms. The director's boasted a cloakroom fitted with a sky-blue lavatory, an astonishing luxury for any public Soviet institution. Comments were made about the obviously foreign clothes that senior officials could buy in special shops. One of the questions asked Yeltsin at a meeting of junior party officials was where he bought his shoes (if the questioner was hoping to catch him out he would have been disappointed. They were made in the Urals and cost only twenty-three roubles).

The contradictory remarks at the congress about party privileges suggested the party's unease on the subject. Geidar Aliyev, questioned by journalists, justified special shops by saying many party members were too busy to go to ordinary shops – a not unreasonable, if scarcely egalitarian, point though the Soviet Union did not claim to be an egalitarian society. A junior Central Committee official denied such shops existed. He said he stood in queues. In fact there had already been rumours the previous year that Gorbachov had moved to limit privileges for the Committee, in particular cancelling the distribution of special food parcels to its cleaners, waitresses and other junior employees. Boris Yeltsin, admitting openly at the congress that it was hurtful to hear people say leaders enjoyed 'special benefits', suggested that those that were 'unjustified' be abolished. Asked after the congress what privileges he had cancelled in the Moscow party committee he offered a significant modification of the traditional reply:

I think the question has been wrongly put. Why only cancel? We have added a thing or two. We have added work, we've increased the number of the [party] bureau meetings. Officials in the Moscow committee now don't work from nine till six but till ten or eleven in the evening and sometimes even to twelve. As for cancelling, to start with we have shut one shop selling consumer goods. I think that's useful. Moscow committee officials will get to have a sharper feel for shortages.

Yeltsin promised to do more, starting with an attack on the use of official cars for taking children to school and wives to the shops. His party officials would be sharing cars whenever possible. But the problem of privilege went beyond the party and the bureaucracy. It was partly a result of the stability the country had enjoyed in the last quarter-century. The better-off groups, from the senior leaders to modest but successful professionals like army officers or industrial managers, had a position they would most likely be able to preserve for their children. At the same time the Jekyll and Hyde quality of the Brezhnev society, with its inefficient official economy and its lively unofficial economy, made it possible for new groups – represented at their best by 'King' the hairdresser, at the worst by the thieving managers of Moscow's shops – to set themselves up too. This seems to have triggered the discontent. Khrushchov had had holiday villas every bit as luxurious as Brezhnev's, but the traditional privileged groups had always been discreet. The topmost leadership was still seldom seen in the ordinary world apart from its ritual public appearances. They were perhaps beyond envy. Envy was also contained by the segregation that was the guiding principle of much of Soviet life. A Central Committee staffer lived in a Committee apartment house, had his dacha in a colony of Committee dachas, went to special shops and took his holidays in special resorts. A writer could live in a world no less exclusive, and so could a ministry official or such labour aristocrats as miners.

The new rich were different because they were visible. Officials from Soviet Central Asia did very well at their comfortable 'embassies' in Moscow but their style of life was seldom observed by ordinary Muscovites. Central Asian traders who made fortunes at Moscow's main market displayed their prosperity with long, lavish lunches at the Uzbekistan restaurant and were disliked for it. The new rich parked their cars in the street, an invitation to envy. Their houses looked all the more ostentatious for being built next to ordinary ones. The pretty black-market clothes of their children excited the schoolchildren of less well-off families. It was difficult to sustain indignation about a party official enjoying himself invisibly in a fine resort one could not enter. It was much easier to get angry about people who made fortunes by renting out expensive rooms to holiday-makers in a seaside town. There was particular indignation that parents visiting children who had been sent away from Chernobyl to holiday camps in the Crimea were having to pay eight roubles a night for a room in a private house: 'someone's grief is someone else's profit.'

The danger was that popular anger against people of this sort would be transferred to the party whose leaders also lived well if for the most part invisibly. A sociologist quoted a disturbing but pertinent question that had been put to him. The newspapers were always writing about dishonest 'speculators' and the like but what about some 'local leaders' who lived in just as much style as these criminals? They too had cars, country houses, gave their children apartments, got them into universities and then into important jobs. Why were they allowed this and others not?

The resentment of the majority of the population that belonged to neither the old nor the new élite might have been contained if the government had paid proper attention to its needs. That it had not was an important theme of Gorbachov's speeches. He spoke angrily of how the belief that all that mattered was to fulfil the plan had 'seeped into our blood', while how the workers lived was considered to be of secondary importance. The result was a society whose inequalities went far beyond the differences in salaries that were supposed to reflect a citizen's contribution to society (a Politburo member received about five times the average wage, a Marshal of the Soviet Union twice as much as that). Stability meant that the children of the successful tended to be successful themselves. Politburo children got good jobs in the academic world (Grishin's daughter; Ustinov's son and daughter; Chernenko's daughter), or in diplomacy (Andropov's son; Gromyko's son and grandson; Anastas Mikoyan's grandson). Gorbachov's daughter was a doctor which most people would have said was a far less desirable profession than the others.

This was only the top of a pyramid of unequal educational opportunities, as Soviet sociologists had begun to admit. The country could not offer all children an 'equal start'. The chance of going on to higher education depended a great deal on where and in what sort of family a child was born. The higher up the educational ladder from kindergarten to university, the more these social differences counted. The majority of students at some of the most prestigious universities and institutes came from only a small number of schools in the capital. Big cities could provide both private tutors (some charging over twenty-five pounds from each member of a two-hour group session) as well as 'special schools', many of the latter giving intensive training in foreign languages and particularly sought after by ambitious professional families. Almost three-quarters of the students at the two institutes that trained future Soviet diplomats were children of well-placed officials. The sons and daughters of famous actors and senior officials were prominent among students at Moscow's theatrical institutes. Favouritism and bribery got young children to Artek, the model pioneer camp in the Crimea that was meant to sum up all that was best in Soviet education. Devices to protect the children of the less well-off, such as easier entry for students who had worked for a year, were manipulated by canny professional parents to the benefit of their offspring. And as a last resort, if parents had neither the right job nor good enough contacts, they could try a bribe. It cost about two and a half thousand pounds to get a student accepted by some medical faculties. The chances of being caught out had for many years been small. Was it surprising that a Soviet cosmonaut should complain that among young people building BAM, the new northern branch of the Trans-Siberian railway, there were very few children of 'great scientists, military chiefs, actors, and leading party, economic and government officials'?

In a country where older people had been brought up in hard and uncertain times there was a tendency to spoil children. Families spent from seventeen to twenty-five thousand roubles on the education and upkeep of a child till the age of eighteen; an astonishing figure remembering that the average annual wage when Brezhnev died in 1982 came to not much over two thousand roubles. If children had uneven educational opportunities they also had uneven health care. The countryside, as might be expected, got the worst. The best was provided to those families of the topmost party and government officials who qualified for treatment by the Fourth Main Administration of the Ministry of Health. Presided over by Yevgeni Chazov, the heart specialist who had been Brezhnev's chief physician, it controlled a country-wide network of twelve hospitals, eight polyclinics, one research institute, one laboratory and fifteen sanatoria. This was medicine on the level of the Western world. Between these extremes the standard of care was usually matched to the importance the government attached to a person's job, with the residents of major cities also among the better cared for.

These gradations would have mattered less if the average standard had been good and there had been no black market medicine. In fact the country's health had started to decline in the 1970s and by the middle of the decade the government stopped publishing statistics that allowed calculations to be made about such things as life expectancy and infant mortality. Foreign estimates suggested that male life expectancy fell from 67 in 1964 to 62 in 1980, and for women from 76 to 73. They seemed borne out by figures, offered by Boris Yeltsin in 1986, showing that the average life expectancy for men and women in Moscow had fallen from 70 in 1983 to 68 two years later. Infant mortality rates over the same period had gone up, though the meaning of this was more disputed. But that all was not well with child care could be seen from a 1980 report by medical specialists in Leningrad where the standard of health might be expected to be above average. It noted that only forty per cent of children under five were really healthy while the same amount often suffered from acute respiratory illnesses. As many as six per cent of children in a smaller survey in Leningrad turned out to have rickets – not a condition usually found in a developed industrial society.

The unevenness of opportunity for good health care was compounded by the development of the black market in medical services. The popular surgeon who needed to be encouraged to operate by a 'present' and the nurse who would only use a good needle for an injection if she was given a chic foreign plastic carrier bag were familiar at least in everyone's imagination. Yevgeni Yevtushenko gave such characters belated punishment in a fierce poem of 1986 (it would not have been published before) about an apparently model nurse who had stolen scarce drugs to sell on the black market:

> How many medicines have been snatched by thieving hands
> From the painful bloody wounds of others!

The more one looked at Soviet society the harder it was to decide what was and what was not just – as the confused Soviet debate on the problem showed. Was it fair that the low rent should be the same for everyone? Did the better-off need such heavily subsidized housing, especially when their flats were often of superior quality and situated in much more desirable areas. It was almost as easy to judge a Muscovite's status by his address as it was the income of a Londoner or New Yorker by theirs. Not surprisingly this was resented. 'Why shouldn't a leading official live on the same level as ordinary workers, why fence themselves off from the masses?' asked a letter published in *Pravda* before the party congress. And yet the rent per square metre of a flat in a fine pre-revolutionary building in Granovsky Lane, where Khrushchov had lived when in power and Molotov, till his death, was the same as for a low-ceilinged, noisy apartment in a pre-fabricated block in the distant new suburb of Chertanovo where both shops and public transport were bad. The same point could be made about heavily subsidized food which, while needed by the average wage-earner, represented an unfair advantage for those who could afford to pay the real production costs.

- Is Making Money Right? -

And was it right that children should inherit fortunes from their parents? There was no inheritance tax on money and only a registration fee of up to ten per cent of value on other estate. The official criterion of 'good' money lay in the distinction between earned and unearned income. Some experts argued that inherited money should be considered 'unearned' because the heirs had not worked for it. They produced statistics to suggest that young families had twice the average amount of consumer durables thanks to help from their parents. Far from being pleased by this they argued it was corrupting the young. The solution they proposed was a 'significant' tax on all inheritance. Some members of the public were horrified by the idea. 'What will be the stimulus to work if a man knows that his children will have to start from the beginning again? . . . After all, we live for our children.' Others applauded it. As a well-known playwright remarked in an attempt to bring some humanity into an increasingly ill-tempered debate, envy was as much a quality of *meshchanstvo*, the evocatively disapproving Russian word for petty bourgeois attitudes, as was money-grubbing. No one paid him much attention.

The fiercest passions were roused by the farmers' private plots. To understand them was to understand why anything connected with money in the Soviet Union led to a tangle of contradictory moral and economic theories. Although tiny (on collective farms they were about one third of a hectare) the plots produced over ten per cent of the food that was sold in the shops and markets. Khrushchov had wanted to abolish them but the country had got over that brief flashback to primitive communism. Yet it still seemed that almost everything the peasant did was bound to be wrong. His private labour was meant to contribute to the nation's food supply, but the more he delivered to market the greater the danger that he would be accused of amassing 'unearned income'. How could it be unearned? The theory was that a peasant family ought to use its plot to grow food for its own needs but could sell any surplus on the private market. In most Russian towns in the summer you did indeed see little lines of country women standing quietly outside state foodshops. They held a few bunches of radishes, a handful of scrubbed baby carrots tied together with cotton, lettuce, parsley or a little fruit. But it was obvious that, in a country where distances were so great, transport so often poor, and the demand for garden produce so high, a system was needed to bring fruit and vegetables to the towns in sufficient quantities. And it had to be unofficial because the government was unable to organize an efficient one itself.

It was not only unofficial. It was also almost entirely illegal. Produce was bought by private middlemen and shipped to market by illegal arrangement in official trucks and planes (as the Azerbaidzhani Geidar Aliyev had discovered for himself when he took over the leadership of his republic). The freight department of Alma-Ata airport for years ran two operations; one legal, the other illegal. The latter sent planeloads of Kazakhstan's southern fruit and vegetables to the towns of Siberia and the Russian north. The markets themselves had their unofficial guilds of full-time retailers, each one of them breaking every day the law against 'speculation' (there were signs, alarming to the authorities, that a significant minority of the population no longer saw anything wrong in these people's work). The system was to a large extent fed by peasants who turned their third of a hectare into a real market garden. That was illegal too. Everyone involved in this vast and astonishingly efficient business were technically making 'unearned income', meaning money made by labour that official morality did not recognize as worthy. It was wrong to grow early strawberries in the Ukraine for the market. A family that did just that and who suffered a car crash on the way home from making a sale were written about as though they had received some form of divine socialist retribution. It was wrong to put all your plot down to flowers even though there was an immense hunger for them in most Russian cities. A village in Krasnodar had a tradition of growing roses. Their gardens were ploughed up and anyone who was a party member was threatened with expulsion if he did not stop growing flowers. That a successful private plot could bring a family an income of three and a half thousand pounds, and sometimes twice and even four times as much, inevitably added to the fervour of the anti-garden lobby.

Why was this so wrong? The experts had many explanations. A peasant who turned his garden into a commercial enterprise would shirk his duties on the collective farm though the rose-growing Communists of Krasnodar denied this. The official farming newspaper argued that the peasant had to pay nothing for the land he was making money out of, and got his water, energy and many of the supplies he needed at controlled state prices, while he sold his produce at market prices that were on average twice those in state shops. The final insult (and the most galling to its readers, the paper claimed) was that no tax was paid on these ill-made profits. Eminent legal authorities made a more precise ideological point. These farmers were not making money so much out of their own labour as by exploiting the free market and its mobile prices. That the market was signalling the demands of consumers was neither here nor there, for such men believed, together with the elderly intellectuals in the play *Look who's arrived!*, that a spontaneous market had no place in the Soviet system.

Yuri Andropov had spoken of the need to develop a 'culture of sensible consumption'. Gorbachov said 'we do not look upon socialism . . . as a consumer society. We will not follow the standards of the Western way of life.' But sociologists admitted that not much thought had been given to what Soviet standards should be. The man who argued most energetically for an inheritance tax complained that not even the greatest experts could tell him what sort of spread in income and possessions between families of the same size was compatible with social justice. It was the formidable Tatyana Zaslavskaya, appearing more and more often in the media from

1985 on, who came up with the most detailed suggestions. Saying outright that the government had ignored the problem of social justice during most of the Brezhnev years, she suggested a series of tough financial measures. She wanted a progressive tax on income and perhaps on property too, the latter to include not only a citizen's house or flat and his country cottage if he had one, but also his car and any other valuable consumer durables (savings bank accounts would presumably be included, for surveys had shown that deposits in a small proportion of these could be worth as much as twenty thousand pounds). Zaslavskaya also proposed differentiated rents on land that was used for private plots. She pointed out that land near a city in the fertile south was far more valuable than land in some village lost in the roadless fields and forests of north Russia. As far as she was concerned this difference represented unearned income for those with good land. 'Let's look truth in the eye,' she told a Soviet journalist, 'if we do not succeed in this struggle people will not believe . . . [that we have] . . . social justice.'

If they did not believe that, the chances for a serious reform of the economy were slim. Gorbachov knew, and so did the experts who championed reform, that people would not put up with its discomforts if they were seen neither to have a purpose nor to be evenly shared. Zaslavskaya was more frank than most about what those discomforts might be. Many people, especially in management at first, would lose their jobs and have to be re-trained. Not only factories and farms but whole districts would develop at a different pace. The less productive ones would fall behind in the provision of social services. There would also be some 'inevitable psychological strain' because of what she called 'the just punishments administered by the rouble'.

Measures introduced by the government in May 1986 were meant to persuade people that the opportunities for 'unearned income' were at last being blocked off. They did not include any of the taxes that had been proposed, perhaps because it had been impossible to devise a system quickly for such a big country. But they did impose new and shocking restrictions on deals involving large sums of cash. Any deal or purchase worth more than five thousand roubles could no longer be done in cash. Instead a money transfer through the State Bank or savings banks would have to be used. Anyone involved in a deal of over ten thousand roubles, or building a house worth more than twenty thousand roubles, would have to present a declaration of how the money had been obtained. Most of the other measures stiffened already existing penalties for such offences as the misuse of official vehicles, bribery, and theft of state property. The register of people involved in cottage industries and services – legal as long as only one person was involved – was to be brought up to date and their income properly taxed. It was asserted that over a million people were making money in this way without registering. There was to be stricter control of the renting of private housing, and of the exchange of flats which was often accompanied by illegal payments. Regulations concerning the internal passports each citizen carried were to be more diligently enforced to make the life of market traders and other undesirable characters difficult. No one had an accurate idea of how many people throughout the country were managing to avoid the legal obligation to work but officials hinted the number was large. Control over the peasant markets was to be balanced by improving the work of the cooperative system that was already meant to (but seldom did) act as an irreproachable middleman between the peasant and the consumer.

The measures took in their sights many of the abuses that caused popular anger, though everything would depend on the intelligence and force with which they were put into practice. Within less than a month the Moscow authorities announced that all Muscovites of working age had to provide their district soviet with a certificate from his or her place of work. The names of those still refusing to work would be passed on to the militia. Within weeks, too, reports were coming in that stricter attention to the regulations governing the sale of private plot produce was emptying some markets and sending up the prices. Peasants were stopped from travelling to markets outside their own districts. In some places people who worked hard on their private plots were even attacked as 'enemies'. Representatives from a Siberian town who tried to buy onions from private growers in Kazakhstan were forced to unload them by local police. Gorbachov himself had to scold farm officials in the Soviet Far East for implying in his presence that every peasant who took produce to market was a 'speculator'. But even he did not want to take off all restrictionss. He wanted peasants to sell what they grew in their gardens through state cooperatives rather than chase after the higher free market prices. He warned against 'grasping attitudes' and that old Soviet demon, 'the psychology of private ownership'. It was not surprising if many local officials had decided that peasants selling fruit at what seemed an exorbitant price by comparison with the state shops deserved to be harassed. The country's traditions and prejudices, and a huge bureaucracy that was used to proving its obedience by none too intelligent zealousness, were bound to lead to excesses.

More important was whether most people would find Gorbachov's stern new world of financial punishments and rewards congenial even if it was, by its own rules, scrupulously fair. As Academician Zaslavskaya pointed out, some would do better than others and it would not always be easy to see the justice in it. The farmers who worked bad land and the employees of an enterprise producing an out-of-date product would indeed – if the system was allowed to bite – be punished by the rouble and might ask if this was socialism. And for all its tough talk the government itself remained ambivalent about money. The idea that man should be morally stimulated to labour for the good of society had deep roots in the Soviet Union. There was an elaborate system of so-called socialist competition in which factories competed among each other to set records. Gorbachov had done his best to put new life into the Stakhanov movement. Named after the Donbas miner who had produced unprecedented amounts of coal in the 1930s, this was supposed to encourage emulation of both the miner himself and other heroes of labour. Stakhanovites were not always popular because their achievements could be used to impose harder norms on other workers.

In fact not even Stakhanovism had been a demonstration of pure proletarian morality. Whatever the great miner's motives the authorities believed that proletarian ardour needed to be fuelled. The evening after Aleksei Stakhanov had mined his record one hundred and two tons of coal the mine's party committee voted to give him a month's salary as bonus; to assign him one of the apartments reserved for technical experts and install a telephone in it; and to give him and his wife free tickets to every film show and other occasion in the miners' club. They would have given him a motor car, too, if they had had one. Instead Stakhanov got a horse and trap with rubber wheels. This had not hurt the image of the miner partly because publicity had always stressed his heroism, and also because as a working class hero he was assumed strong enough to fight off the petty bourgeois instincts that having a telephone and a horse and cart might rouse in others. By contrast the people who were apprehensive about money in the 1980s were decidedly unsure of the ability of Soviet citizens to withstand its temptations. It was the apprehension of older people who had never known the luxuries many young people now took for granted. This was a popular subject for films in which wise old parents came to stay with successful but unhappy young children caught up in a dangerous world of automatic coffee-grinders and fashionably large pet dogs. It also reflected the belief of the schoolteacher inside most Soviet Communists that without a guiding hand the pupils would surely go astray.

This unease about money also reflected powerful myths connected with the Revolution and the hard times the country had lived through. Whatever sophisticated intellectuals might say there were still people who could not understand why money was necessary seventy years after the defeat of capitalism. There were people who believed all children should be brought up communally and the family no longer serve as a social or economic unit. If these were minority beliefs the special vocabulary that had evolved to express doubts about money and possessions was widely used. The common verb 'to have' was dark with undertones of disapproval. A new word, *veshchizm*, literally thing-ism, implied the wrongness of being interested in material things. People described as 'knowing how to live' were people who lived too well for the liking of those talking about them. That they had come by their money legally had nothing to do with it. Such a person might be a man in his late twenties, married and with a son, and living in a three-roomed flat. His salary as a member of a Moscow scientific institute would be below the national average but he gets royalties from books written by his father. He has a car, a Parker pen, a Japanese video recorder. He is intelligent, well-read, and knows how to get tickets to the theatres and concerts most in demand. His son will go to an English-language special school and will soon start tennis lessons.

The young man was real; infuriatingly real to the Soviet journalist who talked to him and who felt he was being treated as an inferior. He had the last word, though, as journalists tend to. He reported that when this 'superman's' mother had died he had asked the hospital to give him her three gold teeth. Such were the moral depths inhabited by someone who 'knew how to live'. Disapproving essays of this kind reflected well-known facts of Soviet life. It was difficult to acquire some if not most consumer goods in an entirely legal way. Anyone who owned a car could hardly keep it running if he did not flirt with black market mechanics. The best economics journal in the country once ran an article suggesting that mastering the difficulties of car ownership was the best way for a man to prove he had true Russian machismo. But even if the new leadership could make it possible for car-owners to become honest again, would they still not be searched for moral flaws? Wouldn't even the money honourably earned by the efficient and productive, when the new reforms were working, still be watched – by some enviously; by others alarmed at its potentially corrupting powers?

> The highest value in the West is money. Or its equivalent, goods. The most respected person in that society is the one who knows how to make money. In our translation – the person 'who knows how to live'. He's the one who tries to convince us that it's indecent for us to look into his purse. Our highest value is the moral man, the harmoniously developed personality. The equality of people. Absolutely not money and not goods . . . The communist ideal is above all the equality of people.

This was the voice of a well-known columnist who specialized in the problems of the young. In 1983 the pages of *Komsomolskaya Pravda* were taken up over several months first with a piece of hers about schoolgirls and then with readers' reactions to it. It had begun with a letter from a girl called Alisa who said she came from a well-off family and was proud of it. She and her friends were prettier, better dressed and brighter than the ordinary girls, whom she laughed at as 'grey mice'. Alisa added that she and her group also did better in exams, knew more about culture and not only attracted all the best-looking boys but awed them into good behaviour (an achievement in the often poorly disciplined Soviet schools of the 1980s). Some of the letters of kids who wrote in to support her were printed but most of the comment was hostile. As for the journalist, she said she was heartened that the sharpest condemnation of these snobbish young people had come from workers in the classic machine building industries, the forge of the 'proletarian type of personality with its developed collectivism and its feeling of fellowship that is the polar opposite of the private property mentality'.

234

It was re-fighting the battles of the past. On one side was the Russian worker, solid and simple in his blue overalls, a spanner in his mighty hand; on the other the bourgeoisie, the 'brand-new, energetic . . . jeans bourgeoisie'. Were these the attitudes the country needed to take into the twenty-first century where, if Gorbachov's hopes for a technological revolution began to come true, there would be much more than jeans to tempt the young and Soviet economic strength would no longer lie in the great factories that were revered as the cradle of proletarian values? At moments like these the Soviet Union seemed to be yearning for the simpler days of Revolutionary propaganda when good and evil were clearly defined. It did not take much for some leaders to slip back into the language of that time. The 'private property mentality', the new party leader of Georgia warned soon after his election in 1985, signalled the existence of a 'reactionary and conservative class. And we must fight this morality with all the weapons of the class war – without compromise, in a principled fashion, without mercy.'

It was an unusually vigorous outburst, but one sensed in some of the other new leaders – Yegor Ligachov, for example, and Boris Yeltsin too – a throwback to the model Communists of the twenties and thirties; straight, tough men for times that were tough but surely simpler than the end of the twentieth century. Mikhail Gorbachov was not immune to the attraction of those days, as when he told an audience of party officials that they deserved to be described, using a 'good word' from the past, as the 'commissars of the present stage of the struggle'.

Was the Soviet past becoming a burden on the Soviet future? Was the home of the world's first communist revolution already a prisoner of its past? Seventy years of achievements and unaccomplished dreams, sacrifices and suffering, since the Revolution had become part of the stability of the state, providing the store of common emotions, beliefs and thoughts that any country needs. If its burden becomes too great a country may try to escape from it by revolution, as the Chinese destroyed Confucian temples and images of Buddha in an attempt to free themselves from the intolerable weight of a long and ancient civilization. But the Russians had used up that option in 1917. The Soviet Union's problem was not the instability that leads to revolution but the stability that makes necessary change difficult. The alternative was to exorcise some of that past by removing some of the mystification and self-deception from it. There were those who hoped this would happen. And there was encouraging logic in the appearance of a new leader with plans for the next century at the moment when an effort of national memory was being made to do justice to a tragic past.

18

Memory and Mother Russia

Hidden in our memory for ever
Are dates, and incidents, and faces . . .
If in the minefield of the past you dig
It's better that you never make mistakes . . .

Vladimir Vysotsky,
1938–1980

'Culture,' the novelist Yuri Nagibin wrote, 'cannot exist outside memory; outside consciousness of the fact that each of us is a chain in the general process of history. The man who does not remember where he comes from cannot become cultured.' Nagibin used a special word for culture – *intelligentnost*, the quality of being a true member of the Russian intelligentsia. Memory entered the meaning of the most precious word in the intelligentsia's vocabulary: *chestny*, used to describe the person who was honourable, who remembered and was loyal to the truth. In a country where political truth had for many decades squeezed out the broader truth, the truth of the honourable man, to be called *chestny* was the greatest compliment of all.

The political truth had seduced many for it contained myths and hopes that were noble: not for nothing had some compared the building of the new Russia to the act of Genesis itself. Even Dr. Zhivago had thought for a time that the Revolution was a piece of 'splendid surgery'. Like the hero of a popular Ilya Ehrenburg novel of the 1930s, such men and women accepted that one had to submit to this partial, official truth or become a traitor. It was a terrible decision to be faced with and those who had the strength to refuse

236

it – and were lucky enough to be remembered – became patron saints for a large part of the intelligentsia. Boris Pasternak provided their motto when he described the poet as 'eternity's hostage captive to time'.

Time with its conditional, political truths was a powerful gaoler but memory could pick his locks. It had already been working for more than twenty years to release the largest group imprisoned in the official version of the country's history. By the time Mikhail Gorbachov became Soviet leader these people were still not free, but at least it was harder to deny their existence and unhappy recent past. The peasants of Russia had for a time been conjured away by the great illusion of the Revolution. Bolshevik rhetoric turned a peasant country – four out of five inhabitants of the newly-created Soviet Union lived in the countryside – into the world's first proletarian state. So great was the romance of industrialization, so persuasive the new proletarian language, that many convinced themselves that the peasant, though still unfortunately numerous, was no longer significant and that his world had no more value. Yet seventy years after the Revolution a third of the population still lived in villages. Over twenty-five million people still worked on the land, though half of these, the employees of the state as opposed to collective farms, had been turned nominally into members of the working class by a trick of ideological book-keeping that was pure revolutionary magic.

It was the country's backwardness (in matters of modern industry) that made the proletarian future seem too good to wait for. The future had to be proclaimed at once. The complaint of Russians in the 1980s that their old cities had been destroyed by ugly modern building would not have made sense to the planners of the 1930s who saw factories as beautiful by definition. When Khrushchov travelled to America in 1959 he expressed greatest admiration for the industrial landscape of New Jersey from which sophisticated Americans tended to avert their eyes as their train approached Manhattan. If a church in Moscow was seized to house some industrial workshop, as often happened, it remained in a way holy: only the gods honoured there had changed. The promise of the industrial future distracted attention from the perversely different present. When peasants came to Moscow to admire the underground railway Stalin was building, they looked at the mosaic ceiling of the station at Mayakovsky Square and saw aeroplanes, dirigibles, and parachutists falling from a bright blue sky. They were meant to be glad that they had been overtaken by history, and that if the present still had its feet on the old Russian earth, the future certainly would not.

The country's dash into the new world unencumbered by memories of the old one that gave birth to it came to an end when Hitler's army attacked in June 1941. Tukhachevsky, genius of the new Red Army, had talked after the Revolution as though he was already commander of an 'army of the international proletariat'. He declared this army would never fight an enemy unaided because it would always be supported by the workers of the country with whose bourgeoisie it was at war. It was an example of how far a brilliant man can be carried away from reality by the excitement of his own ideas. The day that the German soldiers crossed the border two out of three inhabitants of the Soviet Union were still living in villages. The Soviet army that eventually stopped, and then drove back, the Germans was mostly a peasant army, as the armies that fought Russia's invaders had always been. Many of its commanders, beginning with Zhukov, the greatest of them all, were village boys born. Stalin had known the truth of this. 'We are under no illusion,' he told America's wartime ambassador Averell Harriman, 'that they [the Russian people] are fighting for us. They are fighting for Mother Russia.'

The realization, during the terrible days of the Soviet retreat, of who was fighting this war to save Russia drove a clever young writer called Konstantin Simonov, mobilized as a war correspondent, to write a poem of homage and apology to the country he and others like him had forgotten. Many Russians still know its opening lines by heart.

> Do you remember, Alyosha, the roads round Smolensk,
> How the foul rains fell without cease . . .

It was as if Simonov's head had been swept clean of factory chimneys and five year plans and their place taken by 'villages, villages, villages with their graveyards, as though all Russia had come together there'. He imagined the dead old men protecting the living with the sign of the cross, 'praying for their grandchildren who no longer believe in God'. And he realized that this peasant Russia was still the country's heart.

> I think you know that after all the motherland
> Isn't the city house where I merrily lived,
> It's these villages where our grandfathers passed before us
> With the simple crosses over their Russian graves.

And it was a peasant, an imaginary one but all the more real for that, who became the epitome of the Russian fighting man. When Gorbachov attended the celebrations of the fortieth anniversary of the victory in May 1985 he and the rest of the Soviet grandees listened to part of this peasant's story as though it were their own. Invented by the poet (and later great literary editor) Aleksandr Tvardovsky, the peasant soldier Vasili Tyorkin fought the war from start to finish in what he called the 'mother infantry', without losing his Russian patience, generosity or sense of humour. There was a special victory day parade in 1985 and it was opened by troops dressed in wartime uniforms stamping down Red Square. Their khaki capes hung down to the cobblestones and the old Shpagin submachine guns they carried looked as though they had just been delivered from some wartime arms factory working day and night in the Urals. These were Tyorkin's brothers-in-arms, though he might have felt happier with the old soldiers and their families who gathered after the parade in the Moscow parks. The old men had pinned tinkling medals on their best dark suits and there were ghosts among them, too. Small boys, the great-great-grandchildren of vanished Tyorkins, held up faded photographs of young soldiers and signs that asked 'Who knew him?'

In the villages of Russia, the Ukraine and Belorussia most people knew him. Of the twenty million Soviet citizens who are believed to have died in the war most came from the villages, amongst them many women, the old and the very young left behind there when the men went off to fight. Not one soldier returned to Timonikha, the village of Vasili Belov, the writer and friend of the Vologda party leader Drygin who had made himself a hero by offering to retire. Throughout the whole Vologda region less than a third of the soldiers came back, and half of those would die from battlefield wounds and illness. The same was true of hundreds of other Russian villages. The Germans never reached Timonikha but starvation and the illnesses that accompanied it did, killing Belov's grandmother and many others. Much of the countryside never recovered from this shock. The population of the region outside Novgorod, most famous of old Russian cities, was still only a quarter of a million in the early 1980s although it covered as much territory as Belgium. At the outbreak of war it had been almost four times as great.

The first act of the liberators of Novgorod was to rebuild the monument erected in its Kremlin in 1862 to celebrate the thousandth anniversary of the city and the birth of the Russian state (an enterprise also entangled in the demands of political truth, for its designers were not allowed to include the Ukrainian poet Shevchenko among the frieze of great writers and had to fight to keep the too gloomy Gogol there). The Germans had done their best to destroy the monument, mutilating its bronze figures and scattering them in the snow. But it was easier to put the allegorical figures representing Russian Orthodoxy back on the globe at the monument's top, and to replace the great princes and emperors, the soldiers like Suvorov and Kutuzov who had given their name to the war's new medals, together with Gogol and other less disputed literary heroes, than it was to restore the villages. The impulse the war gave to look upon Russian national feeling more kindly eventually led to the founding in 1966 of the All-Russia Society for the Preservation of Historical and Cultural Monuments. Although the government decision to allow its creation may have been connected with what then was seen to be a growing threat from China (the Society's first honorary chairman was the war hero Marshal Chuikov) its rapid increase in membership suggested it was a genuinely popular movement. But the Society's purpose was the preservation of buildings. The villages of Russia were not within its preserve and they continued to decline.

The trouble went back to collectivization, when Stalin forced the peasants into near serfdom (denied internal passports, it became very difficult for them to leave their villages) in order to extract the cheap food and resources he needed for industrialization and the creation of a modern army. Few episodes in Soviet history were so firmly locked up in the prison of official truth as the birth of Soviet socialist farming. Two of the most famous books of officially recognized Soviet literature, Mikhail Sholokhov's *Quiet Flows the Don* and *Virgin Soil Upturned* left no doubt that bringing Stalin's socialism to the villages had been a bloody and tragic business. Max Hayward, the most perceptive of British writers on Russian literature, suggested that the first parts of *Quiet Flows the Don* could, like *Doctor Zhivago*, leave the reader feeling that men's acts were insignificant compared to the timeless processes of nature. Later writing under Stalin about collectivization was not allowed to be so ambiguous. Soviet socialist agriculture was declared a triumph and there was no more to be said.

While the politicians maintained this orthodoxy, writers from the 1960s onwards had tried to allude to the tragedy of rural Russia though some thought it was not enough to free them of the charge of having avoided the 'unanswered questions' about collectivization and the 1930s. Their references had been softened by being in fictional form. But in early 1986 one of the most respected of them, the Belorussian Vasil Bykov, managed in an interview to give an unusually frank non-fictional account of an episode in the tragedy. His latest novel *A Sign of Trouble* had in its Russian translation just won a Lenin Prize. The irony was that this edition of the book had been much more heavily censored than the Belorussian original and was as a result in places incomprehensible. In particular it was impossible to understand why one of the characters committed suicide. The reason had to do with the collectivization Bykov had seen as a boy in his own Belorussian village.

Collectivization, he explained, had been different in different parts of the country and while it may have been true that in Sholokhov's Cossack lands along the Don there were kulaks, rich peasants, to be defeated it was not the case in Belorussia.

. . . in general we didn't have any kulaks, but we still had to de-kulakize. It was impossible to single them out by the amount of land they had – everyone only had a little. All the same they de-kulakized three people who were as poor as everyone else . . . They discovered someone who didn't have one cow but one and a half – a cow and a half – and they put him on the list of those to be dekulakized. Another was put into this category for having once hired labour: a distant relative had helped him during the harvest. Another was singled out, for example, because he had a mare and foal. I was in my second year at school then and I had a friend whose family had been de-kulakized. They had to leave. The boy boasted

240

about it: 'We're going to go on a train, a long way!' and I envied him . . . It was necessary to give seeds to the collective farm for the sowing. And although a commission was set up which went round all the houses and raked the grain literally clean there still wasn't enough for sowing and there were suspicions that people hadn't given all they had and had hidden some. And in order that this hidden grain shouldn't be turned into flour our local ruling idiots broke all the millstones. I remember how they broke ours. They took it outside and smashed it and threw the pieces into the nettles . . .

Bykov's father each night recovered the pieces, bound them together and ground some grain. Then he put the pieces back so that the village authorities would see them when they came by on their daily tour of inspection. The result, Bykov said, was that people started to hate each other.

After all it wasn't unknown strangers who were lording over us but our own village people. And this was among people who had lived for generations in the same village. Suddenly everything went to pieces, broke up, and people began not simply to dislike but to hate each other terribly because it was one group of poor people using violence against other poor people.

It was the reason, Bykov believed, for something that had for years barely been admitted – the collaboration of some peasants with the German occupiers when the latter first arrived. 'Someone or other would go to the [German] police, as I remember now, just to settle accounts with his own people. Many couldn't understand then what fascism was and what it leads to.'

This explained the mysterious suicide in Bykov's novel. The man killed himself out of remorse for what he had done during collectivization. Throughout the country at least a million peasant households, numbering certainly five million people, were identified as kulak and exiled to harsh, uninhabited regions, or labour camps. Most, if not all of them, are believed to have died as a result. It has been called the equivalent of the 'uprooting of a small nation'. Many of them were no richer than the farmers in Bykov's Belorussia. Most were peasants who were a little better-off because they were the better farmers. Kulak came to mean those the régime needed to destroy to put its grip on the villages. The destruction of the so-called kulaks was the prelude of an even greater tragedy when famine followed the brutally enforced collectivization, with millions of country people dying, the brunt of it taken by the Ukraine. Soviet scholars have not been allowed to calculate the damage done but it is possible that as many as fourteen and a half million peasants died between 1930 and 1937.

Bykov was saying nothing that many Russians did not know and that had already been chronicled in unofficial and unpublished histories. But for such remarks to appear in the country's leading literary newspaper only underlined the complete absence of official remorse about those events. Ever since collectivization the true state of affairs in the countryside had been too bad to be admitted. After the war as during it the women continued to bear the heaviest burden on the impoverished farms. There were Russian villages in the late 1940s where old women and their grandchildren worked the fields with cows, and sometimes themselves, harnessed to the plough. The widows of the soldiers who did not return stayed in the villages. They had nowhere else to go. Everything they produced in their own little gardens was taxed. People were often hungry. Stalin watched films in which peasants were played by well-fed actors while only a few miles from his dacha in suburban Moscow there were villages where the windows of houses were stuffed with straw and all the young men – in spite of the passport restrictions – had managed to leave. Some were prepared even to go to prison for a couple of years in the hope that on leaving they would get their passport and be able to settle where they liked. The towns, badly in need of labour after the war, easily bewitched the young out of a countryside where there were few roads, where it was only from the mid-1960s that peasants regularly received payment in money rather than kind, and where the land to all intents and purposes belonged to the local officials and not to the men and women whose ancestors had worked it.

The Stalinist state learned many of its coercive skills in the struggle against the peasant. The peasant in return took up passive resistance as his only defence against a regime whose method of farming was essentially to tax the land. The government found itself ruling the countryside like an absentee landlord through agents whose careers depended on extracting the most they could from the soil in the face of peasant indifference. Eventually no one thought it odd any more that the newspapers in Moscow should print exhortations and instructions every sowing and harvest time. The habit of constant interference died hard, if at all. Even in the spring of 1986, when the outline of Gorbachov's agricultural reforms was clear, a Soviet journalist could find a farm in Belorussia where the district leaders had telephoned with instructions to start sowing the flax (an important local crop) when snow was still falling. When the farm chairman protested he was told, 'Yes, yes, we can see it, it's snowing here too. But all the same just take your seed drill and put it at the edge of the field.' What mattered was not the weather but that a commission had arrived to check up on adherence to the timetable the bosses in regional headquarters had drawn up. And this happened in a republic known for having better than average farming. At the same time, by letting the peasant have his private plot and take produce to market, the authorities tried to encourage the peasant back to his old skills and diligence – the very qualities the system had destroyed.

The memory of Russian writers was focussed above all on one part of the countryside – the Russia of Pskov and Novgorod, Vologda and Yaroslav, Tula and Tver (re-named Kalinin after the Soviet president of the middle years of Stalin's rule, to the abiding displeasure of some of its inhabitants). This was officially known as the *Nechernozemya*, the Non-Black Earth Zone, to distinguish it from the area of darker, richer soils to the south. Most of Russian history lay within the *Nechernozemya* and sixty million people, almost a third of the Soviet population, lived there. This was the Russia whose landscape the painters and writers of the nineteenth century had introduced to the world, its flatness exaggerated by the winter snows, gripped by what Russians called 'roadlessness' in the mud of spring and autumn. If Russia could be said to have a heart, it was here. And yet nowhere were the problems of farming more acute; nowhere did they go more obviously beyond technical matters of agriculture to the health of the Russian nation and to its understanding of itself.

For years this Russian heartland had been neglected. The government directed money towards the reconstruction of war-destroyed industry and towns, to the virgin lands in the East where grain could be grown more cheaply, to the opening up of Siberia. But in the 1970s it took fright at the state of the old Russian countryside and its steady loss of population. Sixty-eight billion roubles were invested in farming in the Non-Black Earth Zone between 1976 and 1984, twice as much as in the preceding ten years. The results were extremely disappointing, as a 1986 survey of Tula showed. Tolstoy's country estate, Yasnaya Polyana, had been in Tula and it was through Tula's fields that he would walk to and from Moscow. The town had for centuries made weapons for Russian soldiers. It had famously withstood the Germans' attack in 1941. Contemporary Tula's farms, though three times better equipped than they had been at the start of the seventies, were producing less milk than sixteen years earlier. The flight of people from the villages had not stopped: a third of Tula's rural population had left for the towns over the last fifteen years. Those that remained were getting older. Almost half of the dairy maids were approaching or beyond pensionable age. The farms were short of twenty-five thousand workers; at harvest time they needed twice as many. Most of the villages were without hard-surface roads. Mud and potholes often made impassable even the better dirt roads that were hopefully called 'big ones'. Some villages had no schools. Natural gas, the new joy of Soviet towns, had not reached most villages. Water usually came from the pump. Drunkenness was common, not least because town workers frequently sacked from factories for their drinking could always get a job on a farm. Children with no local school to go to had to be sent to boarding school, most likely breaking for ever their link with the land.

Village shops were very poor but they were sometimes little better in some of the smaller towns of the *Nechernozemya*. Reporters from *Izvestia* who in the autumn of 1985 visited the town of Trubchevsk in Bryansk region to the west of Moscow, could find no cooking oil, no butter, no sausage, very little fruit or vegetables, and only tinned fish. The local department store could not supply rubber galoshes, essential wear throughout much of the year. The selection of clothes was meagre. There were no shoes at all for babies and young children. Every Friday workers in the town delegated people to go to Moscow to shop, a bus journey of three hundred miles. The overnight train was better – it arrived in Moscow early in the morning making it possible to be at the capital's foodshops when they opened – but tickets were hard to get.

The huge investments of recent years had in some ways made the situation worse. Many small old fields had been abandoned to concentrate on ambitious schemes to create new acreage by draining and improving land. For a while it was policy to abandon some of the smaller villages that were judged to have, as official documents put it, 'no future'. It was not long before this provoked protests. Traditional Russia, peasant Russia, had at last been openly identified as a threatened species. 'I have several times been in abandoned Russian villages. Oh what a sight it is! You never can accept it, never get used to it, at least I never have. After all some of the villages that have been so hurriedly, eagerly, even light-heartedly written off were a thousand years old, perhaps even more. And the saddest sight of all is an abandoned Russian cottage . . .'

The novelist Viktor Astafyev described how once he came across an immaculate *izba* or cottage in one of these deserted villages. There was a padlock on the door, but the departed owners had left everything in order in case someone might still come to live there. They had put an axe, a spade and a broom outside the front door. A faint cross made in chalk could just be seen above the door. Through the window Astafyev made out three ikons on the wall, a stove with a pile of wood beside it, cooking pots. The vanished owners had even left some clothes, a black coat made from a dyed army greatcoat and little jacket made of plush, 'the pride of an earlier generation of fashionable village girls'. There were children's schoolbooks on a shelf and old posters, a famous one of the war-time mother calling on her children to save the Motherland, and another (less effective) of a red-nosed drunk rolling in a ditch with a pig. Opposite stood another cottage, but this had been left as a slum. The owners, Astafyev implied, had already lost their identity before moving. They had left 'without praying at the threshold and bowing to the paternal hearth they were leaving: here was neither god nor memory'.

The grief was not that so much of the Russian countryside was poor, for Russians had always been able to find virtue in poverty. A nineteenth-century poet would rejoice in the wretchedness of villages which for him nevertheless glowed in a way the 'proud foreigner's glance' could never see. He imagined Christ, dressed as a servant, passing through the wretched settlements and blessing them. But something unprecedented had happened now – a line of succession was being broken. Probably no one would ever live again in the cottage Astafyev had seen in the Vologda village of Gridkino, unless perhaps it was an adventurous young intellectual from a big city with a taste for country life. But hadn't the line begun to break earlier, when collectivization cut the peasant's old links with the land, when the land itself was made an orphan? This was a matter so sensitive it could be mentioned only obliquely. One such reference was contained in a debate on the steady degradation of the soil of agricultural Russia. If the experts concerned about this were right it was a major cause of the poor harvests that failed to provide enough feed for the growing livestock herds and forced the government in most years to make huge imports of foreign grain. They argued that fifty years of careless farming – fifty years took one back to the start of collectivization – had so depleted the soil's humus content, an essential component of fertility, that in places it scarcely remained fertile at all. Non-Black Earth Russia, with the poorest soil to start with, had suffered most. The land had been too greedily and carelessly farmed. It had had too many masters. The collective farm at Vasili Belov's Timonikha had had a new chairman on average almost every year since its foundation in 1930. Few of these men had bothered to give back life to the soil with organic fertilizers – it was too much trouble – while artificial ones remained in short supply. The experts, citing as their authority the geologist Vasili Dokuchayev who had pioneered Russian soil science in the nineteenth century, wondered what would happen if the land was not treated with proper knowledge and respect. 'Will a man survive without air, water, food, warmth and light? No, he will not, and the land also will not survive. Here lies the meaning of the cultivation of the land . . . Every little piece of land, every lump of earth needs its special approach, its own caress. These are the spiritual foundations of agriculture.'

The author, an ecologist at the Academy of Sciences, complained that no one had personal responsibility for the land any more. The orphan needed love. It needed farmers who would be answerable for it over generations. The one piece of land for which a peasant did still have responsibility – his private plot – was indeed a miracle of fertility by comparison with most state and collective farms. It was common for these tiny plots to produce twice the yield of a crop like potatoes compared to the state farm next door.

If the ecologist and others who thought like him were right, the Russian countryside had suffered two breaks. At the first, collectivization, the land had been taken away from the responsibility of the men who with their ancestors had worked it for centuries. This brought with it the destruction of much of the spiritual part of peasant life which was based on the land, its cultivation and its seasons. The second break came when, deprived of a meaningful link with their land, the peasants began to desert it for the cities. This experience had to some measure been shared by most other countries as they industrialized but in Russia it was extraordinarily quick and purposefully brutal.

The shock waves had been and were still felt throughout the nation for, as one of the greatest champions of the countryside said, ' . . . all of us have come out of the village. The village represents our primal source and our roots.' The peasant agricultural skills almost disappeared, surviving if at all on the private plots where, a Russian journalist observed, people still remembered the precepts 'received from their grandfathers . . . islands that have remained from the peasant Atlantis. These precepts were derived from staggering industriousness and effort, from a memory retentive of ancestral experience and from a spirit of enterprise – the main components in the concept of a culture of work.'

Old country housekeeping skills were also lost in the movement from demoralized villages into a bleak new world of towns and cities that for the most part offered little real urban civilization. A woman recalled with wonder how her grandmother had managed to feed her peasant family of twelve with a variety of cheap but good dishes. She had lost these skills and lamented the fact. Mention a famous dish of old Russian cooking to a modern Muscovite and a likely response was a sad shake of the head, as though the name had been spoken of a friend long since dead.

Much more was lost than old recipes, as one of the most striking Soviet films of the 1980s made plain. *Family*, the work of Nikita Mikhalkov, among the finest of the younger Soviet directors, told the story of a peasant woman's visit to the city to stay with a daughter who, while no longer a peasant herself, remains clumsy in the art of urban living. An ear-splitting family row ends with the little granddaughter, dressed in her mother's clothes and make-up, doing a savage disco dance with the television switched on, a transistor radio round her neck and earphones on her head. In the film-maker's judgement she is an orphan, cut off for ever from the memory of her ancestors' land and customs, from what Russians had come to call the 'little motherland' that everyone should be warmed by. Mikhalkov made the film to demonstrate what happens to people who are uprooted from one place and cannot put down new roots in another. The same point was made in a memorable story by the much-admired writer Vasili Shukshin about a man who goes every Saturday to the railway station to talk to peasants waiting for a train home. The man had escaped from his village in the 1930s and made a comfortable and none too honest life in the city as a warehouse clerk. As he grew older these weekly conversations became a necessity. He would tell the peasants he wanted to pick a village to retire in; get them to describe where they lived, how the cottages there were built, whether they had proper barns and a bath house as a good *izba* should. He would take out a piece of paper and write down the names and addresses. In fact he never meant to leave the city. But if someone had forbidden him this weekly conversation at the station 'he would have begun going there secretly. He could not do without it now.'

As Russians looked backward to the past there was a temptation to idealize it. Vasili Belov published in 1982 an evocative book called *Harmony* about the disappearing way of life and customs of the peasants of north Russia, generally regarded as the last outpost of the old countryside. It was a celebration of the village trades and the work of the women, of the food and the yearly festivals, of the architecture and equipment of the peasant households. Belov noted down the old songs and poems. And he tried to show the continuity between the living and the dead by printing rows of photographs of modern faces next to peasants' pictures snapped or painted in the nineteenth century. The book left the impression of a life of hard work made meaningful and beautiful by custom and ritual. It was difficult to read it without coming to the conclusion that to sweep all this away, as collectivization had done, was a crime of vast proportions; the loss, indeed, of an Atlantis.

Many did not go as far as Belov. Anyone who knew no more than nineteenth-century novels could guess there was much bad as well as good in the old villages, not least the widespread illiteracy. Serfdom, though far from being a unified system, had scarcely laid the foundations for a healthy country life. For some, too, praising the old countryside smelt of reactionary Russian nationalism, of the cult of a unique Mother Russia, the traditional adversary of the outward-looking Russian intellectual. The condition of the peasant and the land had been pushed into the public mind partly by the activity of a group of talented writers (among them Belov and Rasputin) who were of course read by other members of the intelligentsia rather than peasants themselves. For most of the intelligentsia the peasant was only part of a concern for the wider past, for a history and traditions much of which had fallen victim to the Revolution's demonization of everything that was out of step with it. Official memory was concentrated on a very special past: on the Revolution, on the 'heroic feats' of socialist construction, and above all on the war against Hitler which was the foundation of modern Soviet patriotism. For educated Russians, recovering a much wider past was a necessary step towards restoring the nation to moral health, as the eminent historian Dmitri Likhachov tried to explain:

> Man is a part of society and a part of its history. If he does not keep within himself the memory of the past he destroys part of his personality. By cutting himself off from his national, family and personal roots he condemns himself to wither prematurely. And what if whole layers of society are infected by loss of memory? It tells inevitably on the world of moral behaviour, on people's attitudes to the family, to children, parents and to work, especially to work and to traditions of work.

This explained the interest of a man like Nikita Mikhalkov in the wider past. He also made films about nineteenth-century characters – the fictional Oblomov and Griboyedov, the first great Russian playwright – in the hope of educating a public many of whom knew little about them except their names.

Significant, too, was the scrupulous gathering of material and artefacts for these films, something for which the shockingly rough film about the 1930s *My friend Ivan Lapshin* had also been remarkable. The past that the Revolution and socialist construction was supposed to have blown away was being reconstructed out of the smallest and most insignificant fragments. Aleksei German, the maker of *Lapshin*, hung his own parents' portraits in the flat where much of the film's action takes place. 'It was unthinkable,' he said later, 'to tell lies under their gaze.'

Mikhalkov was conscious of his own background as a member of an intelligentsia family that had had the luck to survive and even prosper in the Revolution. His father was author of the Soviet national anthem and long a none-too-popular prince among official writers; a grandfather had been a pre-Revolutionary avant-garde painter. Nikita Mikhalkov seemed to feel it a personal duty to help young Soviet people recover the 'national aesthetic roots' his family had managed to preserve. 'Young people should be made to reflect,' he said in an interview in 1985, 'that they weren't simply born in 1962 or 1970 . . . but that their appearance on earth was conditioned by an endless train of generations disappearing into the dark ages. It is necessary to listen to the distant voice of the past in order to understand oneself.'

The interviewer broke in: 'I understand perfectly. There has been an unprecedented social upheaval, comparable to a huge tectonic shift. Ask anyone about his family tree and it is a rare person who can go back further than the grandfather.'

To which Mikhalkov replied that he would be happy if young people had so much as the desire to know who their great-great-grandfathers were. Mikhalkov's was one of a growing number of voices demanding that the work of pre-Revolutionary historians be re-published. No edition of Karamzin, father of the Russian historical school, had been published since before 1917 and later historians, unless they were Marxists, had done little better. Recovering the past also involved recovering different interpretations of the past.

The debate on the peasant and the land, on the disappearance of the Russian past and on the often unsatisfactory present that had replaced it, was carried on in public for the most part with carefully restrained feeling and under a watchful censor's eye. But at the Soviet writers' congress in the early summer of 1986 restraint was abandoned. One of the most passionate outbursts came from Yuri Bondarev, respected as a writer of honest novels about the war and whom at one time the Kremlin seemed to be grooming as a future leader of the literary community.

'If we do not stop the destruction of the monuments of our architecture,' Bondarev warned, 'if we do not stop the rape of our earth and rivers, if there is not a moral explosion in our science and criticism, then one fine morning, which will be the last and the one of our funeral, we with our inexhaustible optimism will wake up and understand that the national culture of vast

248

Russia has been wiped out, gone for good, has been done away with, destroyed for ever: her spirit, her love of the land of our fathers, her beauty, her great literature, her painting, philosophy, all will be gone and we shall sit, naked beggars in the ashes, trying to remember the native alphabet that was dear to our hearts and we shall not be able to because thought, and feeling, and happiness and historical memory will all have disappeared.'

This unprecedented, almost hysterical, cry of anguish partly reflected the unease of the country after the recent accident at Chernobyl, but it was not principally meant as a forecast of nuclear apocalypse. Others said the same thing more succinctly. The poet Andrei Voznesensky warned of the 'destruction of spirituality, of the ecology of culture'. The writers' outburst was partly provoked by frustration over a battle that Russian writers – among them Astafyev, the author of *The Fire*, Valentin Rasputin, Belov and Bondarev – had been waging for several years against a giant scheme to divert water from the rivers of north Russia and Siberia to irrigate the parched land of the Ukraine, south Russia and Soviet Central Asia. One writer, Sergei Zalygin, had almost abandoned literary work to fight the battle, which he did with amazing persistence in the press, on television, and in the offices of scientists and bureaucrats. The projects that aroused so much feeling were gigantic pieces of engineering, immensely expensive, and whose consequences for not only Russia's but the world environment were uncertain. They were typical of earlier great Soviet schemes. Soviet man would once again show he was master of nature and at one stroke solve all the country's farming problems (the irrigated lands were supposed to grow the grain the country was having to import).

Many Russians, writers apart, had never liked the plans, and weighty missiles of contradictory scientific expertise had been lobbed back and forth by the two sides. But it was only with the arrival of Gorbachov in power that the opponents of river diversion made progress. The two schemes suffered a setback at the party congress which decided to continue study of their desirability, but not to conduct any preparatory engineering works. This was what had infuriated the writers: one after the other they got up to complain that the ministries reponsible for the diversion schemes were ignoring this decision and trying to press ahead with the first excavations.

The scheme would flood some of the oldest inhabited parts of the north Russia. Academician Likhachov had only recently proposed that the whole region be turned into a museum. Belov forecast the destruction of 'forests and arable land, hay meadows, villages, hamlets, the most ancient monuments'. It was as though the last reserves of patience had been exhausted. The diversion scheme had come to symbolize all that had gone wrong in the Soviet past: vast undertakings careless of both man and nature imposed by a government with too much power and too much confidence in the infallibility of science (the writers accused the president of the Academy of Sciences of being one of the chief villains of the story, and a few months later he retired, though not just because of this affair. He was approaching eighty-four and Soviet science also needed new brooms). Valentin Rasputin, in a story called 'Farewell to Matyora' published in the mid-seventies, had described the flooding of a Siberian village as part of a hydro-electric scheme through the eyes of an old woman whose life was destroyed by having to leave her home. It was appropriate that the first writer to stand on its head the traditional attitude to change in the name of progress should have made the most dramatic gesture to stop the diversion scheme. Linking it with the problem of the pollution of Siberia's Baikal, greatest of Russian lakes, he appealed personally to Gorbachov to intervene 'for the sake of our people'. The writers' clamour was successful. A few weeks later the Politburo ordered all engineering work on the project to be stopped.

There were other official gestures towards the past, too. The renaming of streets from which so many Russian cities had suffered seemed to have come to an end once and for all with the decision in the late summer of 1986 to restore three well-loved old Moscow place names. An announcement at the same time that the memory of the Vietnamese leader Le Duan, who had died in July, would be honoured by naming after him one of the *new* streets on the capital's outskirts seemed to set a more popular pattern for the future. But the greatest gesture Gorbachov had in his power to make to the past was in his policy for the farms. To restore them to health, to give the land back into the responsibility of the people who worked it, would be far more than an economic success. It would be to restore well-being to the very heart of Russia.

Identified first by family and then by career with every official policy since collectivization, Gorbachov seemed an unlikely candidate to repay the Russian Revolution's debt to the land and the men and women who worked it. But he was at last his own master and the idea behind the farm reforms outlined at the party congress was broadly similar to those devised for industry. Central control was to be more intelligent and precise (easier to say than to achieve) while there would be more room for initiative for the actual producers: the best of both worlds again. No one supposed that the state and collective farms could be dismantled, though one of the most intriguing of old Kremlin rumours had it that Gorbachov's patron Fyodor Kulakov proposed something like that to the Politburo, and committed suicide when his colleagues rebuffed him. What would count, in the years ahead, was where Moscow put the emphasis – on the power of the planners and the agricultural bureaucracy, headed since the end of 1985 by a new mega-ministry called the State Agro-Industrial Committee, or on the independence of the farmers. It was plain that Gorbachov had no intention of dumping the responsibility for the farms on one of his Politburo colleagues, as he could have done. Official statements stressed his part in working out the new farm measures. And the official picked to head the new Committee and given the rank of first deputy prime minister, Vsevolod Murakhovsky, was indisputably Gorbachov's man. Though by birth a Ukrainian, Murakhovsky's entire career had been made in Stavropol, first as Gorbachov's senior (he was the older of the two), then as his subordinate. When Gorbachov went to Moscow as Central Committee secretary in 1978 Murakhovsky had taken his place as Stavropol party leader.

The new agricultural chief said things that made ears prick up. They were all the more interesting because he was assumed to be entirely in Gorbachov's confidence. Murakhovsky announced that he had cut by half the staffs of the five ministries merged in his Committee. And he spoke as an enthusiast for the most experimental parts of the new farm programme: making farms financially independent; the use of market pressures to punish and reward; the importance of labour systems that allowed greater initiative to farm workers. The last included a contract system in which groups of workers took responsibility for a part of a farm and were paid according to result, a method Gorbachov had tried when he was running Stavropol. There was also a variation of this system called the 'family contract', under which a single family could undertake to look after so many animals, or cultivate part of a crop. This was the basis of the Chinese agricultural reforms, about which the Soviet press had so far reported gingerly. The arrangement was not completely unknown in the Soviet Union but it had been little used because many officials saw it as the backdoor to the individual peasant farming that Soviet socialism was supposed to have abolished.

Murakhovsky, however, laughed at these fears. 'It doesn't contradict our principles at all. The land is still the state's. The fertilisers and the equipment belong to the collective farm. It's just the work that the single man or his family do. After all, a lathe operator works on his own at his machine.'

The enthusiasts of the family contract saw no limits to its application. In particular they attacked the common view that it would never work on large grain-growing farms. As long as a family had the proper range of equipment, they said, it could do an efficient job. Others explained its advantages in moral language that the defenders of the family farm anywhere in the West might have used.

A man determines much in his own life. But much also depends on his surroundings. And the nearest to him is the family: mother, father, wife, husband, children. What wife doesn't want her husband to be the best, an example to others? What children don't want their father and mother to be the 'very, very best of all'? With us [the speaker was the chairman of one of the few collective farms using the family contract system] they don't just want this, they act. They help their parents to be better. The family shares a common task. And everyone in the family each day and each hour helps the others . . .

Was this not re-establishing a link to the vanishing world that Vasili Belov had celebrated in his book *Harmony*, the world in which the farmer's life had a purpose beyond increasing production of milk and grain? And would not a family, re-attached to its piece of land, treat it with the care that so much Russian land had for decades been deprived of? It was certainly a different world from that of many existing Soviet farms where children hurried to leave home as soon as they could while their parents did a grudging day's work. It would take time to know what would come of these new ideas. The weight of Soviet tradition was against them. It was difficult to fit them into the world both of Soviet myth and of existing popular attitudes, neither of which looked kindly on the family as an independent point of economic achievement. One could almost hear the envious cries of 'kulak!' already raised against those who cultivated their private plots too successfully. The new ideas were hard, too, to reconcile with the interfering habits of bureaucrats; harder still to see where, in the end, they left the party.

As for the writers, it was unclear how far they would pursue their memories. Their outspokenness at the congress about the river diversion plan was partly the result of an easing of censorship that had been felt since the autumn of 1985. When their congress met it was put about, though not announced officially, that Glavlit, the Soviet censor's office, would no longer vet literary works. It did not mean that the writers were free. Control would be exercised by the editors of journals and publishing houses, almost all of whom were party members picked by party authorities (an interesting exception was Sergei Zalygin, hero of the fight against the diversion of Russian rivers, who was to become editor of *Novy Mir*). This was the ordinary system of control in daily newspapers, proof enough of its effectiveness. And though the writers elected a new leader of their union their choice was guided: the authorities had picked the candidate several weeks in advance. Vladimir Karpov had been the editor of a *Novy Mir* much tamed since the days of its great editor Tvardovsky. Karpov was a reliable party man and had been elected a candidate member of the Central Committee at the recent party congress. A wartime hero, he had shown no taste for skirmishes with the Soviet authorities. His was the one speech at the writers' gathering that used memory to a quite different purpose: to sound the old schoolmaster's warning about the dangers of going too far. One should remember, he said, what happened in the 1950s and '60s, 'when we also talked and argued a lot. As it turned out later, forgetting the boundaries between democracy and demagogy sometimes gives birth to very unpleasant consequences. For it was precisely in those years that the literary dissidents made their appearance.'

Only a small group of writers had fought to preserve the disappearing world of rural Russia and the peasant, though they had made up in talent what they lacked in numbers. Many more writers, encouraged to look into the past, thought first of their own dead and wounded. Russian literature and culture, as officially presented, resembled a picture that had been much re-worked, with a good deal of painting out and painting in. The mood was strong that the original should now be restored. As the director of the Moscow Arts Theatre had said, it was time to understand 'the genealogy of all our problems. Let us not be like Aitmatov's "Mankurts" and forget the past. Art is the total memory of the nation, and from this memory, as from a song, not one word can be discarded.'

Aitmatov's 'Mankurts' – this was a reference to the most powerful image for the destruction of memory in modern Soviet literature. Chingis Aitmatov was a bilingual Kirgiz writer who had become one of the masters of modern Russian prose. A man of Oriental shrewdness and discretion, he had nevertheless managed to be accepted as a Russian writer in the greatest sense of being a truth-teller. The mankurts came from his novel *And the day lasts longer than an age*. According to Central Asian legend, they were prisoners who had been turned into slaves by having their heads wrapped in a hood of camel skin which under the sun dried tight as a metal band. Some died. Those that survived became mankurts: 'The mankurt did not know who he was, from what family or tribe he came; he did not know his name, he did not remember his childhood, his father or mother. In a word the mankurt did not recognise himself as a human being.'

Determined not to be 'mankurts', several of the writers called for full honour to be done their famous dead; to great poets like Pasternak, Anna Akhmatova and Osip Mandelstam whose full works had never been printed in Moscow, and to others who had been scratched out entirely from the official portrait of Soviet and Russian culture (thus making a present of them to the West, the venerable Academician Likhachov pointed out). Andrei Voznesensky, who had been Pasternak's protégé, complained that living writers were being forgotten too. He accused literary officials of having rigged the election of delegates to the congress to keep out those people who had had a stormy youth in the 1950s and '60s though just managed to avoid joining the literary dissidents Karpov had referred to. There were others whose names were not mentioned but who must have been in many delegates' minds, among them the talented writers who had been forced to emigrate, most of them in the years when another poet, Yuri Andropov, was directing the KGB.

It was not only the writers who were excited. Paintings of the great Russian moderns, for decades kept in storerooms for fear of corrupting the public's socialist realist taste, began to be exhibited in greater numbers. The film makers had already voted out their old leader – the man whom Gorbachov made public fun of at the party congress – and elected in his place a director whose films the authorities had earlier refused to release. Leading theatre directors were complaining publicly of the restraints under which they had to work. It seemed that Gorbachov felt he could use these artistic worlds to help change the atmosphere in the country, to bring about what was officially called 'the restructuring of the way of thinking and psychology of man himself'. The difficulty of achieving this had become a regular theme of his speeches. He sounded as though he needed all the assistance he could get. But how far his and the creative intelligentsia's interests coincided was not clear. The appointment as new minister of culture of a specialist in party propaganda who had worked under the famously illiberal Grigori Romanov in Leningrad was a reminder that neither Gorbachov nor anyone else had suggested that the arts had an independent mission outside helping the party. The party officials advanced by Gorbachov – Boris Yeltsin, for example – combined a refreshing outspokenness with total confidence in their power and right of command. Yeltsin had criticized the old leadership of the Central Committee's cultural department for not doing enough. It seemed that the old leaders of the cultural establishment were being removed not because they were 'illiberal' but because the new leadership judged them ineffective allies for the tasks ahead.

Memory, though, had already begun to brush on matters of political sensitivity. Voznesensky suggested the time had come to revoke the Stalin decree of 1946 that expelled Anna Akhmatova and the satirist Mikhail Zoshchenko from the Writers' Union and forbade publication of their work. This was the occasion on which Stalin's cultural commissar Zhdanov called the poetess 'a nun and a whore who combines harlotry with prayer'. Why stop there? Why not admit more of the tragic past, instead of imposing as a condition of Soviet loyalty the ability to suffer its memory in silence? If writers could suggest some of the horrors of collectivization, why not rehabilitate one of Stalin's most famous political victims, Nikolai Bukharin, Lenin's most brilliant disciple and an opponent of the ruthless remaking of the countryside who had died in the great purge? Was Gorbachov ready for such things?

He had authorized a more adult approach to that devilishly tricky subject, the history of the party. There was to be a new attempt to write it that showed party history having its mistakes and problems, and even moments of 'backward movement'. But how frank this much-needed re-assessment would be after the party's scholars had argued over it remained to be seen. Gorbachov had begun, in a general way, to admit that the leadership, including himself, 'should bear greater responsibility for what was allowed to happen'. But this was a reference to Brezhnev's omissions, not to Stalin's commissions. He would not admit that anything called 'Stalinism' had existed. He said the word was 'invented by the opponents of communism'. His view of the Soviet past as a series of heroic feats, all the greater for involving sacrifice, suggested he was unlikely to turn against the collectivization on which his own family's fortunes had been built. It was hard to see how he could avoid altogether stepping into the 'minefield of the past'. How far he would risk it was of the greatest interest to those who lived outside the Sixth Continent. Nothing was more likely to improve its standing with the rest of the world than a determination to shed some of the myths and complexes about the Soviet past.

19

Rejoining the World

A man taken blindfold into the streets of Tallinn or Riga, the capitals of the Soviet republics of Estonia and Latvia, would know at once that he is not in Russia. Baltic dampness mixes with the bitterness of coal smoke underlaid by the smell of hops that lingers on old buildings to announce that this is central Europe. These are cities of coffee-drinkers; not the sweet black coffee Russians took from the East but the drink of a diligent, German-influenced world. Museums in Tallinn exhibit fine old coffee pots whose comfortable shapes speak of a middle-class urban culture Russians never knew and many despised even before the Revolution.

In the winter the children of Riga and Tallinn go to school in the dark because the republics keep to Moscow time. 'Of course,' Latvians will say, 'we do have our own Latvian time.' They make it sound like an heirloom too precious to be used. When the Russian Empire acquired these valuable outposts of Europe Catherine the Great advised that they should, 'in the gentlest manner, be brought to the point where they become Russian and stop looking like wolves to the woods'. Nearly three hundred years later they had not known much gentleness from any of their great neighbours nor had they become Russian. The Orthodox cathedral of Alexander Nevsky that stands on the hill around which Lutheran Tallinn is built remains as obvious a piece of imperial architecture today as when it was put up at the end of the last century. Plaques on the walls remember the sailors who sunk on the battleship *Navarin* fighting the Japanese in the Straits of Tsushima in 1905, the first victory of modern Asia over a European power. All the names are Russian except for the ship's Baltic baron captain.

The low houses in the back streets of Dushanbe (once Stalinabad), the capital of Central Asian Tadzhikistan, are of whitewashed mud, their courtyards hidden from the narrow, crooked streets. It is early afternoon and the only person to be seen is a Tadzhik woman spinning cotton outside her door. She wears a scarf on her head, and brightly coloured trousers under her skirt. The mosque is marked by three tall plane trees that grow in its courtyard. Thirty old men sit cross-legged on a wooden verandah that runs the length of the mosque. They are eating flat bread and rice, and drinking tea from blue and turquoise bowls. Most have beards. All wear white turbans or black skullcaps embroidered in white thread. They have tucked their trousers into tall boots and tied sashes at the waist of the long coats that are brightly striped in the colours of English seaside rock: pink, red and white; blue, green and white. They have just finished the daily two o'clock prayers and are in welcoming mood. 'The gates are open. All may come in.' They say Islam is flourishing; a Koran in each house. Were there children who refused to learn it? 'That could never happen.'

If the Soviet Union remains Russia in our minds it is because the variety of the country, outside its Slavic centre, is too great to make a coherent whole. It is hard to identify a Baltic, or a Caucasian, or a Central Asian component in Soviet policy towards the outside world. The Slavs, making up more than two-thirds of the total population, dominate the positions of power within the party, the armed forces and the KGB (whose heads in the five Central Asian republics have seldom been local men). This does not mean the Slavs have been able to dominate the way of life of these acquisitions of the Russian Empire. The institutions of Soviet power are everywhere, but they are as misleading as old-fashioned school uniforms that turn children into an apparently manageable regiment. The little Baltic peoples remain Europe's peaceful guerrillas in a Soviet Union deprived of (some Russians might say saved from) the European experience. The Central Asians, to Moscow's alarm, have repeatedly managed to remake their prim Soviet clothes into something decidedly oriental. Since Brezhnev's death the leaders of all the Asian republics together with thousands of their officials have had to be sacked.

In Uzbekistan, the largest of them, traditions of family and clan loyalty combined with the temptations inherent in any vast bureaucratic state to produce two worlds: the false one of official meetings, speeches and statistics; and the real one where Uzbeks went about their business oblivious of Moscow's rules. Most Uzbeks, like most other Central Asians, lived in villages where Slav influence was superficial and the birth rate far higher than anywhere in Russia. As for their leaders, who knew how to behave among Russians, they took advantage of the easy-going Brezhnev years and when the cotton harvest was poor they simply wrote in glorious statistics. Sharaf Rashidov, first secretary of Uzbekistan for almost a quarter of a century, died before the scandal broke but he did not avoid posthumous disgrace. His body was taken out of its grand tomb in Tashkent and returned to his birthplace. The prime minister who served under him was expelled from the party. The minister directly responsible for the fictitious cotton figures was condemned to death. Two out of every three members of the last Central Committee chosen by Rashidov were removed. Moscow had lost confidence in most of the Uzbek establishment.

The process of turning a vast country of many nationalities into a balanced whole seemed to be getting harder as the years went by. The knowledge that they could not feel quite at home in parts of their own country increased Russian unease about the even more unfamiliar world beyond its borders. 'We have a different climate from the West, a different landscape, a different temperament and character, a different blood, a different physiognomy, a different way of thinking, different beliefs, hopes, pleasures, different relations, different conditions, different history, everything different . . .' The nineteenth-century Slavophile publicist who wrote this rejoiced in the difference. Stalin's revolution in one country increased the sense that there was nowhere else in the world like Russia. The belief common enough before the Revolution that Russian difference was also a sign of superiority, usually of the spiritual kind, seemed to some to have received the scientific backing of Marxism-Leninism. A modern Soviet writer of nationalist tendencies explained the logic: 'Our country has a special road. Dostoyevsky spoke of that. And that is why the revolution was achieved in our country.' Such thoughts were bad Marxism and not allowed officially into print by the party but they found their way often enough indirectly into public life. A prominent Soviet moralist of the 1980s, reflecting on the unfortunate interest of some young Soviet people in Western fashions, was comforted by the thought that 'one and the same nation cannot be first in moral quests, in the desperate daring of building a new society – and also in extravagant fashions'.

The Soviet experience seemed to have continued what many saw as Russia's mission, at immeasurable cost to herself, to protect an ungrateful, uncomprehending European civilization from barbarism. Modern Soviet historians argued that the European stability that made possible the Renaissance and Reformation was built on the 'heavy sacrifice of the Russian people' in holding off the Mongol hordes. 'Western Europe had and still has an unpaid debt towards our Motherland.' Russia, according to the editor of the most popular Soviet illustrated magazine, had performed the same service again by defeating Napoleon and Hitler. By his calculation 'Russia has thrice sacrificed herself to save Europe'.

This resentment towards an ungrateful Europe was combined with an unwillingness in some circles to admit foreign contributions to Russian development. The academic world was in indignant pursuit of adherents of the so-called 'Norman theory', according to which the first Russian state was founded not by a Slav but by the Norseman Rurik, though the latter unfortunately occupied a heroic place in the Novgorod monument to the Russian millenium that was lovingly rebuilt after the war. Jealousy about

257

Russian achievements reached its height in polemics over the Second World War. The selfish and short-sighted manoeuvrings of the European powers leading up to 1939 were interpreted by the Soviet chief of staff Marshal Akhromeyev to mean that 'all of international imperialism' – that is Britain, France and the United States as well as Germany – prepared Hitler's attack on the Soviet Union. According to this view Britain's declaration of war against Germany in 1939 was not only insignificant. It was an 'unjust' war waged in the interests of the British bourgeoisie. It followed that the defeat of Hitler was also a defeat of imperialism in general; that it weakened the West, and proved the 'insuperable stability' of Soviet socialism. These ideas were repeated over and over again in 1985 at the time of the celebration of the fortieth anniversary of the war's end. A film released then and based on the novel *Victory* by Aleksandr Chakovsky, one of the most politically powerful writers in the country, portrayed Churchill and President Truman as devilish characters ready to take up Hitler's work.

While convinced of their country's unique contribution to history official Russians knew that the rest of the world remained for the most part sceptical. This would have made their dealings with the outside world delicate enough. The problem was compounded by the difficulty representatives of authoritarian states have always had in explaining their country to a less than respectful foreign audience. Soviet envoys abroad, in the Brezhnev years, were time and again put in the difficult position of having to deny what they knew to be true. How were they to gain the respect of foreigners while remaining loyal to their country? The Tsars' servants had known this problem too. Fyodor Tyutchev, the nineteenth-century poet who served as a diplomat, warned that it was impossible.

> However much you humble yourself before it, gentlemen,
> You will never win the recognition of Europe:
> In her eyes you will always be
> Not the servants of enlightenment, but serfs.

Soviet officials on the whole followed Tyutchev's advice. Finding it impossible to please, they clammed up or became pugnacious. Few risked trying to explain what it meant to be citizen of a country one loved but at times despaired of, and which history had seemed to lock into patterns that could not be changed.

After the war the burden of Russian resentment shifted from Europe to America. If Russia was different from Europe it seemed even more different from the United States. What comparison could there be between Russia 'with a culture that stretched back centuries and fully reflected the character of her people and their moral foundations' and the 'multi-storey culture' of the Americans? This thought came to a Russian writer of nationalist inclinations in New York as he stood beside the 'gloomy mass' of the Empire State Building and remembered the Kremlin, the ikons of Andrei Rublyov and 'our marvellous songs and fairy tales'. More sophisticated Russians would admit some virtue in social democratic Europe by comparison with the capitalist anarchy they professed to see in America.

The novelist Valentin Rasputin liked to say that of all people the Russians were the most attached to their native soil. It was true that many did not take easily to life outside the country that often exasperated them but to which they recognized they were for ever bound. Not for nothing were the Russian words for family, motherland, nation and nature derived from a common root. Mother Russia had never made it easy for her children to leave home. Even a nineteenth-century liberal like Alexander Herzen had little pleasure living in exile in England although he found a good deal to admire in its way of life. The only things he missed after his years there were Colman's mustard, pickles and mushroom ketchup. Perhaps even that was a lot. Pushkin remembered his friend Prince Sheremetyev complaining, after a European trip, 'It's bad, brother, living in Paris. There's nothing to eat; you can't get black bread for love or money.'

The modern Soviet authorities never stopped delivering lectures about the dangerous attraction of Western manners and gadgets. It was as though blue jeans and rock music had been invented by the Central Intelligence Agency with the sole purpose of subverting the Soviet Union. But, if Rasputin was right, it was doubtful that young Soviet people could be so easily seduced, that a taste for hamburgers would ever completely replace the need for black bread. What was more, the old Russian belief that theirs was a world apart, beyond the comprehension of others, had been raised to a higher order by a communist ideology that divided everything into good and evil. Some Russian writers had begun to question this. 'You will always have enemies,' someone says to the young Bolshevik hero in one of the novels of Yuri Trifonov, the chronicler of the modern intelligentsia. As a youth during the Civil War the hero does not understand what is meant. Years later, as an old man, he sees the light: 'There's one thing I don't understand: it has to be black and white, devils and angels. And there's nothing in between. But everything is in between. There's something of darkness, and of devils, and of angels in everyone . . .'

The Manichean approach to the world persisted, however. Flattering to the Russian sense of being different and misunderstood, it was too useful to the Soviet state to be lightly surrendered. It discounted the West's greater riches by equating them with moral inferiority. It justified the barriers put up against the outside world. It was, in a word, a substitute for the equality with the West the Soviet Union sought but knew it had not yet achieved. Gorbachov, in his report to the twenty-seventh Party Congress, provided a fine example of this approach when after outlining the horrors of imperialism – militarism, fascism and genocide to name a few – he indignantly exclaimed that this was 'the society we are compelled to be neighbours of and to look for ways of cooperation and mutual understanding with'. As the Trifonov hero remarked, 'there's nothing in between'.

The claim to moral superiority was meant to make up for only a temporary lack of equality in other respects. The Soviet leaders had never said it was better to be poor and good than rich and powerful and good. The images Stalin had imposed on the country, like the heavy buildings made of rich materials that he favoured, were not the least ascetic. What was needed was time, and the man who came to dominate Soviet diplomacy in the Brezhnev era had been trained above all to play for time. Andrei Gromyko, foreign minister since 1957, was ambassador in Washington when the Americans exploded the first atom bomb and with it Soviet hopes that the bloody victories won by a now-vast Red Army and the earlier sacrifices Stalin deemed necessary to industrialize at speed, had at last won them equality with the West. Foreigners in Moscow at the time felt the gloom at once. The British embassy reported that 'at a blow the balance which had now seemed set was rudely shaken. Russia was balked by the West when everything seemed to be within her grasp. The three hundred divisions were shorn of much of their value.'

Gromyko's life was largely spent in trying to redress that balance. 'Grim Grom', as he was known in a British Foreign Office that came to regard him with respect and apprehension, developed a style that was above all meant to disguise Soviet weaknesses. Stalin had been a fine teacher here, showing how a country's limited power can be masked by outrageous demands and bluff. Soviet officials would in private marvel at what they called Gromyko's 'oriental bazaar style of negotiations', in which he demanded an astronomic price with such imperiousness that he occasionally got it. Gromyko was patient and completely competent. This was his only power for he had no base whatsoever in the Communist party. Khrushchov, who sometimes took cruel pleasure in teasing him in public, acknowledged that when he called him 'our encyclopedia'. Gromyko's family had suffered in the war – two brothers had died – and Germany remained perhaps the one subject on which he could be tempted to show emotion. Otherwise the rectangular face, with its long upper lip and the corners of the mouth turned down as if in permanent anticipation of disappointment, was one of the great masks of European diplomacy. It did not evoke sympathy, but it imposed respect; and sometimes considerably more respect than the real strength of his country merited.

The peak of Gromyko's career came in 1973 with his appointment to the Politburo. The Kremlin's servant had become one of its masters. This was also the time when Moscow's pursuit of equality with America seemed at last on the verge of success. The Strategic Arms Limitation Treaties of the mid-seventies appeared to have put a brake on American technological superiority, and to make a permanent military stand-off between the superpowers possible. The West, above all a United States disoriented by failure in Vietnam, was on the defensive. It was ready to improve relations with the Soviet Union. And it appeared unwilling to defend its old interests in the Third World. In 1976 Leonid Brezhnev began his report to the party congress with his cry of triumph: 'Comrade delegates . . . the world is changing before our very eyes, and changing for the better.'

In truth Soviet diplomacy was as much a victim of illusion as Soviet domestic policy. The successes of both, to use the fashionable vocabulary of the Gorbachov era, had been extensive rather than intensive. Like the Soviet economy, Moscow's system of alliances was producing quantity rather than quality. The East European regimes, with the exception of the Hungarian, had made little progress in winning the support of the majority of their people. It was hard to see how a single one of them could survive if the Soviet army withdrew and promised never to return. Stalin had brought them into the Soviet fold to protect Russia's flank, but East Europe was no defence against American missiles, and its chronic discontent actually decreased the overall security of the Soviet Union. There was little hope of West Europe losing its suspicion of Moscow as long as the situation in East Europe remained unchanged. The Soviet Union needed its socialist commonwealth in Europe to show that it had followers to lead into the new world. But as statistics these were scarcely more real than the figures Sharaf Rashidov thought up for the cotton harvests of Uzbekistan.

Moscow was also acquiring Marxist-Leninist adherents in the Third World, to the alarm of many in the West. But, while Soviet experts could help set up the security and party organizations that would keep the new leaderships in Ethiopia, Angola and Mozambique in power, they could not provide the funds or techniques needed for these poor countries' economic development. Worst of all was Afghanistan, where the Soviet Union had to commit an army to a war with no end in sight in order to sustain a minority Communist regime. The older Soviet allies, Vietnam and Cuba, had become as dependent on Moscow's subsidies as Soviet farming. And there was also a price to pay for these extensions of Soviet influence. The Chinese, whom Moscow by the beginning of the 1980s needed to woo again, disliked the Soviet troops in Afghanistan, and were even more upset by the behaviour of Moscow's ally Vietnam in Cambodia. As for the Japanese, the other powerful Soviet neighbours in the Far East, Soviet diplomacy treated them one day as the martyrs of Hiroshima and Nagasaki, the next as monsters of a re-born Japanese militarism. When in the spring of 1984 the Japanese celebrated the fiftieth anniversary of the death of the Admiral Togo who sank the battleship *Navarin* and the rest of the Russian navy in the Straits of Tsushima, Moscow denounced it in Tsarist tones as an act hostile 'to Russia, to the Soviet Union and her people'. The anger suggested the degree of Soviet frustration at the failure of their Far Eastern policies. The East was beginning to look as dangerous for the Soviet Union as the West.

The confidence that military parity had been reached once and for all also proved an illusion, for it ignored the Soviet Union's relative technological backwardness. When Ronald Reagan announced that America would exploit its scientific skills to take its defences into space, Moscow reacted like innocence deceived. It was scarcely less of a blow than the news of America's first atom bomb. It was not true, as Russians sometimes claimed, that the Soviet Union had always lagged behind the United States in the technology of the arms race. Moscow knew how to exploit its achievements, as when Soviet scientists put man's first rocket on the moon the day before Khrushchov arrived in America in 1959. But the Russians were always working from a poorer scientific and economic base. Each of their successes represented a proportionately far greater sacrifice. As for President Reagan's plan for space defences, there were Soviet generals who had known such a development was likely. The talented but tiresome Marshal Ogarkov was to publish in 1985 a book that explained how the technology of war had always developed through the challenge and response between offensive and defensive weapons. The book's title, *History teaches vigilance*, could have been read as a warning to improvident politicians.

The old diplomacy whose deficiencies Gromyko's skill had so often managed to hide collapsed with the failure in 1983 of the Soviet campaign to prevent NATO deploying American medium range missiles to match the new Soviet SS20s. It was never clear if Moscow had properly thought through its decision to modernize the missiles it aimed at Europe. Its fight to stop NATO's response was certainly misguided. The old techniques learned from Stalin and Molotov no longer worked. Moscow at first refused to talk, and then let itself be dragged slowly and without dignity into negotiations. The wild campaign alleging that NATO's deployment of the new weapons would push the world to the brink of nuclear war – some Soviet propagandists probably came to believe this was true – was by the last months of 1983 causing so much anxiety inside the Soviet Union itself that it had to be called off. More than one generation of Western officials had been tested since the war by this sort of Soviet offensive. 'The iron enters the soul,' diplomats in Moscow would sometimes say of what it felt like after living through one. The West resented being hectored and shouted at. The Russians felt their concern for peace had once again been scorned.

Gromyko, like a great general, was ready to fight a new campaign. By the time Gorbachov came to power the foreign minister had been to Washington to put together something of what had been smashed in the attempt to stop the NATO missiles. Gromyko's downfall was not so much because of disagreement with the new leader over Soviet strategy. It was that Gorbachov brought both a new urgency to the consideration of Soviet problems and a new confidence that they could be overcome. The combination was a difficult one for the older generation to accept. Utmost discretion about difficulties at home had for them been a precondition for the boasts they made abroad. Gorbachov, while admitting things his elders would never have, was also more cocky than they, and more eager, too, to compete with the West. The first Soviet leader to be a true child of the system, he seemed to regard the country's history since 1917 as a series of stiff exams that had been successfully passed, leaving his generation now qualified for any challenge. 'They predicted that Russia would never rise again after the war. But we coped.' He spoke of his generation's Soviet Union as 'an entirely different country, developed and up to date'. The pride in his voice was unmistakable when he spoke of the talents of Soviet science, some of whose younger stars he had chosen as advisers. Within weeks of Gorbachov becoming general secretary a Western diplomat in Moscow felt able to put a finger on the difference between him and his predecessors. 'Gorbachov doesn't think the Soviet Union has anything to apologise for. He really does think he and his country are equals of the United States. Previous leaders – the Chernenkos and Brezhnevs – always claimed that equality but you sensed they never believed it.'

The confidence was partly based on a traditionally ideological view of the Western world. Gorbachov's accomplished performances abroad included moments when he spoke with a very familiar Soviet voice. It was the voice of a man who for all his strengths found it hard to understand how others saw his country, or to accept that there could be different points of view about its habits and achievements. It was not obvious that he understood, when he visited France in October 1985 on his first visit as leader to the West, what a shift there had been in French attitudes towards the Soviet Union. It was striking to anyone who remembered the romance of the French left with things Soviet that there was no longer a single French intellectual of note who could be presented to him as a friend of Moscow. Nevertheless he chose in his first interview on Western television to lecture the French on the inadequacies of Western democracy, claiming there were more workers and peasants in the Supreme Soviet than in all the Western parliaments where 'workers are not admitted'.

He seemed convinced that westerners could not fail to like the Soviet Union if only they knew it better, making this point to his first international press conference with a naive story about how the eyes of American tourists were opened by a boat trip down the Volga. He would claim that even many Americans saw modern Russia as the world's 'last reservoir of spirituality', an opinion he apparently shared. Reading Dostoyevsky with his wife, he had come across a phrase that particularly pleased him about how of all peoples the Russian heart was the 'most open to fraternity and unity'. He gave as good as he got on human and civil rights. He preferred to take the offensive but, unlike his predecessors, was ready to defend in some detail Soviet policy on such matters as Jewish emigration from the Soviet Union and the isolation of Andrei Sakharov in Gorky. The Soviet Union had no political prisoners, he would say, but 'every state has to defend itself' against those who threaten its security. 'We have an extremely wide freedom of speech and freedom of criticism.' As for Soviet Jews, if there was any other country where Jews had such political and other rights 'I would be very glad to hear about it'. He would not allow that the Soviet Union had any more censorship than other countries. Questions on these subjects clearly annoyed him. A French journalist noted maliciously that when French television asked him about Sakharov his hands tensed so tightly 'one could hear the joints crack'. On another occasion he said, 'The Soviet Union cannot be spoken to the way some people allow themselves to speak to dozens of states and governments with no respect at all. The Soviet Union will put anyone in his place if necessary.' But the liberation of Andrei Sakharov from Gorky in December 1986 suggested he understood the vulnerability of past Soviet polices and disliked the embarrassment it caused him.

Respect was what he was after. On one of his trips round the Soviet Union he was talking about the need 'to put pressure' on the West to agree to disarmament measures when an onlooker shouted, 'Let them be afraid of us!' Gorbachov's reply was, 'Let them not fear us. We don't want to scare them. But let them respect us – yes.' This explained both the pugnaciousness he showed when he felt his country was being sniped at and the human, courteous face he could also turn to the foreign world. He understood it was important for both him and his wife to become media personalities. That she was able to arrive with the self-assurance and some of the glamour of an actress at a state banquet thrown for them at Versailles during their 1985 visit to France counted for much in a world where impressions are formed by television images. By the time of the Reykjavik summit in October 1986 she had so established herself as a personality that she could accompany her husband, although Mrs. Reagan stayed at home. It was a minor revolution in the customs of the Soviet élite. That Gorbachov's first meeting with Ronald Reagan in Geneva in November 1985 showed him holding the public stage quite as elegantly as the American of course counted for even more.

Gromyko abroad had awed but he had never charmed, though westerners who dealt with him over the years developed a certain affection for the man and his predictable ways. Brezhnev on his foreign travels had tried to project the amiable side of great power; not a difficult knack given the right personality. But like his foreign minister – let alone the even more curious Khrushchov – he was obviously a man from another world, a true potentate of the Sixth Continent. There was a part of Gorbachov that seemed at ease abroad. President Mitterand suggested this when he called him the first modern man to lead the Soviet Union. Some Soviet people quite quickly sensed and appreciated it too. Even before the Geneva meeting man-in-the-street interviews on Soviet television had Russians expressing optimism about East-West relations 'because our comrade Gorbachov is now respected by the whole world, not just ourselves'.

Gorbachov was 'modern' in his confidence about Soviet ability to compete with the West. On his visit to London in 1984 he had puzzled a British minister with the remark that 'if you send us a flea, we will put horseshoes on it'. Russians at once knew what he meant. It was a reference to a story by the nineteenth-century writer Nikolai Leskov about a clockwork flea, so small it could only be seen through a microscope, that Tsar Alexander I had bought in London as proof of the superiority of British craftsmen. The story's later twists and turns were what made it interesting. The next Tsar, according to Leskov, 'had great confidence in the Russian people' and he looked for Russian craftsmen to equal the English feat. Four smiths from the weapon-making town of Tula, working without microscopes or special tools, put metal shoes on the flea's feet. The Tsar was so pleased that he sent one of them to London to show the British 'what sort of craftsmen we have in Tula'. The smith was impressed by British methods but he refused to let the British train him because he believed his skill derived from his Orthodox faith ('Our books are fuller than yours,' he told them, 'and our faith is fuller'). After a drunken voyage home the smith sent a message to the Tsar telling him the English no longer cleaned their musket barrels with brick dust, something the Tsars' generals, not liking to get their white gloves dirty, had failed to discover for themselves. The message never reached the Tsar. The Russian army continued to damage its musket barrels by scrubbing them with brick dust and lost the Crimea War to Britain.

The story was an anthology of Russian complexes about the outside world and their ability to match it. Gorbachov appeared to be the first Soviet leader who had all the old Russian impulse to compete but far fewer of the old doubts about the ability to do so. Unlike the older leaders he did not seem to accept, as though it were a law of nature, that some things were beyond the Soviet Union. Nikita Khrushchov had liked to tell the story about the flea but, as we have seen, he could still produce 'one's own shit smells of raspberries' as his argument for building a Soviet car rather than borrowing a Western model. Gorbachov could never have said such a thing. He wanted Soviet cars not just to be equal to any in the world but to be the best, to be the 'trend-setter in world car fashions'. It was an astonishing thought for a Soviet leader to offer, though pleasing to those who thought the Brezhnev policy of importing technology, like Alexander I's admiration of the English flea, an insult to Russian skills (the president of the Academy of Sciences talked angrily about the 'plague of imports'). Gorbachov's demand followed logically from Andropov's argument that Soviet-style socialism would only win adherents by the results it achieved at home. This meant a revolution throughout Soviet technology because, Gorbachov believed, 'the battle is being fought on the technological front all over the world'. When the Soviet machine-tool industry was ordered in 1986 to come up to the best world standards within seven years, Gorbachov's Politburo colleague Lev Zaikov proudly called it 'a revolutionary task' without its like in modern times.

The modernization of the economy needed time and money, and a great deal of the latter was being diverted to defence. Twenty years before

Gorbachov became general secretary a man who was later to become one of his economic advisers, Abel Aganbegyan, had written an analysis of Soviet economic difficulties that found its way into *samizdat*. He pointed out that the Soviet Union had to match American military production with an economy that had only half the potential of the American. And he estimated that a third or more of the Soviet workforce was tied up in defence production. The burden could have been scarcely less in the mid-1980s, when according to Western calculations the Soviet government was having to spend on defence twice as much of the wealth it produced as the United States. Soviet experts would complain privately, during Andropov's year of power, that hopes for new economic programmes had already been spoilt by President Reagan's bigger military budgets. The public Soviet position on the president's strategic defence initiative was that it could be cheaply countered. In private, people were not always so sure. Gorbachov admitted in one of his first speeches as party leader that his modernization plans were 'complicated by the fact that we are compelled to invest *immense* [author's italics] funds into defence' (as though Gorbachov had given too much away, the printed text of the speech changed 'immense' into 'the necessary'). On another occasion he named as the two most serious 'objective difficulties', by which he meant difficulties not caused by the Soviet Union's own mismanagement, the demographic situation with its consequent shortage of labour and 'the arms race that has been forced upon us'.

Several times Gorbachov referred to the fear, often expressed in Moscow since Reagan's election, that the American defence programme was meant to 'drain the Soviet Union economically and weaken it politically'. In his private talks with President Reagan in Geneva he spent a good deal of time trying to persuade the American this was a misconception. He argued that while 'there was a time when our society had a different potential and lesser capacities' the modern Soviet Union had 'tremendous capacities and this misconception is simply a hindrance to conducting a realistic policy'. Western experts differed on how well the Soviet economy had to perform to continue matching American military programmes. But it was hard to find anyone who doubted the Soviet establishment would go on trying, and very likely succeed, whatever the cost. It was in one of his impromptu conversations that Gorbachov seemed to speak the popular mind on this. He had been visiting a war memorial and started talking about the country's need for peace: 'It is difficult to handle the imperialists. If we had been weak, nobody would have talked to us. [Cries from the crowd of "of course!"] However much it costs our people to spend on defence, never, wherever I have been in the Soviet Union, have I heard anyone saying, Mikhail Sergeyevich, let's abandon defence and move everything to consumer goods.'

Was not the urgency Gorbachov brought to Soviet foreign policy evidence of his anxiety to reduce that burden as much as possible? He liked to say that his plans for modernizing the economy were proof that Moscow had neither the time nor means for military adventures. The main idea behind his programme of economic and social reform was to make sure the country reached the highest world levels of technology as quickly as possible. Hence the slogan 'acceleration'. The consequences of failing to do so would – for a competitive Russia – be catastrophic. Unexpected developments in world trade threatened to reduce the possibility of speeding modernization with technology purchases abroad. The fall in the price of oil, Moscow's chief hard currency earner, had brought home the foolishness of a great industrialized power relying on raw material exports. Collapsing oil prices also damaged Soviet arms sales to the oil-producing Middle East (in 1984 the Soviet Union had sold more weapons than the United States). The urgency of the need to take these pressures off the Soviet Union matched to the personality of the man explained why it was not enough for Gorbachov merely to outline a new foreign strategy. Gorbachov needed to control this strategy himself and to pick the men to carry it out. Andrei Gromyko had at last to go.

Gromyko, in 1985, showed little sign in public that he was seventy-six. He had a natural hardiness (as a young man he had wanted to be a pilot) and maintained it by a strict regime: exercises every morning, back to his dacha outside Moscow each evening. For years British diplomats had jokingly ended their letters with the words 'yours till Gromyko turns grey'. The grey hairs were still hard to spot, though it was said that he had found it hard to keep up with the faster pace of Kremlin life set by Gorbachov. Gromyko's public performances showed a man who enjoyed showing he was still master of his world. That was part of the trouble. Since Brezhnev's last years foreign policy had been become more and more his preserve. When Chernenko was leader and the two men met important foreigners it was Gromyko who usually led the unscripted part of the talks. He had also become something of a bully with his staff, frequently expressing dissatisfaction with their work and losing his temper with them even in the presence of foreigners. Soviet diplomats joked, ruefully, that *grom* in Russian meant thunder. After he had left the foreign ministry other things were whispered. He was said to have turned the ministry into his *knyazhestvo*, his principality, and to have become extremely sensitive to anything he considered to be interference with it.

This was a serious matter because Soviet foreign policy was not meant to be the preserve of Soviet diplomats. The Communist party should in theory have inspired and guided the foreign ministry as every other branch of government, but this had been ignored under Brezhnev. The Central Committee's own 'foreign ministry', its international department, had to make do with the most ideological parts of Soviet foreign strategy, such as relations with foreign Communist parties and national liberation movements. Apart from making ideological points it did not seem to have much impact on East-West relations. Gromyko and the international department's long-time head, Boris Ponomaryov, were known to dislike each other. Ponomaryov, four years older than the foreign minister, was also Stalin-trained. The Yugoslav ambassador had been amazed to see Stalin's picture still on the wall of his Central Committee office two years after Khrushchov secretly denouncing his crimes. As well preserved as Gromyko, and in his own field as knowledgeable, Ponomaryov's peculiar skill was interpreting the entrails of world events in the light of Marxist-Leninist wisdom. Given the ideological foundations of the Soviet system it gave him the power of an old high priest tucked in the back room of the great temple; often tiresome, but difficult to ignore.

Gorbachov's assault on these awesome men and their empires was subtle and devastating. Gromyko, the ally in the skirmishes for Chernenko's succession, was elevated in the summer of 1985 to be Soviet head of state and replaced by the Georgian party leader Eduard Shevardnadze. Did Gromyko ever imagine that the new young leader would shift him upstairs, away from the control of foreign policy? Before long he found himself making journeys round the Soviet Union – something he had seldom done before – and as head of state receiving foreign visitors sufficiently important to be formally honoured but of little interest as negotiating partners. The new job brought him a bitter honour.

Shevardnadze's appointment was at first puzzling. The Georgian had long been spotted as an enterprising and innovative party leader whom Gorbachov would very likely favour, but he had no experience of foreign affairs. Its meaning became clear at the party congress the next year when Ponomaryov was replaced as head of the international department by Anatoli Dobrynin, for the previous twenty-four years the Soviet ambassador in Washington. Given Shevardnadze's lack of experience and Dobrynin's unmatchable expertise it was clear that the Central Committee would become the dominant mind in policy-making. It was a typically deft Gorbachov ruse to persuade Gromyko to hand over the foreign ministry to another Politburo member rather than to the great diplomat who for several years had been the most talked of rival for his job.

Shevardnadze, by his easy Georgian and uncombative style, was able to make an agreeable impression without doing very much. The change was so great that western diplomats had to pinch themselves to make sure they were dealing with a Soviet foreign minister. It was also a signal to younger Soviet diplomats that there were sunnier models to follow than Gromyko. An expert in personnel matters from the Central Committee who had been inserted into the foreign ministry as a deputy minister to Shevardnadze drew up plans for a re-shuffle of most of the ministry's jobs that eventually took place in 1986. The groundwork of change was completed by the abolition of another Central Committee department that under Brezhnev became the Kremlin's spokesman's office. Its head, Leonid Zamyatin, had been Moscow's voice to the world since Khrushchov's day. Sharp-tongued, suspicious, and more like a prosecuting counsel than public relations man, Zamyatin's style was to cow critics rather than win friends. His departure seemed to be a signal too.

The first dramatic move in Gorbachov's attempt to break the pattern of East-West relations came with his announcement, before the Geneva summit, that Soviet nuclear tests would be suspended. He followed this in the new year with a time-table for complete world nuclear disarmament by the end of the century. All nuclear devices would be destroyed and a 'universal accord on ensuring that these weapons are never revived again' would be drawn up. At the party congress in February Gorbachov called this programme a 'fusion of the philosophy of shaping the security of the world in the nuclear and space age with a platform of specific actions'. Pursuing this programme would be 'the central direction' of Soviet foreign policy in the future. It was essentially this programme that the Soviet leader – in a daring moment of diplomatic *shturmovshchina*, storming – tried to impose on President Reagan at their meeting in Reykjavik. Self-confident, in a hurry, he was behaving in what some would say was a recognisably Russian way. True to old Soviet methods, he offered Reykjavik's failure as evidence of American moral inferiority.

Gorbachov matched this with another programme which he called an 'all-embracing system of international security'. Its military element included his nuclear and other disarmament proposals plus a general renunciation of the use of force, the dissolution of military alliances and reduction of military budgets. The plan also had political, economic and 'humanitarian' components that hinted at Soviet diplomacy's new tactics. There was to be 'just political settlement' of international conflicts and cooperation against 'international terrorism'. There should be a 'new world economic order', the 'just settlement' of the problems of international debt, and cooperation on the solution of 'global problems on which the fate of civilization depends'. The 'humanitarian sphere' apparently meant 'dissemination of the ideas of peace, disarmament and international security'; more 'objective information' about the world; expansion of international cooperation – 'while respecting the laws of every country' – on the 'political, social and personal rights of the human being'.

This came to be known in Moscow as the 'new political thinking'. The question was, how new? Was it the start of a Soviet attempt to move away from its view of the world as a football pitch on which 'communist' and 'capitalist' teams were fated to play according to the rules of 'peaceful coexistence' until history blew the whistle and the 'capitalists' disappeared never to return? Or was it only a new competitive strategy, better adapted to the more sophisticated skills of the new Soviet team and the changing tactics of the opposing one?

By the mid-1980s the Soviet view of America was veering back and forth between the sentimental and the savage. When an American schoolgirl called Samantha Smith was invited to the Soviet Union by Yuri Andropov in 1983 the propagandists' fascination with her went beyond the call of duty, suggestive of a longing for an impossibly uncomplicated relationship with the West and above all the United States. Moscow's constant propaganda about a threatening, malevolent outside world, added to Russian uncertainty about those who did not live like them, made it seem miraculous that a pretty, friendly girl could emerge from such a menacing place (a reaction mirrored by western pleasure at meeting 'human' Russians). When Samantha Smith was killed two years later in an aircrash a poem in *Pravda* immortalized her as:

> Clever, charming, quite unusual
> Bright in soul and in allure.
> Such was once great Dante's Beatrice
> Sweet Juliet, too, could have been her.

Later a mountain in the Caucasus was renamed in the American girl's honour.

The savage view was well put by Aleksandr Yakovlev, for ten years Soviet ambassador in Canada until Andropov chose him in 1984 to run IMEMO, the chief Soviet foreign affairs institute. Yakovlev argued that Ronald Reagan was only continuing the anti-Soviet line of all post-war US presidents and the American 'messianism' that he saw as plaguing the United States from its earliest days. America's 'defence' of democracy was a cover for the 'establishment of the American totalitarian regime wherever possible throughout the whole world'.

The apostles of 'American freedom' are not embarrassed by the piratical wars which the United States has been and is waging, by its genocide towards the Indians, by racism, the persecution of trade unions, the use of child labour, organised crime, cultural degeneracy, or by the concentration of all power in the hands of a narrow group of super-rich and all the other 'charms' of the American way of life.

Yakovlev accused this American élite of being unable to adapt to a changed world. The 'American century' was already disappearing but it only remembered that 'yesterday it was almost a dictator, admiring its own strength, sated and self-confident, pluming itself on its wealth, ready to buy and to kill if it became necessary'.

Such thoughts were evidence of how passionately Soviet officials resented the rival that in the past they had been forced to accept was the more powerful. And they were certainly not a disqualification for success under Gorbachov. He had met Yakovlev during a trip to Canada in 1983 and later promoted him to be his chief of propaganda and secretary of the Central Committee: an influential figure in the new foreign strategy. With Reagan's coming to power Soviet strategists both in public and private added deeply gloomy military expertise to Yakovlev's theme. The Americans, they argued, had never accepted the idea of nuclear parity. They had never really believed in the nuclear philosophy of 'mutually assured destruction', but only used it as a smokescreen behind which to plan the military defeat of the Soviet Union. Such specialists insisted that America still hoped to achieve the nuclear first strike capability needed to win a war (American hardliners harboured an identical fear about Soviet strategy).

But there was another view as well-informed on American life as Yakovlev's (he had spent time as an exchange student at Columbia University) but which saw the two countries' relationship as much more complicated, and potentially fruitful, than just bitter competition. Such a view, often ill-defined, was common among that part of the intelligentsia which found Marxist-Leninist axioms resistable. It was movingly, if sentimentally, expressed in a rock opera with lyrics and scenario by the poet Andrei Voznesensky that opened in Moscow in 1981. This told the story of a Russian trader and explorer who, voyaging to California in the early nineteenth century, falls in love with a Spanish American girl. The affair, ending tragically, becomes the symbol of the unhappy American-Russian relationship. The show ended with the hero and heroine addressing the audience: 'Two souls, borne in space for one hundred and fifty lonely years, we implore you for concord.' It was immensely popular and the authorities, sniffing controversy, as was their habit on such occasions limited it to two or three performances a month.

There were people within the party establishment who, in private, seemed far closer to Voznesensky's longing for concord than to Yakovlev's contempt of the American way of life. They would argue that America and the Soviet Union were not natural enemies; that there were no life and death issues between them, no territorial or economic claims. The two countries could be compared to boxers, but not to gladiators: they would not go into the ring against each other if that meant getting killlled. Overall the two countries were more like 'rivals and partners'; rivals because two great civilizations could not avoid some rivalry; but partners, too, because the survival of both increasingly depended on the solution of global problems. Was Gorbachov making the same point when he said that 'confrontation is not an inborn defect in [US-Soviet] relations. It is an anomaly'?

Such people argued that the East-West relationship had to be based on compromises by both sides. And compromise was a word much used in the 'new political thinking'. A Soviet correspondent who watched the start of the two leaders' first meeting at Geneva described how a Soviet colleague wished Gorbachov good luck. The Russian suggested he wish the American the same, adding: 'We must reach agreements together. If someone insists only on getting his own way, I'm not sure this will be correct, that it will look like a decision. We are very inter-dependent.'

Anatoli Dobrynin, Gorbachov's most important adviser in foreign strategy, explained that the 'new political thinking' was based on 'the inter-dependence of survival – the unbreakable unity of the historical fates of all

271

world states in the face of a possible nuclear conflict'. Echoing the opinion of many westerners since nuclear weapons first appeared he argued that traditional approaches to national security were outmoded. 'The new political thinking presupposes a qualitatively higher level of flexibility in foreign policy, a readiness to make reasonable compromises with one's negotiating partner.'

What should be a dialogue between the super-powers, Dobrynin complained, had too often been replaced by 'an ideological monologue astonishingly similar to the speech of a prosecutor in court'. This was ostensibly a crack at the Americans but it also sounded, probably intentionally, like a description of many a past Soviet diplomatic performance. The old foreign policy was also discreetly criticized for having ignored what in the now fashionable language was called 'unused reserves' which, if exploited, might make compromise agreements possible. Gorbachov's more supple approach to verification and inspection of arms agreements was offered as an example of this.

Past Soviet statesmanship, reflecting the leadership's lack of self-confidence about matching the Americans, had relied on the traditional weapons of the weaker side: stubbornness, secrecy, deception. Elevating compromise into a policy reflected Gorbachov's greater self-confidence as well as the urgent Soviet need to reduce the expense of arms competition. The other element in the new thinking – its 'global' dimension – was also a rejection of the Gromyko approach. The appointment of a new foreign policy team, including the despatch as ambassador to Washington of a diplomat with no American experience and less than fluent English, was read by many as a sign that Moscow would give less importance to relations with the United States. In one of his first statements on foreign affairs Gorbachov himself had said he would not look at the world only 'through the prism' of the US-Soviet relationship. But the shift in Soviet emphasis was more subtle than that. Dobrynin, in his twenty years in Washington, had received a unique education in global as well as American affairs – there were few better places for that than the American capital. He could see the countless forms of American involvement in the world. He would have appreciated the way American power was underpinned by intellectual and cultural influence that affected most countries whether their rulers liked it or not. Arguably this was simply the influence of modernity, but that was no comfort to the Russians who in that case evidently were not on the side of the modern.

Moscow was a backwater by comparison. The Soviet Union had chosen to remain a prisoner within the confines of the Sixth Continent. When it did venture out its face was usually suspicious. Dobrynin argued that the new diplomacy called for 'a multi-measure approach' which was what Gorbachov had outlined in his 'all-embracing system of international security'. This was a script that gave the Soviet Union a proper part on the world stage. It suggested a more active Soviet role in the international economy, and in the solution of environmental and ecological problems. It allowed for more Soviet openness on human rights, which Dobrynin had seen the West use countless times to attack his country, doing considerable damage to its reputation. This script was remarkably free from talk of 'the correlation of world forces', the code phrase of the Brezhnev years for what was assumed to be the tilting of world power in Moscow's favour. Moscow's emphasis was now on the common threat to all countries. Soviet civilian experts were being brought more and more into the discussion of military matters.

But the 'new thinking' remained competitive. The programme for complete nuclear disarmament by the end of the century, however much it represented a genuine keenness to reduce the nuclear threat, was clearly also designed as a thick stick with which world opinion could beat the Reagan administration. The new thinking was also an attempt to set a Soviet agenda for the world. By getting more deeply involved in international economic relations, in talks about human rights and increased contacts and exchange of information, the Soviet government would try to influence the criteria of the debate. It promised no concessions whatsoever on the Soviet bloc. Gorbachov's stated policy for East Europe was to bind it more tightly than ever into a single economy with the Soviet Union. Dobrynin warned the West that it had to accept the 'process of headlong changes in the world', but he excepted the Soviet bloc from the laws of change. The Soviet alliance was still declared eternal. History, Dobrynin announced, was not to be 'rewritten'. Gorbachov himself chose Warsaw to declare that any attempt to 'tear this or that country out of the Socialist commonwealth means to encroach on not just the will of a nation but on the whole post-war order, and in the final account on peace itself'. This approach, one was left to understand, had nothing in common with the American attempt to turn parts of the world into its 'fiefdom', one of Gorbachov's favourite complaints.

Dobrynin ended his analysis of the 'new thinking' by laying down the correct attitude to 'capitalism'. The Soviet Union had 'its own idea of the historical fate of the capitalist order. But as a state we do not place before us the aim of overthrowing capitalism in other countries. This flows from our readiness for peaceful coexistence with them.'

It was difficult to see how this differed from what had been the Soviet position since Khrushchov's day. It left untouched the Manichean drive behind the Soviet view of the world. One of the Politburo members to speak most strongly on the need for new foreign tactics was the KGB chief Viktor Chebrikov. He declared 'immobility and routine' to be 'alien' to a Soviet foreign policy that needed 'flexibility and boldness'. He also called for 'a balance of reasonable compromises'. Yet Chebrikov also led the way in characterizing the West as the nightmare across the border that had to be stopped from infiltrating Soviet minds.

It was on such logic that the Sixth Continent was built. It was the justification for the Communist party. It was the basis of the Soviet view of a world in which two systems were fated to compete. Khrushchov, referring to Leskov's story of the flea, had talked of 'putting shoes on capitalism'. Gorbachov said, 'Let each of the social systems prove its advantages through its example.' It was a view flattering to Moscow and Washington, the protagonists in this drama, but arguably more and more irrelevant to the rest of the world. It was flattering to Gorbachov both as Russian and Communist. Averell Harriman, who had known Stalin better than any other American, said he had been unable to tell whether Stalin ever distinguished between the promotion of the interests of the Russian state and the advancement of Communism. It was striking that the men doing well under Gorbachov combined the austereness and energy of commissars from the 1930s with a new sensitivity to Russian voices.

Whether the Soviet Union could re-join a world it had so triumphantly broken away from in 1917 would be decided by the changes Gorbachov was making inside the country. A Soviet Union whose population lived on the same level as the rest of the industrialized world would not have to see every trivial western gadget as a threat to Communism and Mother Russia. A Soviet government that could harness the resourcefulness and energy of its people rather than treat them as perpetual schoolchildren would be more self-confident as well as more prosperous. A Communist party that was closer to squaring the circle of tolerating democracy in a one-party state might not need to use the world beyond the Sixth Continent's borders as a bogeyman to instil obedience. The possibilities fascinated but it would need years for them to become realities. The definite news from Russia was that the country's leadership understood the need for change. The boundaries of that change could still not be mapped. Sacred habits and traditions seemed to be threatened, but some equally sacred prejudices were still being nourished. Only when the Soviet Union at last knew what it wanted to be itself would it also know the terms on which it wanted to live with the rest of the world.

Notes

The following abbreviations are used in the notes:
SWB – Summary of World Broadcasts produced by the BBC Monitoring Service.
RL – Radio Liberty Research Bulletin.
I refer to two unpublished sources. Interviews and conversations held in the Soviet Union where the speaker's identity is for obvious reasons not revealed are characterized as author's interview. Notes from a diary kept during my 1982–5 Moscow posting are referred to as *Moscow Diary*.

Translations from the Russian are almost all my own except when the reference is to the Summary of World Broadcasts. I have tried for simplicity rather than strict consistency in the transliteration of Russian words and names. Notably I have used Gorbachov, Ligachov, Khrushchov, because that is how they are pronounced, with the last syllable stressed.

All numbers refer to page numbers in text

Chapter 1

2 Kutakhov – *Moscow Diary*.
5 Gorky – *Izvestia* 18.4.86.
6 'frontline soldiers' – quoted in Zhores Medvedev, *Gorbachev*. London 1986, p. 216.
7 Chelyabinsk – *Sovietskaya Rossiya* 11.2.86.
7 Kuibyshev – *Literaturnaya Gazeta* 16.4.86.
9 telephone – *Stenotchot*, 26th Party Congress. Moscow 1981, Vol. 1 p. 332.
9 Presidium member – *Moscow Diary*.
10 Chakovsky – *Pravda* 6.11.81.

Chapter 2

12 Medunov – *Pravda* 24.8.82.

13 Medunov speech – *Stenotchot*, 26th Party Congress. Moscow 1981, Vol. 1 pp. 226–30.

13 Yeltsin – *Pravda* 27.2.86.

14 investigations – *Komsomolskaya Pravda* 7.6.86.

14 construction teams – *Sovietskaya Rossiya* 6.6.86.

14–16 Krasnodar scandals – *Literaturnaya Gazeta* 25.3.81; *Sovietskaya Rossiya* 22.3.83, 26.4.84, and 29.1.85; *Kommunist* 4/1985.

15 foodshop bribes – *Izvestia* 30.5.86.

16 Medunov's part – *Pravda* 23.1.84.

16 headline – *Observer News Service* 19.5.82.

16–17 Galina stories – Zhores Medvedev, *Andropov*. London 1983, pp. 93–8, and *Moscow Diary*.

17–18 Brezhnev jokes – *Moscow Diary*.

18 Brezhnev – author's interviews.

19 dagger – author's interview.

19 samovar – *Moscow Diary*.

Chapter 3

21 poet (A. Voznesensky) – *Literaturnaya Gazeta* 2.7.86.

22 Vysotsky – A. German, *Literaturnaya Gazeta* 18.6.86.

22 Pozhar – *Nash Sovremennik* 7/1985.

24 Interregnum (*Mezhdutsarstviye*) – *Novy Mir* 4/1982.

25 illusions – A. German, *Literaturnaya Gazeta* 18.6.86.

25 shopping – *Moscow Diary*.

26 Department Store (*Univermag*) – *Novy Mir* 8–10/1982.

26 slush fund – *Izvestia* 7.8.86.

26 unpopular professions – *Literaturnaya Gazeta* 7.5.86.

27 Shcholokov and the militia – *Moscow Diary*, *Pravda* 30.7.83 and 1.3.86, SWB (Soviet TV) 10.11.85 and SWB (Moscow Radio) 25.5.86.

28 Krasnodar – *Sovietskaya Rossiya* 22.3.83.

29 Ryazan – Roy Medvedev and Zhores Medvedev, *Khrushchev: The years in Power*. New York 1975, chapter 9.

29 Baku – *Literaturnaya Gazeta* 14.5.86.

29–30 Vaksberg – *Literaturnaya Gazeta* 7.5.86.

30 Moldavia – *Literaturnaya Gazeta* 9.4.86.

31 Moscow newspaper – *Literaturnaya Gazeta* 9.10.85.

31 Central Asia – Boris Yeltsin *Pravda* 27.2.86.

31–2 Aliyev – *Moscow Diary*.

32 Rostov – *Izvestia* 6.2.86.

32 trial – SWB (Soviet TV) 8.2.86.

33 Burlatsky – op. cit.

34 Gorbachov – *Pravda* 28.2.86 and 7.3.86.

Chapter 4

35 Andropov – author's interviews.

36 Maclean – *Moscow Diary*.

37 rumours – author's interviews and *Moscow Diary*.
37 Suslov's death – Zhores Medvedev, *Andropov*. London 1983, pp. 95–6.
37 Suslov – author's interview.
38 Andropov – SWB (Moscow Radio) 22.4.82.
38 Leningrad magazine – *Daily Telegraph* 4.3.82.
38 Andropov poem – SWB (Soviet TV) 15.6.85.
38 Soviet poets – *Literaturnaya Gazeta* 2.7.86.
39–40 Andropov on Lenin and Dzerzhinsky – *Sovietskaya Rossiya* 13.2.84.
40 Chebrikov – *Pravda* 1.3.86.
41 Brezhnev in Azerbaidzhan – SWB (Moscow Radio) 26.9.82.
42 Chernenko in Tbilisi – SWB (Moscow Radio) 29.10.82.
42 weather planes – SWB (Moscow Radio) 24.1.85.
42–4 Andropov's election – author's interviews and *Moscow Diary*.
44 Chernenko – Tass 12.11.83.
44–5 funeral – author's interviews.

Chapter 5

46–7 fictional village – Pantaleimon Romanov, *Rus*. Moscow 1930, volume 3, chapter 9.
47 Ivan Bunin, *Zhizn Arsyeneva*. Works in three volumes, Moscow 1984, volume 3, p. 77.
47 economist – *Observer News Service* 2.12.83.
48 railways – *Pravda* 4.3.86.
48 Apatity – *Moscow Diary, Pravda* 4.10.84.
48 unsuitable machinery – *Eko* 2/1986.
50 farm debts – *Voprosy Istorii* 2/1986.
50–1 economic problems – *Eko* 8/1985.
51 plastic pipes – B. Paton *Pravda* 5.3.86.
52 subsidies – RL 295/86.
52 programme – *Programma KPSS*. Moscow 1976. p. 93.
53 television – *Moscow Diary*.
53 'exhaustion and boredom' – *Pravda* 16.5.86.
54 foreign trade dangers – *Kommunist* 14/1984.
55 Ogarkov – *Kommunist* 10/1981 and *Pravda* 9.5.84.
55 Solomentsev – *Pravda* 1.3.86.

Chapter 6

56–7 'In the Politburo' – *Pravda* 11.12.82.
58 police in Moscow – *Moscow Diary*.
58 Sandunovskaya – V. A. Gilyarovsky, *Moskva i Moskvichi*. Moscow 1983, p. 254.
58 manager – *Moscow Diary*.
59 ambassador – *Moscow Diary*.
59 'whipping the horse' – author's interview.
59 'a kind man' and jokes – *Moscow Diary*.
59–60 Aliyev – *Moscow Diary*.
60 railways – *Problems of Communism*. Nov–Dec 1985.
61 Andropov – *Moscow Diary*.
61 Shcholokov – *Voyenny Entsiklopedicheski Slovar*. Moscow 1983.
62 presidency – author's interviews.
63 opposition – *Kommunist* 18/1982 and V. Chikin in *Sovietskaya Rossiya* 21.1.83.

65 rules – *Ustav KPSS*. Moscow 1981 pp. 51–3.
65–6 arrests – RL 341/82 and author's interviews.
66 Maclean – *Moscow Diary*.

Chapter 7

The texts of the Andropov speeches referred to are in his *Izbranniye Rechi*, Moscow 1983 and also in *Pravda* 16.8 and 27.12.83. I have also used the articles by V. Chikin in *Sovietskaya Rossiya* 21.11.82, 21.1, 5.2 and 30.3.83, and in *Kommunist* 6/1983.
71 Igor Andropov – SWB (Soviet TV) 15.6.85.
75 levelled salaries – *Eko* 8/1985.
77 pop groups – *Stenotchot*, June 1983 Central Committee plenum. Moscow 1983 p. 69.
78 New laws – *Vedomosti RSFSR* 37/1983 and *Vedomosti SSSR* 3/1984.

Chapter 8

80 Turgenev – from V. S. Pritchett, *The Gentle Barbarian*. London 1977, p. 25.
81 revised programme – *Pravda* 7.3.86.
81 letter – *Komsomolskaya Pravda* 13.2.85.
82 Irina Ratushinskaya, *No, I'm not afraid*. London 1986, p. 71.
82 'Plato and Aristotle' – *Komsomolskaya Pravda* 13.2.85.
83 *Kommunist* 8/1983.
83 Nesterenko – *Moscow Diary*.
84 Vadim Pechenev, *Sotsialistichesky ideal i realny sotsializm*. Moscow 1984, p. 183.
84 border guards – SWB (Soviet TV) 28.5.86 and *Pravda* 28.5.86.
85 criticism of TV – *Pravda* 19.5.86.
86 seven hundred million – *Pravda* 15.6.83.
86 tee shirts – *Kommunist* 4/1984.
87 Ogarkov – *Kommunist* 10/1981.
87 *Sovietskaya Rossiya* 27.4.83.
87 Sverdlovsk – *Sovietskaya Rossiya* 6.6.86.
88 farms – *Sotsiologicheskiye Issledovaniya* 2/1986.
89 'radical formula' – *Voprosy Filosofii* 2/1984.
89 'remoteness' – *Pravda* 26.2.86.
89 resolution – *Pravda* 22.8.86.

Chapter 9

90 Andropov's economic policy – see *Izbranniye Rechi* and his talk with party veterans *Pravda* 16.8.83.
90 cutting labour force, the Shchokino experiment – *Observer News Service* 9.3.83.
90 Shevardnadze – *Stenotchot*, June 1983 Central Committee plenum. Moscow 1983 p. 64.
92 Chikin – *Sovietskaya Rossiya* 21.1.83.
93 retirement – *Izvestia* 1.12.85.
93 Gromyko – author's interview.
94 Machiavelli – author's interview.
94–5 Romanov – author's interviews and *Moscow Diary*. At theatre, *Izbranniye Rechi*. Moscow 1983, p. 458.

95–6 dachas and presents – *Moscow Diary*.
96 Ligachov background – RL 183/85 and V. Rasputin in *Sovietskaya Kultura* 19.3.85.
97 rumours – author's interviews, *Moscow Diary*.
97 autopsy report – *Pravda* 11.2.84.
97 Kadar – SWB (Soviet TV) 15.6.85.
97 seriously ill – *International Herald Tribune* 30.7.85.
98 suicide – *Moscow Diary*.
98 Shcholokov's son – *Komsomolskaya Pravda* 9.7.83.
98 Sokolov – *Izvestia* 30.5.86. Lefortovo – *Moscow Diary*.
99 Chebrikov and change – see especially *Pravda* 7.11.85.
100 Cuban crisis – F. Burlatsky in *Literaturnaya Gazeta* 22.11.83.
101 vigilance – *Observer News Service* 2.11.83.
101 war scare – author's interviews.
101 Brezhnev anniversary – *Pravda* 10.11.83.
102 party elections – *Pravda* 30.8.83.
102–3 election reports and results – *Pravda* 14.8, 13.10, 3 and 13.11.83, and 22.1.84.
103 five more years and Andropov's last weeks – author's interviews.
103 plenum speech – *Pravda* 27.12.83.
104 poem – *Sovietskaya Kultura* 20.6.85.
104 Chikin – *Sovietskaya Rossiya* 21.1.84.

Chapter 10

105 new law – central press 19.6.83.
106 Aliyev – *Izvestia* 18.6.83. and *Pravda* 8.6.86.
106 discipline measures *Pravda* 7.8.83.
107 Bondarev – *Sovietskaya Rossiya* 28.5.83.
107 ten per cent – *Observer News Service* 7.5.85.
107 scientists – *Sovietskaya Rossiya* 12.1.85.
108 adviser – Pechenev op. cit. p. 294.
108 Polish events – RL 474/82. Photograph – *Sovietskaya Rossiya* 1.4.83.
108–9 factory school – *Observer News Service* 16.3.84.
110 Lapshin – *Literaturnaya Gazeta* 18.6.86.
111 parents' wish – *Observer News Service* 16.3.84.
111 Zaslavskaya – copy of paper in author's possession.
112 labour shortage – *Literaturnaya Gazeta* 7.3.84.
112 Far East differential – *Eko* 3/1986.
112 Moscow migrants – Boris Yeltsin in *Arkhiv Samizdata* No. 5721.
112 work rhythm – *Sovietskaya Rossiya* 14.12.82 and *Sotsiologicheskiye Issledovaniya* 1/1984.
112 survey of workers – *Sotsiologicheskiye Issledovaniya* 1/1986.
112 Zaslavskaya – see *Eko* 7/1985 and 3/1986.
114 brigades – *Sovietskaya Rossiya* 2.8.83.
115 other voices – *Kommunist* 8/1983.
116 *Eko*'s investigation – *Eko* 8/1985.
116–8 Shabashniks – *Izvestia* 17.4.85, 15.6.85, 14.12.85, 21.3.86 and 15.4.86. Also *Kommunist Tadzhikistana* 7.1.86 and *Problems of Communism* Nov-Dec 1985.

Chapter 11

119 funeral commission – SWB (Moscow Radio) 10.2.84.

119–20 first impressions – *Moscow Diary*.
120 young Russian – *Moscow Diary*.
120 an intellectual – author's interview.
121 Chikin – *Sovietskaya Rossiya* 13.2.84.
122 Gorbachov supporter – author's interview.
123 Vienna summit – author's interviews.
123 Gromyko and Chernenko – author's interviews.
123–4 Chernenko's background – *The Observer* 19.2.84; Chernenko's foreword to English edition of collected speeches, London 1984; *Krasnaya Zvezda* 21.7.84.
124 Communists' education – *Spravochnik Partiinogo Rabotnika*. Moscow 1984, p. 344.
124 'cunning and dodgy' – Moshe Lewin, *The Making of the Soviet System*. London 1985, p. 239.
125 Brezhnev on Chernenko – SWB (Moscow Radio) 24.9.81.
125 Shevchenko – *International Herald Tribune* 22.2.84.
125–6 Chernenko's speeches – *Izbranniye Rechi*. Moscow 1984, passim.
126 Zavidovo – *Moscow Diary*.
127 Women's day – *Moscow Diary*.
127 Molotov – *Moscow Diary*; Tass 2.7.86; *Times Literary Supplement* 18.7.86.
128 meeting in Central Committee – *Pravda* 7.3.84.
128 Gorbachov proposes – *Pravda* 12.4.84. (compared with nomination of Gromyko *Pravda* 3.7.85.).
129 Marshal's star – RL 179/84. Chernenko's Order of Lenin – *Pravda* 28.9.84.
129–30 Chernenko the border guard – *Krasnaya Zvezda* 10.4.84. and *Ogonyok* 22/1984.
    Outpost of Youth – SWB (Moscow Radio) 12.1.85.

Chapter 12

131 Ogarkov – author's interviews.
131–2 Tukhachevsky – *Pravda* 16.2.83.
132 Petrov – author's interview.
132 relevant Ogarkov writings – *Izvestia* 8.5 and 22.9.83; *Krasnaya Zvezda* 23.2 and 23.9.83, 9.5.84; *Kommunist* 10/1984; *Istoria Uchit Bditelnost* Moscow 1985.
133 Ustinov and Stalin – author's interview.
134 Ustinov's motorbike – *Sovietskaya Rossiya* 1.3.85.
134 Romanov – *Pravda* 25.12.84.
134 Brezhnev in a crisis – author's interview.
135 Party membership – Ellen Jones, *Red Army and Society*. Boston 1985, p. 127.
135 exhibition – *Moscow Diary*.
136–7 rank badges – John Erickson, *The Road to Berlin*. London 1983, pp. 38ff.
    medals – *Ordena i medali SSSR*. Moscow 1982, passing.
137 Nevsky – *Pravda* 18.7.84.
137 St. George's Cross – *Krasnaya Zvezda* 5.1.85 and 31.3.85.
137 law on awards – *Vedomosti Verkhovnogo Sovieta SSSR* 10/1985.
138 Pushkin and Suvorov – *Voinskiye Ritualy*. Moscow 1981, pp. 11ff.
138 bayonet – *Sovietskaya Rossiya* 18.11.82.
138 Tolubko – *Pravda* 19.11.82.
138 draft and training – *Krasnaya Zvezda* 1.10.83 and *Jones* op. cit. pp. 153 and 157.
139 corrupt colonel – *Krasnaya Zvezda* 1.10.83.
139 Thermidor – author's interview.
139 song – *Sovietsky Voin* 17/1984.
139 romantic authoritarianism – Stephen Cohen ed., *An End to Silence*. New York 1982, p. 171.

140 Lizichev – *Krasnaya Zvezda* 6.6.86.
140 Afghan cliché – *Komsomolskaya Pravda* 2.3.84.
140–1 song – *Sovietsky Voin* 4/1984.
141 nurses – *Komsomolskaya Pravda* 6.2.83.
141 a very good youth – *Pravda* 3.6.86.
141 welcome – *Literaturnaya Gazeta* 23.4.86.
141–2 invalid – *Komsomolskaya Pravda* 26.2.84 and 28.4.84.
142 beret song – *Sovietsky Voin* 16/1985.
142 Chepik – *Pravda* 2.8.84.
143 contras – *Komsomolskaya Pravda* 24.9.85 and 8.1, 17.1 and 16.4.86. RL 241/86.
143 six regiments – SWB (Moscow Radio) 13.10.86.
144 Guards – *Sovietskaya Rossiya* 19.10.86.
144 books – *Trud* 23.1.85.
144 Prokhanov – *Literaturnaya Gazeta* 17.11.82, 28.8.85 and *Pravda* 21.6.86.
144 Ligachov – *Kommunist* 16/1985.

Chapter 13

146 September ceremony – *Pravda* 28.9.84.
147 assistants' resignations – *Izvestia* 25.4.86 and RL 398/85.
147 Chernenko's health – author's interview, *Moscow Diary*.
147 Shcholokov's death – *International Herald Tribune* 17.12.84.
148 Sokolov – *Izvestia* 1.8.84 and *International Herald Tribune* 18.7.84.
148 Tank city – *Kommunist* 16/1984.
149 American Communist – *The Observer* 25.11.84.
149 Tsedenbal – *Pravda* 24.8.84 and author's interview.
149 Chikin – *Sovietskaya Rossiya* 2.9.84.
150 Tikhonov – *Pravda* 24.10.84.
150 diversion suspended – *Izvestia* 20.8.86.
150 Politburo – *Pravda* 16.11.84.
151 dachas – author's interview.
151–2 Sokolov and Moscow shops – *Izvestia* 21.8.84, 30.5 and 7.8.86; *Sovietskaya Rossiya* 11 and 13.9.86; *Arkhiv Samizdata* No. 5271.
152 taxis – *Sovietskaya Rossiya* 8.6.86.
152 car repairs – *Izvestia* 8.6.86.
153 architecture – *Izvestia* 3 and 22.5.86.
153–4 Lenin Library – *Pravda* 13.4.86; *Literaturnaya Gazeta* 26.3.86.
154 Voznesensky – *Literaturnaya Gazeta* 2.7.86.
154 Politburo – *Pravda* 15.8.86.
154–5 criticism of Grishin – *Pravda* 15.11.85, 25 and 26.1.86, 30.3.86. *Izvestia* 8.4.86. *Sovietskaya Rossiya* 26.1.86. *Partiinaya Zhizn* 5/1986. Yeltsin in *Arkhiv Samizdata* No. 5271. SWB (Soviet TV) 24.1.86.
155 Gorbachov's retort – *Le Monde* 20.2.86.
155 Order of Lenin – *Pravda* 5.10.84.
155 nominations – RL 72/1984.
156 Commander-in-Chief – SWB (Soviet TV) 22.2.85 and *Pravda* 23.2.85.
156 rumours – *Moscow Diary*.
156 Chernenko on TV – SWB (Soviet TV) 24 and 28.2.85.
157 telephone talk – *Moscow Diary*.

Chapter 14

158 Andropov – SWB (Soviet TV) 15.6.85.
158–9 Gorbachov's background – Zhores Medvedev, *Gorbachev*. London 1986.
 Introduction to Mikhail S. Gorbachev, *A Time for Peace*. New York 1985.
159 unusual passage – *Pravda* 11.12.84.
160–1 London anecdotes – *The Observer* 23.12.84.
161 in France – BBC Radio Four. *Analysis* 26.2.86.
161 deaths in Stavropol – Robert Conquest, *The Harvest of Sorrow*. London 1986, p. 280.
162 'tempering' – SWB (Soviet TV) 19.9.86.
162 Komsomol – SWB (Soviet TV) 26.7.86.
163 Mlynar – *L'Unita* 9.4.85.
163 'The Big Deal' – Vera Dunham, *In Stalin's Time*. New York 1976, ch. 1.
164–5 Gromyko – *Materialy Vneocherednogo Plenuma* (11.3.85). Moscow 1985.
165–6 Politburo – author's interviews.
166 Chebrikov – *Pravda* 7.11.85.
166 'knowledgeable Russian' – author's interview.
167 leader – *Partiinaya Zhizn* 11/1985.
167 Chernenko's death – *Pravda* 26.4.85. Decree – Medvedev op. cit. p. 21.
167–8 Place names – *Literaturnaya Gazeta* 25.6.86.
168 Politburo and drink – *Pravda* 5.4.85.
168 samizdat on drink – RL 39/85.
168 new measures – *Pravda* 17.5.85. Divorce – RL 267/86.
169–70 anecdotes – *Moscow Diary*.
170 Gorbachov's village – SWB (Soviet TV) 8.4.86.
170 Gorbachov in Moscow – Medvedev op. cit. p. 184 and author's interviews.
171 Stavropol walkabouts – *Time* 9.9.85.
171–3 Gorbachov in Leningrad – SWB (Soviet TV) 16.5.85; SWB (Moscow Radio) 21.5.86;
 Partiinaya Zhizn 11/1985; author's interviews.
171–4 Gorbachov on tour – SWB (Soviet TV) 25, 26 and 27.6.85; 4, 6 and 7.9.85; *Pravda* 26.6,
 12.7, 7.11 and 11.9.85.
175 Hammer – *International Herald Tribune* 29.5.86.
175 Stakhanovite meeting – *Pravda* 21 and 22.9.85.

Chapter 15

176–7 Shakhmatov – *Literaturnaya Gazeta* 8.12.86.
177 'my close comrade' – *Partiinaya zhizn* 1/1986.
177 Sobolev – *Pravda* 28.7.85.
178 Party statistics here and elsewhere are taken from *Pravda* 26.9.83 and *Spravochnik
 Partiinogo Rabotnika*. Moscow 1984.
178 Army and Party – Erickson op. cit. p. 401.
179 Dzerzhinsky – *Kommunist* 13/1985.
179 Yeltsin – *Arkhiv Samizdata* No. 5271.
179–80 Kirov – *Sovietskaya Rossiya* 26.3.86 *Komsomolskaya Pravda, Pravda, Izvestia* and
 Krasnaya Zvezda all 27.3.86.
180 Party intellectuals – *Pravda* 8.7.86.
181 junior official – *Moscow Diary*.
181 getting into headquarters – *Pravda* 28.9.86.
181–2 secretaries – *Pravda* 29.3.85.
182 own home – *Pravda* 17.6.86.

182 Chabanov – *Pravda* 17.6.86.
183 'railway trucks' – Yeltsin *Pravda* 27.2.86.
183 farmer – *Izvestia* 23.3.85.
183 barley – *Pravda* 19.7.84.
184 instructions – *Sovietskaya Rossiya* 18.8.83.
184 'a political decision' – author's interview.
184 fantasy world – *Pravda* 7 and 31.7.83, 27.11.83, 15.10.84 and 6.7.86.
185–6 Mysnichenko – *Literaturnaya Gazeta* 19.2.84.
186 Gorbachov – *Pravda* 26.2.86.
187 school magazines – William Clark, *From Three Worlds*. London 1986, p. 37.
187 Gorbachov – SWB (Soviet TV) 26.6.85.
187 nineteen million – *Pravda* 26.2.86.
188 Ligachov – *Pravda* 13.6.85.
188 ministry committees – SWB (Soviet TV) 11.6.85.
188 debate on Party rules – *Sovietskaya Rossiya* 4 and 13.2.86.
  Kommunist 17 and 18/1985 and 1–3/1986.
  election practices – *Pravda* 25.6 and 9.10.85.
190 new article in Criminal Code – *Izvestia* 25.12.85 and *Literaturnaya Gazeta* 1.8.86.
190 few prosecutions for suppressing criticism – *Izvestia* 25.12.85.
191 Gorbachov – *Pravda* 16.10.85.
191 'constitutional right' – *Pravda* 24.4.86.
191 'infallibility' – *Pravda* 19.4.86.
192 Chernobyl – *Pravda* 17.6.86.
192 sacked officials – *Sovietskaya Rossiya* 26.6.86.
192 'gentlefolk' – *Kommunist* 14/1985.
192 Nenashev – RL168/86.
192 Yeltsin – *Pravda* 27.6.86.
193 'Our trouble' – *Izvestia* 23.3.85.
193 letter to Central Committee – *Sovietskaya Rossiya* 16.2.86.
193 editor – *Kommunist* 14/1985.
193 thirty cuts – SWB (Soviet TV) 18.9.86.
193 'Bolshevik frankness' – *Pravda* 24.4.85.
193 no parties – SWB (Soviet TV) 31.7.86.
193 'proper names' – SWB (Soviet TV) 31.12.85.
193 apprehensive officials – SWB (Soviet TV) 26.7.86.
194 'wasn't in secret' – *Pravda* 6.7.86 also *Pravda* 21.6.86 and *Sovietskaya Rossiya* 11.6.86.
194 Chernobyl – *Komsomolskaya Pravda* 21.3.86, *Izvestia* 17.4.86 and *Pravda* 16.5.86.
194 'tighten the nut' – SWB (Soviet TV) 26.7.86.
194 These two passages are by P. N. Tkachev, quoted from Franco Venturi, *The Roots of Revolution*. London 1960, chapter 16.
195 'compensation' – *Pravda* 17.6.86.
195 control – *Pravda* 24.4.85.

Chapter 16

198 acceleration – SWB (Soviet TV) 26.6.86.
198 'wait a minute' – SWB (Soviet TV) 26.7.86.
198 'torment' – *Sovietskaya Rossiya* 27.7.86.
198 'solid' – *The Observer* 17.3.86.
198 Mitterand – *Le Monde* 9.7.86.
198–9 Mrs. Gorbachov – RL 304/86, Tass 22.6.86 and *Moscow Diary*.
  'Who's running the country?' – *Moscow Diary*.

199 Vozhd – *Moscow Diary*.
200 pensions – RL 98/85 and *Izvestia* 28.5.85.
201 alcohol decree – *Pravda* 17.5.85.
201 Romanov at congress – *Le Monde* 28.2.86.
202 impatient – *Pravda* 17.6.86.
202 Tikhonov letter – *Pravda* 28.9.85.
203 *Kommunist* 9/1985.
203–4 Vologda – *Pravda* 23.9.85 and *Sovietskaya Rossiya* 25.1.86.
204–5 Grishin's new job – Yeltsin *Arkhiv Samizdata* No. 5721.
205 press attack on Grishin – *Sovietskaya Rossiya* 21.7, 18.8 and 8.9.85.
205 Galperina – Medvedev op. cit. p. 172.
206 'See the perspective' – *Pravda* 17.11.85.
206 last fight – author's interview.
206 Yeltsin – *Arkhiv Samizdata* No. 5721.
206 presidency – *Pravda* 12.4.84 and 3.7.85.
207–8 reports on party congress – *Pravda* 26.2–9.3.86.
208 Yevtushenko – *Pravda* 9.9.85.
209 'inert stratum' – *Pravda* 13.2.86.
210 'ship's wheel' – *Literaturnaya Gazeta* 2.7.86.
210 Zaslavskaya – copy in author's possession and *Eko* 7/1985.
211 Afanasyev – SWB (Czech TV) 10.6.86.
211 'fight' – *Pravda* 17.6.86.
211 'struggle' – SWB (Soviet TV) 1.10.86.
211 Chernobyl fight – *La Repubblica* 31.5.86.
211 ridiculing – SWB (Soviet TV) 7.4.86.
211 'not every truth' – *Izvestia* 15.2.86.
212 speeches – *Pravda* 17.6.86. His sayings during the Far East trip are most fully recorded in SWB (Soviet TV) 26, 27 and 31.7.86 and SWB (Moscow Radio) 29 and 30.7.86.
212 Krasnoyarsk – *Izvestia* 11.6.86.
212 procurator general – *Zhurnalist* 5/1986.
212 Pskov – *Pravda* 13.6 and 14.7.86.
213 taxis – *Literaturnaya Gazeta* 23.7.86.
213 Kazakhstan – *Pravda* 18.12.85 and 5.3.86. *Kazakhstanskaya Pravda* 7. 8 and 10.2.86.
213 dirty tricks – *Pravda* 11.7.86.
213 Molotov – Tass 2.7.86.
215 soviets – *Literaturnaya Gazeta* 23.4.86 and author's interview.
215 decree on soviets – *Pravda* 30.7.86.
216 Lenin quote – G. Shakhnazarov *Kommunist* 10/1979.
216 competitive appointments *Pravda* 4.3.85 and *Literaturnaya Gazeta* 8.4.86.
216–7 Burlatsky – *Literaturnaya Gazeta* 1.10.86.

Chapter 17

218 Gorbachov – SWB (Soviet TV) 26.7.86.
219 Zinovyev – quoted in E. H. Carr, *The Bolshevik Revolution*. London 1952, vol. 2 p. 262–3.
219 metro at loss – *Arkhiv Samizdata* No. 5721.
220 savings accounts – *Narodnoye Khozyaistvo SSSR v 1983*. Moscow 1984.
221 economic journalist's ideal – *Novy Mir* 6/1985.
222 'departure' – *Pravda* 26.2.86.
222 'eternal truths' – SWB (Soviet TV) 31.7.86.
222 'ship is socialism' – *Foreign Affairs* 3/1986.

222 advisers – BBC Radio Four *Analysis* 26.2.86.
222 restructuring is revolution – SWB (Soviet TV) 31.7.86.
222 'dilemma' – *Eko* 6/1986.
222 'sensibility' – *Eko* 5/1986.
223 letter – *Pravda* 13.2.86.
223–4 writer – *Moscow Diary*.
224 robbing the rich – *Literaturnaya Gazeta* 21.5.86.
224 sociologist – *Kommunist* 13/1986.
224 no privileges – Boris Ponomaryov in *Pravda* 10.5.86.
224 Central Committee – *Moscow Diary*.
224 blue lavatory – *Arkhiv Samizdata* No. 5721.
225 official and privileges – *The Times* 11.3.86.
225 Gorbachov and Central Committee privileges – author's interview.
226 Chernobyl – *Pravda* 10.6.86.
226 leaders like speculators – *Literaturnaya Gazeta* 7.5.86.
226 Gorbachov – SWB (Soviet TV) 31.7.86.
226–7 educational opportunities – *Eko* 3/1986; *Voprosy Istorii* 1/1986; *Izvestia* 18.2 and 3.5.86; *Moskovskaya Pravda* 20.7.86; *Sovietskaya Rossiya* 2.2, 19.3 and 20.4.86; and *Pravda* 31.7.86.
227–8 health care – *Soviet Economy in the 1980s* (for Joint Economic Committee of US Congress) Washington 1982, part 2 pp. 224 and 235.
228 Yevtushenko – *Pravda* 8.6.86.
228 letter – *Pravda* 10.2.86.
229 taxation – *Pravda* 20.10.85 and *Komsomolskaya Pravda* 7.6 and 7.8.85.
229–30 Alma-Ata – *Izvestia* 13.8.85.
230 Krasnodar – *Pravda* 11.2.86.
230 income from gardens – *Komsomolskaya Pravda* 10.10.85.
230 official farming paper – *Selskaya Zhizn* 18.1.86.
230 legal authorities – *Kommunist* 10/1986.
230 Gorbachov – SWB (Soviet TV) 21.11.85.
230 income and justice – *Voprosy Filosofii* 5/1985.
230 Zaslavskaya – *Izvestia* 18.4.86.
231 savings banks – *Literaturnaya Gazeta* 7.5.86.
231 measures – *Pravda* 28.5.86.
231 unregistered – SWB (Moscow Radio) 6.6.86.
232 not working – *Kommunist* 10/1986.
232 Moscow registration – RL 279/86.
232 Gorbachov – SWB (Soviet TV) 17.9.86.
232 excesses – *Pravda* 14.7.86.
233 Stakhanov – *Pravda* 3.3.86.
233 is money necessary? – SWB (Soviet TV) 14.6.86.
233 communal upbringing – *Komsomolskaya Pravda* 17.5.86.
233 knowing how to live – *Sovietskaya Rossiya* 13.6.86.
234 machismo – *Eko* 5/1985.
234 the author is Ye. Losoto in *Komsomolskaya Pravda* 30.8, 18.9, 13 and 29.11, and 1.12.83; and 27.7.84.
235 Georgia – RL 271/86.
235 Gorbachov – SWB (Soviet TV) 31.7.86.

Chapter 18

236 Vysotsky – Vladimir Vysotsky, *Pesni i Stikhi*. New York 1983, vol. 2 p. 59.
236 Nagibin – *Komsomolskaya Pravda* 23.4.86.
238 Stalin – G. R. Urban ed., *Stalinism*. London 1982, p.41.
238 Simonov – Konstantin Simonov, *Sobraniye Sochineniya*. Moscow 1966–70, vol. 1 p. 271.
238–9 Tyorkin in Red Square – *Moscow Diary*.
239 Belov – *Nash Sovremennik* 6/1985 and *Literaturnaya Gazeta* 2.7.86.
240 Hayward – Max Hayward, *Writers in Russia 1917–1978*. London 1983, p. 159.
240 'unanswered questions' – O. Suleimenov in *Literaturnaya Gazeta* 2.7.86.
240–1 Bykov – *Literaturnaya Gazeta* 14.5.86.
241 uprooting – Lewin op. cit. pp. 223–4.
241 deaths – see discussion in Conquest op. cit. Chapter 16.
242 post-war villages – *Izvestia* 9.2.86.
242 prison for passport – Belov in *Nash Sovremennik* op. cit.
242 flax – *Literaturnaya Gazeta* 28.5.86.
242–3 Tula – Izvestia 6, 7 and 9.2.86.
244 Astafyev – *Literaturnaya Gazeta* 30.5.84.
244 poet – F. I. Tyutchev, *Sochineniya*. Moscow 1984, vol. 1 p. 171.
245 experts – *Novy Mir* 8/1984, *Nash Sovremennik* 2/1985.
245 champion – Fyodor Abramov, quoted in Edward Allworth ed., *Ethnic Russia in the USSR*. London 1980.
246 'Atlantis' – *Izvestia* 11.8.86.
246 grandmother – *Pravda* 8.4.84.
246 Shukshin – Vasili Shukshin, *Rasskazy*. Moscow 1979, p. 266.
247 Harmony – Vasili Belov, *Lad*. Moscow 1982.
247 historian – D. Likhachov, *Zametki o Russkom*. Moscow 1984, p. 31.
248 German – *Literaturnaya Gazeta* 18.6.86.
248 Mikhalkov – *Sovietskaya Kultura* 16.3.85.
248–9 Bondarev and Voznesensky – *Literaturnaya Gazeta* 2.7.86.
249 Likhachov – *Kommunist* 1/1986.
249 Belov – *Literaturnaya Gazeta* 2.7.86.
250 Le Duan – SWB (Moscow Radio) 6.8.86.
250–1 Murakhovsky – *Literaturnaya Gazeta* 22.1.86 and *Kommunist* 6/1986.
251 grain – *Pravda* 20.3.86.
251 family contract farm – *Izvestia* 27.7.86.
252 'kulak' cries – *Izvestia* 10.8.86.
252 censorship – author's interview and *The Guardian* 28.6.86.
252 Karpov – *Literaturnaya Gazeta* 2.7.86.
253 director (O. Yefremov) – *Pravda* 21.2.86.
253 'Mankurts' – Chingis Aitmatov, *Buranny Polustanok* (alternative title). Moscow 1981, p. 106.
253 restructuring – *Pravda* 21.6.86.
254 Yeltsin – *Pravda* 27.2.86.
254 Gorbachov admits – SWB (Moscow Radio) 30.7.86.
254 'Stalinism' – *Pravda* 8.2.86.

Chapter 19

255–6 Baltic and Central Asia – *Moscow Diary*.
256 Uzbeks – RL 94/86, 297/86 and Tass 27.8.86.

257 unfamiliar world – from Norman Davies, *God's Playground*. London 1981, vol. 2 p. 90.
257 Dostoyevsky – from Stephen Cohen op. cit. p. 221.
257 'one and the same nation' – *Komsomolskaya Pravda* 8.1.84.
257 'heavy sacrifice' – S. Tikhvinsky *Sovietskaya Rossiya* 22.7.84.
257 'thrice sacrificed' – *Izvestia* 7.7.83.
258 Akhromeyev – *Kommunist* 3/1985.
258 'unjust' – *Pravda* 22.4.85.
258 'insuperable' – *Pravda* 26.4.85.
258 Tyutchev – op. cit. vol. 1 p. 362.
258 'multi-story' – *Izvestia* 7.7.83.
259 Sheremetyev – A. S. Pushkin, *Izbranniye Sochineniya*. Moscow 1980, vol. 2 p. 658.
259 Yuri Trifonov, *Starik*. Moscow 1979, pp. 22 and 47.
260 British Embassy – quoted in David Holloway, *The Soviet Union and the Arms Race*.
      London 1983, p. 19.
260 'oriental bazaar' – author's interview.
261 Togo – *Pravda* 26.5.84.
263 'we coped' – SWB (Soviet TV) 25.6.86.
263 'different country' – SWB (Moscow Radio) 30.7.86.
263 diplomat – author's interview.
263 French interview – SWB (Soviet TV) 1.10.85.
263 press conference – SWB (Soviet TV) 4.10.85.
263 spirituality – SWB (Moscow Radio) 19.9.86.
263–4 Jews – *Pravda* 8.2.86.
264 cracking joints – *Liberation* 2.10.85.
264 'let them respect us' – SWB (Soviet TV) 8.4.86.
264 Mitterand – *Le Monde* 11.7.86.
265 flea – *The Observer* 23.12.84.
265 car fashions – SWB (Soviet TV) 8.4.86.
265 'plague' – *Pravda* 27.2.86.
265 battle – SWB (Soviet TV) 31.7.86.
265 Zaikov – *Pravda* 9.8.86.
266 Aganbegyan – Stephen Cohen op. cit. p. 225.
266 experts – author's interviews.
266 'immense' – SWB (Soviet TV) 11.6.85 and *Pravda* 12.6.85.
266 difficulties – *Pravda* 8.2.86.
266 drain the economy – SWB (Soviet TV) 18.8.86.
266 'misconception' – SWB (Soviet TV) 21.11.85.
266 'handle the imperialists' – SWB (Moscow Radio) 30.7.86.
267 'military adventures' – SWB (Soviet TV) 26.6.85.
267 arms sales – *International Herald Tribune* 15.5.85.
267 Gromyko's ways – author's interviews.
268 Ponomaryov – Veljko Micunovic, *Moscow Diary*. London 1980, p. 386.
269 timetable – *Izvestia* 16.1.86.
269 Congress report – *Pravda* 26.2.86.
269–70 Samantha – *Pravda* 6.10.85 and Tass 5.10.86.
270 Yakovlev – *MEMO* 1/1984.
271 strategists – for example M. Milshtein *SShA* 11/1984 and G. Trofimenko 1/1985.
271 Andrei Voznesensky, *Yunona i Avos*. Moscow (no date).
271 rivals and partners – author's interview.
271 anomaly – *Pravda* 8.4.85.
271 Gorbachov in Geneva – S. Kondrashov *Izvestia* 17.3.86.
271–3 Dobrynin – *Kommunist* 9/1986.
272 reserves – Ye. Primakov *Literaturnaya Gazeta* 5.2.86.

272 prism – *Pravda* 18.4.85.
273 Warsaw – *Izvestia* 1.6.86.
273 fiefdom – SWB (Soviet TV) 21.11.85.
273 Chebrikov – *Pravda* 7.11.85 and 1.3.86.
274 social systems – SWB (Soviet TV) 21.11.85.
274 Harriman – G. R. Urban op. cit. p. 61.

Index

289

DATE DUE

DEMCO 38-297